The John Fahey Handbook
Vol. 2

THE JOHN FAHEY HANDBOOK

with a complete illustrated
discography and labelography of
FONOTONE & TAKOMA RECORDS

VOL. 2

CLAUDIO GUERRIERI

Foreword by Malcolm Kirton

Copyright © 2014 by Claudio Guerrieri

1st Edition, 2014

JohnFaheyHandbook@gmail.com

ISBN-10: 0-9853028-1-X (paperback)

ISBN-13: 978-0-9853028-1-8 (paperback)

Library of Congress Control Number: 2014910971

The copyright of the original record label and cover designs is retained by the individual record companies and their designers. The albums are reproduced here for the purposes of historical study.

The author and publisher have made every reasonable effort to credit all those who have been involved in the design and production of each record label and cover, and have made every reasonable effort to contact all copyright holders of material reproduced in this book. Any omissions or errors that may have occurred are inadvertent and anyone who has not been contacted is invited to write to the publisher so that a full acknowledgement may be made in subsequent editions of this work.

All rights reserved. No part of this publication may be reproduced, stored in a retrieval system, or transmitted in any form or by means electronic, mechanical, photocopying, recording or otherwise, without the prior written permission of the publisher.

Takoma is a registered trademark of the Concord Music Group, Inc.

Takoma Records album covers, labels and booklets courtesy of the Concord Music Group, Inc.

Front cover illustration: John Fahey in Hollywood, Los Angeles, CA, 1967.
Photograph: 1967 © Marvin Lyons

To my father Renato,
To my brother Ernesto.
Although they are gone
They never seem far away.

Contents

Volume 2

Foreword	xi
Acknowledgements	xv
Introduction	xvii
Glossary	xix

5) JOHN FAHEY DISCOGRAPHY – ORIGINAL ISSUES (CONT.):

Key to the Discography section	1
Fonotone: 1968	3
Yellow Princess	4
The Elektra Demo Tape	29
A March For Martin Luther King	31
Epithalamium	32
Finlandia E.P.	34
Ragtime Ralph	36
The New Possibility	37
Fonotone: 1970	56
America	58
Of Rivers And Religion	72
After The Ball	81
Fare Forward Voyagers	90
The Essential John Fahey	102
Old Fashioned Love	108
Christmas With John Fahey, Vol. II	120
Best of John Fahey, 1959-1977	129
John Fahey Visits Washington, D.C.	145
Yes! Jesus Loves Me	158
Live In Tasmania	162
Christmas Guitar, Volume One	171
The Guitar Of John Fahey	175
Railroad I	179
Popular Songs Of Christmas And New Year's	187
Let Go	191
Fonotone: 1985	197
Rainforests, Oceans And Other Themes	200
Christmas Guitar	203
I Remember Blind Joe Death	205
God, Time And Causality	211
Jouluyö, Juhlayö	213
The John Fahey Christmas Album	214
Old Girlfriends And Other Horrible Memories	218
The New Possibility / Christmas With John Fahey, Vol II	220
Return Of The Repressed	223

Morning / Evening	225
City Of Refuge	226
The Mill Pond	228
Womblife	232
The Epiphany Of Glenn Jones	234
Things To Come	236
Georgia Stomps, Atlanta Struts, And Other Contemporary Dance Favorites	237
Best Of The Vanguard Years	240
Hitomi	241
Good Luck	243
KBOO Radio Live Session	245
John Fahey Trio – Vol. 1	246
Red Cross	247
Hard Time Empty Bottle Blues	252
Of Rivers And Religion & After The Ball	253
The Best Of John Fahey, Vol. 2: 1964-1983	255
The Great Santa Barbara Oil Slick	258
Americana Masters	260
Americana Masters, Vol. 2	263
Americana Masters, Vol. 3	264
On Air	266
Some Summer Day	267
The Sunny Side Of The Ocean	268
Sea Changes And Coelacanths	269
Addendum	272
Vanguard Visionaries: John Fahey	273
Twilight On Prince Georges Avenue	274
Live At Studio KAFE	275
Some Sunny Day	276
The Guitar Masters Collection: John Fahey	277
Pick It Baby	278
John Fahey Concert: The Great American Music Hall	279
Your Past Comes Back To Haunt You	280
The Definitive John Fahey	285
The Transcendental Waterfall: Guitar Excursions 1963-1967	286
Christmas Soli	293
John Fahey at Amazingrace: 8/24/74	294
John Fahey at The Great American Music Hall: 10/10/74, set 1	294
John Fahey at The Great American Music Hall: 10/10/74, set 2	295
John Fahey at Amazingrace: 8/15/75	295
John Fahey at Amazingrace: 8/16/75	296
John Fahey at The Great American Music Hall: 7/14/76, set 1	296
John Fahey at The Great American Music Hall: 7/14/76, set 2	297
John Fahey at The Great American Music Hall: 11/2/76, set 2	297
John Fahey at The Great American Music Hall: 10/31/79	298

6) JOHN FAHEY DISCOGRAPHY – COLLABORATIONS:

Contemporary Guitar	299
Tony Thomas: Old Style Texas & Oklahoma Fiddlin'	304
Canned Heat: Living The Blues	310
Memphis Swamp Jam	312
Leo Kottke – Peter Lang – John Fahey	318
Jo Ann Kelly with J. Fahey, W. Mann, J. Miller & A. Siedler	334
Give Me Wings	337
Guitar Heaven	339
Jo Ann Kelly: Retrospect (1964-1972)	340
Lori Carson: Shelter	342
Stories From The Hearth: World Folk Stories, Vol. 1	344
Miss Murgatroid: Myoclonic Melodies	345
Halana: Vol. 1, No. 3	346
The Red Crayola: Live 1967	346
Miss Murgatroid: Drill – What's The Curse?	347
Kim's Bedroom	348
More Music, Less Parking: WFMU Live From Jersey City	349
Jack Nitzsche: Three Piece Suite	350
Jeff Fuccillo: Disturbed Strings	351
Loren Connors: Sails	352
Friends Of Fahey Tribute	352
The Great Koonaklaster Speaks	353

7) JOHN FAHEY DISCOGRAPHY – COMPILATIONS:

Compilations	354

8) JOHN FAHEY VIDEOS:

Videos	375

APPENDICES:

A) John Fahey in Movie & TV Soundtracks	391
B) Live Unofficial Recordings & Videos	390
C) Concerts - Gigs	392
D) John Fahey Writings	425
E) Fahey on the Front Page	428
F) Fahey Songs According to Guitar Chord Tuning	430
G) Guitars Used by John Fahey	434
H) Takoma Records Catalogues	436
I) Takoma Records LP Weight	440
J) Sävel Records	441

References	442
Picture Credits & Acknowledgements	443
Index	444

Foreword

"An intellectual says a simple thing in a hard way. An artist says a hard thing in a simple way." --Charles Bukowski

"I've always been a lazy bum in the Outgroup. . . . I worked many long and arduous years to get into this situation. I put up with many hardships. I went without a lot of things the Ingroup members possess or 'have' in some sense."
--John Fahey, "The Historical Subjectivity of The Guitar," *Grinning Idiot* (1982)

* * *

Of all the legendary figures in the century of American popular music, it is difficult to think of a greater enigma than John Fahey. Maverick, prankster, visionary, entrepreneur, researcher — he was all of these and more. A conceptualist before the term became accepted, Fahey created an elaborate self-mythology from the unlikely material of a white-collar Maryland upbringing, carving out his own niche in American music, forged from the obscure and outmoded styles of archaic blues and country.

Fahey began as an unabashed amateur, a "primitive," and remained throughout his life a restless explorer and artificer. When musical inspiration flagged he used whatever means or media came to hand.

To those who judge music on the basis of technical knowledge or virtuosity John Fahey's reputation may appear overblown. Yet the "American Primitive Guitar" genre he pioneered in the 1950s has proven to have a depth and vigor nobody could have predicted.

Fahey's legacy continues to inspire guitarist-composers of two generations and young listeners are still being captivated by the power and passion of his best music.

Guitarist Daniel Hecht eloquently voiced what it is about Fahey's music that moves people so:

"It was Fahey's magic, not Segovia's, Fahey's personality or *élan vital*, that put me inside the music. Fahey invited me to step inside the sound of a solo guitar . . . into a virtual 3-D space with fascinating auditory phenomena occurring above, below, to every side. Suspended among fireworks in the night sky: I think that's how Fahey heard it and therefore how he conveyed it to us." (www.danielhecht.com)

* * *

I remember first hearing John Fahey (probably in late 1968) on John Peel's *Top Gear* radio show. Peel had spent seven years working in the U.S. and when he returned to Britain, among the records he brought back was *The Great San Bernardino Birthday Party*. Via his radio shows Peel became a keen advocate of Fahey's music. In 1968 "Sail Away Ladies" and "The Death of the Clayton Peacock" made an immediate impact on receptive young ears, eager for novel sounds. Even at the first encounter, Fahey's music enthralled.

There were lots of other guitar players around at the time of course, and some of those who played in similar "fingerpicking" styles showed decidedly more technical ability. Fahey was different though. His music seemed to come from a different time and place – it sounded progressive but simultaneously as old as the hills.

The sound of the guitar was unforgettable: so vivid and three-dimensional you could imagine your ear was pressed to the soundboard. Fahey's rhythmic feel was an integral part of his music; he borrowed the term 'syncopation' to describe the unhurried, laid-back swing he adopted from old time players like his hero, Charley Patton.

His playing showed a unique blend of power and tenderness, and by contrast the British school of filigree, virtuosic picking sounded irresolute and effete. Fahey sounded tough, uncompromising – he was Plain School, the Ernest Hemingway of the guitar.

The sleeve notes and the mythology, as in the booklet that came with *The Transfiguration of Blind Joe Death* (issued in the UK in 1968), only deepened the spell cast by the music.

For those who, like Claudio Guerrieri, came to John Fahey's music 40 or more years ago (around the time this volume's chronology begins) information about so-called "underground" artists was hard to come by. Although he toured the UK in 1969, and Italy and Germany in the early '70s, Fahey remained a mysterious and little-known cult figure. The Takoma LPs were almost impossible to find in Europe outside of a few specialist import stores. Before the advent of the Internet it was a rare event to come into contact with anyone who had even heard of John Fahey, let alone owned any of his records. (So much so that one German fan advertised in the U.S. and British music press, seeking contact with other fans and collectors.)

At that time, access to the fount of information that is *The John Fahey Handbook* would have been unimaginable.

Things are very different now. In the 13 years since John Fahey's death there has been a steady stream of re-releases, tributes, articles and publications. Almost all of his records are currently in print and available at the click of a mouse.

In the past two years alone Fahey fans have had their hearts gladdened by a box set of Fahey's Fonotone recordings (many of them previously unreleased), a documentary film (James Cullingham's *In Search of Blind Joe Death*), and the publication of the first book-length biography (Steve Lowenthal's *Dance of Death*).

Not the least of these offerings was the first volume of Claudio Guerrieri's *John Fahey Handbook*. The book was (and is) a revelation, and few can have anticipated the sheer scope, the astonishing amount of research and scholarship that went into it. Part discography, part biography, it set the bar for future works of popular music scholarship. Guerrieri's *magnum opus* represents some 40 years of collecting and investigative work; rarely has any artist been accorded this level of dedication.

The *Handbook Volume 1* became immediately *the* requisite guide to the tangled skeins of Fahey's recorded output, and to the complex histories of the Takoma and Fonotone record labels. Claudio's meticulous investigations provided us with more factual information about John Fahey's life and musical odyssey than even obsessive fans had previously been able to uncover.

And now the author has gifted us with the rest of the story!

Volume 2 charts the greater part of Fahey's output, from *The Yellow Princess* (whose story is told in detail) through to the posthumously issued *Red Cross*, spanning the creative high of 1968-72, the troubled middle years of the 1980s and Fahey's renaissance as an icon of the alternative music movement in the late '90s.

The work of this period was of decidedly uneven quality, encompassing the magnificent heights of *Fare Forward Voyagers* as well as the nadir of *I Remember Blind Joe Death*.

While it is likely that Fahey will be remembered by posterity more for the Takoma recordings he affected to despise than for the 'industrial noise' work of his late career, Claudio is not concerned with issues of quality here, and wisely has kept to his brief: to deliver the facts, Just The Facts. The core of the book is, again, a detailed catalogue of recordings issued and re-issued, this time including complete information on the many and various compilations, collaborations, re-packagings and more. Once again, we are given a wealth of bonus material in the form of sidebars and appendices.

One of the highlights of *Volume 1* was the author's detailed analysis of the enigmatic sleeve notes for *The Voice of The Turtle,* with its elaborate crypto-biography and cast of characters from Fahey's life. While there is nothing to compare to *The Voice of The Turtle* in the period covered here, Guerrieri has amply compensated with the inclusion of sidebars on illustrator Patrick Finnerty; cowboy fiddler Tony Thomas; references to trains in *Railroad I,* and other assorted arcana.

If you ever wondered about the identity of the lady on the cover of *Old Fashioned Love* or where and when Fahey performed his first concert, the answers are here. Fahey aficionados will surely love the asides, many of them fascinating in their own right.

Also included is a chronology of concerts, a listing of songs by guitar tuning, a list of Takoma Records catalogues and more. (There is even a graph showing the fluctuating weight of Takoma vinyl LPs according to when they were manufactured!)

All of the above makes *Volume 2* an essential companion to *Volume 1*, an indispensible guide to the puzzle that was John Fahey.

Malcolm Kirton
North Yorkshire, UK
November, 2014

Acknowledgements

This book could not have taken shape without the help of all those who contributed with their support, insights, and especially patience in answering my many questions.

I am immensely grateful to Bill Belmont of Takoma Records/Fantasy Records/Concord Music Group and Joe Bussard of Fonotone Records who supported the project and allowed the representation of John Fahey's recordings. Special thanks also go to Mitchell Greenhill and Melody Fahey of the John Fahey Trust; Sam Charters (and the Samuel & Ann Charters Archives of Blues and Vernacular African American Musical Culture, Thomas J. Dodd Research Center, University of Connecticut); and Fred Jasper at Vanguard Records.

A heartfelt thanks goes to all those who have courteously assisted me in my inquiries over the years, and to those who have given permission to use illustrations or quotes in the book, including Vicki Artimovich, Mark Berresford, Stephen Brower, Patricia Cloar, Thomas Curtis, Eugene "ED" Denson, Alix Elias, Max Elias, Janet Lebow Fahey, Andy Field, Nick Fritsch of Lyrichord Records, David Gardner, Robert Gardner, David Lance Goines, Stefan Grossman, Robert Hakalski, John Van Hamersveld, Barret Hansen, Ralph Hawkins, Tony Herrington (*Wire* magazine), Georgia Higley, Importantrecords, Ralph Johnston, Glenn Jones, Malcolm Kirton, Roz Larman (*Folkscene* magazine), Alicia Bay Laurel, Robert Anthony Lee, James Lindbloom of Roaratorio Records, Marvin Lyons, Country Joe McDonald, Nancy McLean Suniewick, Charles McVicker, Jon Monday, Paul Mooney, Mark D. Moss of *Sing Out!*, Barbara Namkin, Barry Olivier, Stephanie Pyren, Timo Saarviki, Richard Sales of Glasswing Media, Charlie Schmidt, William Scott, Dalles Sherwood, Phil Spiro, Jeff Tiedrich, Andy Tucker, Harry M. Tuft, Susan Turner and family, William Vandivier, Carol Burchuk Warden, Tom Weller, David Wilson, and George Winston.

I was helped by Kirstin Eshelman at the Thomas J. Dodd Research Center, University of Connecticut; Matthew Turi at the Southern Folklife Collection, Wilson Library, University of North Carolina at Chapel Hill; Stephanie Smith of Folkways Records; Marilyn Masler of The Memphis Brooks Museum of Art; Judith Gray at the Folklife Center of the Library of Congress; Margaret Brady at the University of Utah; Rick Romagosa of the *San Francisco Chronicle*; Oscar Epaillat at Corbis; Jan Alderton of the Cumberland Times-News; Tomas Fong at Heritage Microfilm/NewspaperARCHIVE; and Jennifer Bertani at WNET.

Special thanks go to Ralph Lawson, a second-degree cousin of John Fahey and grandson of Russell Blaine Cooper, who kindly provided photographs of Fahey's ancestral family; and to Susan Turner who graciously shared her correspondence with Fahey as well as her photographs.

I am indebted to Glenn Jones for allowing me to use his archive of John Fahey documentary material, and to Malcolm Kirton for sharing a copy of the "Notes to the Engineer" regarding the *Voice of the Turtle* recording session.

Pictures of some of the records were contributed by Glenn Jones, Nora Smith, Vicki Artimovich, Bill Scott, Malcolm Kirton, and Warren Hodgdon.

Many thanks go to Glenn Jones and Nora Smith for proofreading the manuscript; to Glenn Jones and Malcolm Kirton for writing the forewords; and to Byron Coley for contributing the back cover blurb.

Several CD booklets and liner notes are a first-rate source of information regarding John Fahey's discography. Notable is the booklet in *The Legend of Blind Joe Death* (Takoma TAKCD-8901-2) written by Glenn Jones, and the notes written by Barry Hansen that accompany the anthology *Return of the Repressed* (Rhino R2 71737).

Additional information and material about John Fahey's discography can be found at several excellent and highly recommended Fahey-related websites such as www.johnfahey.com run by Melissa Stephenson and The International Fahey Committee (Paul Bryant, Chris Downes, Malcolm Kirton and Tom Kremer); Stephen Cooper's blog at www.johnfahey.blogspot.com; and the John Fahey chat group at FaheyGuitarPlayers@yahoogroups.com. Also, the book included in the John Fahey CD set *Your Past Comes Back To Haunt You [The Fonotone Years 1958-1965]*, Dust-to-Digital DTD-21, 2011, is an excellent source of information about Fahey's musical beginnings. The illustrated discography of Takoma Records, as well as many other blues-related record labels, can be found on the superlative website www.wirz.de/music/american.htm by Stefan Wirz.

Two notable additions to the story of John Fahey have been recently issued: the documentary film *In Search Of Blind Joe Death: The Saga Of John Fahey* by James Cullingham (Tamarack Productions, 2013), and the biography *Dance of Death: The Life of John Fahey, American Guitarist* by Steve Lowenthal (Chicago Review Press, 2014).

INTRODUCTION

This manual intends to provide a complete and systematic account of the discographical journey by the American acoustic steel-string guitarist John Fahey (1939-2001). Its principal aim is to present an accurate and trustworthy testimony of every known recording issued by John Fahey, each annotated with its discriminating peculiarities. Notably, the attempt has been made to distinguish between all the various editions of an officially issued recording — be it on vinyl, cassette tape, 8-track tape, compact disc, or video format — and to place them in accurate chronological order.

The two-volume book opens with a succinct biography of John Fahey, as well as an attempt to lay down his genealogical background. We then have a discussion of Takoma Records and Fonotone Records, and their respective record output — Fonotone being the first label for which Fahey recorded, while Takoma his own label created in 1959. This is followed by a full discographical list that may be used as a quick reference to John Fahey's oeuvre.

A significant portion of volume 1 is dedicated to the labelography of Takoma Records and Fonotone Records. These two record companies issued the majority of Fahey's records, most of which had multiple editions produced over time. Each label affixed to the discs is closely examined, and every one of its variations are classified and organized in a sequential order.

After reviewing hundreds of labels and the entire Takoma catalogue, a classification of its labels is here proposed. This will serve as a guide to decipher the chronological order of John Fahey's record output.

The labelography of Fonotone Records was recently introduced in the book accompanying the John Fahey CD set *Your Past Comes Back To Haunt You* (Dust to Digital DTD-21, 2011). Here it is updated and accompanied by the most complete catalogue known of Fonotone Records itself.

Regarding the vinyl LPs, it was desired to give a representation of any noteworthy variation occurring among their labels and album jackets.

John Fahey's discographical musical output can be divided into three main categories:

(1) <u>Original Issues</u>: this includes records that were issued with only Fahey music and contain original material. Also included are his *Best Of* records and repackaged editions of previous records, but only if pertaining to Fahey's music exclusively, as well as records in which Fahey is the principal artist (e.g., The John Fahey Trio).

Volume 1 of this two-volume book set ends with *The Voice of the Turtle* album from 1968, and Volume 2 picks up in mid-1968 with Fahey's later Fonotone issues and *The Yellow Princess*.

(2) <u>Collaborations</u> are those records in which Fahey plays guitar as an accompanist to other musicians. Also included here are records by other artists in which Fahey is present on one or more tracks with

original and not previously released material (i.e., compilations with original music).

(3) Compilations are those records by assorted artists in which one or more tracks are by Fahey playing tunes that have been previously released elsewhere (i.e., compilations with previously-issued material).

Towards the end of each volume of this book set are several appendices that complement the discussions in the book and present some interesting information that was utilised to reach the conclusions in the discographical analysis. In volume 2, there is also a long but partial list of concerts performed by Fahey from 1964 to 2000, and a list of non-official and/or live recordings that circulate among fans. The latter, although often of low-fidelity, are interesting snapshots of Fahey's musical career on stage, as well as a document of his interaction with the audience.

Finally, may this book be a tribute to John Fahey's enterprising vision of a record label dedicated to acoustic steel-string guitar music; to the music record industry that allowed Fahey's music to remain alive; and to those who understood and believed in the significance of his guitar playing and compositions.

The blues scholar Phil Spiro stated in 1967 that "the best way to enjoy John Fahey is to play the record and forget about the details." Indeed, John Fahey's music may well take you upon a fascinating journey.

GLOSSARY & ABBREVIATIONS

Labels

BD:	black dull
BL:	black with lines
BS:	black shiny
BSB:	black shiny bold
BSM:	black shiny medium
BST:	black shiny thin
Da:	dragon black
Di:	dragon white
Do:	dragon gold
Du:	dragon blue
O:	orange

Records

BJD:	Blind Joe Death
DC:	Death Chants
DHGB:	Days Have Gone By
DOD:	Dance of Death
GSBBP:	Great San Bernardino Birthday Party
TOBJD:	Transfiguration of Blind Joe Death
VOT:	Voice of the Turtle

Jacket Covers

Countries

AUS:	Australia
CAN:	Canada
ENG:	England
EU:	Europe
FIN:	Finland
FRA:	France
GER:	Germany
HOL:	Holland / Netherlands
IRE:	Ireland
ITA:	Italy
JAP:	Japan
SCO:	Scotland
SWI:	Switzerland
UK:	United Kingdom
US:	United States

Other

TPJHS: Takoma Park Junior High School.
MBHS: Montgomery Blair High School.
NWHS: Northwestern High School.
EAN-13: European Article Number barcode
UPC: Universal Product Code barcode
DTD: Dust-to-Digital
w: with
wo: without

THE JOHN FAHEY HANDBOOK

with a complete illustrated
discography and labelography of
FONOTONE & TAKOMA RECORDS

VOL. 2

*"I'm merely an entertainer who likes to play tricks.
Listen to the record.
I produced it.
I know it's a good record.
Don't worry about the notes."*

John Fahey

(from a deleted section of the original *The Yellow Princess* notes, 1967)

Chapter 5

JOHN FAHEY DISCOGRAPHY
– ORIGINAL ISSUES –
(CONTINUED)

KEY to the
JOHN FAHEY DISCOGRAPHY SECTION

: This is the chronological number given to each edition of an LP. Each edition varies primarily according to the label used. However, when a record is found with a mastering or a jacket cover that is prior or subsequent to that of its label edition, it is then given a "variant" edition number (e.g., variant #2a). If a certain edition is also found with a second unique jacket or mastering, then it is given a *bis* issue number (e.g., DC #4 bis).

Release date: The earliest documentable date that a particular edition was released to the public.

Edition: This indicates the issue number as well as, in parentheses, the version of label, jacket, and mastering used for that edition [e.g., 7th edition (label #7, jacket #5, songs #2)].

Catalog number: This is the record company's catalog number, usually the one printed on the label. There are instances when there is a discrepancy between a new catalog # (e.g., on the matrix #) and an old catalog # (e.g., on the label). In such cases, preference is given to the label.

Format: Diameter size, record speed, mono vs stereo, of the vinyl platter.

Jacket cover: This may correspond to the type of jacket (e.g., blue-1018, see glossary) or to the sequential edition number.

- **Front cover**: List of features that aid in distinguishing the various editions from one other.
- **Spine**: Text written on the spine of the album cover.
- **Back cover**: same as front cover.

Cover credit: Person credited for the front cover image or design.

Label code: Type of label used for each edition (see Labelography section for Takoma Records).

Matrix #: The numbers and letters etched or stamped in the run-off space of the vinyl disc. Each time the matrix number changes, this indicates that a new mastering of the record was made. In early Takoma albums, the SSL symbol in the dead wax corresponds to Sierra Sound Laboratories (see Appendix B).

Songs: This is the version of the songs pressed from a specific master. The number corresponds to the sequential order of the master used. If a record issue has songs that are different because they were re-recorded, it is given a different number (e.g., 1, 2, etc). If a record was re-mastered but with the same songs as the previous edition, then it is given a suborder number (e.g., 1-a, 1-b, 1-c, etc). After the song version #, the number of tracks on each side is given in parentheses [e.g., (6+5)]. A list of the song titles with their time duration then follows.

Recording Dates: This is the actual recording date of the tracks for that record. Occasionally the recording date is much earlier than the first release date (e.g., see Dance of Death #1).

Booklet: This indicates whether or not a booklet accompanied the record and, if multiple versions of the booklet were issued, which version was contained with that particular LP edition.

Producer: The person given as producer of the album.

Of note: Any significant or interesting feature that characterizes that particular issue of the record. Extra space can be used by the reader.

*   *   *   *   *   *   *   *   *   *

A similar format is used for non-LP issues (4- or 8-track tape, cassette tape, open reel tape, and CD).

In the upper-right corner of each entry is the country of origin of the recording. This is left blank for all US issues.

If a jacket cover is used with two or more labels, its image is depicted only with the first label it was issued with.

FONOTONE 6801

Original release date: 1968
Artist name: John Fahey
Recording Date: April 15, 1960
Songs:
   A1 – Guitar Solo by John Fahey – Titel [sic] Unknown   2:57
   B1 – Guitar Solo by John Fahey – Titel [sic] Unknown   3:25

Edition: 1ˢᵗ
Catalog number: 6801
Format: 7" 45 rpm on acetate disc (? hole)
Label: type #8 from 1970-1985
Matrix #: F.T. 6801-A
           F.T. 6801-B

Of note: (1) *Guitar Solo #1* is a version of "Revelations on the Banks of the Pawtuxent." (2) *Guitar Solo #2* is a version of "Night Train to Valhalla."

THE YELLOW PRINCESS

#1

Release date: late 1968 or January 1969
Edition: 1st issue (label #1, jacket #1, songs #1) - promo
Catalog number: VSD-79293
Format: 12" LP, 33⅓ rpm, stereo
Jacket cover: 1st
   - **Front cover**: STEREO; VSD-79293
   - **Spine**: VSD-79293   JOHN FAHEY "THE YELLOW PRINCESS"   VANGUARD
   - **Back cover**:   VSD-79293   STEREO
Cover credit: Chuck McVicker / Jules Halfant / Jeff Lovelace
Label: Vanguard – White; STEREO   (not for sale)

Matrix #:   VSD-79293A   XSV143775-1A
              VSD-79293B   XSV143776-3A
Songs: version #1-a (5+4)

A1 – The Yellow Princess	4:49
A2 – View (East From The Top Of The Riggs Road/B & O Trestle)	4:54
A3 – Lion	5:03
A4 – March! For Martin Luther King	3:40
A5 – The Singing Bridge Of Memphis Tennessee	2:49
B1 – Dance Of The Inhabitants Of The Invisible City Of Bladensburg	4:07
B2 – Charles A. Lee: In Memoriam	3:58
B3 – Irish Setter	7:14
B4 – Commemorative Transfiguration and Communion at Magruder Park	5:59

Recording Dates: Sierra Sound Laboratories, Berkeley, CA, in June, 1968.
Producer: John Fahey and Barret Hansen
Liner Notes: yes
Of Note: (1) The back liner notes mention the word "Raga" instead of "Dance" for song B1. In November, 1968, Fahey had asked that the track title be corrected since it should read "Raga of . . ." This did not happen. (2) On the label, the time of A3 is 5:08. (3) For track A4, the label omits the exclamation point in the title, which is thus written as "March for Martin Luther King."

DANCE OF THE INHABITANTS OF THE INVISIBLE CITY OF BLADENSBURG

This piece is a remake (with session rock musicians) of the song "Dance Of The Inhabitants of The Palace Of King Phillip XIV" from *Death Chants, Breakdowns & Military Waltzes*. The latter was issued in one version only, which was used on all the various editions of the *Death Chants* album. Furthermore, these are reworkings of the Fonotone-era piece "Smoky Ordinary Blues" (Fonotone 6150) from 1961. Thus the following are titles for the same tune:
- Smoky Ordinary Blues
- Dance Of The Inhabitants Of The Palace Of King Philip XIV
- Dance Of The Inhabitants Of The Invisible City Of Bladensburg
- Raga Of The Inhabitants Of The Invisible City Of Bladensburg

The title of "Dance Of The Inhabitants Of The Invisible City Of Bladensburg" is derived from that of a classical music piece called "The Legend Of The Invisible City of Kitezh" by Rimsky-Korsakov.

THE SINGING BRIDGE OF MEMPHIS, TENNESSEE

This song is a combination of the guitar music of John Fahey, an electric bassoon, the sound of freight cars passing over a railroad bridge, and an "old phonograph record." The record used is "Quill Blues" by Big Boy Cleveland (Gennett 6106-B; recorded April 12, 1927). The quill is also known as a syrinx or panpipes. Fahey utilizes a two-minute section (from 0'21" to 2'23") from the original 78 rpm record.

#2

Release date: late 1968 or January 1969
Edition: 2nd issue (label #2, jacket #1, songs #1)
Catalog number: VSD-79293
Format: 12" LP, 33⅓ rpm, stereo
Jacket cover: 1st
 - **Front cover**: STEREO; VSD-79293
 - **Spine**: VSD-79293   JOHN FAHEY "THE YELLOW PRINCESS"   VANGUARD
 - **Back cover**: VSD-79293   STEREO
Cover credit: Chuck McVicker / Jules Halfant / Jeff Lovelace
Label: Vanguard – Gold; STEREO

Matrix #: XSV143775-1E   VSD 79293 A
              VSD-79293B   XSV143776-3A
Songs: version #1-a (5+4)

A1 – The Yellow Princess	4:49
A2 – View (East From The Top Of The Riggs Road/B & O Trestle)	4:54
A3 – Lion	5:03
A4 – March! For Martin Luther King	3:40
A5 – The Singing Bridge Of Memphis Tennessee	2:49
B1 – Dance Of The Inhabitants Of The Invisible City Of Bladensburg	4:07
B2 – Charles A. Lee: In Memoriam	3:58
B3 – Irish Setter	7:14
B4 – Commemorative Transfiguration and Communion at Magruder Park	5:59

Recording Dates: Sierra Sound Laboratories, Berkeley, California, in June 1968.
Producer: John Fahey and Barret Hansen
Liner Notes: yes
Of note: (1) On the label, the time of A3 is 5:08. (2) For track A4, the label omits the exclamation point in its title.

#3

Release date: Early 1969 (UK)
Edition: 3rd issue (label #3, jacket #2, songs #1)
Catalog number: SVRL. 19033
Format: 12" LP, 33⅓ rpm, stereo
Jacket cover: 2nd
  - **Front cover**: *no* STEREO; Vanguard logo.
  - **Spine**: VANGUARD • JOHN FAHEY • THE YELLOW PRINCESS • SVRL 19033
  - **Back cover**: SVRL 19033; no picture.
Cover credit: Chuck McVicker / Jules Halfant
Label: Vanguard – Black

Matrix #: SVRL 19033 AN1 420
    SVRL 19033 BN1 420
Songs: version #1-b (5+4)

A1 – The Yellow Princess	4:49
A2 – View (East From The Top Of The Riggs Road/B & O Trestle)	4:54
A3 – Lion	5:03
A4 – March! For Martin Luther King	3:40
A5 – The Singing Bridge Of Memphis Tennessee	2:49
B1 – Dance Of The Inhabitants Of The Invisible City Of Bladensburg	4:07
B2 – Charles A. Lee: In Memoriam	3:58
B3 – Irish Setter	7:14
B4 – Commemorative Transfiguration and Communion at Magruder Park	5:59

Recording Dates: Sierra Sound Laboratories, Berkeley, California, in June 1968.
Producer: John Fahey and Barret Hansen
Liner Notes: yes (with minor changes to the wording)
Of note: (1) The back liner notes now mention the word "Dance" for song B1. (2) For track A4, the label now adds the exclamation point in the title.

#4

Release date: 1969 (Australia)
Edition: 4th issue (label #4, jacket #3, songs #1)
Catalog number: VSD-79293
Format: 12" LP, 33⅓ rpm, stereo
Jacket cover: 3rd
  - **Front cover**: STEREO; VSD-79293
  - **Spine**: VSD-79293   JOHN FAHEY "THE YELLOW PRINCESS" VANGUARD
  - **Back cover**: VSD-79293   STEREO;
         "Astor Radios, Radiograms and Television" at bottom center.
Cover credit: Chuck McVicker / Jules Halfant / Jeff Lovelace
Label: Vanguard – Red

Matrix #: VSD-79293-A   (etched)
             VSD-79293-B2   (etched)
Songs: version #1-c (5+4)
A1 – The Yellow Princess   4:49
A2 – View (East From The Top Of The Riggs Road/B & O Trestle)   4:54
A3 – Lion   5:03
A4 – March! For Martin Luther King   3:40
A5 – The Singing Bridge Of Memphis Tennessee   2:49
B1 – Dance Of The Inhabitants Of The Invisible City Of Bladensburg   4:07
B2 – Charles A. Lee: In Memoriam   3:58
B3 – Irish Setter   7:14
B4 – Commemorative Transfiguration and Communion at Magruder Park   5:59
Recording Dates: Sierra Sound Laboratories, Berkeley, California, in June 1968.
Producer: John Fahey and Barrett Hansen
Liner Notes: yes
Of note: (1) On the label, the time of A3 is 5:08. (2) Astor Records was a record label based in Melbourne and was the Australian distributor for Vanguard.

#5

Release date: 1970   (Canada)
Edition: 5th issue (label #5, jacket #4, songs #1)
Catalog number: VSD-79293
Format: 12" LP, 33⅓ rpm, stereo
Jacket cover: 4th
  - **Front cover**: STEREO; VSD-79293
  - **Spine**: VSD-79293   JOHN FAHEY "THE YELLOW PRINCESS" VANGUARD
  - **Back cover**:   VSD-79293   STEREO; Ampex Music of Canada
Cover credit: Chuck McVicker / Jules Halfant / Jeff Lovelace
Label: Vanguard – Tan; STEREO

Matrix #: VSD 79293 A   XSV-143775   TG   (etched)
                       VSD-79293-B2   TG   (etched)
Songs: version #1-c (5+4)
A1 – The Yellow Princess   4:49
A2 – View (East From The Top Of The Riggs Road/B & O Trestle)   4:54
A3 – Lion   5:03
A4 – March! For Martin Luther King   3:40
A5 – The Singing Bridge Of Memphis Tennessee   2:49
B1 – Dance Of The Inhabitants Of The Invisible City Of Bladensburg   4:07
B2 – Charles A. Lee: In Memorium   3:58
B3 – Irish Setter   7:14
B4 – Commemorative Transfiguration and Communion at Magruder Park 5:59
Recording Dates: Sierra Sound Laboratories, Berkeley, California, in June 1968.
Producer: John Fahey and Barrett Hansen
Liner Notes: yes
Of note: (1) On the label, the time of A3 is 5:08. (2) The label misspells track B2 as "In Memorium." (3) The label mentions Sam Charters as the producer, and not as executive producer. (4) In October 1970, Vanguard signed a contract that gave Ampex access to the manufacture and distribution of its catalog in Canada.

#6

Release date: 1975
Edition: 6th issue (label #6, jacket #1, songs #1)
Catalog number: VSD-79293
Format: 12" LP, 33⅓ rpm, stereo
Jacket cover: 1st
  - **Front cover**: STEREO; VSD-79293
  - **Spine**: VSD-79293   JOHN FAHEY "THE YELLOW PRINCESS" VANGUARD
  - **Back cover**:   VSD-79293   STEREO
Cover credit: Chuck McVicker / Jules Halfant / Jeff Lovelace
Label: Vanguard – Yellow Marble

Matrix #: XSV143775-1F   (stamped)
          V SD 79293 B   XSV143776-3F   (stamped)
or
          XSV143775-1H   (etched)
          VSD 79293B   XSV143776-3K   (etched)

Songs: version #1-a (5+4)
A1 – The Yellow Princess   4:49
A2 – View (East From The Top Of The Riggs Road/B & O Trestle) 4:54
A3 – Lion   5:03
A4 – March! For Martin Luther King   3:40
A5 – The Singing Bridge Of Memphis Tennessee   2:49
B1 – Dance Of The Inhabitants Of The Invisible City Of Bladensburg 4:07
B2 – Charles A. Lee: In Memoriam   3:58
B3 – Irish Setter   7:14
B4 – Commemorative Transfiguration and Communion at Magruder Park 5:59

Recording Dates: Sierra Sound Laboratories, Berkeley, California, in June 1968.
Producer: John Fahey and Barret Hansen
Liner Notes: yes
Of note: (1) On the label, the time of A3 is 5:08. (2) For track A4, the label omits the exclamation point in the title.

#7

Release date: 2006 (Italy)
Edition: 7th issue (label #7, jacket #5, songs #1)
Catalog number: VSD-79293
Format: 12" LP, 33⅓ rpm, stereo
Jacket cover: 5th
  - **Front cover**: STEREO; VSD-79293
  - **Spine**: VSD•79293   JOHN FAHEY "THE YELLOW PRINCESS" VANGUARD
  - **Back cover**:   VSD-79293   STEREO; COMET logo
Cover credit: Chuck McVicker / Jules Halfant / Jeff Lovelace
Label: Vanguard – Copper; STEREO

Matrix #: VSD 79293   A   33 RPM
          VSD 79293   B   33 RPM
Songs: version #1-d (5+4)
A1 – The Yellow Princess   4:49
A2 – View (East From The Top Of The Riggs Road/B & O Trestle)   4:54
A3 – Lion   5:03
A4 – March! For Martin Luther King   3:40
A5 – The Singing Bridge Of Memphis Tennessee   2:49
B1 – Dance Of The Inhabitants Of The Invisible City Of Bladensburg   4:07
B2 – Charles A. Lee: In Memoriam   3:58
B3 – Irish Letter   7:14
B4 – Commemorative Transfiguration and Communion at Magruder Park   5:59
Recording Dates: Sierra Sound Laboratories, Berkeley, California, in June 1968.
Producer: John Fahey and Barret Hansen
Of note: (1) Comet Records is an Italian reissue label and distributor for several Vanguard releases. (2) Notice the label's misspelling of track B4 "Irish Setter" as "Irish Letter"!

#8

Release date: 2007 (UK)
Edition: 8th issue (label #8, jacket #6, songs #1)
Catalog number: VSD-79293
Format: 12" LP, 33⅓ rpm, stereo
Jacket cover: 6th
  - **Front cover**: STEREO; VSD-79293
        Pure Pleasure sticker on plastic shrink
  - **Spine**: VSD-79293   JOHN FAHEY "THE YELLOW PRINCESS" VANGUARD
  - **Back cover**: VSD-79293   STEREO
        "Manufactured by www.purepleasurerecords.com" on bottom.
Cover credit: Chuck McVicker / Jules Halfant / Jeff Lovelace
Label: Vanguard – Golden-green - STEREO

Matrix #: VSD-79293-A   15820.1 (3)
              VSD-79293-B   15820.2 (3)
Songs: version #1-e (5+4)
A1 – The Yellow Princess   4:49
A2 – View (East From The Top Of The Riggs Road/B & O Trestle)   4:54
A3 – Lion   5:03
A4 – March for Martin Luther King   3:40
A5 – The Singing Bridge Of Memphis Tennessee   2:49
B1 – Dance Of The Inhabitants Of The Invisible City Of Bladensburg   4:07
B2 – Charles A. Lee: In Memorium   3:58
B3 – Irish Setter   7:14
B4 – Commemorative Transfiguration and Communion at Magruder Park   5:59
Recording Dates: Sierra Sound Laboratories, Berkeley, California, in June 1968.
Producer: John Fahey and Barret Hansen
Of note: (1) On the label, the time for track A3 is 5:08. (2) The record was issued as a limited edition on 180 gram vinyl. (3) The label misspells track B2 as "In Memorium"; for track A5 the word "Tennessee" is lacking one "e"; and for track A4 the label omits the exclamation point in its title.

#9

Release date: 2010
Edition: 9th issue (label #9, jacket #7, songs #1)
Catalog number: VSD-79293
Format: 12" LP, 33⅓ rpm, stereo
Jacket cover: 7th
  - **Front cover**: STEREO; 60th anniversary sticker on plastic shrink.
  - **Spine**: VSD-79293   JOHN FAHEY "THE YELLOW PRINCESS"   VANGUARD
  - **Back cover**:   VSD-79293   STEREO; bar code.
Cover credit: Chuck McVicker / Jules Halfant / Jeff Lovelace
Label: Vanguard – Silver - STEREO

Matrix #: S-71303   79293-1-A
         S-71304   79293-1-B
Songs: version #1-f (5+4)

A1 – The Yellow Princess	4:49
A2 – View (East From The Top Of The Riggs Road/B & O Trestle)	4:54
A3 – Lion	5:03
A4 – March! For Martin Luther King	3:40
A5 – The Singing Bridge Of Memphis Tennessee	2:49
B1 – Dance Of The Inhabitants Of The Invisible City Of Bladensburg	4:07
B2 – Charles A. Lee: In Memoriam	3:58
B3 – Irish Setter	7:14
B4 – Commemorative Transfiguration and Communion at Magruder Park	5:59

Recording Dates: Sierra Sound Laboratories, Berkeley, California, in June 1968.
Producer: John Fahey and Barret Hansen
Liner Notes: yes
Of note: (1) This is the first time that the spelling of the track titles on the label matches the ones on the back cover. (2) This was issued in a limited edition of 500 copies for Vanguard's 60th anniversary and for Record Store Day on April 17, 2010. (3) The S-##### matrix number suggests that this was pressed by Rainbo Records in 2010.

THE YELLOW PRINCESS
John Fahey
Vanguard VSD79293
Produced by John Fahey and
Harrett Hansen

The Yellow Princess; View (East from the top of the Riggs Road/B&O Trestle); Lion; March! For Martin Luther King; The Singing Bridge of Memphis, Tennessee; Dance of the Inhabitants of the Invisible City of Bladensburg; Charles A. Lee; In Memoriam; Irish Setter; Commemorative Transfiguration and Communion at Magruder Park.

That in <u>The Yellow Princess</u> John Fahey sounds much the same as he did five years ago should not be an obstacle toward an appreciation of what he has recorded here. The fantasies he plays and the forms he plays in on his solo acoustic guitar may no longer be revolutionary in impact but some of them at least have substance to them.

The first side of the album contains the rewarding works. The title tune, which is based on a theme of Saint-Saens, is a pleasant improvisation on both the musical theme and its subject, a clipper ship. "View..." is a plodding tune with little to recommend it, but "Lion," written for Fahey's tomcat, combines vigorous strumming passages a la Leadbelly with "Swing Low, Sweet Chariot" to make a nicely proportioned memoriam.

Ralph Earle's review of *The Yellow Princess* **in "The Broadside of Boston" from June 18, 1969 (cont.)**

Reproduced with kind permission of Ralph Earle and David Wilson.

"March! For Martin Luther King" is particularly effective. Accompanied by organ, electric bass and snare drum, it is stately, reverent, and respectful, yet it retains spirit. It does not slog or shuffle along, and the use of the glissando from the minor to the major third adds just the proper amount of color to the piece, a sensitive response to King's death.

"The Singing Bridge of Memphis, Tennessee" is quite literally that. Fahey has mixed traffic, people, and Nature sounds and noises with his own delicate playing in the background and a bluesy whistle in the foreground (like Ed Young and the Southern Fife and Drum Corps) to make the bridge sing. Somewhat similar in tone to opening scenes of a motion picture, it is nevertheless an effective use of music concrete.

The second side is difficult to appreciate. The cuts meander in and out of focus and in and out of tune. The fact that the title "Dance of the Inhabitants of the Invisible City of Bladensburg" is a steal from Stravinsky's Firebird ballet (for "Bladensburg" substitute Stravinsky's "Kitzeh") reveals nothing about the work. "Irish Setter" quotes "Night on Bald Mountain" and "Commemorative Transfiguration..." quotes the hymn "All Creatures of Our God and King," but both to no discernable end.

The liner notes by Fahey are thoughtful and stimulating, but they do not help the understanding of his more personal exercises here. And since Fahey himself writes "the listener need not concern himself with the problems in the life of the creative artist," the cuts have to stand on their own merits. With the definite exception of "March!..." and "The Singing Bridge...," they stand unsteadily at best and often fall.

Ralph Earle

Reel-to-Reel Tape issue

Release date: 1969
Catalog number: X-9293
Format: reel tape, 4-track, 3¾ ips
Cover: STEREO; *no* catalog number
Original Cover credit: Chuck McVicker
Songs: version #1 (9)

1 – The Yellow Princess	4:49
2 – View (East From The Top Of The Riggs Road/B & O Trestle)	4:54
3 – Lion	5:03
4 – March! For Martin Luther King	3:40
5 – The Singing Bridge Of Memphis, Tennessee	2:49
6 – Dance Of The Inhabitants Of The Invisible City Of Bladensburg	4:07
7 – Charles A. Lee: In Memoriam	3:58
8 – Irish Setter	7:14
9 – Commemorative Transfiguration and Communion at Magruder Park	5:59

Original Producer: John Fahey and Barret Hansen
Recording Dates: same as LP #1
Of note: (1) On the tape's label, the producer is given as Sam Charters.

Tape re-issue

#1

Release date: ? 1993
Catalog number: CV-79293
Format: cassette tape
Cover: STEREO; VSD-79293
Original Cover credit: Chuck McVicker
Songs: version #1 (5+4)

A1 – The Yellow Princess	4:49
A2 – View (East From The Top Of The Riggs Road/B & O Trestle)	4:54
A3 – Lion	5:03
A4 – March! For Martin Luther King	3:40
A5 – The Singing Bridge Of Memphis Tennessee	2:49
B1 – Dance Of The Inhabitants Of The Invisible City Of Bladensburg	4:07
B2 – Charles A. Lee: In Memoriam	3:58
B3 – Irish Setter	7:14
B4 – Commemorative Transfiguration and Communion at Magruder Park	5:59

Original Producer: John Fahey and Barret Hansen
Recording Dates: same as LP #1
Of note: (1) Vanguard is now a WELK Record Group company.
(2) The cassette's cover retains the catalogue number of the LP. (3) The UPC code on the back is: 015707929349.

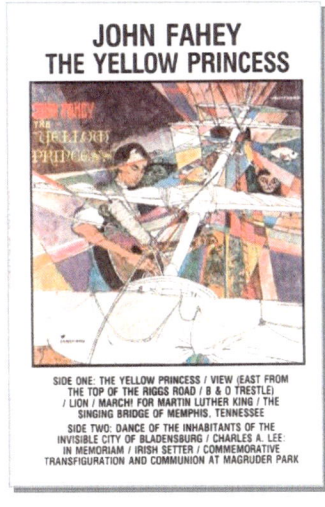

CD re-issue

#1

Release date: ? 1993
Catalog number: VMD-79293
Format: CD
Cover: STEREO; VSD-79293.   **Disc label**: Silver

Original Cover credit: Chuck McVicker
Songs: version #1 (9)

1 – The Yellow Princess	4:49
2 – View (East From The Top Of The Riggs Road/B & O Trestle)	4:54
3 – Lion	5:03
4 – March! For Martin Luther King	3:40
5 – The Singing Bridge Of Memphis Tennessee	2:49
6 – Dance Of The Inhabitants Of The Invisible City Of Bladensburg	4:07
7 – Charles A. Lee: In Memoriam	3:58
8 – Irish Setter	7:14
9 – Commemorative Transfiguration and Communion at Magruder Park	5:59

Recording Dates: same as LP #1
Remastering: not mentioned
Original Liner Notes: yes (reproduced)
Original Producer: John Fahey and Barret Hansen
Reissue Producer: not given
Of note: (1) Vanguard is now a WELK Record Group company. (2) The CD's cover retains the catalogue number of the LP. (3) The UPC code on the back cover is: 015707929325.

#2

Release date: 2000 (Italy)
Catalog number: VMD-79293
Format: CD - digipak
Cover: STEREO; VMD-79293.

Disc label: Tan

Original Cover credit: Chuck McVicker
Songs: version #1 (9)

1 – The Yellow Princess	4:49
2 – View (East from the Top Of The Riggs Road/B & O Trestle)	4:54
3 – Lion	5:03
4 – March! for Martin Luther King	3:40
5 – The Singing Bridge Of Memphis, Tennessee	2:49
6 – Dance of the Inhabitants of the Invisible City of Bladensburg	4:07
7 – Charles A. Lee: in Memoriam	3:58
8 – Irish Letter	7:14
9 – Commemorative Transfiguration and Communion at Magruder Park	5:59

Recording Dates: same as LP #1
Remastering:
Original Liner Notes: yes (reproduced)
Original Producer: John Fahey and Barret Hansen
Reissue Producer: Comet Records, Italy
Of note: (1) Notice the misspelling on the cover and label of "Irish Setter" as "Irish Letter"! (2) The front cover has the correct catalogue # VMD-79293 that matches the one on the label. (3) The EAN-13 code on the back cover is: 8026575293526.

#3

Release date: 2001 (Japan)
Catalog number: KICP 773
Format: CD
Cover: STEREO; *no* catalog number   **Disc label**: Yellow / black

Original Cover credit: Chuck McVicker
Songs: version #1 (9)

1 – The Yellow Princess	4:49
2 – View (East From The Top Of The Riggs Road/B & O Trestle)	4:54
3 – Lion	5:03
4 – March! For Martin Luther King	3:40
5 – The Singing Bridge Of Memphis Tennessee	2:49
6 – Dance Of The Inhabitants Of The Invisible City Of Bladensburg	4:07
7 – Charles A. Lee: In Memoriam	3:58
8 – Irish Setter	7:14
9 – Commemorative Transfiguration and Communion at Magruder Park	5:59

Recording Dates: same as LP #1
Remastering:
Original Liner Notes: yes (reproduced)
New Liner Notes: yes (in Japanese)
Original Producer: given as Samuel Charters
Reissue Producer: King Record Co., Tokyo, Japan
Of note: (1) The correct time of 5:08 for track A3 is written on the inside pages of the booklet. (2) The EAN-13 code on the obi strip is: 4988003257163.

#4

Release date: 2004 (UK)
Catalog number: VMD 79293
Format: CD
Cover: *no* STEREO; *no* catalog number.   **Disc label**: Yellow / red

Original Cover credit: Chuck McVicker
Songs: version #1 (9)

1 – The Yellow Princess	4:49
2 – View (East From The Top Of The Riggs Road/B & O Trestle)	4:53
3 – Lion	5:06
4 – March! For Martin Luther King	3:39
5 – The Singing Bridge Of Memphis Tennessee	2:49
6 – Dance Of The Inhabitants Of The Invisible City Of Bladensburg	4:06
7 – Charles A. Lee: In Memoriam	3:58
8 – Irish Setter	7:14
9 – Commemorative Transfiguration and Communion at Magruder Park	6:00

Recording Dates: same as LP #1.
Remastering:
Original Liner Notes: yes (reproduced)
New Liner Notes: by Rob Chapman
Original Producer: John Fahey and Barret Hansen
Reissue Producer: Vanguard, a WELK music group company; marketed by ACE Records.
Of note: (1) The UPC code on the back cover is: 029667005821.

#5

Release date: 2006
Catalog number: 79795-2
Format: CD
Cover: STEREO; *no* catalog number.   **Disc label**: Purple / silver

Original Cover credit: Chuck McVicker (not given on front cover)
Songs: version #2 (12)
1 – The Yellow Princess	4:53
2 – View (East From The Top Of The Riggs Road/B & O Trestle)	4:56
3 – Lion	5:10
4 – March! For Martin Luther King	3:43
5 – The Singing Bridge Of Memphis, Tennessee	2:53
6 – Dance Of The Inhabitants Of The Invisible City Of Bladensburg	4:10
7 – Charles A. Lee: In Memoriam	4:02
8 – Irish Setter	7:17
9 – Commemorative Transfiguration and Communion at Magruder Park	6:00
10 – The John Fahey Sampler, Themes and Variations	8:43
11 – Fare Forward Voyagers, 1965	4:53
12 – Steel Guitar Medley	9:23

Recording Dates: 1-9: same as LP #1; 10-12: August 1965.
Remastering: Stephen Brower
Original Liner Notes: yes (reproduced)
New Liner Notes: by M. Ward and Glenn Jones
Original Producer: John Fahey and Barret Hansen
Reissue Producer: Vanguard, a WELK music group company.
Of note: (1) This issue contains the three tunes from the Elektra demo tape made in 1965.
(2) The UPC code on the back cover is: 15707979528.
(3) A promo CD with a silver disc label and without a cover was issued →

#6

Release date: 2006 (UK)
Catalog number: VMD 79795
Format: CD
Cover: STEREO (cropped at top); VSD-79293. **Disc label**: Purple / red

Original Cover credit: Chuck McVicker
Songs: version #2 (12)

1 – The Yellow Princess	4:53
2 – View (East From The Top Of The Riggs Road/B & O Trestle)	4:56
3 – Lion	5:10
4 – March! For Martin Luther King	3:43
5 – The Singing Bridge Of Memphis, Tennessee	2:53
6 – Dance Of The Inhabitants Of The Invisible City Of Bladensburg	4:10
7 – Charles A. Lee: In Memoriam	4:02
8 – Irish Setter	7:17
9 – Commemorative Transfiguration and Communion at Magruder Park	6:00
10 – The John Fahey Sampler, Themes and Variations	8:43
11 – Fare Forward Voyagers, 1965	4:53
12 – Steel Guitar Medley	9:23

Recording Dates: 1-9: same as LP #1; 10-12: August 1965.
Remastering: Stephen Brower
Original Liner Notes: yes (reproduced)
New Liner Notes: by M. Ward and Glenn Jones
Original Producer: John Fahey and Barret Hansen
Reissue Producer: Vanguard, a WELK music group company; marketed by ACE Records.
Of note: (1) This issue contains the three tunes from the Elektra demo tape made in 1965. (2) The UPC code on the back cover is: 029667020329.

"YELLOW PRINCESS" - The Painting

"The Yellow Princess was a magnificent Clipper ship with golden sails, ivory prow, jade hull and jeweled mast-head; . . ."

The original painting reproduced on the front cover was made by Charles (Chuck) McVicker. It is a 20" x 22" acrylic painting on illustration board, and is unsigned.

Charles T. McVicker (born 1930) is a painter and illustrator, and a retired Professor of Art at the College of New Jersey. He grew up in the suburbs of Pittsburgh, Pennsylvania, and studied Fine Art at The Principia College and at the Art Center College of Design in Los Angeles.

McVicker was a freelance illustrator in New York City when he was commissioned in 1968 by Vanguard Records to illustrate the cover of the *Yellow Princess* album. He never met John Fahey, and for the painting he used a photograph of him. The various elements of the painting were suggested by the subjects in the song titles and notes. He worked for the art director of Vanguard Records, Jules Halfant, for whom he made one other album cover ("Mahler: Symphony No. 3", Vanguard VCS-10072/3, 1969). One can notice the same technique used in the paintings for the two album covers.

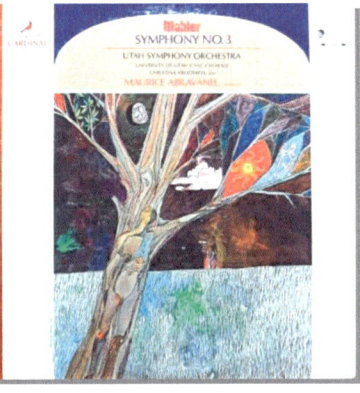

At the time, the work of commissioned artists was generally not returned to them. Thus, this painting remained in Halfant's collection until his death in 2001. McVicker stated that he was very pleased with the painting and enjoyed making it because he was given free rein to do as he wished.

 "Lion" – Fahey's orange tom-cat.

 "View" – the B & O trestle

 "March! For Martin Luther King"

"And in that lake lived an enormous turtle . . . his shell painted by moss and pulp."

 ". . . but there are a few carp and cat-fish . . ."

The Making of *THE YELLOW PRINCESS*

The Yellow Princess is a record that evolved directly from the previous year's album *Requia*. Most of its songs had been already hatched in January 1967, and its notes had been initially written for *Requia*, but later modified to agree with the final selection of songs on the *Requia* album.

Moreover, several of the songs on *The Yellow Princess* were initially titled or considered as requia:

    Requiem for Charles A. Lee → Charles A. Lee: In Memoriam
    Requiem for Lion → Lion
    Requiem for Martin Luther King → March! For Martin Luther King
    Irish Setter → dedicated to the passing of one of Fahey's dogs.

At the January 1967 recording session at Hollywood Sound Recorders, Los Angeles, John Fahey had recorded "Irish Setter" (7'34"), "Requiem for Charles A. Lee" (7'50"), and "Requiem for Lion" (4'50"). The album version of these three songs have the times: 7'14", 3'58", and 5'08", respectively. The difference in duration suggests that they were either shortened from the original or re-recorded. Barret Hansen confirms that they were indeed re-recorded in June of 1968.

In February 1968, John Fahey and Sam Charters discussed the new contract for this album with Vanguard. The following month Charters went to Berkeley and met up with Fahey. After the uneasy relation they had had in releasing *Requia*, Sam Charters, who was also committed to other artists, decided to list himself only as executive producer for Fahey's second Vanguard release. John Fahey thus asked Barry Hansen to be the producer of *The Yellow Princess*.

By then, Fahey had already selected most of the pieces that he wanted to record. He had also decided that he wanted to make the album at Sierra Sound Labs in Berkeley where he had often recorded in the past and because he felt more comfortable there. Fahey wanted to re-make four pieces that he had recorded at the Hollywood session of January 1967 – "Requiem for Charles A. Lee," "Lion," "Irish Setter" and "Yellow Princess." He also played some newly composed pieces to Hansen, including "Requiem for Martin Luther King" which he had written soon after the assassination of King on April 4, 1968. The latter was also planned for a 45 rpm issue.

In mid-April, Fahey travelled east for a concert tour in Pennsylvania, New York City, and Boston. Thereafter, he dropped out of school and was ready to dedicate himself completely to the project. Barry Hansen made the arrangements for a recording session and they found an electric bassoon player for the "Singing Bridge" cut.

The entire *The Yellow Princess* album was recorded at Sierra Sound Labs in Berkeley during the week of June 4, 1968, with the sole exception of the sound effects used in "The Singing Bridge" that John had previously taped. These would be dubbed onto a multi-track tape at Sierra Sound and mixed according to John's instructions.

The first track to be recorded on the first day of recording, June 4, was the title track "Yellow Princess." A song with this same title had been recorded at the January 1967 taping as a 4'56" long piece. It had a middle section which was in 3/4 waltz time. However, neither Charters nor Fahey were happy with it, and Fahey admitted to botching the splice job on it. The middle waltz section was referred to as the "Bastrop Waltz" and in an early version of the *Requia* album liner notes, when referring to the song "Yellow Princess," a crossed-out sentence by Fahey stated: "The mid-section 'Bastrop Waltz' has absolutely nothing to do with Bastrop, Louisiana, except that I completed that 3/4 part of the song in that city." Indeed, the engineer notes for that January 1967 session appended the phrase "(introducing the Bastrop Waltz)" to its title. This piece was eventually eliminated from the *Requia* album. The new version of "The Yellow Princess," which by now had shed its middle waltz section, is the version (lasting 4'49") that we are familiar with on the LP of the same name. An interesting guitar piece called "Bastrop Waltz" is present on a circulating bootleg tape and probably is the "Yellow Princess #1" version.

After listening to the playback of Take 1 of "Yellow Princess," everybody was happy with it and they moved on to the the next songs. Amongst these were two tracks with added musicians. The idea of bringing aboard the extra musicians to ambitiously remake "Bladensburg" was Barry Hansen's. John was not enthusiastic at first but agreed to go along with it. Once the musicians were booked, Fahey found use for them also on "March! For Martin Luther King."

The additional musicians were Jay Ferguson and Mark Andes, members of the rock band Spirit; Matt Andes; as well as Kevin Kelley, a part-time member of the Rising Sons, The Byrds and, later on, of Fever Tree. Jay Ferguson and the two Andes brothers (sons of the actor Keith Andes, who notably played Marilyn Monroe's boyfriend in the movie *Clash By Night*) were introduced to Fahey by their longtime friend Hansen. These three musicians had started their first band in high school (along with Denny Bruce, future president of Takoma Records!), and would later form the group Jo Jo Gunne.

The two tracks with added musicians were recorded on Wednesday, June 6, 1968. The evening before, Robert F. Kennedy had been shot in Los Angeles. Mark, Matt, Jay, Kevin and Barry Hansen were all watching television in their hotel when it happened, and were all shocked, having been through the assassinations of John F. Kennedy and Martin Luther King, Jr. John Fahey, who was staying elsewhere, tried not to show that he was upset the next day. They were all distracted, but nevertheless they soldiered on.

As for "The Dance of the Inhabitants of the Invisible City of Bladensburg," its last portion was originally a couple of minutes longer. After hearing the playback a few times, Fahey insisted that most of the "rock" part be edited out. Barry somewhat reluctantly went along with it.

After the sessions were wrapped at Sierra Sound, the tapes were sent to Vanguard Records in New York. The album was mastered and prepared for release there.

In November the record was almost ready. Fahey had received the liner notes to *The Yellow Princess* and asked for some corrections to be made, such as adding the names and record company of the session musicians. However, in the title listing for side 2 (upper right corner of back liner notes), "Dance of the …. Bladensburg" was supposed to be corrected to "Raga of the ….. Bladensburg," but it never was, probably because by then it was too late.

By December, John Fahey was planning his 3rd Vanguard record *Epithalamium*.

CHARLES A. LEE: IN MEMORIAM

This tune is dedicated to the father of Fahey's friend R. Anthony Lee ("Flea"). His father's name is actually Charles F. Lee (Charles Foster Lee) and not Charles A. Lee. He was born on July 29, 1906, in Cleveland, Ohio. He became a chemical engineer after graduating in 1928 from Case Institute of Technology.

Charles F. Lee worked as a fish biologist and fisheries industry troubleshooter for the U.S. Fish and Wildlife Service at College Park, Maryland, as well as for the U. S. Department of Interior's Bureau of Commercial Fisheries. He also worked on foreign assignments in Scotland, Egypt, Argentina, Chile, Peru, and the Netherlands to work on aid programs and research in this field.

Over three decades he published many articles and books dedicated to the science of fisheries, such as:
"Composition of cooked fish dishes" (1954)
"Menhaden Industry" (1961)
"Soft-Crab Industry" (1962)
"Oyster Industry of Chesapeake Bay, South Atlantic, & Gulf of Mexico" (1963)
"Crab Industry of Chesapeake Bay and the South" (1964)

In the notes to *The Yellow Princess*, Fahey states that Charles Lee was murdered in Brazil. This is sadly quite true. In February 1966, Lee moved with his wife and daughter to the coastal town of Recife in northeastern Brazil for a two-year stint as a representative of the U.S. Agency for International Development. On September 1, 1966, he was stabbed to death by an apartment house custodian and his cousin in a dispute over thievery. Indeed, Lee's home had been burglarized three times by unknowns since he had arrived. The murder culprits were arrested soon after the crime.

Charles F. Lee was a learned man of gentle nature, and John Fahey was quite fond of him.

The Saga of the Elektra Demo Tape

The Elektra Demo saga is a work in progress, of which the final chapter has yet to be written.

Item #25 of the *Dance of Death* notes states that in August 1965 Fahey, along with Bill Barth and "Mysterious" Al Wilson, cut a guitar instruction LP illustrating various traditional styles for Elektra Records in New York City. This is confirmed by a short notice in the September 15, 1965 issue of *The Broadside of Boston*:

> ***JOHN FAHEY stopped in New York to record a few cuts for a Guitar Styles Project album***The first re-

At this session, Fahey also recorded five of his own guitar pieces for Elektra, two of which had Al Wilson on veena:

- On the Banks of the Owchita
- Sail Away Ladies

The remaining three pieces by Fahey on solo guitar were called:

- Revolt of the Brontosaurus
- Delta Serenade
- Green, Green

This Elektra demo session never yielded a record, and Fahey apparently wanted the tape sent back to him. His request must have gone unanswered, so much so that an unconventional and anonymous ad was posted in the 1966 issue of *The Little Sandy Review*:

In 2006, *The Yellow Princess* was reissued on a CD that contained an extra three tracks deemed to be the lost Fahey demo songs that he had made for Elektra. These were found on a tape that was stored in the Vanguard vaults. But since the tape box had no track listing, the songs were given temporary titles by producer Glenn Jones after playing them for guitarist Charlie Schmidt:

> #10 – The John Fahey Sampler, Themes and Variations   8:43
> #11 – Fare Forward Voyagers, 1965   4:53
> #12 – Steel Guitar Medley   9:23

Several years later additional information surfaced since the release of *The Yellow Princess* CD re-issue. What is now known is that the Elektra demo tape had been indeed returned to Fahey back in March of 1967 by Sam Charters.

The following are excerpts from letters exchanged between John Fahey and Sam Charters in early 1967.

March 23, 1967: Sam Charters writes, "I am enclosing the letter that I got from Elektra. The tape of the three selections was with it, and I am sending it to you by separate package. The Revolt of the Brontosaurus is a gem. . . . Perhaps we could use it for the next record."

March 31, 1967: Fahey answers, "Good great wonderful you got the tapes out of Elektra. I think we should probably use Revolt of Brontosaurus but change the title . . . ."

April 11, 1967: Sam sent a dub and writes, "I kept the master copy here so we can use the 12-string piece . . . ."

Late April, 1967: Fahey answers, "Have listened to the Elektra tapes & believe we should use the twelve string cut most definitely (although you must realize that there are short sections alluding to two other songs I have recorded, but three-fourths of it are all new) . . . and most of the bottleneck cut is pretty good."

This epistolary correspondence between Fahey and Charters furnishes the following facts about the three songs:

(1) One of the tracks is a 12-string guitar piece titled "Revolt of the Brontosaurus." This may well correspond to "The John Fahey Sampler: Themes & Variations" on the 2006 CD reissue.

(2) The second track is a bottleneck piece. This could be the "Delta Serenade" (a/k/a "Steel Guitar Medley").

(3) As for the third track, no details are known but, by exclusion, it should be "Green, Green" (a/k/a "Fare Forward Voyagers, 1965").

A MARCH FOR MARTIN LUTHER KING
B/W SINGING BRIDGE

Release date: late 1968
Catalog number: VRS-35076
Format: 7" 45 rpm, stereo
Matrix #: ZTSP-221001   34-4   8-68
             ZTSP-221002   34-4   8-68
Songs: A1 – A March For Martin Luther King   3:40
           B1 – Singing Bridge   2:46
Recording Dates: June 1968 (mastered in August 1968)

Of note: In the early part of 1968, John Fahey went into a funk. He dropped out of school and even asked to be released from his Vanguard contract since he did not feel he had enough music left in him for two more albums. And once sales of *Requia* stalled, he did not believe that Vanguard would make any money from him anyhow.

However, things looked brighter when concert gigs on the East Coast came up. Then, in April of 1968, Martin Luther King, Jr., was assassinated. John Fahey had great admiration for the man and he began the process of writing a "Requiem for M.L.K." He now became serious about reviving his contract with Vanguard Records and spurring them to produce a new album which would include this requiem.

This 45 rpm was issued as a promotional record only. Its series number (VRS-35---) indicates that a commercial release was contemplated, but probably cancelled when it did not stir up much interest. Fahey had his own issues and had previously expressed his impressions about the release of a 45 rpm record of his music, (presumably from the *Requia* album), and said that it would have been a waste of money and that he did not believe there was "anything sufficiently palatable for mass cultural consumption."

EPITHALAMIUM

THE 3ʳᴰ VANGUARD ALBUM

The idea for this album was hatched after the production of *The Yellow Princess* album was complete.

In late September of 1968, John Fahey had proposed a re-issue on Vanguard of *The Transfiguration of Blind Joe Death*. Two of its songs would be eliminated ("Poor Boy" was already on *Dance of Death*; and Fahey did not care for "My Station Will Be Changed After While"). He wanted to retain its jacket cover and keep the booklet as well. Fahey also wanted to re-record *Dance of Death* for Vanguard. For this reason he put on hold any Takoma re-recording of *Dance of Death*. These two ideas were not accepted by Vanguard Records since they preferred to issue records with new material, and considered *Dance of Death* as too good a record to mess with.

Thereafter, the plan was to record a 3ʳᵈ Vanguard album. This was going to be a "light" album with orchestral arrangements and strings, along with guitar solo pieces.

John Fahey planned to be in New York City (Dec-Jan, 1969) to do some recording. He already had recorded some material at Sierra Sound Labs with Bob DeSousa. However, Fahey was perplexed on how to incorporate string arrangements with his songs. Sam Charters proposed that he contact Ed Bogas (who had worked on albums by Country Joe & The Fish and Joe Byrd's United States of America) in Berkeley.

By December, Fahey had come up with a list of tunes for the album, which would be titled *Epithalamium*. This is a Greek word (a/k/a Epithalamion) that refers to the wedding or nuptial bed, and likely is a reference to the fact that Fahey had just married the previous year. In the *Voice of the Turtle* booklet (section VII) a reference is made to a song called 'Epithalamion' "which is still in progress" (as of 1968), and he curiously says that it is not a song inspired by a woman.

The planned song list was the following:

A1 – Epithalamium
A2 – Two Hawaiian songs for guitar
A3 – The Okefenokee Swamp Raintree (piano piece with orchestra)
A4 – Theme and Variations for Guitar from Dvorak's 4ᵗʰ Symphony
A5 – New Orleans Shuffle
A6 – Charley Bradley's 1066 (with strings or orchestra)
A7 – collage (see below)
    B1 – Bottleneck piece in open G (with organ drone)
    B2 – Requiem for Molly, part 5
    B3 – Guitar solo, long improvisation on the hymn "Come Labor On".

His plan was to now record tracks A1, A4, B1 and B3 at one of the California studios (Sierra Sound in Berkeley or Western in Hollywood). A3 was a piano piece written by Fahey, to be played by a session player whom he nicknamed "QuickPencil" since he could not remember his name. A6 is a tune similar to "Jim Lee Blues." He even planned a "Singing Bridge"-type collage (A7) with "echo blasts from some large tunnels and alligators in the Okefenokee swamp bellowing when the weather starts to change, and one french horn and one trumpet."

This album was never produced.

Charley Bradley's 1066 (ten sixty-six) was an unissued song by Charley Patton. Son House explained its origin in an interview he gave to John Fahey, Barrett Hansen and Mark Levine in Venice, California on May 7, 1965. It refers to a train that came out of Memphis and went to Vicksburg, passing through Clarkesville. Charley Bradley was the railroad engineer and 1066 was the engine number.

A song with this title would be issued posthumously on Fahey's *Red Cross* album in 2003.

SÄVEL – FINLANDIA E.P.

Release date: April 1968   (Finland)
Catalog number: SÄ 1518
Format: 7" EP, 33⅓ rpm, stereo
Matrix #: SÄ 1518 A
          SÄ 1518 B
Songs:
  A1 – Finlandia   3:15   (a)
  A2 – Night Train To Valhalla   2:26   (a)
    B1 – A Raga Called Pat   6:22   (b)
Recording Dates: (a) April 8, 1966 – Takoma Studios, Berkeley, California.
(b) June 12, 1966 – Ash Grove, Los Angeles, California.
Producer: Pekka Gronow

These are supposedly three songs from the LP *Days Have Gone By*.

Side A

"FINLANDIA" is identical to "We Would Be Building" on the LP *Days Have Gone By*, except that it is the complete and longer version.

"NIGHT TRAIN TO VALHALLA" is not the song by this title, but actually a never-before issued John Fahey tune called "Television Song (or Rag)."

Ralph Cameron Johnston (a/k/a Ragtime Ralph – see page 36) issued a very similar version "Ragtime Piece in G – a/k/a Television Blues" on his album *Volume Four* in 1982. Ralph had learned it from a tape of Fahey tunes that Joe Bussard had sent him, and then from Fahey himself when he met him in Vancouver.

Fahey had previously recorded this as: (1) "Thing in G (The Television Song)" at Arhoolie Studios in Berkeley, California, on April 13, 1964; (2) "The Television Song" at Adelphi Studios in Silver Springs, Maryland, in the summer of 1964; (3) "Television Song / Rag" at Topanga, California, in early June, 1965; and (4) "Television Rag" at Takoma Studios in Berkeley, California, on April 8, 1966.

Side B

"A RAGA CALLED PAT" is a different mix of "A Raga Called Pat, part 1" from *Days Have Gone By*. Notably, the first minute-long segment of guitar is brought to the forefront. The guitar portion was presumably recorded at the Ash Grove on June 12, 1966.

THE STORY BEHIND THE FINNISH E.P.

In the 1960s, Pekka Gronow, an ethnomusicologist from Finland who had studied in the United States, read about John Fahey and collected all his LPs on Takoma. He was intrigued by his interpretation of the Finnish national anthem "Finlandia" by Jean Sibelius (a/k/a "We Would Be Building" on the 1967 album *Days Have Gone By*) and wrote to him about the possibility of publishing this tune in Finland. John Fahey was very agreeable and sent Gronow the master tape.

The single was originally planned for release on Pekka Gronow's **Eteenpäin!** label, but difficulties arose when getting the publisher's clearance for the compositions. And so it was decided to seek the cooperation of the label **Sävel**. It was distributed by Finnlevy.

Since the tracks were not marked very clearly on the tape, an error occurred when identifying them. This led to the fortuitous inclusion of the previously unissued track "Television Rag" instead of "Night Train To Valhalla." The master tape was returned to Fahey at the time, and the single did not sell much. It is unclear if Fahey ever got any royalties from it. Legend has it that the song "Finlandia" was temporarily banned from Finnish national radio since it was not an exact or proper, note-for-note rendition of the national anthem.

RAGTIME RALPH

Ralph Cameron Johnston (a/k/a Ragtime Ralph a/k/a Blind Brand X) was born in 1952 in Regina, Saskatchewan, Canada. He fell under the spell of John Fahey after seeing him on the *Guitar, Guitar* TV show in 1969. He eventually moved to New Westminster, British Columbia, where he released three EPs of acoustic guitar music under the name of Ragtime Ralph in 1982.

When Fahey came to play at the 5th Annual Folk Music Festival in Vancouver, he and his wife Melody stayed at Ralph's place. Ralph received guitar lessons from Fahey and also learned how to play his "Television Rag." Fahey showed interest in releasing Ralph's LP *Volume 4* on Takoma Records, but later backed out after accusing Ralph of using him to get into the music business. Ralph then decided to release the album himself in 1982.

Ralph also recorded six sides for Joe Bussard's Fonotone with the group The Backporch Drifters. In 1982, John recorded Ralph's arrangement of "Away In A Manger" on his Varrick Christmas album, which made him quite proud. Ralph later played in a surf band called The Surfdusters, several of whose pieces can be heard on episodes of the TV cartoon show *Spongebob Squarepants*. He also played in the duo Quonset.

In the 1990s Ralph, now known as Blind Brand X and having moved to Vancouver, began issuing home-made CDs of his guitar music, most of which he dedicated to his hero John Fahey:

Ragtime Ralph: *Lost Blues 1929-1934*	CD	2008
Blind Brand X: *Black Dog Blues*	CD	2008
Ragtime Ralph: *Volume 4*	CD	2009
The Backporch Drifters: *Raiders of the Lost Porch*	CD	2009
Ragtime Ralph: *Unearthed: Ragtime Ralph Live...Feb 28, 1981*	CD	2009
Blind Brand X: *Yesterday I'll Be Happy*	CD	2009
Blind Brand X & Dixie X: *Wreck of the Ol' 78*	CD	2010
RC Johnston: *The Fahey Project*	mp3	2012
RC Johnston: *Aloha, Mahalo*	mp3	2014

These have been offered gratis to his fans or made available for download.

The many album jackets of *Ragtime Ralph - Volume Four* (3 LPs, and one CD on far right), the album that contains Ralph's rendition of Fahey's "Television Song."

THE NEW POSSIBILITY
JOHN FAHEY'S GUITAR SOLI CHRISTMAS ALBUM

#1
Release date: November 1968
Edition: 1st issue (label #1, jacket #1, songs #1)
Catalog number: C-1020
Format: 12" LP, 33 1/3 rpm, stereo
Jacket cover: 1st
  - **Front cover**: cream; textured; red "T" logo.
  - **Spine**: THE NEW POSSIBILITY   JOHN FAHEY   TAKOMA C-1020
  - **Back cover**: liner notes;
        Berkeley Graphic Arts union logo.
Cover credit: Tom Weller
Label: BL⁹

Matrix #: 1020-A
        1020-B
Songs: version #1-a (8+6)

A1	Joy To The World	1:52
A2	What Child Is This?	3:02
A3	Medley: Hark, The Herald Angels Sing; O Come All Ye Faithful	3:10
A4	Auld Lang Syne	2:01
A5	The Bells Of Saint Mary's	2:10
A6	Good King Wenceslas	1:10
A7	We Three Kings Of Orient Are	1:50
A8	God Rest Ye Merry Gentlemen Fantasy	3:00
B1	The First Noel	2:12
B2	Christ's Saints Of God Fantasy	10:12
B3	It Came Upon A Midnight Clear	1:28
B4	Go I Will Send Thee	3:00
B5	Lo How A Rose E'er Blooming	3:45
B6	Silent Night, Holy Night	1:14

Recording Dates: 1968
Back Liner Notes: yes (this also came with the 1968 Takoma catalogue).
Producer: John Fahey
Of note: (1) Track A8 is actually 2'42" long.

#2
Release date: 1969
Edition: 2nd issue (label #2, jacket #1, songs #1)
Catalog number: C-1020
Format: 12" LP, 33 1/3 rpm, stereo
Jacket cover: 1st
  - **Front cover**: cream; textured; red "T" logo.
  - **Spine**: THE NEW POSSIBILITY   JOHN FAHEY   TAKOMA C-1020
- **Back cover**: liner notes; Berkeley Graphic Arts union logo.
Cover credit: Tom Weller
Label: BD^2

Matrix #: 1020-A
  1020-B
Songs: version #1-a (8+6)
Recording Dates: 1968
Back Liner Notes: yes
Producer: John Fahey

The "textured" album cover for this first version was an idea of Tom Weller. Since Fahey came across as more of an intellectual Christian, Weller did away with images of mangers and wise men, and used only images of rather severe crosses. He made the prints with *linocuts* (similar to woodcuts, but using linoleum instead of wood). Weller printed the covers in Berkeley and decided to use *laid paper* which gave a ribbed texture and a nice tactile element to the album. Later versions would be printed on glossy paper, unfortunately.

CHRISTMAS ALBUM REVELATION

In 1984 Fahey stated: "When going through the old 78s in a record store in Winston-Salem in 1958, I came upon box after box of *White Christmas* by Bing Crosby. It was July and they were already stocking up. Couldn't get enough of them. The idea of making a guitar Christmas album got into my brain." (Daniel Gewertz, *Boston Herald*, 1984).

Regarding his interpretation of the Christmas carols, Fahey said: "Those I had to sit down and pretty much learn, although I knew most of them already from going to church so much! In fact most of the hymns are in standard key of C — almost like a record of studies in the key of C." (Michael Grenfell, *Guitar*, 1984)

Fahey's hunch paid off. As an example, in the 2nd half of 1981, Takoma sold 4500 LPs of the New Possibility, 2000 LPs of Xmas volume 2, but just over 100 copies of his Volumes 1-3 combined.

Not only did this become his best selling record ever, but John Fahey will be in the company of Bing Crosby on no less than eight Christmas CD compilations.

#3
Release date: 1969
Edition: 3rd issue (label #3, jacket #2, songs #1)
Catalog number: C-1020
Format: 12" LP, 33 1/3 rpm, stereo
Jacket cover: 2nd
  - **Front cover**: cream; textured; red "T" logo.
  - **Spine**: THE NEW POSSIBILITY   JOHN FAHEY   TAKOMA C-1020
  - **Back cover**: liner notes; *no* printer's union logo.
Cover credit: Tom Weller
Label: O

Matrix #: 1020-A
              1020-B
Songs: version #1-a (8+6)
Recording Dates: 1968
Back Liner Notes: yes
Producer: John Fahey
Of note: (1) The label says monaural, but the record is stereo.

#4
Release date: 1971
Edition: 4th issue (label #4, jacket #2, songs #1)
Catalog number: C-1020
Format: 12" LP, 33 1/3 rpm, stereo
Jacket cover: 2nd
  - **Front cover**: cream; textured; red "T" logo.
  - **Spine**: THE NEW POSSIBILITY   JOHN FAHEY   TAKOMA C-1020
  - **Back cover**: liner notes; *no* printer's union logo
Cover credit: Tom Weller
Label: Da[1]
Matrix #: 1020-A
              1020-B
Songs: version #1-a (8+6)
Recording Dates: 1968   **Back Liner Notes**: yes
Producer: John Fahey   **Of note**: (1) The label says monaural, but the record is stereo.

#5

Release date: 1971
Edition: 5th issue (label #5, jacket #2, songs #1)
Catalog number: C-1020
Format: 12" LP, 33 1/3 rpm, stereo
Jacket cover: 2nd
  - **Front cover**: cream; textured; red "T" logo.
  - **Spine**: THE NEW POSSIBILITY   JOHN FAHEY   TAKOMA C-1020
  - **Back cover**: liner notes; *no* printer's union logo.
Cover credit: Tom Weller
Label: Da^2
Matrix #: 1020-A
             1020-B
Songs: version #1-a (8+6)
Recording Dates: 1968
Back Liner Notes: yes
Producer: John Fahey

#6

Release date: 1972
Edition: 6th issue (label #6, jacket #2, songs #1)
Catalog number: C-1020
Format: 12" LP, 33 1/3 rpm, stereo
Jacket cover: 2nd
  - **Front cover**: cream; textured; red "T" logo.
  - **Spine**: THE NEW POSSIBILITY   JOHN FAHEY   TAKOMA C-1020
  - **Back cover**: liner notes; *no* printer's union logo.
Cover credit: Tom Weller
Label: Du^1
Matrix #: 1020-A
             1020-B
Songs: version #1-a (8+6)
Recording Dates: 1968
Back Liner Notes: yes
Producer: John Fahey

#7

Release date: 1974
Edition: 7th issue (label #7, jacket #2, songs #1)
Catalog number: C-1020
Format: 12" LP, 33 1/3 rpm, stereo
Jacket cover: 2nd
  - **Front cover**: cream; textured; red "T" logo
  - **Spine**: THE NEW POSSIBILITY   JOHN FAHEY   TAKOMA C-1020
  - **Back cover**: liner notes; *no* printer's union logo
Cover credit: Tom Weller
Label: Da^{3K}
Matrix #: 1020-A
         1020-B
Songs: version #1-a (8+6)
Recording Dates: 1968
Back Liner Notes: yes
Producer: John Fahey
Of note: (1) some have jacket #3.

#8

Release date: 1976
Edition: 8th issue (label #8, jacket #2, songs #1)
Catalog number: C-1020
Format: 12" LP, 33 1/3 rpm, stereo
Jacket cover: 2nd
  - **Front cover**: cream; textured; red "T" logo
  - **Spine**: THE NEW POSSIBILITY   JOHN FAHEY   TAKOMA C-1020
  - **Back cover**: liner notes; *no* printer's union logo
Cover credit: Tom Weller
Label: Da^{3G}
Matrix #: 1020-A
         1020-B
Songs: version #1-a (8+6)
Recording Dates: 1968
Back Liner Notes: yes
Producer: John Fahey

#9

Release date: 1976
Edition: 9th issue (label #9, jacket #3, songs #1)
Catalog number: C-1020
Format: 12" LP, 33 1/3 rpm, stereo
Jacket cover: 3rd
  - **Front cover**: white; semi-glossy; red "T" logo.
  - **Spine**: THE NEW POSSIBILITY   JOHN FAHEY   TAKOMA C-1020
  - **Back cover**: liner notes; *no* printer's union logo.
Cover credit: Tom Weller
Label: Da^3

Matrix #: 1020-A
              1020-B
Songs: version #1-a (8+6)
Recording Dates: 1968
Back Liner Notes: yes
Producer: John Fahey

#10

Release date: 1977
Edition: 10th issue (label #10, jacket #4, songs #1)
Catalog number: C-1020
Format: 12" LP, 33 1/3 rpm, stereo
Jacket cover: 4th
  - **Front cover**: white; semi-glossy; red "T" logo
  - **Spine**: THE NEW POSSIBILITY   JOHN FAHEY   TAKOMA C-1020
  - **Back cover**: *no* liner notes; *no* printer's union logo
Cover credit: Tom Weller
Label: Da$^{3S\text{-}K}$

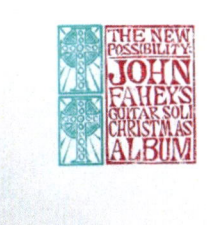

Matrix #: 1020-A
              1020-B
Songs: version #1-a (8+6)
Recording Dates: 1968
Back Liner Notes: no
Producer: John Fahey
Of note: (1) **Variant 9a** (label #10, jacket #5, songs #1). (2) Glenn Jones once asked John Fahey why he deleted the liner notes to this album. Fahey answered "Oh, I just didn't feel that way any more."

#11

Release date: 1978
Edition: 11th issue (label #11, jacket #5, songs #1)
Catalog number: C-1020
Format: 12" LP, 33 1/3 rpm, stereo
Jacket cover: 5th
   - **Front cover**: cream; textured; brown "T" logo
   - **Spine**: THE NEW POSSIBILITY   JOHN FAHEY   TAKOMA C-1020
   - **Back cover**: *no* liner notes; *no* printer's union logo
Cover credit: Tom Weller
Label: Di

  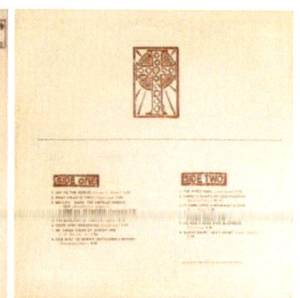

Matrix #: 1020-A
            1020-B
Songs: version #1-a (8+6)
Recording Dates: 1968
Back Liner Notes: no
Producer: John Fahey
Of note: (1) **Variant 11a**: (label #11, jacket #5a, songs #2) comes with a TAK 7020 sticker on back cover.
Its songs are version #2 with matrix numbers:
      T1   TAK-7020-A   (1) >
      T1   TAK-7020-B   (1) >
It also has the 1st "T-shirt Ad" inner record sleeve with Takoma catalogue up to D-1064 (see page 122).

#12

Release date: 1979
Edition: 12th issue (label #12, jacket #6, songs #2)
Catalog number: TAK-7020
Format: 12" LP, 33 1/3 rpm, stereo
Jacket cover: 6th
  - **Front cover**: cream; glossy; *no* "T" logo
  - **Spine**: TAK 7020   THE NEW POSSIBILITY • JOHN FAHEY
        TAKOMA RECORDS   PRINTED IN U.S.A.
  - **Back cover**: *no* liner notes; *no* printer's union logo;
        "Takoma Records Distributed by Chrysalis"
Cover credit: Tom Weller
Label: Do[1]

Matrix #: T1   TAK-7020-A   (1)   >
              T1   TAK-7020-B   (1)   >
Songs: version #1-b (8+6)

A1 – Joy To The World	1:52
A2 – What Child Is This?	3:02
A3 – Medley: Hark, The Herald Angels Sing; O Come All Ye Faithful	3:10
A4 – Auld Lang Syne	2:01
A5 – The Bells Of Saint Mary's	2:10
A6 – Good King Wenceslas	1:10
A7 – We Three Kings Of Orient Are	1:50
A8 – God Rest Ye Merry Gentlemen Fantasy	3:00
B1 – The First Noel	2:12
B2 – Christ's Saints Of God Fantasy	10:12
B3 – It Came Upon A Midnight Clear	1:28
B4 – Go I Will Send Thee	3:00
B5 – Lo How A Rose E'er Blooming	3:45
B6 – Silent Night, Holy Night	1:14

Recording Dates: 1968
Back Liner Notes: no
Producer: John Fahey

#13

Release date: 1983
Edition: 13th issue (label #13, jacket #7, songs #3)
Catalog number: TAK-7020
Format: 12" LP, 33 1/3 rpm, stereo
Jacket cover: 7th
  - **Front cover**: cream; glossy; *no* "T" logo
  - **Spine**: TAK 7020   THE NEW POSSIBILITY • JOHN FAHEY
        TAKOMA RECORDS   PRINTED IN U.S.A.
  - **Back cover**: *no* liner notes; *no* printer's union logo;
        "Takoma Records ... marketed by Allegiance Records"
Cover credit: Tom Weller
Label: Do^2

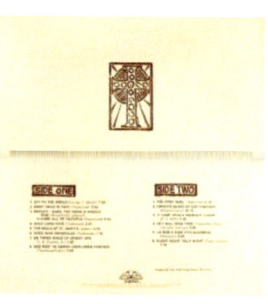

Matrix #: TAK-1-7020   G-1   PRC-1-1-2   A   MASTERED BY CAPITOL
              TAK-2-7020   G-1   PRC-1-1-2   B   MASTERED BY CAPITOL
Songs: version #1-c (8+6)

A1 – Joy To The World	1:52
A2 – What Child Is This?	3:02
A3 – Medley: Hark, The Herald Angels Sing; O Come All Ye Faithful	3:10
A4 – Auld Lang Syne	2:01
A5 – The Bells Of Saint Mary's	2:10
A6 – Good King Wenceslas	1:10
A7 – We Three Kings Of Orient Are	1:50
A8 – God Rest Ye Merry Gentlemen Fantasy	3:00
B1 – The First Noel	2:12
B2 – Christ's Saints Of God Fantasy	10:12
B3 – It Came Upon A Midnight Clear	1:28
B4 – Go I Will Send Thee	3:00
B5 – Lo How A Rose E'er Blooming	3:45
B6 – Silent Night, Holy Night	1:14

Recording Dates: 1968
Back Liner Notes: no
Producer: John Fahey

#14

Release date: 1987
Edition: 14th issue (label #14, jacket #7, songs #1)
Catalog number: SF-72720
Format: 12" LP, 33 1/3 rpm, stereo
Jacket cover: 7th
  - **Front cover**: cream; glossy; *no* "T" logo
  - **Spine**: TAK 7020   THE NEW POSSIBILITY • JOHN FAHEY
        TAKOMA RECORDS   PRINTED IN U.S.A.
  - **Back cover**: *no* liner notes; *no* printer's union logo;
        "Takoma Records ... marketed by Allegiance Records";
        Sticker with SF-72720
Cover credit: Tom Weller
Label: Do^3

Matrix #:
ST-1-72720   G-1   O   B-28504-G1   Δ17570   1-1   MASTERED BY CAPITOL
ST-2-72720   G-1   O   B-28505-G1   Δ17570-X 1-1 MASTERED BY CAPITOL
Songs: version #1-d (8+6)

A1 – Joy To The World	1:52
A2 – What Child Is This?	3:02
A3 – Medley: Hark, The Herald Angels Sing; O Come All Ye Faithful	3:10
A4 – Auld Lang Syne	2:01
A5 – The Bells Of Saint Mary's	2:10
A6 – Good King Wenceslas	1:10
A7 – We Three Kings Of Orient Are	1:50
A8 – God Rest Ye Merry Gentlemen Fantasy	3:00
B1 – The First Noel	2:12
B2 – Christ's Saints Of God Fantasy	10:12
B3 – It Came Upon A Midnight Clear	1:28
B4 – Go I Will Send Thee	3:00
B5 – Lo How A Rose E'er Blooming	3:45
B6 – Silent Night, Holy Night	1:14

Recording Dates: 1968
Back Liner Notes: no
Producer: John Fahey

Non-Takoma LP re-issue

#1

Release date: 1976 (England)
Catalog number: Sonet SNTF 702
Format: 12" LP, 33 1/3 rpm, stereo
Jacket cover:
  - Front cover: cream; glossy; Sonet and Takoma logos.
  - Spine: JOHN FAHEY   THE NEW POSSIBILITY   SNTF 702
  - Back cover: liner notes; Sonet logo.
Cover credit: Tom Weller
Label: pyramid

Matrix #: SNTF 702   A-2ΔG
              SNTF 702   B-1ΔG
Songs: version #1-e (8+6)

A1 – Joy To The World	1:52
A2 – What Child Is This?	3:02
A3 – Medley: Hark, The Herald Angels Sing; O Come All Ye Faithful	3:10
A4 – Auld Lang Syne	2:01
A5 – The Bells Of Saint Mary's	2:10
A6 – Good King Wenceslas	1:10
A7 – We Three Kings Of Orient Are	1:50
A8 – God Rest Ye Merry Gentlemen Fantasy	3:00
B1 – The First Noel	2:12
B2 – Christ's Saints Of God Fantasy	10:12
B3 – It Came Upon A Midnight Clear	1:28
B4 – Go I Will Send Thee	3:00
B5 – Lo How A Rose E'er Blooming	3:45
B6 – Silent Night, Holy Night	1:14

Recording Dates: 1968
Back Liner Notes: yes
Producer: John Fahey

#2

Release date: 1977   (England)
Catalog number: Sonet SNTF 702
Format: 12" LP, 33 1/3 rpm, stereo
Jacket cover:
  - **Front cover**: cream; glossy; Sonet and Takoma logos.
  - **Spine**: JOHN FAHEY   THE NEW POSSIBILITY   SNTF 702
  - **Back cover**: liner notes; Sonet logo.
Cover credit: Tom Weller
Label: mountains

Matrix #: SNTF 702   A-2ΔG
              SNTF 702   B-1ΔG
Songs: version #1-e (8+6)

A1 – Joy To The World	1:52
A2 – What Child Is This?	3:02
A3 – Medley: Hark, The Herald Angels Sing; O Come All Ye Faithful	3:10
A4 – Auld Lang Syne	2:01
A5 – The Bells Of Saint Mary's	2:10
A6 – Good King Wenceslas	1:10
A7 – We Three Kings Of Orient Are	1:50
A8 – God Rest Ye Merry Gentlemen Fantasy	3:00
B1 – The First Noel	2:12
B2 – Christ's Saints Of God Fantasy	10:12
B3 – It Came Upon A Midnight Clear	1:28
B4 – Go I Will Send Thee	3:00
B5 – Lo How A Rose E'er Blooming	3:45
B6 – Silent Night, Holy Night	1:14

Recording Dates: 1968
Back Liner Notes: yes
Producer: John Fahey

8-Track re-issue

#1
Release date: 1968
Catalog number: C-1020
Format: 8 track stereo
Cover: THE NEW POSSIBILITY.
Original Cover credit: Tom Weller

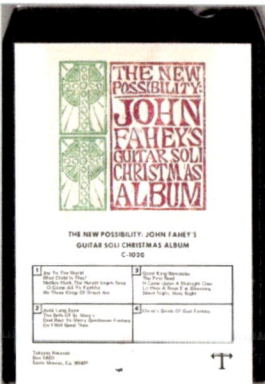

Songs: version #1 (4+4+5+1)
A1 – Joy To The World
A2 – What Child Is This?
A3 – Medley: Hark, The Herald Angels Sing;
        O Come All Ye Faithful
A4 – We Three Kings Of Orient Are
  B1 – Auld Lang Syne
  B2 – The Bells Of Saint Mary's
  B3 – God Rest Ye Merry Gentlemen Fantasy
  B4 – Go I Will Send Thee
    C1 – Good King Wenceslas
    C2 – The First Noel
    C3 – It Came Upon A Midnight Clear
    C4 – Lo How A Rose E'er Blooming
    C5 – Silent Night, Holy Night
      D1 – Christ's Saints Of God Fantasy

Recording Dates: 1968
Manufacturer: Takoma Records

#2
Release date: 1979
Catalog number: 8TA-7020
Format: 8 track stereo
Cover: THE NEW POSSIBILITY.

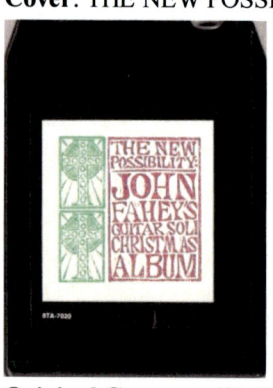 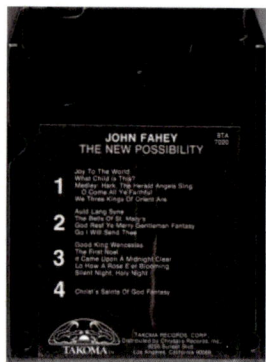

Original Cover credit: Tom Weller
Songs: version #1 (4+4+5+1)
Recording Dates: 1968   **Manufacturer**: Takoma Records

Tape re-issue

#1
Release date: 1979
Catalog number: CTA 7020
Format: cassette tape
Cover: black
Original Cover credit: Tom Weller
Songs: version #1 (8+6)
A1 – Joy To The World
A2 – What Child Is This?
A3 – Medley: Hark, The Herald Angels Sing; O Come All Ye Faithful
A4 – We Three Kings Of Orient Are
A5 – Auld Lang Syne
A6 – The Bells Of Saint Mary's
A7 – God Rest Ye Merry Gentlemen Fantasy
A8 – Go I Will Send Thee
    B1 – Good King Wenceslas
    B2 – The First Noel
    B3 – It Came Upon A Midnight Clear
    B4 – Lo How A Rose E'er Blooming
    B5 – Silent Night, Holy Night
    B6 – Christ's Saints Of God Fantasy

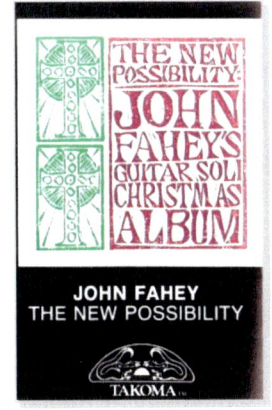

Recording Dates: 1968   **Of note**: (1) Distributed by Chrysalis.

#2
Release date: 1983
Catalog number: CTA 7020
Format: cassette tape
Cover: cream
Original Cover credit: Tom Weller
Songs: version #2 (8+6)
A1 – Joy To The World
A2 – What Child Is This?
A3 – Medley: Hark, The Herald Angels Sing; O Come All Ye Faithful
A4 – Auld Lang Syne
A5 – The Bells Of Saint Mary's
A6 – Good King Wenceslas
A7 – We Three Kings Of Orient Are
A8 – God Rest Ye Merry Gentlemen Fantasy
    B1 – The First Noel
    B2 – Christ's Saints Of God Fantasy
    B3 – It Came Upon A Midnight Clear
    B4 – Go I Will Send Thee

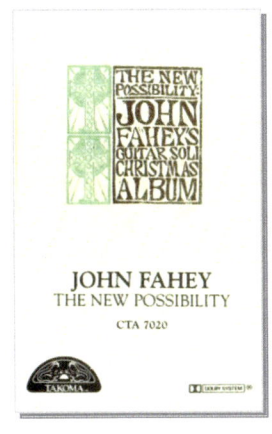

B5 – Lo How A Rose E'er Blooming
B6 – Silent Night, Holy Night

Recording Dates: 1968
Of note: (1) Manufactured by Allegiance. (2) The song order reverts to the original sequence on the LP.

#3
Release date: 1987
Catalog number: 4XF 72720
Format: cassette tape
Cover: cream; track titles.
Original Cover credit: Tom Weller
Songs: version #2 (8+6)
  same as cassette #2.
Recording Dates: 1968
Of note: (1) Manufactured by Allegiance. (2) The UPC code on the back cover is: 022397272044.

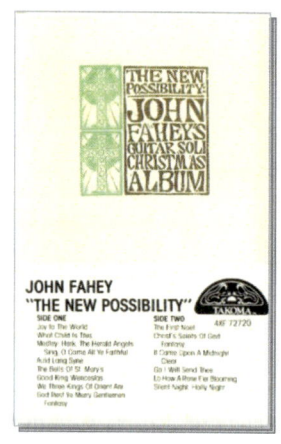

#4
Release date: 1994
Catalog number: Essex ESC-7061
Format: cassette tape
Cover: blue; lion & sheep.
Original Cover credit: Stephanie Pyren
Songs: version #3 (7+7)
A1 – Joy To The World
A2 – What Child Is This?
A3 – Medley: Hark, The Herald Angels Sing /
           O Come All Ye Faithful
A4 – Auld Lang Syne
A5 – The Bells Of Saint Mary's
A6 – Good King Wenceslas
A7 – Christ's Saints Of God Fantasy
    B1 – We Three Kings Of Orient Are
    B2 – God Rest Ye Merry Gentlemen Fantasy
    B3 – The First Noel
    B4 – It Came Upon A Midnight Clear
    B5 – Go I Will Send Thee
    B6 – Lo How A Rose E'er Blooming
    B7 – Silent Night, Holy Night

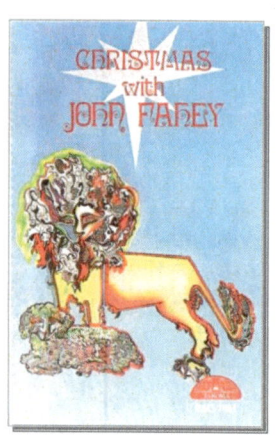

Recording Dates: 1968
Of note: (1) This has a slightly different song order compared to the original LP. (2) Even though the cover picture is from the 1975 album *Christmas with John Fahey Vol II* (note the absence of "Vol II"), the songs are all from *The New Possibility*. (3) The UPC code on the back cover is: 084646706144.

CD re-issue

#1
Release date: 1986
Catalog number: TAKCD 7020
Format: CD

#2
Release date: 1987
Catalog number: CDP-72720
Format: CD
Cover: cream; *no* Takoma logo.   **Disc label**: Silver

Original Cover credit: Tom Weller
Songs: version #1 (14)

1 – Joy To The World	1:52
2 – What Child Is This?	3:02
3 – Medley: Hark, The Herald Angels Sing, O Come All Ye Faithful	3:10
4 – Auld Lang Syne	2:01
5 – The Bells Of Saint Mary's	2:10
6 – Good King Wenceslas	1:10
7 – We Three Kings Of Orient Are	1:50
8 – God Rest Ye Merry Gentlemen Fantasy	3:00
9 – The First Noel	2:12
10 – Christ's Saints Of God Fantasy	10:12
11 – It Came Upon A Midnight Clear	1:28
12 – Go I Will Send Thee	3:00
13 – Lo How A Rose E'er Blooming	3:45
14 – Silent Night, Holy Night	1:14

Recording Dates: 1968
Remastering: Michael Boshears
Original Liner Notes: no
Original Producer: John Fahey
Reissue Producer: not given

Of note: (1) The track listing is confusing. The list detailed above is the one found on the tray card and insert.
The CD label and the actual tracks on the CD have the sequence: 1, 2, 3, 7, 4, 5, 8, 12, 6, 9, 11, 13, 14, 10.
(2) The UPC code on the back cover is: 022397272020.
(3) Made in Japan for Allegiance Records.
(4) Some CDs were housed in a generic Allegiance CD long box.

#3

Release date: 1994
Catalog number: Essex   ESD-7061
Format: CD
Cover: blue; lion & sheep; Takoma dragon logo.   **Disc label**: White

Original Cover credit: Stephanie Pyren
Songs: version #1 (14)

1 – Joy To The World	1:52
2 – What Child Is This?	3:02
3 – Medley: Hark, The Herald Angels Sing, O Come All Ye Faithful	3:10
4 – Auld Lang Syne	2:01
5 – The Bells Of Saint Mary's	2:10
6 – Good King Wenceslas	1:10
7 – Christ's Saints Of God Fantasy	10:12
8 – We Three Kings Of Orient Are	1:50
9 – God Rest Ye Merry Gentlemen Fantasy	3:00
10 – The First Noel	2:12
11 – It Came Upon A Midnight Clear	1:28
12 – Go, I Will Send Thee	3:00
13 – Lo, How A Rose E're Blooming	3:45
14 – Silent Night, Holy Night	1:14

Recording Dates: 1968
Remastering: Michael Boshears
Original Liner Notes: no
Original Producer: John Fahey
Reissue Producer: not given
Of note: (1) This CD, like its corresponding cassette, has a slightly different order of the songs compared to the one on the original LP. (2) Even though the cover picture is from the 1975 album *Christmas with John Fahey Vol II* (note the absence of "Vol II"), the songs are all from *The New Possibility*. (3) On the tray notes and the disc label, the title of track 13 is mistakenly written with "E're" instead of "E'er". (4) The track listing is confusing. The above list is the one found on the tray card, CD label, and the CD digital listing. The actual tracks on the CD follow a different sequence: 1, 2, 3, 4, 5, 6, 8, 10, 9, 7, 11, 12, 13, 14. (5) The UPC code on the back cover is: 084646706120.

FONOTONE 70001

Original release date: 1970
Artist name: John Fahey
Recording Date: 1965
Songs: 9+5

A1 – Bottleneck Blues (a/k/a Rainy Days Down Metzerott Road)	2:59
A2 – O Jesus I Have Promised	3:07
A3 – Untitled #1	1:09
A4 – Untitled #2 / O Jesus I Have Promised	3:24
A5 – I Am a Rake and Rambling Boy	1:46
A6 – Goodbye Old Paint #1 / Whoopee-Ti-Yi-Yo	1:26
A7 – Goodbye Old Paint #2	1:01
A8 – Simple Gifts	0:53
A9 – Untitled #3	1:38
B1 – Western Medley	6:01
B2 – Bury Me Not On The Lone Prairie	1:42
B3 – Goodbye Old Paint #3	1:16
B4 – Durgan Park	2:07
B5 – The Bitter Lemon	2:46

Catalog number: 70001
Format: 12" 33⅓ rpm on acetate disc (1 hole)
Label: type #8 from 1970-85
Matrix #: FONOTONE L.P. 70001-A F.M.
           FONOTONE L.P. 70001-B F.M.

Of note: (1) No track titles were provided on the original LP. The titles given here come from the CD / book set *Your Past Comes Back To Haunt You* (DTD-21). (2) Some issues have the alternate title *The Early Years of John Fahey* (see DTD-21).

FONOTONE 70002

Original release date: 1970
Artist name: John Fahey
Recording Date: Summer 1965
Songs: 6+3

A1 – Brenda's Blues	1:49
A2 – St. Patrick's Hymn	1:52
A3 – Bicycle Built For Two	1:24
A4 – The Blues You Saved For Me	1:35
A5 – House Carpenter	1:30
A6 – How Long	2:25
B1 – The Portland Cement Factory At Monolith, California	4:32
B2 – You Take The E Train [The Last Steam Engine Train]	2:33
B3 – I Sing A Song Of The Saints Of God	3:14

Catalog number: 70002
Format: 10" 33⅓ rpm on acetate disc (1 hole)
Label: type #8 from 1970-85
Matrix #: F.t. 70002-A
          F.T. 70002-B

Of note: (1) No track titles were provided on the original LP. The titles given here come from the CD / book set *Your Past Comes Back To Haunt You* (DTD-21). (2) Some issues have the alternate title *The Early Years of John Fahey*. (3) Pictured below is a test pressing of the album.

AMERICA

#0

Release date: 1971 (test pressing only)
Edition: demo issue (label #0, jacket #0, songs #1)
Catalog number: C-1030
Format: Double 12" LP, 33 1/3 rpm, stereo
Jacket cover: none
Label: white; track titles handwritten by John Fahey

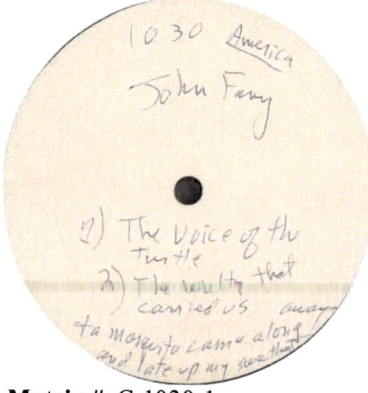 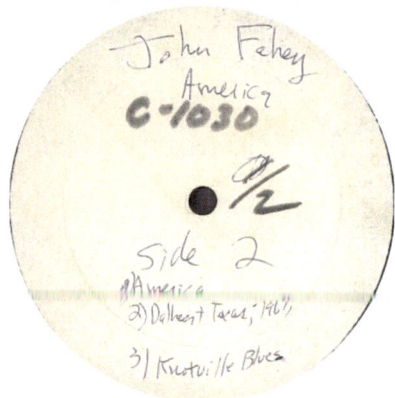

Matrix #: C-1030-1
   C-1030-2
   C-1030-3 (presumably)
   C-1030-4 (presumably)
Songs: version #1 (2+3+?+?)

A1 – The Voice of the Turtle	15:42
A2 – The Waltz That Carried Us Away & A Mosquito Came Along And Ate Up My Sweetheart	5:49
B1 – America	7:40
B2 – Dalhart, Texas; 1967	11:01
B3 – Knoxville Blues	3:07
C – ?	
D – ?	

Recording Dates: January 31, 1971, at Larrabee Sound, Los Angeles, California. Mastered at Location Recorders, Burbank, California.
Of note: (1) In 1980, Fahey stated to his friend Jürgen Kleine "Originally, the America album was to contain two records. I did not issue the second record because I felt it [was] too depressing, except for the waltz from the 3rd movement [of] Dvorak's 8th symphony (not the ninth). A test pressing was made but I do not have it." (2) In 1986, musician George Winston paid 10¢ for a copy he found in a used record store. He noted the title *America* written in Fahey's handwriting on the label, and that it had about ten tracks, many more than the usual four. He would later give the record to Bill Belmont, then at Fantasy Records, who would use it to issue the CD with the complete track list.

#1

Release date: 1971
Edition: 1st issue (label #1, jacket #1, songs #2)
Catalog number: C-1030
Format: 12" LP, 33 1/3 rpm, stereo
Jacket cover: 1st - gatefold
   - **Front cover**: "The Turtle in the Millpond"
   - **Spine**: JOHN FAHEY   AMERICA   TAKOMA C-1030
   - **Back cover**: "The Destruction of Takoma Park, Maryland, 20012"
Cover credit: Patrick Finnerty
Label: O

 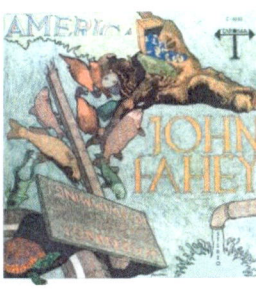 

Matrix #: C-1030-1
                 C-1030-2B
Songs: version #2-a (2+2)
A1 – The Voice of the Turtle
A2 – The Waltz That Carried Us Away And Then A Mosquito Came And Ate Up My Sweetheart
   B1 – Mark 1:15
   B2 – Knoxville Blues
Recording Dates: same as LP #0
Booklet: yes
Producer: John Fahey
Of note: (1) The booklet inside contains ink and pen drawings by Patrick Finnerty which depict trips to the Mojave Desert that Fahey made with Finnerty in the spring and summer of 1970. They were created between September 6 and October 27, 1970, after Patrick returned to his home in Sylmar, California. Depicted on panel #2 is Boron, a city on the western edge of the Mojave Desert. The photographs reproduced in the booklet of *The Great Santa Barbara Oil Slick* and on page 68 of the book in *Your Past Comes Back To Haunt You* show Fahey on a later trip in September, 1970, possibly to restore the rescued tortoises to a safe natural habitat somewhere in the Mojave Desert. One can see the same walking cane, pith helmet, and Fahey's shirt pocket protector in Finnerty's drawings. The album cover was also designed by Patrick Finnerty and is dated July 2, 1971.
(2) The front cover depicts an apocalyptic environmental calamity, *AMERICA* sinking, and an overturned wooden sign that says: "WARNING! – DUE TO

EXCESSIVE SEWAGE – POLLUTION IN THESE WATERS – NO SWIMMING!"
(3) In January 1972, Fahey said, "I write my own songs and try to express the soul of our nation, and of man in the twentieth century in a classical but syncopated manner." (*Daily Bruin*, 1972)

PATRICK FINNERTY

William Patrick Finnerty is an artist-draftsman who illustrated books and articles written by scholars in the anthropology department of UCLA. He also participated in local archaeological excavations and even authored a monograph in this field: *Community Structure and Trade at Isthmus Cove: A Salvage Excavation on Catalina Island* (Pacific Coast Archaeological Society Occasional Paper, #1, 1970). Finnerty drew maps of excavation grounds in which one can find features that he used in the panels for the *America* booklet.

Below is an excerpt of one of his illustrations from this scientific paper. One can see several elements that are similar to those in the *America* booklet, such as the meter, the graphics, and the numerical cataloguing of artifacts, as well as Finnerty's standard signature at the bottom.

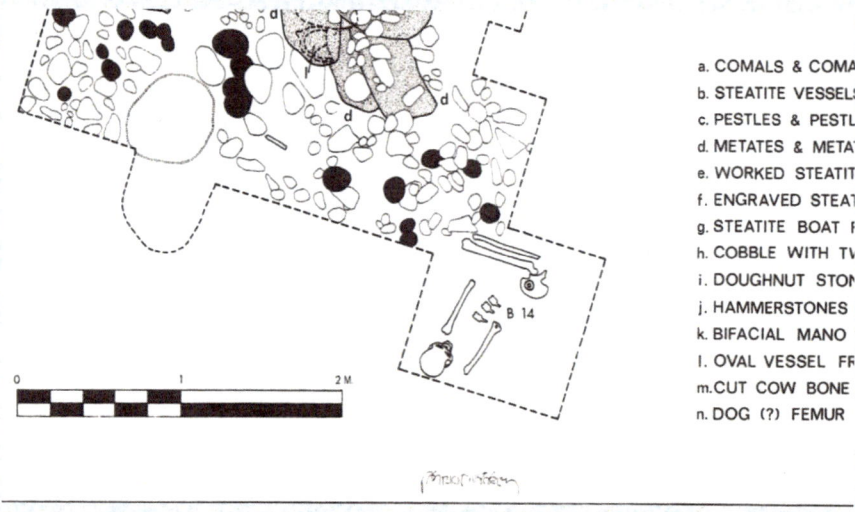

a. COMALS & COMA
b. STEATITE VESSEL
c. PESTLES & PESTL
d. METATES & META
e. WORKED STEATIT
f. ENGRAVED STEAT
g. STEATITE BOAT F
h. COBBLE WITH T\
i. DOUGHNUT STOP
j. HAMMERSTONES
k. BIFACIAL MANO
l. OVAL VESSEL FR
m. CUT COW BONE
n. DOG (?) FEMUR

A comparison with the series of drawings by Finnerty titled "In the Desert with the Tortoises" in the *America* booklet, especially plates 1, 10 and 11, reveals why it is no surprise that this is reminiscent of a scientific and archaeological expedition.

The original title of the *America* album was "Ecology." This was written in the upper left hand corner of the front cover illustration. However, Fahey decided to change this to "America" and Finnerty designed the new title name and pasted it over the old one.

The story of how Patrick Finnerty became the artist for this record began when Finnerty, who knew Fahey's work, one day called him after finding his number listed in the local phone book. He told Fahey how the cover art of his Takoma albums did not adequately represent his music, and that he could do a better job. Fahey invited him down to the Takoma studio, and thereafter asked him if he wanted to join him on a mission to rescue tortoises. So Finnerty accompanied John on three or four trips to the Mojave desert, once with Patrick's then-girlfriend whom he had met at a Fahey concert at McCabe's.

Finnerty illustrated the story of the turtle rescue mission in his drawings, for which he was given complete freedom, and even wrote a story to be included with the artwork. Fahey eventually chose, to Finnerty's dismay, not to include the story (which is now apparently lost). Finnerty would afterwards find that Fahey's choices, regarding both the album's title and his story, were appropriate and intuitive. And he also felt that the song "Voice of the Turtle" is one of the musical masterpieces of the 20th century. As to the fate of Finnerty's illustrations, they were in his possession for a long time but were given to a friend and are now probably lost.

Patrick Finnerty has been described as a laconic Irishman and was known for his drafting skills, eye for detail, and patience. He was also interested in physics, a hobby that included reading scientific articles in the UCLA physics library and corresponding with scholars in the field. This explains the drawing along the sidebar in the front inner cover, beneath the title list. As clarified by Finnerty himself, what we have is a sort of "atomic pool table" where the billiard balls are labeled with the symbols of subatomic elementary particles, such as the proton, K mesons, Pi mesons, Lambda hyperon, and the last discovered Omega minus hyperon.

Another curiosity is seen on the back inner cover where Finnerty drew a hand holding a fish. The Greek word "ixous", which means "fish" or "Jesus," is written on its flank. Not that Fahey and Finnerty had deep religious conversations during their trips, but Finnerty knew of his intellectual knowledge and interest in religious matters. Interestingly, the type of fish depicted is a muskellunge, a northern pike that was a favorite of Finnerty.

Patrick Finnerty also illustrated the covers of Peter Lang's first album on Takoma (C-1034) and his second album on Flying Fish Records (FF 014). He went on to be a scientific illustrator for many archaeological and anthropological papers, and worked for the UCLA, Getty Museum, and the Los Angeles County Museum of Art.

#2

Release date: 1971
Edition: 2nd issue (label #2, jacket #1, songs #2)
Catalog number: C-1030
Format: 12" LP, 33 1/3 rpm, stereo
Jacket cover: 1st - gatefold
  - **Front cover**: "The Turtle in the Millpond"
  - **Spine**: JOHN FAHEY   AMERICA   TAKOMA C-1030
  - **Back cover**: "The Destruction of Takoma Park, Maryland, 20012"
Cover credit: Patrick Finnerty
Label: Da^2

Matrix #: C-1030-1
           C-1030-2B
Songs: version #2-a (2+2)
A1 – The Voice of the Turtle
A2 – The Waltz That Carried Us Away And Then A Mosquito Came And Ate
    Up My Sweetheart
  B1 – Mark 1:15
  B2 – Knoxville Blues
Recording Dates: same as LP #0
Booklet: yes
Producer: John Fahey

MARK 1:15

"Mark 1:15" refers to chapter 1, verse 15, of the Gospel according to Mark in the New Testament. It quotes Jesus and his message of salvation: "The time is fulfilled, and the Kingdom of God is at hand: repent ye, and believe the Gospel." This alludes to the sending of the Messiah after the destruction of the reign of sin, and in its place the kingdom of God will be established after repentance for past sins.

One might loosely interpret the album cover as depicting the sins of environmental pollution as well as the destruction of Fahey's evil past in Takoma Park, and the warnings of the wise old turtle. The conclusion is portrayed by Finnerty in the last plate with Fahey leading the tortoises to salvation.

#3

Release date: 1972
Edition: 3rd issue (label #3, jacket #1, songs #2)
Catalog number: C-1030
Format: 12" LP, 33 1/3 rpm, stereo
Jacket cover: 1st - gatefold
  - **Front cover**: "The Turtle in the Millpond"
  - **Spine**: JOHN FAHEY   AMERICA   TAKOMA C-1030
  - **Back cover**: "The Destruction of Takoma Park, Maryland, 20012"
Cover credit: Patrick Finnerty
Label: Du[1]

Matrix #: C-1030-1
        C-1030-2B
Songs: version #2-a (2+2)
A1 – The Voice of the Turtle
A2 – The Waltz That Carried Us Away And Then A Mosquito Came And Ate Up My Sweetheart
  B1 – Mark 1:15
  B2 – Knoxville Blues
Recording Dates: same as LP #0
Booklet: yes
Producer: John Fahey

#4

Release date: 1976
Edition: 4th issue (label #4, jacket #1, songs #2)
Catalog number: C-1030
Format: 12" LP, 33 1/3 rpm, stereo
Jacket cover: 1st - gatefold
  - **Front cover**: "The Turtle in the Millpond"
  - **Spine**: JOHN FAHEY   AMERICA   TAKOMA C-1030
  - **Back cover**: "The Destruction of Takoma Park, Maryland, 20012"
Cover credit: Patrick Finnerty
Label: Da³

Matrix #: C-1030-1
           C-1030-2B
Songs: version #2-a (2+2)
A1 – The Voice of the Turtle
A2 – The Waltz That Carried Us Away And Then A Mosquito Came And Ate Up My Sweetheart
  B1 – Mark 1:15
  B2 – Knoxville Blues
Recording Dates: same as LP #0
Booklet: yes
Producer: John Fahey

KNOXVILLE BLUES

"Knoxville Blues" is a country-blues tune played by Sam McGee (Vocalion B 15326) and recorded in New York City on April 17, 1926. Fahey plays this tune (which is in 4/4 time) quite fast, and yet at a much slower speed than McGee himself. After an intro played in 3/4 time, Fahey starts the "Knoxville Blues" tune only at 1'12" into the piece.

Non-Takoma LP re-issue

#1

Release date: 1972   (England)
Record company: Sonet
Catalog number: SNTF 628
Format: 12" LP, 33 1/3 rpm, stereo
Jacket cover: *no* gatefold
  - **Front cover**: "The Turtle in the Millpond"; Sonet & Takoma logos.
  - **Spine**: JOHN FAHEY   AMERICA   SNTF 628
  - **Back cover**: "The Destruction of Takoma Park, Maryland, 20012"
Cover credit: Patrick Finnerty
Label:

 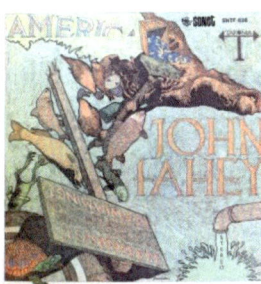 

Matrix #: SNTF   628   A-3◊X
              SNTF   628   B-2◊X
Songs: version #2-b (2+2)
A1 – The Voice of the Turtle
A2 – The Waltz That Carried Us Away & Then A Mosquito Came And Ate Up My Sweetheart
  B1 – Knoxville Blues
  B2 – Mark
Recording Dates: same as LP #0
Booklet: no
Producer: John Fahey
Of note: (1) Although the vinyl has the correct song sequence, the titles of side two are inverted on the label and the back cover. (2) "Mark 1:15" is now just titled "Mark."

#2

Release date: 2009
Record company: 4 Men with Beards
Catalog number: 4m117
Format: double 12" LP, 33 1/3 rpm, stereo
Jacket cover: gatefold
  - **Front cover**: "The Turtle in the Millpond"
  - **Spine**: JOHN FAHEY   AMERICA   4M117
  - **Back cover**: "The Destruction of Takoma Park, Maryland, 20012"; #/3000.
Cover credit: Patrick Finnerty
Label:

 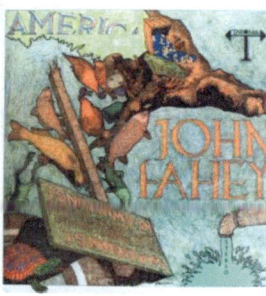 

Matrix #: 4m117A   S-69354   PSM-SF
　　　　　　4m117B   S-69355   PSM-SF
　　　　　{ 4m117C   S-69356   PSM-SF　　　　　　　　　(erroneous master)
　　　　　{ 4m117-C   RE-1   S-69356   RE-1   PSM-SF   (new master)
　　　　　　4m117D   S-69357   PSM-SF

Songs: version #3 (7+2+2+2)
A1 – Jesus Is A Dying Bed Maker
A2 – Amazing Grace
A3 – Song #3
A4 – Special Rider Blues
A5 – Dvorak
A6 – Jesus Is A Dying Bed Maker
A7 – Finale
　B1 – America
　B2 – Dalhart, Texas, 1967
　　C1 – The Voice of the Turtle
　　C2 – The Voice That Carried Us Away & Then A Mosquito Came
　　　　　And Ate Up My Sweetheart
　　　D1 – Mark 1:15
　　　D2 – Knoxville Blues
Recording Dates: same as LP #0
Booklet: yes
Original Producer: John Fahey

Of note: (1) This is a 180 gm issue and a limited edition of 3000 copies. (2) The early issue numbers have a production error whereby Side C is identical to Side D. (3) The song title "The WALTZ That Carried Us Away . . ." is written as "The VOICE That Carried Us Away . . ." (3) Just like the CD version, "Mark 1:15" is about 2 minutes shorter than the original. (4) The matrix number suggests that this album was mastered in 2009 by Rainbo Records in Canoga Park, California.

THE WALTZ THAT CARRIED US AWAY AND THEN A MOSQUITO CAME AND ATE UP MY SWEETHEART

The title of this song was borrowed and modified from the combination of the titles to the following two 78 rpm Cajun records:

"The Waltz That Carried Me To My Grave" by **Joseph F. Falcon**, recorded on Friday, April 27, 1928, New Orleans, Louisiana (Joseph Falcon on accordion and vocals and his future wife Cleoma Breaux on guitar).

"A Mosquito Ate Up My Sweetheart" by the **Segura Brothers**, recorded on Sunday, December 16, 1928, New Orleans, Louisiana (Dewey Segura on accordion and vocals and Edier Segura on triangle).

8-Track re-issue

#1

Release date: 1973
Catalog number: C 8122-1030
Format: 8-track stereo
Cover: "The Turtle in the Millpond"; Takoma logo.

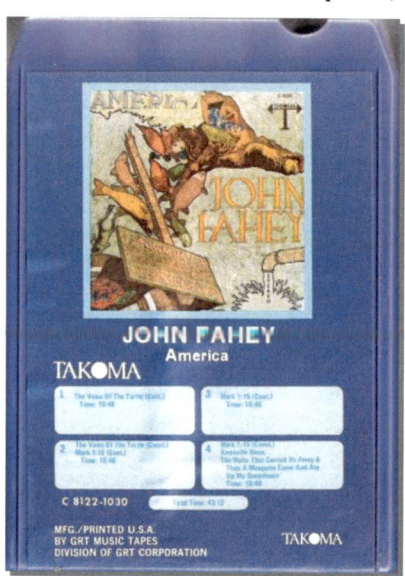

Original Cover credit: Patrick Finnerty
Songs: version #2 (4)
A1 – The Voice of the Turtle (cont.)
    B1 – The Voice of the Turtle (concl.)
    B2 – Mark 1:15 (cont.)
        C1 – Mark 1:15 (cont.)
            D1 – Mark 1:15 (concl.)
            D2 – Knoxville Blues
            D3 – The Waltz That Carried Us Away & Then A Mosquito
                  Came And Ate Up My Sweetheart
Recording Dates: same as LP #0
Manufacturer: Takoma Records; distributed by GRT
Of note: (1) In early 1973, Takoma signed a tape distribution agreement with GRT Corp. In mid 1974, the deal was terminated and Takoma then distributed its own 8-track tapes.

#2

Release date: 1974
Catalog number: 1030-8
Format: 8-track stereo
Cover: "The Turtle in the Millpond"; Takoma-Devi logo.

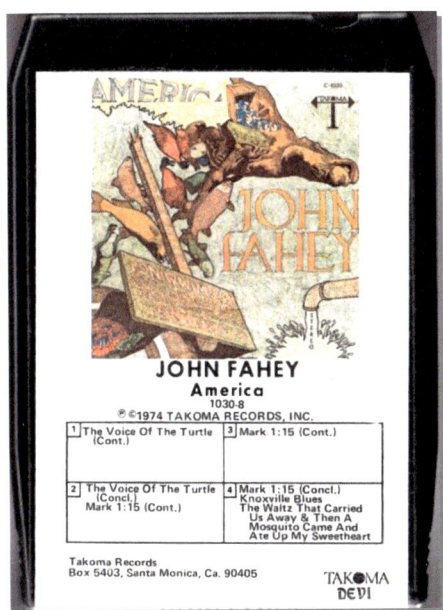

Original Cover credit: Patrick Finnerty
Songs: version #2 (4)
A1 – The Voice of the Turtle (cont.)
    B1 – The Voice of the Turtle (concl.)
    B2 – Mark 1:15 (cont.)
        C1 – Mark 1:15 (cont.)
            D1 – Mark 1:15 (concl.)
            D2 – Knoxville Blues
            D3 – The Waltz That Carried Us Away & Then A Mosquito
                Came And Ate Up My Sweetheart
Recording Dates: same as LP #0
Manufacturer: Takoma – Devi Records

CD re-issue

#1
Release date: 1998
Catalog number: TAKCD-8903-2
Format: CD
Cover: "The Turtle in the Millpond".

Disc label: Green

Original Cover credit: Patrick Finnerty
Songs: version #1 (13)

1 – Jesus Is A Dying Bedmaker	4:20
2 – Amazing Grace	2:18
3 – Song #3	1:48
4 – Special Rider Blues	3:03
5 – Dvorak	3:42
6 – Jesus Is A Dying Bedmaker 2	3:23
7 – Finale	3:10
8 – America	7:40
9 – Dalhart, Texas, 1967	11:01
10 – Knoxville Blues	3:07
11 – Mark 1:15	14:13
12 – Voice of the Turtle	15:42
13 – The Waltz That Carried Us Away and Then A Mosquito Came And Ate Up My Sweetheart	5:49

Recording Dates: same as LP #0
Remastering: Joe Tarantino, Fantasy Studios, Berkeley, California.
Original Booklet: yes (reproduced)
New liner notes: yes, by Charles M. Young
Original Producer: John Fahey
Reissue Producer: Bill Belmont
Of note: (1) The title of tracks #1 and #6 should read "Jesus is a Dying-Bed Maker." Otherwise it has a completely distorted meaning. (2) "Mark 1:15" is about two minutes shorter than the original. Bill Belmont shortened the song so as to fit the entire 2 LP set on one CD. (3) The UPC code on the back cover is: 025218890328.

#2

Release date: 1998 (UK)
Catalog number: CDTAK 8903
Format: CD
Cover: "The Turtle in the Millpond"   **Disc label**: Light green

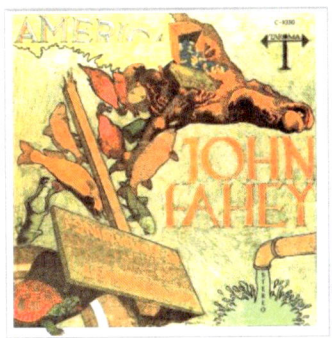

Original Cover credit: Patrick Finnerty
Songs: version #1 (13)

1 – Jesus Is A Dying Bedmaker	4:20
2 – Amazing Grace	2:18
3 – Song #3	1:48
4 – Special Rider Blues	3:03
5 – Dvorak	3:42
6 – Jesus Is A Dying Bedmaker 2	3:23
7 – Finale	3:10
8 – America	7:40
9 – Dalhart, Texas, 1967	11:01
10 – Knoxville Blues	3:07
11 – Mark 1:15	14:13
12 – Voice of the Turtle	15:42
13 – The Waltz That Carried Us Away and Then A Mosquito Came And Ate Up My Sweetheart	5:49

Recording Dates: same as LP #0
Remastering: Joe Tarantino, Fantasy Studios, Berkeley, California.
Original Booklet: yes (reproduced)
New liner notes: yes, by Charles M. Young
Original Producer: John Fahey
Reissue Producer: Bill Belmont
Of note: (1) The title of song #1 and #6 should read "Jesus is a Dying-Bed Maker." Otherwise it has a completely distorted meaning. (2) "Mark 1:15" is about two minutes shorter than the original. (3) Marketed and distributed by Ace Records. (4) The UPC code on the back cover is: 029667980326.

OF RIVERS AND RELIGION

#1

Release date: 1972
Edition: 1st issue (label #1, jacket #1, songs #1) - promo issue
Catalog number: Reprise   MS-2089
Format: 12" LP, 33 1/3 rpm, stereo
Jacket cover: 1st
   - **Front cover**: die cut
   - **Spine**: MS 2089   Of Rivers and Religion / John Fahey and his Orchestra
            0598 – (P) © 1972 Warner Bros. Records Inc. – Printed in USA
   - **Back cover**: song titles
Cover credit: Ed Thrasher
Label: promo - white

  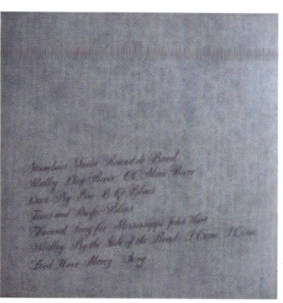

Matrix #: MS 2089   31423-A   1C
              MS 2089 B   31424-1A

Songs: version #1-a (4+4)

A1 – Steamboat Gwine 'Round De Bend		4:15
A2 – Medley: Deep River / Ol' Man River		6:45
A3 – Dixie Pig Bar-B-Q Blues		3:55
A4 – Texas And Pacific Blues		4:30
	B1 – Funeral Song For Mississippi John Hurt	4:20
	B2 – Medley: By The Side Of The Road / I Come, I Come	6:05
	B3 – Lord Have Mercy	2:28
	B4 – Song	5:22

Recording Dates: 1972
Liner notes: yes, by Nat Hentoff (some have a promotional insert).
Producer: John Fahey and Denny Bruce
Of note: (1) A UK edition with catalogue # K44213 is mentioned in at least one review article, but this has not been verified. (2) The duration of track A2 is in reality 5:45. (3) The exact release date was August 15, 1972.

#2

Release date: 1972
Edition: 2nd issue (label #2, jacket #1, songs #1)
Catalog number: Reprise   MS-2089
Format: 12" LP, 33 1/3 rpm, stereo
Jacket cover: 1st
  - **Front cover**: die cut
  - **Spine**: MS 2089   Of Rivers and Religion / John Fahey and his Orchestra   0598 – (P) © 1972 Warner Bros. Records Inc. – Printed in USA
  - **Back cover**: song titles

Cover credit: Ed Thrasher
Label: tan

Matrix #: MS 2089   31423-1
         MS 2089   31424-1

or

         MS 2089   T   31423-1-1
         MS 2089   T1 31424-1-1

or

         MS 2089   T1 31423-1-2
         MS 2089   T1 31424-1-1

Songs: version #1-b (4+4)
Recording Dates: 1972
Liner notes: by Nat Hentoff; some also have a promotional insert.
Producer: John Fahey and Denny Bruce
Of note: (1) The front cover picture (actually the inner sleeve seen through the die cut) was taken at Disneyland in Anaheim, California, and represents the log raft that one takes to get to Tom Sawyer's Island. One can see the Old Mill in the background. A religious ceremony (? wedding) is being enacted on the raft. And the course of water that the raft crosses to get to the island is called the Rivers of Americas. Thus, the picture aptly matches the title *Of Rivers and Religion*.

#3

Release date: 1973   (Australia)
Edition: 3rd issue (label #3, jacket #2, songs #2)
Catalog number: Reprise   MS-2089
Format: 12" LP, 33 1/3 rpm, stereo
Jacket cover: 2nd
  - **Front cover**: not die cut
  - **Spine**: MS 2089   Of Rivers and Religion / John Fahey and his Orchestra
      (P) © 1972 Warner Bros. Records Inc.
  - **Back cover**: song titles + liner notes by Nat Hentoff
Cover credit: Ed Thrasher
Label: yellow

Matrix #: MX170413   MS 2089-1
              MX170414   MS 2089-2
Songs: version #1-c (4+4)

A1 – Steamboat Gwine 'Round De Bend	4:15
A2 – Medley: Deep River / Ol' Man River	6:45
A3 – Dixie Pig Bar - Bar-B-Q Blues	3:55
A4 – Texas And Pacific Blues	4:30
B1 – Funeral Song For Mississippi	4:20
B2 – Medley: By The Side Of The Road / I Come, I Come	6:05
B3 – Lord Have Mercy	2:28
B4 – Song	5:22

Recording Dates: 1972
Liner notes: by Nat Hentoff.
Producer: John Fahey and Denny Bruce
Of note: (1) Notice the errors in the titles A3 and B1 on the label.
(2) Manufactured in Australia.

#4

Release date: 1987 (England)
Edition: 4th issue (label #4, jacket #3, songs #3)
Catalog number: Edsel ED 216
Format: 12" LP, 33 1/3 rpm, stereo
Jacket cover: 3rd
  - **Front cover**: not die cut; Tom Sawyer Island
  - **Spine**: JOHN FAHEY AND HIS ORCHESTRA • OF RIVERS AND RELIGION EDSEL • ED 216
  - **Back cover**: song titles + liner notes by Nat Hentoff
Cover credit: Ed Thrasher
Label: pink-to-white

  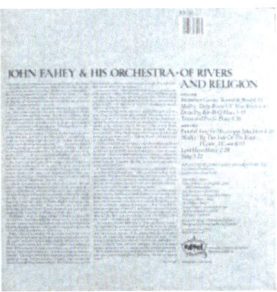

Matrix #: ED-216-A-1   A PUSKU PRIME CUT
         ED-216-B-1
Songs: version #1-c (4+4)
Recording Dates: same as #1
Liner notes: yes, by Nat Hentoff.
Producer: John Fahey and Denny Bruce
Of note: (1) Edsel is a division of Demon Records.

The session musicians that accompany John Fahey on this album are:

Chris Darrow:	second guitar, fiddle, dobro, mandolin
Joel Druckman:	double bass
Jack Feierman:	trumpet
Nappy La Mare:	banjo
Alan Reuse:	banjo
Joanne Grauer:	piano, calliope
Joe Darensbourgh:	clarinet
Ira Nepus:	trombone

They appear on tracks A3, A4 and B3.

#5

Release date: 2014
Edition: 5th issue (label #5, jacket #4, songs #4)
Catalog number: Reprise   MS-2089
Format: 12" LP, 33 1/3 rpm, stereo
Jacket cover: 4th
  - **Front cover**: not die cut
  - **Spine**: MS 2089   Of Rivers and Religion / John Fahey and His Orchestra (P) © 1972—Warner Bros. Records Inc.
  - **Back cover**: song titles + promotional liner notes
Cover credit: Ed Thrasher
Label: tan - red

  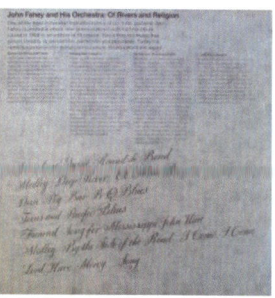

Matrix #: MS 2089-1   A   S-87583
              MS 2089-1   B   S-87584
Songs: version #1-d (4+4)

A1 – Steamboat Gwine 'Round De Bend	4:15
A2 – Medley: Deep River / Ol' Man River	6:45
A3 – Dixie Pig Bar-B-Q Blues	3:55
A4 – Texas And Pacific Blues	4:30
B1 – Funeral Song For Mississippi John Hurt	4:20
B2 – Medley: By The Side Of The Road / I Come, I Come	6:05
B3 – Lord Have Mercy	2:28
B4 – Song	5:22

Recording Dates: 1972
Liner notes: yes, but from the original promotional insert only.
Producer: John Fahey and Denny Bruce
Of note: (1) 180 gram limited edition. (2) Manufactured by Rhino Records; exclusively distributed by Scorpio Music, Inc. (3) The S-##### matrix number in the dead wax suggests that this album was pressed in 2013 by Rainbo Records in Canoga Park, California.

Reel-to-Reel Tape issue

Release date: 1972
Catalog number: RST 2089-C
Format: reel tape, 4-track, 7½ ips, stereo
Cover: Tom Sawyer Island at Disneyland
Original Cover credit: Ed Thrasher
Songs: version #1 (4+4)

A1 – Steamboat Gwine 'Round De Bend	4:15
A2 – Medley: Deep River / Ol' Man River	6:45
A3 – Dixie Pig Bar-B-Q Blues	3:55
A4 – Texas And Pacific Blues	4:30
B1 – Funeral Song For Mississippi John Hurt	4:20
B2 – Medley: By The Side Of The Road / I Come, I Come	6:05
B3 – Lord Have Mercy	2:28
B4 – Song	5:22

Original Producer: John Fahey and Denny Bruce
Recording Dates: 1972
Of note: (1) The duration of track A2 is actually 5:45.

CD re-issue

#1

Release date: 1999 (Japan)
Catalog number: WPCR-10357
Format: CD
Cover: Tom Sawyer Island at Disneyland   **Disc label**: Silver

Original Cover credit: Ed Thrasher
Songs: version #1 (8)
1 – Steamboat Gwine 'Round De Bend	4:14
2 – Medley: Deep River / Ol' Man River	5:45
3 – Dixie Pig Bar-B-Q Blues	3:59
4 – Texas And Pacific Blues	4:31
5 – Funeral Song For Mississippi John Hurt	4:21
6 – Medley: By The Side Of The Road / I Come, I Come	6:04
7 – Lord Have Mercy	2:28
8 – Song	5:22

Recording Dates: 1972
Original Liner Notes: no
New liner notes: yes (in Japanese)
Original Producer: John Fahey and Denny Bruce
Reissue Producer: Warner Music Japan, Inc.
Of note: (1) The EAN-13 code on the obi strip is: 4943674007820

#2

Release date: 2001
Catalog number: CCM-212-2
Format: CD
Cover: Tom Sawyer Island at Disneyland   **Disc label**: Yellow

Original Cover credit: Ed Thrasher
Songs: version #1 (8)

1 – Steamboat Gwine 'Round De Bend	4:15
2 – Medley: Deep River / Ol' Man River	6:45
3 – Dixie Pig Bar-B-Q Blues	3:55
4 – Texas And Pacific Blues	4:30
5 – Funeral Song For Mississippi John Hurt	4:20
6 – Medley: By The Side Of The Road / I Come, I Come	6:05
7 – Lord Have Mercy	2:28
8 – Song	5:22

Recording Dates: 1972
Original Liner Notes: yes (reproduced)
New liner notes: yes; by Richie Unterberger
Original Producer: John Fahey and Denny Bruce
Reissue Producer: Gordon Anderson; Rhino - Collectors' Choice Music, Inc.
Of note: (1) The duration of track #2 is actually 5:45. (2) The UPC code on the back cover is: 617742021226.

One may encounter this 7" 45 rpm record by a certain John Fahey. It carries the tunes "Beal na mBlath" b/w "Beside The Shannon Stream" and was issued in 1972 on the Irish label Solo Records (Solo 103).

This is not our John Fahey, but rather a folk singer from Ireland who goes by the same name. This appears to be the only record issued by the Irish "John Fahey."

AFTER THE BALL

#1

Release date: 1973
Edition: 1st issue (label #1, jacket #1, songs #1) - promo issue
Catalog number: Reprise   MS-2145
Format: 12" LP, 33 1/3 rpm, stereo
Jacket cover: 1st
  - **Front cover**: circular promotional copy sticker
  - **Spine**: MS 2145   JOHN FAHEY / AFTER THE BALL
      0598 (P) 1973 WARNER BROS. RECORDS INC. PRINTED IN USA
  - **Back cover**: song titles; MS 2145
Cover credit: Sherman Weisburd
Label: promo - white

 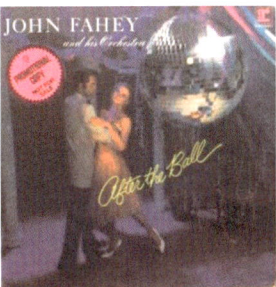 

Matrix #: 1 ~   MS 2145   31609-A -1B
             1 ~   MS 2145   31610-B   1A
Songs: version #1-a (4+6)

A1 – Horses	2:04
A2 – New Orleans Shuffle	3:14
A3 – Beverly	4:44
A4 – Om Shanthi Norris	5:47
B1 – I Wish I Knew How It Would Feel To Be Free	2:33
B2 – When You Wore A Tulip (And I Wore A Big Red Rose)	2:30
B3 – Hawaiian Two-Step	2:38
B4 – Bucktown Stomp	2:11
B5 – Candy Man	1:24
B6 – After The Ball	3:39

Recording Dates: *circa* March 1973
Liner notes: no
Producer: John Fahey and Denny Bruce

#2

Release date: 1973
Edition: 2nd issue (label #2, jacket #1a, songs #2)
Catalog number: Reprise   MS-2145
Format: 12" LP, 33 1/3 rpm, stereo
Jacket cover: 1st
  - **Front cover**: no promotional sticker
  - **Spine**: MS 2145   JOHN FAHEY / AFTER THE BALL
       0598 (P) 1973 WARNER BROS. RECORDS INC. PRINTED IN USA
  - **Back cover**: song titles; MS 2145
Cover credit: Sherman Weisburd
Label: tan

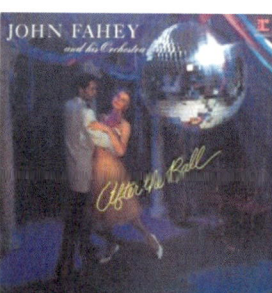

Matrix #:   MS • 2145   31609-1
           MS • 2145   31610 • 1 X
Songs: version #1-b (4+6)

A1 – Horses	2:04
A2 – New Orleans Shuffle	3:14
A3 – Beverly	4:44
A4 – Om Shanthi Norris	5:47
B1 – I Wish I Knew How It Would Feel To Be Free	2:33
B2 – When You Wore A Tulip (And I Wore A Big Red Rose)	2:30
B3 – Hawaiian Two-Step	2:38
B4 – Bucktown Stomp	2:11
B5 – Candy Man	1:24
B6 – After The Ball	3:39

Recording Dates: same as LP #1
Liner notes: no; some have a promotional insert.
Producer: John Fahey and Denny Bruce

#3

Release date: 1973 (UK)
Edition: 3rd issue (label #3, jacket #2, songs #3)
Catalog number: Reprise K 44246
Format: 12" LP, 33 1/3 rpm, stereo
Jacket cover: 2nd
  - **Front cover**:
  - **Spine**: JOHN FAHEY/AFTER THE BALL   REPRISE RECORDS   K44246
  - **Back cover**: song titles; K 44246
Cover credit: Sherman Weisburd
Label: yellow

 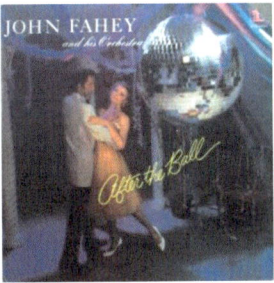 

Matrix #: K 44246 A1
         K 44246 B1
Songs: version #1-c (4+6)

A1 – Horses	2:04
A2 – New Orleans Shuffle	3:14
A3 – Beverly	4:44
A4 – Om Shanthi Norris	5:47
B1 – I Wish I Knew How It Would Feel To Be Free	2:33
B2 – When You Wore A Tulip (And I Wore A Big Red Rose)	2:30
B3 – Hawaiian Two-Step	2:38
B4 – Bucktown Stomp	2:11
B5 – Candy Man	1:24
B6 – After The Ball	3:39

Recording Dates: same as LP #1
Liner notes: no
Producer: John Fahey and Denny Bruce

The session musicians that accompany John Fahey on tracks A2, A4, B1, B3, B5 and B6 are:

Chris Darrow:	guitar, fiddle	Britt Woodman:	trombone
Joel Druckman:	bass	Johnny Rotella:	alto sax
Jack Feierman:	trumpet	Peter Jameson:	guitar
Allen Reuse:	banjo, mandolin, uke	Joe Darensbourgh:	clarinet

#4

Release date: 1973   (Australia)
Edition: 4th issue (label #4, jacket #3, songs #4)
Catalog number: Reprise   MS-2145
Format: 12" LP, 33 1/3 rpm, stereo
Jacket cover: 3rd
  - **Front cover**:
  - **Spine**: MS 2145   JOHN FAHEY / AFTER THE BALL
       (P) 1973   WARNER BROS. RECORDS INC.
  - **Back cover**: song titles; MS 2145; thin black bar on bottom.
Cover credit: Sherman Weisburd
Label: yellow

 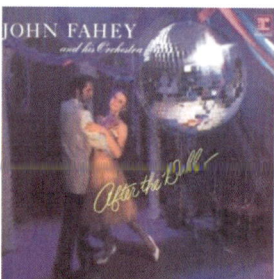 

Matrix #: A   MX170643   MS2145-1
            A   MX170644   MS2145-2
Songs: version #1-d (4+6)

A1 – Horses	2:04
A2 – New Orleans Shuffle	3:14
A3 – Beverly	4:44
A4 – Om Shanthi Norris	5:47
B1 – I Wish I Knew How It Would Feel To Be Free	2:33
B2 – When You Wore A Tulip (& I Wore A Big Red Rose)	2:30
B3 – Hawaiian Two-Step	2:38
B4 – Bucktown Stomp	2:11
B5 – Candy Man	1:24
B6 – After The Ball	3:39

Recording Dates: same as LP #1
Liner notes: no
Producer: John Fahey and Denny Bruce
Of note: (1) Manufactured in Australia.

HAWAIIAN TWO-STEP

On *After The Ball*, John Fahey plays the tune "Hawaiian Two-Step" along with session musicians. Fahey will play it solo when he re-records it as "Spanish Two-Step" for *The Best Of John Fahey: 1959-1977* album, and as "Tasmanian Two-Step" on *Live in Tasmania*.

Fahey stated that he got this tune from a record by Herschel Brown (probably Herschel Brown & L. K. Sentell "Spanish Rag" on OKeh 45484, recorded in Atlanta, Georgia, on March 19, 1929). Yet, Fahey's piece in open G is remarkably similar to the guitar duet "Spanish Fandango" by John Dilleshaw and The String Marvel, which was recorded in Atlanta, Georgia, on March 22, 1929, and issued as OKeh 45328. Like Fahey's tune, Dilleshaw plays it in 4/4 time.

This song has an interesting story. It was created by Henry Worrall, a musician born in Liverpool, England, in 1825. He moved to the USA in 1835 and finally settled in Cincinnati, Ohio. There he became a music professor and wrote guitar music sheets and instruction books. In 1860 he copyrighted "Spanish Fandango" which was to be played in open G tuning. It was originally a tune in 3/4 time. This piece became one of the favorite guitar songs that guitarists in the late 1800s would learn from tutorial books, so much so that the word "Spanish" tuning became synonymous with the open G guitar tuning.

Another song that was copyrighted by Henry Worral was "Sebastopol." He had composed it several years before while the Crimean War was raging (1853-1856). The song commemorated the year-long siege of Sebastopol (later known as Sevastopol) which was home to the Russian Black Sea Fleet and posed a threat to the Mediterranean Sea and the European nations. This time, the guitar was to be tuned in open D. This song became vastly popular as well, and the open D tuning became thus known as "Vastopol" tuning.

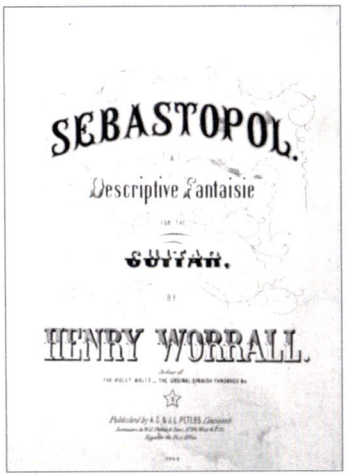

CD re-issue

#1

Release date: 1999   (Japan)
Catalog number: WPCR-10307
Format: CD
Cover: **Disc label**: Silver

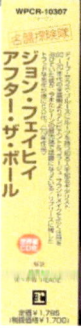  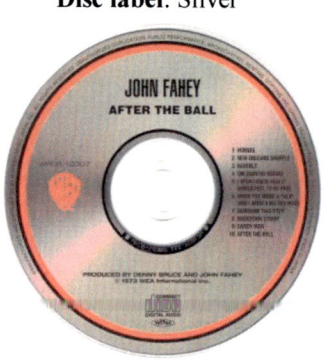

Original Cover credit: Sherman Weisburd
Songs: version #1 (10)

1 – Horses	2:04
2 – New Orleans Shuffle	3:14
3 – Beverly	4:44
4 – Om Shanthi Norris	5:47
5 – I Wish I Knew How It Would Feel To Be Free	2:33
6 – When You Wore A Tulip (And I Wore A Big Red Rose)	2:30
7 – Hawaiian Two-Step	2:38
8 – Bucktown Stomp	2:11
9 – Candy Man	1:24
10 – After The Ball	3:39

Recording Dates: same as LP #1
New liner notes: yes (in Japanese)
Original Producer: John Fahey and Denny Bruce
Reissue Producer: Warner Music Japan, Inc.
Of note: (1) The EAN-13 code on the obi strip is: 4943674005697.

#2

Release date: 2001
Catalog number: CCM-213-2
Format: CD
Cover: **Disc label**: Yellow

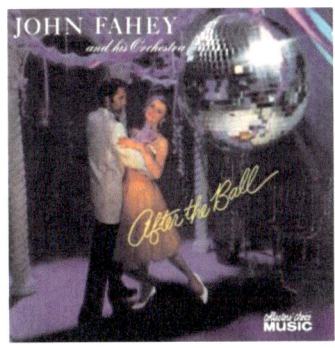

Original Cover credit: Sherman Weisburd
Songs: version #1 (10)

1 – Horses	2:04
2 – New Orleans Shuffle	3:14
3 – Beverly	4:44
4 – Om Shanthi Norris	5:47
5 – I Wish I Knew How It Would Feel To Be Free	2:33
6 – When You Wore A Tulip (And I Wore A Big Red Rose)	2:30
7 – Hawaiian Two-Step	2:38
8 – Bucktown Stomp	2:11
9 – Candy Man	1:24
10 – After The Ball	3:39

Recording Dates: same as LP #1
New liner notes: yes; by Richie Unterberger
Original Producer: John Fahey and Denny Bruce
Reissue Producer: Gordon Anderson; Rhino - Collectors' Choice Music, Inc.
Of note: (1) The UPC code on the back cover is: 617742021325.

NEW ORLEANS SHUFFLE

The jazz tune "New Orleans Shuffle" is adapted from the version played by the Halfway House Dance Orchestra. It was written by the group's pianist, Bill Whitmore, and recorded in New Orleans on September 25, 1925. It was initially issued on the 78 rpm Columbia 541-D.

The Halfway House Orchestra varied in its line-up. For this recording, it was composed of band leader Albert Brunies (cornet), Charlie Cordella (clarinet), Bill Whitmore (piano), Bill Eastwood (banjo), and Leo Adde (drums).

This group took its name from the "Halfway House" Roadhouse and Dance Hall, so named because it was located halfway between New Orleans and Lake Pontchartrain

AFTER THE BALL

This Victorian-era song was written in 1891 by Charles K. Harris (1867-1930). It is a classic waltz in 3/4 time, and it became the best selling sheet music in Tin Pan Alley's history.

Its lyrics narrate the lost love of a man after he sees his sweetheart in the arms of another during a dance. He could not see past his jealousy and refused her explanations. After she died, he discovered that this man was only her brother.

Fahey's version is basically a non-guitar piece, played by the orchestra only. In March 1973, Fahey said: "The last song we're going to do is the complete version of 'After The Ball Is Over' which is real long and most people don't know it."

FARE FORWARD VOYAGERS
(SOLDIER'S CHOICE)

#1

Release date: 1973
Edition: 1st issue (label #1, jacket #1, songs #1)
Catalog number: C-1035
Format: 12" LP, 33 1/3 rpm, stereo
Jacket cover: 1st
  - Front cover: paisley, tapestry; T-logo
  - Spine: JOHN FAHEY   FARE FORWARD VOYAGERS
          (SOLDIER'S CHOICE)   TAKOMA C-1035
  - Back cover: song titles
Cover credit: Jon Monday
Label: Du²

 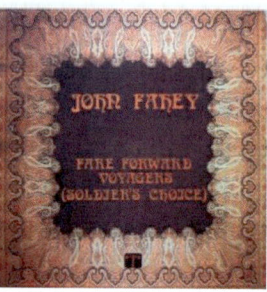 

Matrix #: C-1035-A   SG
          C-1035-B   SG
Songs: version 1-a (2+1)
A1 – When The Fire And The Rose Are One   13:55
A2 – Thus Krishna On The Battlefield   6:36
    B1 – Fare Forward Voyagers   23:42
Recording Dates: Recorded at United Recording Corp., Hollywood, California,
                 & mastered at Location Sound, Burbank, California.
Booklet: none (some have the Yogaville West insert).
Producer: John Fahey
Of note: (1) "SG" in the matrix number stands for the initials of the mastering engineer Steve Guy. (2) The title of the album uses the Arnold Bocklin typefont.

FARE FORWARD VOYAGERS

The three song titles in *Fare Forward Voyagers* are derived from several passages in *The Four Quartets* by T. S. Eliot (1945)[1].

1) From *The Dry Salvages*:

'Fare forward.
          O voyagers, O seamen,
You who came to port, and you whose bodies
Will suffer the trial and judgement of the sea
Or whatever event, this is your real destination.'
So Krishna, as when he admonished Arjuna
On the field of battle.
                  Not fare well,
But **fare forward, voyagers**.

2) From *Little Gidding*:

And all shall be well and
All manner of thing shall be well
When the tongues of flames are in-folded
Into the crowned knot of fire
And the fire and the rose are one.

(SOLDIER'S CHOICE)

The album's subtitle is a reference to the *Bhagavad Gita*. This story is part of the Hindu epic *Mahabharata*. The *Gita* tells the tale of a great warrior, Prince Arjuna, who at the moment of battle has doubts as to what the right thing to do is. His charioteer is Lord Krishna, who counsels him. After their philosophical dialogue, the warrior decides to fight.

---

[1] Source: T. S. Eliot, "Four Quartets" Harvest Books/Harcourt, New York (1971).

#2

Release date: 1977
Edition: 2nd issue (label #2, jacket #1, songs #1)
Catalog number: C-1035
Format: 12" LP, 33 1/3 rpm, stereo
Jacket cover: 1st
  - **Front cover**: paisley, tapestry; T-logo
  - **Spine**: JOHN FAHEY   FARE FORWARD VOYAGERS
        (SOLDIER'S CHOICE)   TAKOMA C-1035
  - **Back cover**: song titles
Cover credit: Jon Monday
Label: Du^{2S}

Matrix #: C-1035-A   SG
             C-1035-B   SG
Songs: version 1-a (2+1)
A1 – When The Fire And The Rose Are One   13:55
A2 – Thus Krishna On The Battlefield   6:36
    B1 – Fare Forward Voyagers   23:42
Recording Dates: Recorded at United Recording Corp., Hollywood, California, & mastered at Location Sound, Burbank, California.
Booklet: no
Producer: John Fahey

A sample of the original paisley shawl used for the album cover of *Fare Forward Voyagers* (see also next page).

#3

Release date: 1979
Edition: 3rd issue (label #3, jacket #2, songs #2)
Catalog number: TAK-7035
Format: 12" LP, 33 1/3 rpm, stereo
Jacket cover: 2nd
  - Front cover: paisley, tapestry; dragon logo
  - Spine: TAK-7035   JOHN FAHEY • FARE FORWARD VOYAGERS
     (SOLDIER'S CHOICE) TAKOMA RECORDS   PRINTED IN USA
  - Back cover: song titles; black bar at bottom
Cover credit: Jon Monday
Label: Do[1]

 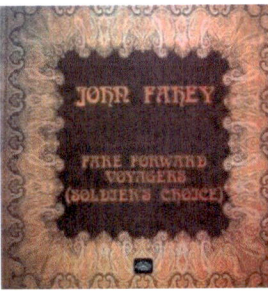 

Matrix #: T   TAK-7035-A   (2)   >
          T   TAK-7035-B   (2)   >
Songs: version 1-b (2+1)
A1 – When The Fire And The Rose Are One   13:55
A2 – Thus Krishna On The Battlefield   6:36
   B1 – Fare Forward Voyagers   23:42
Recording Dates: Recorded at United Recording Corp., Hollywood, California
                 & mastered at Location Sound, Burbank, California.
Booklet: no
Producer: John Fahey

The album cover image is taken from an antique paisley shawl that Jon Monday owned at the time. It was made on a jacquard loom in Europe (probably in the 1800s in Scotland or France). These were produced using the patterns seen on hand-woven silk or wool shawls made in British India and Kashmir in the 1600s.

Jon had been collecting paisley tapestries since the 1960s and suggested using this particular one because the black area in the center allowed for the placement of the text. The original shawl was 5 x 5 feet. Even though the black center of the tapestry measures 7 x 7 inches on the album cover, this same area was 3 x 3 feet on the original shawl.

The shawl was later damaged by moths and subsequently recycled to make quilts. A remnant of it is illustrated on the previous page.

#4

Release date: 1983
Edition: 4th issue (label #4, jacket #?, songs #?)
Catalog number: TAK-7035
Format: 12" LP, 33 1/3 rpm, stereo
Jacket cover: ?
 - **Front cover**:
 - **Spine**:
 - **Back cover**:
Cover credit: Jon Monday
Label: Do^2

Matrix #:

Songs: 1-c?
A1 – When The Fire And The Rose Are One   13:55
A2 – Thus Krishna On The Battlefield   6:36
  B1 – Fare Forward Voyagers   23:42
Recording Dates: Recorded at United Recording Corp., Hollywood, California, & mastered at Location Sound, Burbank, California.
Booklet:
Producer: John Fahey
Of note: (1) The image pictured above of this label is of low quality since it was the only one available at this time. This is due to the fact that this label version appears hard to come by.

#5
Release date: 1987
Edition: 5th issue (label #5, jacket #2a, songs #4)
Catalog number: ST-72735
Format: 12" LP, 33 1/3 rpm, stereo
Jacket cover: 3rd
  - **Front cover**: paisley tapestry; dragon logo
  - **Spine**: TAK-7035   JOHN FAHEY • FARE FORWARD VOYAGERS
       (SOLDIER'S CHOICE) TAKOMA RECORDS   PRINTED IN USA
  - **Back cover**: song titles; black bar at bottom; sticker with ST-72735
Cover credit: Jon Monday
Label: Do³

Matrix #: ST-1-72735 G-1 Q B-28719-G1 Δ17800 1-1 MASTERED BY CAPITOL
        ST-2-72735 G-1 Q B-28720-G1 Δ17800-X 1-1 MASTERED BY CAPITOL
Songs: version 1-d (2+1)
A1 – When The Fire And The Rose Are One   13:55
A2 – Thus Krishna On The Battlefield   6:36
    B1 – Fare Forward Voyagers   23:42
Recording Dates: Recorded at United Recording Corp., Hollywood, California,
        & mastered at Location Sound, Burbank, California.
Booklet: no
Producer: John Fahey

Jon Monday in the control booth of Takoma Studios circa 1978.

Non-Takoma LP re-issue

#1

Release date: 1974   (England)
Record company: Sonet
Catalog number: SNTF 656
Format: 12" LP, 33 1/3 rpm, stereo
Jacket cover:
  - **Front cover**: paisley, tapestry; Sonet logo
  - **Spine**: JOHN FAHEY   FARE FORWARD VOYAGERS   SONET SNTF 656
  - **Back cover**: song titles; white bar at bottom; Sonet logo
Cover credit: Jon Monday
Label: red-orange

 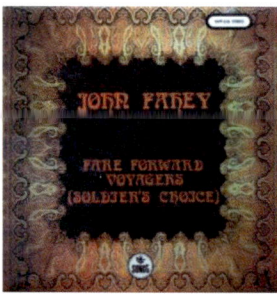 

Matrix #: SNTF 656   A-1ΔG
              SNTF 656   B-1ΔG
Songs: version #1-e (2+1)
A1 – When The Fire And The Rose Are One   13:55
A2 – Thus Krishna On The Battlefield   6:36
      B1 – Fare Forward Voyagers   23:42
Recording Dates: Recorded at United Recording Corp., Hollywood, California,
                   & mastered at Location Sound, Burbank, California.
Booklet: no
Producer: John Fahey

8-Track re-issue

#1

Release date: 1973 (England)
Catalog number: Sonet Y8SN 656
Format: 8-track stereo
Cover: paisley, tapestry; Sonet logo

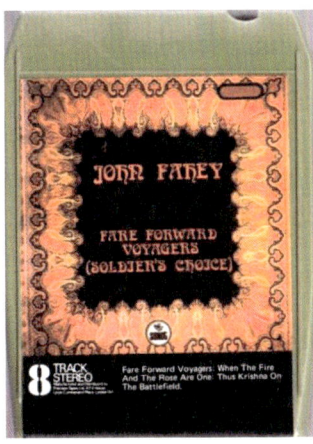  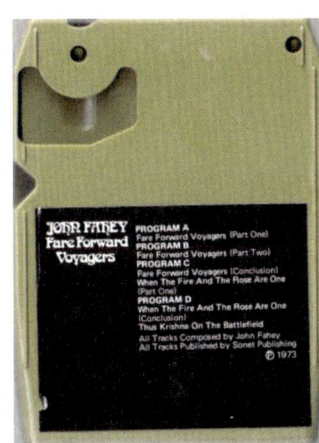

Original Cover credit: Jon Monday
Songs: version #2 (3)
A1 – Fare Forward Voyagers (Part One)
    B1 – Fare Forward Voyagers (Part Two)
        C1 – Fare Forward Voyagers (Conclusion)
        C2 - When The Fire And The Rose Are One (Part One)
            D1 – When The Fire And The Rose Are One (Conclusion)
            D2 – Thus Krishna On The Battlefield
Recording Dates: same as LP #1
Manufacturer: Sonet Records (England)

#2

Release date: 1974
Catalog number: Takoma 1035-8
Format: 8-track stereo
Cover: paisley, tapestry
Original Cover credit: Jon Monday
Songs: version #1 (3)
A1 – When The Fire And The Rose Are One (Cont.)
B1 – When The Fire And The Rose Are One (Concl.)
B2 –Thus Krishna On The Battlefield
B3 – Fare Forward Voyagers (Cont.
C1 – Fare Forward Voyagers (Cont.)
D1 – Fare Forward Voyagers (Concl.)
Recording Dates: same as LP #1
Manufacturer: Takoma Records

John Fahey in the recording studio for the *Fare Forward Voyagers* session (1973). He is playing his Recording King guitar.

Tape re-issue

#1

Release date: 1973 (England)
Catalog number: Sonet ZCSN 656
Format: cassette tape
Cover: paisley, tapestry
Original Cover credit: Jon Monday
Songs: version #2 (1+2)
A1 – Fare Forward Voyagers
B1 – When The Fire And The Rose Are One
B2 – Thus Krishna On The Battlefield
Recording Dates: same as LP #1
Of note: (1) This tape has an alternate track sequence.

#2

Release date: 1987
Catalog number: Takoma 4XT72735
Format: cassette tape
Cover: paisley, tapestry
Original Cover credit: Jon Monday
Songs: version #1 (2+1)
A1 – When The Fire And The Rose Are One
A2 – Thus Krishna On The Battlefield
B1 – Fare Forward Voyagers
Recording Dates: same as LP #1
Of note: (1) The UPC code on the back cover is: 022397273546.

#3

Release date: 1992
Catalog number: Shanachie SH-99005
Format: cassette tape
Cover: vintage airplane.
Cover credit: (Art director: Stefan Grossman)
Songs: version #1 (2+1)
A1 – When The Fire And The Rose Are One
A2 – Thus Krishna On The Battlefield
B1 – Fare Forward Voyagers
Recording Dates: same as LP #1
Of note: (1) The UPC code on the back cover is: 016351990242.

CD re-issue

#1

Release date: 1992
Catalog number: Shanachie 99005
Format: CD
Cover: vintage airplane.

Disc label: Silver

Cover credit: (Art director: Stefan Grossman)
Songs: version #1 (3)
1 – When The Fire And The Rose Are One   13:55
2 – Thus Krishna On The Battlefield   6:36
3 – Fare Forward Voyagers   23:42
Recording Dates: same as LP #1
Remastering: Robert Vosgien, CMS Digital
Original Producer: John Fahey
Reissue Producer: not mentioned
Of note: (1) The UPC code on the back cover is: 016351990525.
(2) Some CDs were housed in a Shanachie CD longbox. The cardboard box was 12" tall so that it could fit in the LP bins of record stores.

#2

Release date: 2007 (UK)
Catalog number: CDTAK 7035
Format: CD
Cover: paisley; tapestry; *no* logo   **Disc label**: Blue

Original Cover credit: Jon Monday
Songs: version #1 (3)
1 – When The Fire And The Rose Are One   13:51
2 – Thus Krishna On The Battlefield   6:34
3 – Fare Forward Voyagers   23:39
Recording Dates: same as LP #1
Liner notes: yes (by Kris Needs)
Remastering: Rob Shread, Sound Mastering Ltd., CMS Digital
Original Producer: John Fahey
Reissue Producer: not mentioned
Of note: (1) The UPC code on the back cover is: 029667029421. (2) The Yogaville West booklet is reproduced in the booklet.

THE ESSENTIAL JOHN FAHEY

#1

Release date: 1974
Edition: 1st issue (label #1, jacket #1, songs #1)
Record company: Vanguard
Catalog number: VSD 55/56
Format: double 12" LP, 33 1/3 rpm, stereo
Jacket cover: 1st (gatefold sleeve)
  - **Front cover**: Fahey on chair with mirror
  - **Spine**: VSD 55/56   THE ESSENTIAL JOHN FAHEY   VANGUARD
  - **Back cover**: song titles
Cover credit: Marvin Lyons
Label: Vanguard - Gold (yellowish); STEREO

 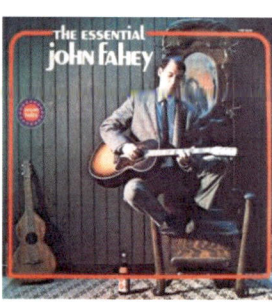 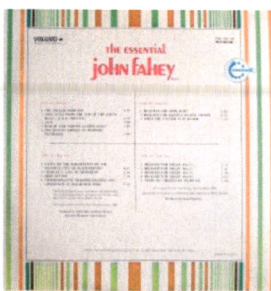

Matrix #: VSD 55 A-1A
             VSD 55 B-1A
             VSD 56 A-1A
             VSD 56 B-1A

Songs: version #1 (5+4+3+5)

A1 – The Yellow Princess	4:49
A2 – View (East From The Top Of The Riggs Road/B&O Trestle)	4:54
A3 – Lion	5:08
A4 – March! For Martin Luther King	3:40
A5 – The Singing Bridge Of Memphis, Tennessee	2:49
B1 – Dance Of The Inhabitants Of The Invisible City Of Bladensburg	4:07
B2 – Charles A. Lee: In Memoriam	3:58
B3 – Irish Setter	7:14
B4 – Commemorative Transfiguration and Communion at Magruder Park	5:59
C1 – Requiem For John Hurt	5:05
C2 – Requiem For Russell Blaine Cooper	8:51
C3 – When the Catfish is in Bloom	7:37
D1 – Requiem for Molly, Part 1	7:35
D2 – Requiem for Molly, Part 2	7:41
D3 – Requiem for Molly, Part 3	2:28

D4 – Requiem for Molly, Part 4   2:55
D5 – Fight On Christians, Fight On   1:54
Recording Dates: 1967-1968
Back Liner Notes: none
Original Producer: John Fahey, Barret Hansen, Sam Charters.
Of note: (1) The label mistakenly states the duration of track D4 as 1:54.
(2) This compilation is a combination of *The Yellow Princess* and *Requia*.
(3) The album features two unused Marvin Lyon photos from the 1967 session that yielded the cover for the album *Requia*. The front cover picture was taken in the home sudio of Lyons in Hollywood, California. This house was torn down years ago. The photograph shows Fahey holding his Bacon & Day guitar as well as his Kona Hawaiian guitar propped up against the wall. In the mirror of the funky chair (a hall tree bench with mirror and hat rack) is the reflection of Fahey's first wife Jan Lebow.

#2

Release date: 1975
Edition: 2nd issue (label #2, jacket #1, songs #1)
Record company: Vanguard
Catalog number: VSD 55/56
Format: double 12" LP, 33 1/3 rpm, stereo
Jacket cover: 1st (gatefold sleeve)
  - **Front cover**: Fahey on chair with mirror
  - **Spine**: VSD 55/56   THE ESSENTIAL JOHN FAHEY   VANGUARD
  - **Back cover**: song titles
Cover credit: Marvin Lyons
Label: Vanguard – Yellow Marbled

Matrix #: VSD 55 A-1E
           VSD 55 B-1D
           VSD 56 A-1E
           VSD 56 B-1D
Songs: version #1 (5+4+3+5)
Recording Dates: 1967-1968
Back Liner Notes: none
Original Producer: John Fahey, Barret Hansen, Sam Charters.
Of note: (1) The label mistakenly states the duration of track D4 as 1:54.

#3

Release date: 1978 (England)
Edition: 3rd issue (label #3, jacket #2, songs #2)
Record company: Vanguard / Pye
Catalog number: VSD 55
Format: double 12" LP, 33 1/3 rpm, stereo
Jacket cover: 2nd (gatefold sleeve)
- **Front cover**: similar to *Requia* cover
- **Spine**: JOHN FAHEY   REQUIA/YELLOW PRINCESS   VANGUARD VSD 55
- **Back cover**: song titles
Cover credit: Marvin Lyons
Label: Vanguard - Gold

Matrix #: VSD 55/56 A1 ΔT
VSD 55/56 B1 ΔT
VSD 55/56 C1 ΔT
VSD 55/56 D1 ΔT
Songs: version #2 (3+5+5+4)

A1 – Requiem For John Hurt	5:05
A2 – Requiem For Russell Blaine Cooper	8:51
A3 – When the Catfish is in Bloom	7:37
B1 – Requiem for Molly, Part 1	7:35
B2 – Requiem for Molly, Part 2	7:41
B3 – Requiem for Molly, Part 3	2:28
B4 – Requiem for Molly, Part 4	2:55
B5 – Fight On Christians, Fight On	1:54
C1 – The Yellow Princess	4:49
C2 – View (East From The Top Of The Riggs Road/B&O Trestle)	4:54
C3 – Lion	5:03
C4 – March! For Martin Luther King	3:40
C5 – The Singing Bridge Of Memphis, Tennessee	2:49
D1 – Dance Of The Inhabitants Of The Invisible City Of Bladensburg	4:07
D2 – Charles A. Lee: In Memoriam	3:58
D3 – Irish Setter	7:14
D4 – Commemorative Transfiguration and Communion at Magruder Park	5:59

Recording Dates: 1967-1968

Inside Liner Notes: by John Tobler
Original Producer: John Fahey, Barret Hansen, Sam Charters.
Of note: (1) This compilation is a combination of *Requia* and *The Yellow Princess*. The sequence order of the songs is chronologically more accurate in this issue. (2) The front cover is the same picture used for *Requia*, but this time it has the correct orientation, so that Fahey appears right-handed.

8-Track re-issue

Release date: 1974
Record company: Vanguard
Catalog number: Y8VBD 55
Format: 8-track stereo
Cover: Fahey on chair with mirror.

Original Cover credit: Marvin Lyons
Songs: version #1 (5+4+3+5)
A1 – The Yellow Princess
A2 – Lion
A3 – Charles A. Lee: In Memoriam
A4 – Commemorative Transfiguration and Communion at Magruder Park
A5 – Fight On Christians, Fight On
    B1 – March! For Martin Luther King
    B2 – The Singing Bridge Of Memphis, Tennessee
    B3 – Irish Setter
    B4 – When the Catfish is in Bloom
        C1 – Requiem For John Hurt
        C2 – Requiem For Russell Blaine Cooper
        C3 – Requiem for Molly, Part 1
            D1 – Requiem for Molly, Part 2
            D2 – Requiem for Molly, part 3
            D3 – Requiem for Molly, part 4
            D4 – View
            D5 – Dance Of The Inhabitants
Recording Dates: same as LP #1
Manufacturer: Precision Tapes Ltd., London

CD re-issue

#1

Release date: 1993
Catalog number: VCD-55/56
Format: CD
Cover: Fahey on chair with mirror.   **Disc label**: Silver

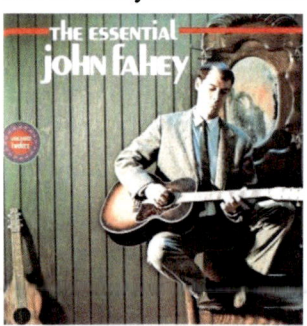

Original Cover credit: Marvin Lyons
Songs: version #1 (13)

1 – The Yellow Princess	4:49
2 – View (East From The Top Of The Riggs Road/B&O Trestle)	4:54
3 – Lion	5:08
4 – March! For Martin Luther King	3:40
5 – The Singing Bridge Of Memphis, Tennessee	2:49
6 – Dance Of The Inhabitants Of The Invisible City Of Bladensburg	4:07
7 – Charles A. Lee: In Memoriam	3:58
8 – Irish Setter	7:14
9 – Commemorative Transfiguration and Communion at Magruder Park	5:59
10 – Requiem For John Hurt	5:05
11 – Requiem For Russell Blaine Cooper	8:51
12 – When the Catfish is in Bloom	7:37
13 – Fight On Christians, Fight On	1:54

Recording Dates: same as LP #1
Remastering:
Liner Notes: none
Original Producer: John Fahey, Barry Hansen, Sam Charters.
Reissue Producer: not given
Of note: (1) This compilation is a combination of *The Yellow Princess* and *Requia* with the exclusion, however, of the 4-part "Requiem for Molly." (2) The UPC code on the back cover is: 015707555623.

#2

Release date: 1993 (Germany)
Record company: Vanguard / Zyx
Catalog number: VCD-55/56 S
Format: CD
Cover: Fahey on chair with mirror.   **Disc label**: White & Silver

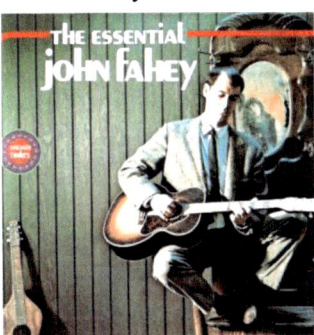

Original Cover credit: Marvin Lyons
Songs: version #1 (13)

1 – The Yellow Princess	4:49
2 – View (East From The Top Of The Riggs Road/B&O Trestle)	4:54
3 – Lion	5:08
4 – March! For Martin Luther King	3:40
5 – The Singing Bridge Of Memphis, Tennessee	2:49
6 – Dance Of The Inhabitants Of The Invisible City Of Bladensburg	4:07
7 – Charles A. Lee: In Memoriam	3:58
8 – Irish Setter	7:14
9 – Commemorative Transfiguration and Communion at Magruder Park	5:59
10 – Requiem For John Hurt	5:05
11 – Requiem For Russell Blaine Cooper	8:51
12 – When the Catfish is in Bloom	7:37
13 – Fight On Christians, Fight On	1:54

Recording Dates: same as LP #1
Remastering:
Liner Notes: none
Original Producer: John Fahey, Barry Hansen, Sam Charters.
Reissue Producer: none given
Of note: (1) This compilation is a combination of *The Yellow Princess* and *Requia* with the exclusion, however, of the 4-part "Requiem for Molly." (2) The UPC code on the back cover is: 090204505425.

OLD FASHIONED LOVE

#1
Release date: 1975
Edition: 1st issue (label #1, jacket #1, songs #1)
Catalog number: C-1043
Format: 12" LP, 33 1/3 rpm, stereo
Jacket cover: 1st
 - **Front cover**: Anna Held
 - **Spine**: OLD FASHIONED LOVE   JOHN FAHEY & HIS ORCHESTRA   TAKOMA C-1043   STEREO
 - **Back cover**: *no* catalogue number
Cover credit: Eric Monson
Label: Da^{3G}

Matrix #: C 1043-A (P) Takoma Records
C 1043-B (P) Takoma Records
Songs: version 1-a (3+5)

A1 – In A Persian Market		7:41
A2 – Jaya Shiva Shankarah		4:59
A3 – Marilyn		6:33
	B1 – The Assassination Of Stephan Grossman	2:11
	B2 – Old Fashioned Love	3:30
	B3 – Boodle Am Shake	3:17
	B4 – Keep Your Lamps Trimmed & Burning	3:06
	B5 – Dry Bones In The Valley	8:52

Recording Dates: 1975. A1-A3 recorded at Blue Rock Studios, NYC; B1-B5 recorded at United/Western Recorders, Hollywood, CA.
Booklet: none
Producer: John Fahey and Doug Decker
Of note: (1) Two titles are slightly different on the label: B3 is "Boodle-Am-Shake" and B4 is "Keep Your Lamp Trimmed & Burning." (2) The full title of track B5 is "Dry Bones In The Valley (I Saw The Light Come Shining 'Round And 'Round)." (3) Tracks A1-A3 are guitar duets by John Fahey and Woody Mann. Tracks B2-B4 consist of John Fahey accompanied by the orchestra. Tracks B1 and B5 are the only Fahey guitar solos.

The front cover image of *Old Fashioned Love* is a turn-of-the-century portrait of the seductive Anna Held (1873-1918), wife of Florenz Ziegfield.

Her fame was shaped by Ziegfield's publicity stunts, her hour-glass corseted figure, the famous milk baths, and her signature song "I Just Can't Make My Eyes Behave." She would be the one to suggest the Folies Berger-style of revue that would become the *Ziegfield Follies*.

In this photograph from 1901, Anna Held is wearing a high-necked salmon-colored dress and a large hat with ostrich feathers. She used this costume for her show *The Little Duchess* which ran in theaters nationwide from October 1901 to May 1903.

#2

Release date: 1975 (Australia)
Edition: 2nd issue (label #2, jacket #2, songs #2)
Catalog number: C-1043
Format: 12" LP, 33 1/3 rpm, stereo
Jacket cover: 2nd
  - **Front cover**: Anna Held; *no* "& HIS ORCHESTRA"
  - **Spine**: OLD FASHIONED LOVE   JOHN FAHEY   TAKOMA C-1043 STEREO
  - **Back cover**: C-1043 in upper right corner; Electric Records in bottom left corner.
Cover credit: Eric Monson
Label: Da^{AUS}

Matrix #: C 1043 A   Δ
              C 1043 B   Δ
Songs: version 1-b (3+5)

A1 – In A Persian Market	7:41
A2 – Jaya Shiva Shankarah	4:59
A3 – Marilyn	6:33
B1 – The Assassination Of Stephan Grossman	2:11
B2 – Old Fashioned Love	3:30
B3 – Boodle Am Shake	3:17
B4 – Keep Your Lamps Trimmed & Burning	3:06
B5 – Dry Bones In The Valley	8:52

Recording Dates: Same as LP #1
Booklet: none
Producer: John Fahey and Doug Decker
Of note: (1) The wording "& HIS ORCHESTRA" is notably eliminated on the front cover. (2) Manufactured and distributed under licence from Takoma Records by Electric Records, a record company based in Melbourne, Australia.

#3

Release date: 1979
Edition: 3rd issue (label #3, jacket #3, songs #3)
Catalog number: TAK-7043
Format: 12" LP, 33 1/3 rpm, stereo
Jacket cover: 3rd
  - **Front cover**: Anna Held
  - **Spine**: TAK-7043   John Fahey & His Orchestra • Old Fashioned Love
        TAKOMA RECORDS   PRINTED IN U.S.A.
  - **Back cover**: TAK-7043 in upper right corner
Cover credit: Eric Monson
Label: Do[1]

 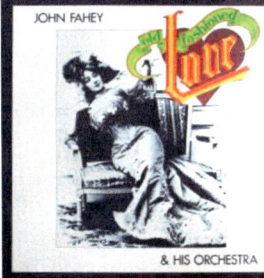 

Matrix #: 1 T   TAK-7043-A (1)
           T 1   TAK-7043-B (2)
Songs: version 1-c (3+5)
Recording Dates: Same as LP #1
Booklet: none
Producer: John Fahey and Doug Decker
Of note: (1) Two titles are slightly different on the label: B3 is "Boodle-Am-Shake" and B4 is "Keep Your Lamp Trimmed & Burning."

Music sheet for
"In A Persian Market"
by Albert W. Ketelbey
from 1920.

#4

Release date: 1987
Edition: 4th issue (label #4, jacket #4, songs #4)
Catalog number: ST-72743
Format: 12" LP, 33 1/3 rpm, stereo
Jacket cover: 4th
  - **Front cover**: Anna Held
  - **Spine**: D11G 72743   John Fahey & His Orchestra • Old Fashioned Love
        TAKOMA RECORDS   PRINTED IN U.S.A.
  - **Back cover**: D11G 72743 with bar code in upper right corner
Cover credit: Eric Monson
Label: Do^3

 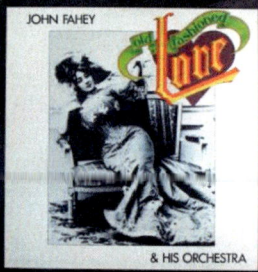 

Matrix #: ST-1-72743   G-1   Q B-29558-G1   Δ18718 1-1   MASTERED BY CAPITOL
          ST-2-72743   G-2   Q B-29559-G2   Δ18718-X 1-1   MASTERED BY CAPITOL
Songs: version 1-d (3+5)
Recording Dates: Same as LP #1
Booklet: none
Producer: John Fahey and Doug Decker
Of note: (1) The titles on the label are now identical to the titles on the back cover.

Dry Bones In The Valley
(I Saw The Light Come Shining 'Round And 'Round)

The song's title and its subtitle are derived from the lyrics of "Dry Bones" by Bascom Lamar Lunsford (see AAFM):

"I saw
 I saw the light from heaven, a-shining all around
 I saw the light come shining, I saw the light come down

 When Moses saw that-a burning bush, he walked **round and round**
 Then the Lord said to Moses "You's treadin' holy ground."

 I saw
 I saw the light from heaven, a-shining all around
 I saw the light come shining, I saw the light come down

 Dry bones in that valley, got up and took a little walk
 The deaf could hear and the dumb could talk"

Non-Takoma LP re-issue

#1

Release date: 1975   (England)
Record Company: Sonet
Catalog number: SNTF 688
Format: 12" LP, 33 1/3 rpm, stereo
Jacket cover:
  - Front cover: Anna Held; SONET logo
  - Spine: OLD FASHIONED LOVE   JOHN FAHEY & HIS ORCHESTRA   SNTF-688
  - Back cover: SNTF 688 in upper right corner
Cover credit: Eric Monson
Label: red & orange

Matrix #: SNTF 688 A-1ΔG
              SNTF 688 B-1ΔG
Songs: version 1-d (3+5)

A1 – In A Persian Market	7:41
A2 – Jaya Shiva Shankarah	4:59
A3 – Marilyn	6:33
B1 – The Assassination Of Stephan Grossman	2:11
B2 – Old Fashioned Love	3:30
B3 – Boodle Am Shake	3:17
B4 – Keep Your Lamps Trimmed & Burning	3:06
B5 – Dry Bones In The Valley	8:52

Recording Dates: Same as LP #1
Booklet: none
Producer: John Fahey and Doug Decker
Of note: (1) The titles on the label are identical to the titles on the back cover.

8-Track re-issue

#1

Release date: 1975
Catalog number: C-1043
Format: 8-track stereo
Cover: Anna Held.

Original Cover credit: Eric Monson
Songs: version #1 (8)
A1 – In A Persian Market
A2 – The Assassination Of Stephan Grossman
    B1 – Marilyn
    B2 – Old Fashioned Love
        C1 – Boodle Am Shake
        C2 – Keep Your Lamps Trimmed & Burning
        C3 – Jaya Shiva Shankarah (Cont.)
            D1 – Jaya Shiva Shankarah (Concl.)
            D2 – Dry Bones In The Valley
Recording Dates: same as LP #1
Manufacturer: Takoma Records

Tape re-issue

#1

Release date: 1987
Catalog number: 4XT- 72743
Format: cassette tape
Cover: Anna Held
Original Cover credit: Eric Monson
Songs: version 1 (3+5)
A1 – In A Persian Market
A2 – Jaya Shiva Shankarah
A3 – Marilyn
    B1 – The Assassination Of Stephan Grossman
    B2 – Old Fashioned Love
    B3 – Boodle Am Shake
    B4 – Keep Your Lamps Trimmed & Burning
    B5 – Dry Bones In The Valley
Recording Dates: same as LP #1

#2

Release date: 1990
Catalog number: SHANACHIE 99001
Format: cassette tape
Cover: Anna Held.
Original Cover credit: Eric Monson
Songs: version 2 (4+4)
A1 – Old Fashioned Love
A2 – In A Persian Market
A3 – Keep Your Lamps Trimmed & Burning
A4 – Dry Bones In The Valley
    B1 – Boodle Am Shake
    B2 – The Assassination Of Stephan Grossman
    B3 – Jaya Shiva Shankarah
    B4 – Marilyn
Recording Dates: same as LP #1
Of note: (1) The UPC code on the back cover is: 016351990143.
(2) The sequence of the songs is completely different here.

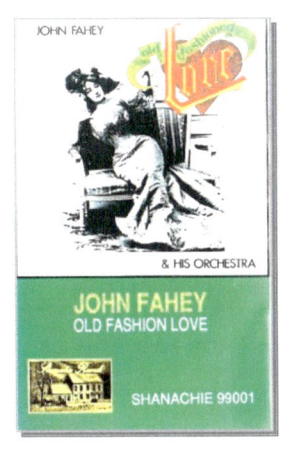

CD re-issue

#1

Release date: 1987
Catalog number: Takoma CDP-72743
Format: CD
Cover: Anna Held.   **Disc label**: Silver

Original Cover credit: Eric Monson
Songs: version #1 (8)
1 – In A Persian Market	7:46
2 – Jaya Shiva Shankarah	5:07
3 – Marilyn	6:37
4 – The Assassination Of Stephan Grossman	2:14
5 – Old Fashioned Love	3:38
6 – Boodle Am Shake	3:27
7 – Keep Your Lamps Trimmed & Burning	3:17
8 – Dry Bones In The Valley	7:58

Recording Dates: same as LP #1
Remastering: Michael Boshears
Liner Notes: none
Original Producer: John Fahey and Doug Decker
Reissue Producer: none given
Of note: (1) Track 8 "Dry Bones In The Valley" is shortened by one minute on this and all future CD issues.
(2) Some CDs were housed in a generic Allegiance CD longbox. This was a short-lived and environmentally unfriendly way to package CDs in the 1980s and early 1990s. The box was 12" tall so that it could fit in the LP bins of record stores.
(3) The UPC code on the back cover is: 022397274321.

#2

Release date: 1990
Catalog number: Shanachie 99001
Format: CD
Cover: Anna Held.   **Disc label**: Silver

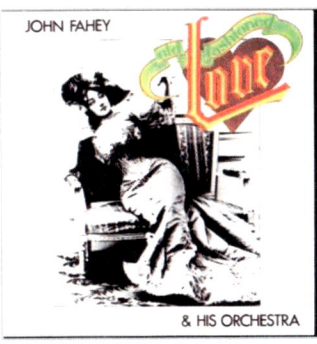

Original Cover credit: Eric Monson
Songs: version #2 (8)
1 – Old Fashioned Love	3:33
2 – In A Persian Market	7:43
3 – Keep Your Lamps Trimmed & Burning	3:08
4 – Dry Bones In The Valley	7:54
5 – Boodle Am Shake	3:20
6 – The Assassination Of Stephan Grossman	2:14
7 – Jaya Shiva Shankarah	5:01
8 – Marilyn	6:36

Recording Dates: same as LP #1
Remastering: Robert Vosgien
Liner Notes: none
Original Producer: John Fahey and Doug Decker
Reissue Producer: none given
Of note: (1) Some CDs were housed in a Shanachie CD longbox. This was a short-lived and environmentally unfriendly way to package CDs in the 1980s and early 1990s. The box was 12" tall so that it could fit in the LP bins of record stores.
(2) The sequence of the songs is similar to the Shanachie tape edition.
(3) The UPC code on the back cover is: 016351990129.

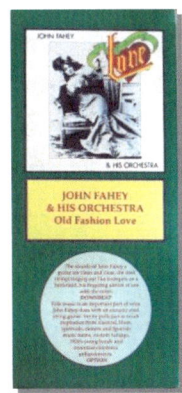

#3

Release date: 2003
Catalog number: Takoma TAKCD-6511-2
Format: CD
Cover: Anna Held.   **Disc label**: Red

Original Cover credit: Eric Monson
Songs: version #1 (8)
1 – In A Persian Market	7:41
2 – Jaya Shiva Shankarah	4:59
3 – Marilyn	6:33
4 – The Assassination Of Stephan Grossman	2:11
5 – Old Fashioned Love	3:30
6 – Boodle Am Shake	3:17
7 – Keep Your Lamps Trimmed And Burning	3:06
8 – Dry Bones In The Valley	7:50

Recording Dates: same as LP #1
Remastering: Joe Tarantino (Fantasy Studios, Berkeley, California)
Liner Notes: by Samuel Charters
Original Producer: John Fahey and Doug Decker
Reissue Producer: none given
Of note: (1) The UPC code on the back cover is: 025218651127.

#4

Release date: 2003 (UK)
Catalog number: Takoma CDTAK 6511
Format: CD
Cover: Anna Held.　　　　　　　　　　**Disc label**: Deep red

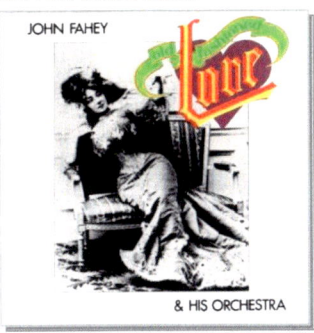

Original Cover credit: Eric Monson
Songs: version #1 (8)

1 – In A Persian Market	7:41
2 – Jaya Shiva Shankarah	4:59
3 – Marilyn	6:33
4 – The Assassination Of Stephan Grossman	2:11
5 – Old Fashioned Love	3:30
6 – Boodle Am Shake	3:17
7 – Keep Your Lamps Trimmed And Burning	3:06
8 – Dry Bones In The Valley	7:50

Recording Dates: same as LP #1
Remastering: Joe Tarantino (Fantasy Studios, Berkeley, California).
Liner Notes: by Samuel Charters
Original Producer: John Fahey and Doug Decker
Reissue Producer: none given
Of note: (1) Marketed and distributed by ACE Records. (2) The UPC code on the back cover is: 029667985123.

#5

Release date: 2003 (Japan)
Record company: P-Vine Records
Catalog number: PCD-3281
Format: CD
Of note: (1) The CD, its tray card and booklet are actually the ACE Records edition from the UK (CDTAK 6511). This is packaged with an obi strip and attached booklet that contains the translation of the original CD booklet in Japanese. (2) The EAN-13 code on the obi strip is: 4995879032817.

CHRISTMAS WITH JOHN FAHEY, VOL II

#1

Release date: 1975
Edition: 1st issue (label #1, jacket #1, songs #1)
Catalog number: C-1045
Format: 12" LP, 33 1/3 rpm, stereo
Jacket cover: 1st
  - **Front cover**: lion-sheep; Takoma "T" logo
  - **Spine**: CHRISTMAS WITH JOHN FAHEY   VOL. II   TAKOMA C-1045
  - **Back cover**: C-1045
Cover credit: Stephanie Pyren
Label: Da³ᴳ

Matrix #: C 1045-A   Re-1
              C 1045-B   Re-1
Songs: version 1-a (5+2)
A1 – Oh Holy Night   3:31
A2 – Christmas Medley (Oh Tannenbaum, Angels We Have Heard
                      On High, Jingle Bells)   3:34
A3 – Russian Christmas Overture   6:49
A4 – White Christmas   5:03
A5 – Carol Of The Bells   2:41
    B1 – Christmas Fantasy – Part I   11:42
    B2 – Christmas Fantasy – Part II   12:28
Recording Dates: Recorded at United/Western Recording, Hollywood, CA.
           Mastered at Fidelatone Mfg. by Bruce Leek
Booklet: none
Producer: John Fahey and Doug Decker
Of note: (1) Tracks A1, A2, A3 & A5 are duets with Rick Ruskin.
(2) Regarding side two, Fahey stated: "A masterpiece in my own opinion."

#2

Release date: 1976
Edition: 2nd issue (label #2, jacket #1, songs #1)
Catalog number: C-1045
Format: 12" LP, 33 1/3 rpm, stereo
Jacket cover: 1st
  - **Front cover**: lion-sheep; Takoma "T" logo
  - **Spine**: CHRISTMAS WITH JOHN FAHEY   VOL. II   TAKOMA C-1045
  - **Back cover**: C-1045
Cover credit: Stephanie Pyren
Label: Da³

Matrix #: C 1045-A   Re-1
            C 1045-B   Re-1
Songs: version 1-a (5+2)
A1 – Oh Holy Night   3:31
A2 – Christmas Medley (Oh Tannenbaum, Angels We Have Heard
              On High, Jingle Bells)   3:34
A3 – Russian Christmas Overture   6:49
A4 – White Christmas   5:03
A5 – Carol Of The Bells   2:41
     B1 – Christmas Fantasy – Part I   11:42
     B2 – Christmas Fantasy – Part II   12:28
Recording Dates: same as LP #1
Booklet: none
Producer: John Fahey and Doug Decker

STEPHANIE PYREN

The art for the album cover of *Christmas with John Fahey Vol. II* was painted by Stephanie Pyren. She created it with India ink and gouache paint on board. At the time, she was combining the art of rock posters with metaphysics, and her symbolism included the images of a lion (strong & aggressive), a lamb (gentle, child), and a star (the giving spirit and all that represents the meaning of Christmas). The painting remained in possession of Fahey or Takoma Records, but its whereabouts today are unknown. Pyren also painted the cover art for Joseph Byrd's *A Christmas Yet To Come* on Takoma Records.

#3

Release date: 1978
Edition: 3rd issue (label #3, jacket #1, songs #1)
Catalog number: C-1045
Format: 12" LP, 33 1/3 rpm, stereo
Jacket cover: 1st
  - **Front cover**: lion-sheep; Takoma "T" logo
  - **Spine**: CHRISTMAS WITH JOHN FAHEY   VOL. II   TAKOMA C-1045
  - **Back cover**: C-1045
Cover credit: Stephanie Pyren
Label: Di

Matrix #: C 1045-A   Re-1
C 1045-B   Re-1
Songs: version 1-a (5+2)
A1 – Oh Holy Night   3:31
A2 – Christmas Medley (Oh Tannenbaum, Angels We Have Heard
             On High, Jingle Bells)   3:34
A3 – Russian Christmas Overture   6:49
A4 – White Christmas   5:03
A5 – Carol Of The Bells   2:41
    B1 – Christmas Fantasy – Part I   11:42
    B2 – Christmas Fantasy – Part II   12:28
Recording Dates: Recorded at United/Western Recording, Hollywood, CA.
             Mastered at Fidelatone Mfg. by Bruce Leek
Booklet: none
Producer: John Fahey and Doug Decker
Of note: (1) **Variant 3a** (label #3, jacket #2, songs #2); this issue comes with the first "T-shirt Ad" inner record sleeve with Takoma catalogue up to D-1064.

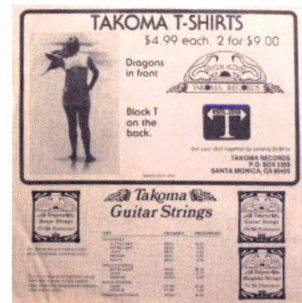

#4

Release date: 1979-80
Edition: 4th issue (label #4, jacket #2, songs #2)
Catalog number: TAK-7045
Format: 12" LP, 33 1/3 rpm, stereo
Jacket cover: 2nd
  - **Front cover**: lion-sheep; Takoma "T" logo
  - **Spine**: CHRISTMAS WITH JOHN FAHEY   VOL. II   TAKOMA C-1045
  - **Back cover**: C-1045, but with TAK-7045 sticker
Cover credit: Stephanie Pyren
Label: Do[1]

Matrix #: T 1   TAK-7045-A   (2)   >
           1 T   TAK-7045-B   (1)   >
Songs: version 1-b (5+2)

A1 – Oh Holy Night	3:31
A2 – Christmas Medley (Oh Tannenbaum, Angels We Have Heard On High, Jingle Bells)	3:34
A3 – Russian Christmas Overture	6:49
A4 – White Christmas	5:03
A5 – Carol Of The Bells	2:41
B1 – Christmas Fantasy – Part I	11:42
B2 – Christmas Fantasy – Part II	12:28

Recording Dates: Recorded at United/Western Recording, Hollywood, CA.
                      Mastered at Fidelatone Mfg. by Bruce Leek
Booklet: none
Producer: John Fahey and Doug Decker
Of note: (1) This issue comes with the second "T-shirt Ad" inner record sleeve with Takoma catalogue up to TAK-7076.

#5

Release date: 1979-80
Edition: 5th issue (label #5, jacket #3, songs #2)
Catalog number: TAK-7045
Format: 12" LP, 33 1/3 rpm, stereo
Jacket cover: 3rd
  - **Front cover**: lion-sheep; *no* Takoma logo
  - **Spine**: TAK-7045   JOHN FAHEY • CHRISTMAS WITH JOHN FAHEY   VOL. II   TAKOMA RECORDS   PRINTED IN U.S.A.
  - **Back cover**: TAK-7045; dragon logo; "… Distributed by Chrysalis …"
Cover credit: Stephanie Pyren
Label: Do[1-var]

Matrix #: T 1   TAK-7045-A   (2)   >
           1 T   TAK-7045-B   (1)   >
Songs: version 1-b (5+2)

A1 – Oh Holy Night	3:31
A2 – Christmas Medley (Oh Tannenbaum, Angels We Have Heard On High, Jingle Bells)	3:34
A3 – Russian Christmas Overture	6:49
A4 – White Christmas	5:03
A5 – Carol Of The Bells	2:41
B1 – Christmas Fantasy – Part I	11:42
B2 – Christmas Fantasy – Part II	12:28

Recording Dates: Recorded at United/Western Recording, Hollywood, CA. Mastered at Fidelatone Mfg. by Bruce Leek
Booklet: none
Producer: John Fahey and Doug Decker
Of note: (1) The label is a variant of Do[1] due to the fact that the artist's name and song titles are printed lower on the label.

#6

Release date: 1983
Edition: 6th issue (label #6, jacket #4, songs #1)
Catalog number: TAK-7045
Format: 12" LP, 33 1/3 rpm, stereo
Jacket cover: 4th
  - **Front cover**: lion-sheep; *no* Takoma logo
  - **Spine**: TAK-7045   JOHN FAHEY • CHRISTMAS WITH JOHN FAHEY
      VOL. II   TAKOMA RECORDS   PRINTED IN U.S.A.
  - **Back cover**: TAK-7045; dragon logo; "… Marketed by Allegiance …"
Cover credit: Stephanie Pyren
Label: Do^2

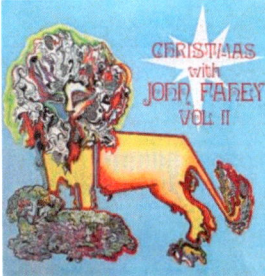

Matrix #: PRC̶   TAK 7045 C̶-̶1̶0̶4̶5̶ – A   Re-1-1-3-◊
         PRC̶   TAK 7045 C̶-̶1̶0̶4̶5̶ – B   Re-1
Songs: version 1-a (5+2)

A1 – Oh Holy Night	3:31
A2 – Christmas Medley (Oh Tannenbaum, Angels We Have Heard On High, Jingle Bells)	3:34
A3 – Russian Christmas Overture	6:49
A4 – White Christmas	5:03
A5 – Carol Of The Bells	2:41
B1 – Christmas Fantasy – Part I	11:42
B2 – Christmas Fantasy – Part II	12:28

Recording Dates: Recorded at United/Western Recording, Hollywood, CA.
          Mastered at Fidelatone Mfg. by Bruce Leek
Booklet: none
Producer: John Fahey and Doug Decker
Of note: (1) The matrix numbers indicate that the same masters of LP #1 and #2 were utilised, albeit with new mothers/stampers that were produced at the Philips Recording Company pressing plant.

#7

Release date: 1987
Edition: 7th issue (label #7, jacket #5, songs #3)
Catalog number: SF-72745
Format: 12" LP, 33 1/3 rpm, stereo
Jacket cover: 5th
  - **Front cover**: lion-sheep; *no* Takoma logo
  - **Spine**: TAK-7045   JOHN FAHEY • CHRISTMAS WITH JOHN FAHEY VOL. II   TAKOMA RECORDS   PRINTED IN U.S.A.
  - **Back cover**: TAK-7045 covered by SF-72745 sticker; dragon logo
Cover credit: Stephanie Pyren
Label: Do^3

Matrix #: SF ~~ST~~-1-72745   G-2   Q B-28506-G2   Δ 17571   1-1   MASTERED BY CAPITOL
           SF ~~ST~~-2-72745   G-1   Q B-28507-G1   Δ 17571-X   1-1   MASTERED BY CAPITOL
Songs: version 1-c (5+2)
A1 – Oh Holy Night   3:31
A2 – Christmas Medley (Oh Tannenbaum, Angels We Have Heard
                        On High, Jingle Bells)   3:34
A3 – Russian Christmas Overture   6:49
A4 – White Christmas   5:03
A5 – Carol Of The Bells   2:41
    B1 – Christmas Fantasy – Part I   11:42
    B2 – Christmas Fantasy – Part II   12:28
Recording Dates: Recorded at United/Western Recording, Hollywood, CA.
                    Mastered at Fidelatone Mfg. by Bruce Leek
Booklet: none
Producer: John Fahey and Doug Decker

Tape re-issue

#1

Release date: 1983
Catalog number: CTA-7045
Format: cassette tape
Cover: lion-sheep.
Original Cover credit: Stephanie Pyren
Songs: version 1 (5+2)
A1 – Oh Holy Night
A2 – Christmas Medley (Oh Tannenbaum, Angels
    We Have Heard On High, Jingle Bells)
A3 – Russian Christmas Overture
A4 – White Christmas
A5 – Carol Of The Bells
  B1 – Christmas Fantasy – Part I
  B2 – Christmas Fantasy – Part II
Recording Dates: same as LP #1

#2

Release date: 1987
Catalog number: 4XF- 72745
Format: cassette tape
Cover: lion-sheep.
Original Cover credit: Stephanie Pyren
Songs: version 1 (5+2)
A1 – Oh Holy Night
A2 – Christmas Medley (Oh Tannenbaum, Angels
    We Have Heard On High, Jingle Bells)
A3 – Russian Christmas Overture
A4 – White Christmas
A5 – Carol Of The Bells
  B1 – Christmas Fantasy – Part I
  B2 – Christmas Fantasy – Part II
Recording Dates: same as LP #1
Of note: (1) The UPC code on the back cover is: 022397274543.

CD re-issue

#1

Release date: 1986
Catalog number: Takoma TAKCD 7045
Format: CD

#2

Release date: 1987
Catalog number: Takoma CDP-72745
Format: CD
Cover: lion-sheep. **Disc label**: Silver

Original Cover credit: Stephanie Pyren
Songs: version #1 (7)
1 – Oh Holy Night
2 – Christmas Medley (Oh Tannenbaum, Angels We Have Heard On High, Jingle Bells)
3 – Russian Christmas Overture
4 – White Christmas
5 – Carol Of The Bells
6 – Christmas Fantasy – Part I
7 – Christmas Fantasy – Part II
Recording Dates: same as LP #1
Remastering: Michael Boshears
Liner Notes: none
Original Producer: John Fahey and Doug Decker
Reissue Producer: none given
Of note: (1) The CD's digital track list combines track 6 and 7 into one long 24'12" track called "Christmas Fantasy, Pt. 1." (2) Some were packaged in a 5½" x 12" generic Allegiance Records CD cardboard longbox. (3) The UPC code on the back cover is: 022397274529.

THE BEST OF JOHN FAHEY, 1959-1977

#1

Release date: 1977
Edition: 1st issue (label #1, jacket #1, songs #1 or 2)
Catalog number: C-1058
Format: 12" LP, 33⅓ rpm, stereo
Jacket cover: 1st
  - **Front cover**: Fahey with Martin guitar
  - **Spine**: JOHN FAHEY   THE BEST OF JOHN FAHEY   1959-1977
       TAKOMA   C-1058   STEREO
  - **Back cover**: TAK●MA   REC●RDS at bottom right corner
Cover credit: Steven J. Cahill
Label: Da^{3S-G}

Matrix #: side 1a: C 1058-A   RE   TAKOMA   SIDE 1   145
         or   **side 1b**:   C 1058-A   RE   TAKOMA   SIDE 1   145   no2

         side 2a: TAKOMA   145   SIDE 2   C 1058-2   (RE)
         or   **side 2b**:   C 1058-B   RE   TAKOMA   SIDE 2   145   no2
Songs: version 1-a / b (7+8)
A1 – Sunflower River Blues   3:15   (b)
A2 – St. Louis Blues   3:12   (a)
A3 – Poor Boy A Long Way From Home   2:22   (a)
A4 – When The Spring Time Comes Again   3:53   (b)
A5 – Some Summer Day   3:21   (b)
A6 – Spanish Dance   2:00   (b)
A7 – Take A Look At That Baby   1:21   (b)
    B1 – I'm Going To Do All I Can For My Lord   1:18   (a)
    B2 – The Last Steam Engine Train   2:14   (c)
    B3 – In Christ There Is No East Or West   2:39   (a)
    B4 – Give Me Cornbread When I'm Hungry   3:08   (c)
    B5 – Dance Of The Inhabitants Of The Palace Of
         King Philip XIV Of Spain   3:11   (e)
    B6 – Revolt Of The Dyke Brigade   2:45   (d)

B7 – On The Sunny Side Of The Ocean	3:40	(d)
B8 – Spanish Two Step	2:12	(e)

Recording Dates:
(a) from *Blind Joe Death*, 3rd version (1967)
(b) from *Death Chants, Breakdowns & Military Waltzes*, 2nd version (1967)
(c) from *Dance of Death* (issued 1965 – recorded in 1964)
(d) from *Leo Kottke / Peter Lang / John Fahey* (1974)
(e) previously unissued (1977)

Booklet: no (but is associated with the book *The Best of John Fahey (1959-1977)* by John Fahey, Guitar Player Books, 1978)

Producer:

Of note:
(1) The matrix numbers are a combination of either 1a/2a, 1b/2a, or 1b/2b.

(2) Some words on the label are spelled differently than on the cover – i.e., Goin' on the label for track B1, and Philip on the back cover for track B5. This will be repeated in all future issues of Takoma labels.

(3) Track A4 "When The Spring Time Comes Again" actually lasts 4:50.

(4) Track B4 is the *short* version of "Give Me Cornbread When I'm Hungry" and is the first time this version appears on disc.

(5) Track B5 "Dance Of The Inhabitants Of The Palace Of King Philip XIV Of Spain" – see next page.

(6) Track B6 "Revolt of the Dyke Brigade" actually lasts 2:50. It is the same version from *Leo Kottke / Peter Lang / John Fahey* except that it is 9" shorter since the last strummed chord is faded out earlier.

(7) Track B8 "Spanish Two Step" is the only never-before issued song on this album. However, it is a re-make of "Hawaiian Two-Step" from *After The Ball* in 1973. It takes its origin from "Spanish Fandango" by John Dilleshaw and The String Marvel, from Atlanta, Georgia, recorded in March 1929 on Okeh 45328.

(8) Even though several songs here were issued in different versions on John Fahey's 1959 debut album *Blind Joe Death*, nothing on this *Best Of* album was recorded prior to 1964. And by 1977, Fahey had issued 16 albums, but the *Best Of* . . . samples only 4 of these.

(9) John Fahey is holding his Martin D-76 guitar in the front cover picture.

Dance of the Inhabitants of the Palace of King Phillip XIV

Track B5 "Dance Of The Inhabitants Of The Palace Of King Phillip XIV Of Spain" is a newly recorded version of the one issued on *Death Chants, Breakdowns & Military Waltzes*.

Even though the 2002 CD re-issue of *The Best Of John Fahey* states that it was recorded in 1977, it is presumed that this comes from a 1975 session in which Fahey re-recorded this piece. In fact, a two-track, 15 inch-per-second, reel-to-reel tape recorded on February 12, 1975, and titled "Fahey – Dance of Inhabitants" contains the section "Bladensburg stomp with improv – several good takes." Its fourth take is identical to the version of "Dance Of The Inhabitants Of The Palace Of King Phillip XIV Of Spain" on the *Best Of . . .* album.

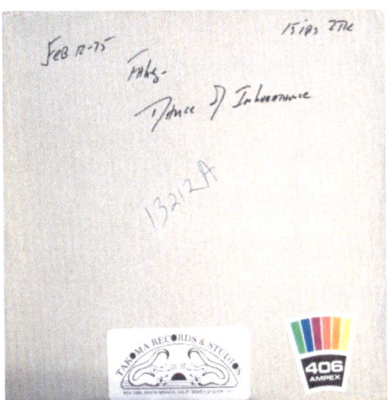
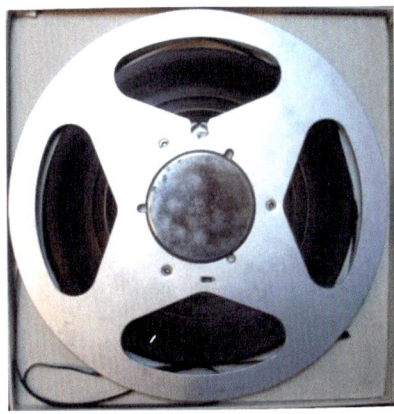

The title of this song makes reference to an imaginary King Philip XIV of Spain. No such king existed. This name appears to be a combination of those of King Phillip II of Spain (1527-1598) and King Louis XIV of France (1638-1715). They are both famous for having created huge and extravagant palaces: *El Escorial* near Madrid, and *Versailles* near Paris, respectively.

"Dance Of The Inhabitants Of The Palace Of King Phillip XIV Of Spain" from *The Best Of John Fahey, 1959-1977* album is included in the 2004 CD compilation *The Roots Of Led Zeppelin* as one of the "classic tracks that inspired Britain's most legendary rock band." It is hard to say if this song is the basis of a specific Led Zeppelin tune, but some are of the opinion that it inspired the slide guitar riff in the song "In My Time Of Dying" on Led Zeppelin's sixth album *Physical Graffiti* from 1975.

#2

Release date: 1979
Edition: 2nd issue (label #2, jacket #2, songs #3)
Catalog number: TAK-7058
Format: 12" LP, 33⅓ rpm, stereo
Jacket cover: 2nd
  - **Front cover**: Fahey with Martin guitar
  - **Spine**: TAK 7058   JOHN FAHEY • THE BEST OF JOHN FAHEY 1959-1977   TAKOMA RECORDS D PRINTED IN U.S.A.
  - **Back cover**: Takoma dragon logo; TAK 7058 in upper right corner
Cover credit: Steven J. Cahill
Label: Do[1]

 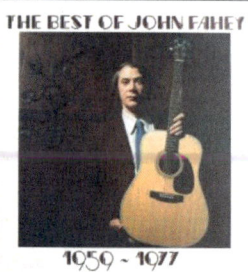 

Matrix #: T1   TAK-7058-A   (1)   >
              T1   TAK-7058-B   (2)   >
Songs: version 1-c (7+8)
Recording Dates: same as LP #1
Booklet: none (but is associated with the book by Guitar Player Books)
Producer:

#3

Release date: 1983
Edition: 3rd issue (label #3, jacket #2, songs #4)
Catalog number: TAK-7058
Format: 12" LP, 33⅓ rpm, stereo
Jacket cover: 2nd
  - **Front cover**: Fahey with Martin guitar
  - **Spine**: TAK 7058   JOHN FAHEY • THE BEST OF JOHN FAHEY
         1959-1977   TAKOMA RECORDS D PRINTED IN U.S.A.
  - **Back cover**: Takoma dragon logo; TAK 7058 in upper right corner
Cover credit: Steven J. Cahill
Label: Do^2

Matrix #: PRC   TAK   ℄-7058-A   RE 1-1-2-1   TAKOMA   SIDE 1   145
      PRC 1-1-1-1 TAK   ℄-7058-B-RE   PRC-C   TAKOMA   145   SIDE 2
Songs: version 1-d (7+8)
Recording Dates: same as LP #1
Booklet: none (but is associated with the book by Guitar Player Books)
Producer:

#4

Release date: 1984 (England)
Edition: 4th issue (label #4, jacket #3, songs #5)
Catalog number: TKMLP 6004
Format: 12" LP, 33⅓ rpm, stereo
Jacket cover: 3rd
  - **Front cover**: Fahey with Martin guitar
  - **Spine**: TKMLP 6004   JOHN FAHEY/THE BEST OF JOHN FAHEY 1959-1977
  - **Back cover**: Takoma dragon logo; TKMLP 6004 in upper right corner;
          black horizontal bar at bottom; PRT logo box.
Cover credit: Steven J. Cahill
Label: Do^{UK}

Matrix #: TKMLP-6004-A2
             TKMLP-6004-B2
Songs: version 1-e (7+8)
A1 – Sunflower River Blues
A2 – St. Louis Blues
A3 – Poor Boy A Long Way From Home
A4 – When The Spring Time Comes Again
A5 – Some Summer Day
A6 – Spanish Dance
A7 – Take A Look At That Baby
  B1 – I'm Going To Do All I Can For My Lord
  B2 – The Last Steam Engine Train
  B3 – In Christ There Is No East Or West
  B4 – Give Me Cornbread When I'm Hungry
  B5 – Dance Of The Inhabitants Of The Palace Of King Philip XLV Of Spain
  B6 – Revolt Of The Dyke Brigade
  B7 – On The Sunnyside Of The Ocean
  B8 – Spanish Two Step
Recording Dates: same as LP #1
Booklet: none (but is associated with the book by Guitar Player Books)
Of note: (1) On the label, track B5 is misspelled as "King Philip XLV" (45th) instead of XIV (14th).

#5

Release date: 1987
Edition: 5th issue (label #5, jacket #4, songs #6)
Catalog number: ST-72758
Format: 12" LP, 33⅓ rpm, stereo
Jacket cover: 4th
  - **Front cover**: Fahey with Martin guitar
  - **Spine**: TAK 7058   JOHN FAHEY • THE BEST OF JOHN FAHEY
            1959-1977   TAKOMA RECORDS D PRINTED IN U.S.A.
  - **Back cover**: Takoma dragon logo;
            TAK 7058 in upper right corner;
            ST-72758 sticker;
            Allegiance Records address.
Cover credit: Steven J. Cahill
Label: Do³

Matrix #: ST-1-72758 G-1   Q B-28249-G1   Δ 17308   1-1 MASTERED BY CAPITOL
         ST-2-72758 G-1   Q B-28250-G1   Δ 17308-X 1-1
Songs: version 1-f (7+8)
Recording Dates: same as LP #1
Booklet: none (but is associated with the book by Guitar Player Books)
Producer:
Of note: (1) The word "Springtime" for track A4 is, for the first time, spelled as such on label.

Non-Takoma LP re-issue

#1

Release date: early 1977   (England)
Record company: Sonet
Catalog number: SNTF 733
Format: 12" LP, 33⅓ rpm, stereo
Jacket cover:
  - **Front cover**: Fahey with Martin guitar
  - **Spine**: JOHN FAHEY   THE BEST OF JOHN FAHEY   1959-1977   SNTF 733
  - **Back cover**: Sonet & Takoma dragon logo;
                    SNTF 733 in upper right corner
Cover credit: Steven J. Cahill
Label: mountains

Matrix #: SNTF 733   A-1 ◇ G
              SNTF 733   B-1 ◇ G
Songs: version #1-g (7+8)
Recording Dates: same as Takoma LP #1
Booklet: none
Producer:
Of note: (1) The spelling of the tracks on the labels is identical to the list on the back cover.

#2

Release date: late 1977　　　　　　　　　　　　　　　　(England)
Record company: Sonet
Catalog number: SNTF 733
Format: 12" LP, 33⅓ rpm, stereo
Jacket cover:
 - **Front cover**: Fahey with Martin guitar
 - **Spine**: JOHN FAHEY　THE BEST OF JOHN FAHEY　1959-1977　SNTF 733
 - **Back cover**: Sonet & Takoma dragon logo;
　　　　　　SNTF 733 in upper right corner
Cover credit: Steven J. Cahill
Label: pyramid

Matrix #: SNTF 733   A-1 ◇ G
　　　　　　SNTF 733   B-1 ◇ G
Songs: version #1-g (7+8)
Recording Dates: same as Takoma LP #1
Booklet: none
Producer:
Of note: (1) The spelling of the tracks on the labels is now identical to the list on the back cover.

#3

Release date: 1977   (West Germany)
Record company: Metronome
Catalog number: 0069.053
Format: 12" LP, 33⅓ rpm, stereo
Jacket cover:
  - **Front cover**: Fahey with Martin guitar; catalogue # in upper right corner
  - **Spine**: THE BEST OF JOHN FAHEY   0069.053
  - **Back cover**: Sonet & Takoma dragon logo;
            0069.053 in upper right corner;
            'Metronome Musik GMBH' on bottom center.
Cover credit: Steven J. Cahill
Label: black

 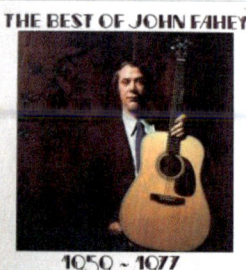 

Matrix #: 0701   919   S1   320
           0701   919   S2   320
Songs: version #1-h (7+8)
Recording Dates: same as Takoma LP #1
Booklet: none
Producer:
Of note: (1) The spelling of the tracks on the labels is identical to the list on the back cover.

8-Track re-issue

#1

Release date: 1979
Catalog number: 8TA-7058
Format: 8-track stereo
Cover: Fahey with Martin guitar.

 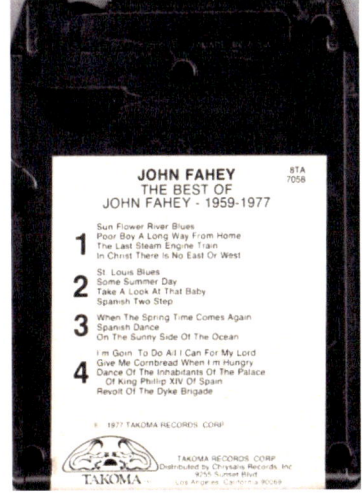

Original Cover credit: Steven J. Cahill
Songs: version #1 (4+4+3+4)
A1 – Sun Flower River Blues
A2 – Poor Boy A Long Way From Home
A3 – The Last Steam Engine Train
A4 – In Christ There Is No East Or West
   B1 – St. Louis Blues
   B2 – Some Summer Day
   B3 – Take A Look At That Baby
   B4 – Spanish Two Step
     C1 – When The Spring Time Comes Again
     C2 – Spanish Dance
     C3 – On The Sunny Side Of The Ocean
        D1 – I'm Goin' To Do All I Can For My Lord
        D2 – Give Me Cornbread When I'm Hungry
        D3 – Dance Of The Inhabitants Of The Palace Of King Phillip XIV
           Of Spain
        D4 – Revolt Of The Dyke Brigade
Recording Dates: same as Takoma LP #1
Manufacturer: Takoma Records

Tape re-issue

#1

Release date: 1984 (UK)
Catalog number: ZCTKM 6004
Format: cassette tape
Cover: Fahey with Martin guitar
Original Cover credit: Steven J. Cahill
Songs: version #1 (7+8)
A1 – Sunflower River Blues
A2 – St. Louis Blues
A3 – Poor Boy A Long Way From Home
A4 – When The Spring Time Comes Again
A5 – Some Summer Day
A6 – Spanish Dance
A7 – Take A Look At That Baby
   B1 – I'm Going To Do All I Can For My Lord
   B2 – The Last Steam Engine Train
   B3 – In Christ There Is No East Or West
   B4 – Give Me Cornbread When I'm Hungry
   B5 – Dance Of The Inhabitants Of The Palace Of King Phillip XIV Of Spain
   B6 – Revolt Of The Dyke Brigade
   B7 – On The Sunny Side Of The Ocean
   B8 – Spanish Two Step
Recording Dates: same as Takoma LP #1
Of note: (1) On the cassette label, track B5 is misspelled as "King Phillip XLV" (45th) instead of XIV (14th). (2) Marketed and distributed by PRT [Precision Records & Tapes].
(3) The EAN-13 code on the back cover is: 5011664600449.

#2

Release date: 1987
Catalog number: 4XT 72758
Format: cassette tape
Cover: Fahey with Martin guitar
Original Cover credit: Steven J. Cahill
Songs: version #1 (7+8)
Recording Dates: same as Takoma LP #1

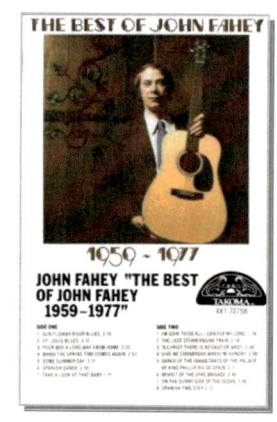

CD re-issue

#1

Release date: 1986
Catalog number: TAKCD 7058
Format: CD
Cover: Fahey with Martin guitar.   **Disc label**: silver

Original Cover credit: Steven J. Cahill
Songs: version #1 (15)
1 – Sun Flower River Blues
2 – St. Louis Blues
3 – Poor Boy A Long Way From Home
4 – When The Spring Time Comes Again
5 – Some Summer Day
6 – Spanish Dance
7 – Take A Look At That Baby
8 – I'm Gonna To Do All I Can For My Lord
9 – The Last Steam Engine Train
10 – In Christ There Is No East Or West
11 – Give Me Cornbread When I'm Hungry
12 – Dance Of The Inhabitants Of The Palace Of King Phillip XIV Of Spain
13 – Revolt Of The Dyke Brigade
14 – On The Sunny Side Of The Ocean
15 – Spanish Two Step
Recording Dates: same as Takoma LP #1
Remastering: none given
Reissue Producer: not mentioned
Of note: (1) Bizarrely, the sequence of the songs on the CD disc is actually:
1, 3, 9, 10, 2, 5, 7, 15, 4, 6, 14, 8, 11, 12, 13.   (2) The title of the song "I'm Gonna To Do All I Can For My Lord" has the 2nd word spelled <u>Going</u> in the booklet, <u>Goin'</u> on the back cover, and <u>Gonna</u> on the disc label. (3) The CD was made in Japan for Allegiance Records. (4) No UPC code on the back cover.

#2

Release date: 1987
Catalog number: CDP-72758
Format: CD
Cover: Fahey with Martin guitar.   **Disc label**: silver

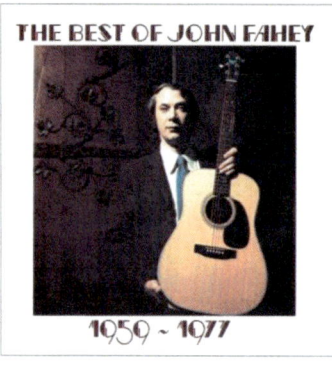

Original Cover credit: Steven J. Cahill
Songs: version #1 (15)
1 – Sun Flower River Blues
2 – St. Louis Blues
3 – Poor Boy A Long Way From Home
4 – When The Spring Time Comes Again
5 – Some Summer Day
6 – Spanish Dance
7 – Take A Look At That Baby
8 – I'm Gonna To Do All I Can For My Lord
9 – The Last Steam Engine Train
10 – In Christ There Is No East Or West
11 – Give Me Cornbread When I'm Hungry
12 – Dance Of The Inhabitants Of The Palace Of King Phillip XIV Of Spain
13 – Revolt Of The Dyke Brigade
14 – On The Sunny Side Of The Ocean
15 – Spanish Two Step
Recording Dates: same as Takoma LP #1
Remastering: none given
Reissue Producer: not mentioned
Of note: (1) Here, too, the sequence of the songs on the CD disc is actually: 1, 3, 9, 10, 2, 5, 7, 15, 4, 6, 14, 8, 11, 12, 13. (2) The title of the song "I'm Gonna To Do All I Can For My Lord" has the 2nd word spelled <u>Going</u> in the booklet, <u>Goin'</u> on the back cover, and <u>Gonna</u> on the disc label. (3) The CD label has the CDP # while the cover has the TAKCD #. (4) The CD was made in Japan for Allegiance Records. (5) The UPC code on the back cover sticker is: 022397275823.

#3

Release date: 2002
Catalog number: TAKCD-8915-2
Format: CD
Cover: Fahey with Martin guitar.   **Disc label**: white

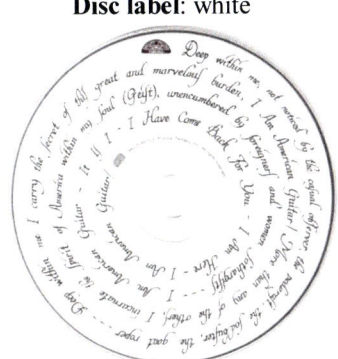

Original Cover credit: Steven J. Cahill
Songs: version #2 (18)

1 – Sunflower River Blues	3:19
2 – St. Louis Blues	3:16
3 – Poor Boy Long Ways From Home	2:24
4 – When The Springtime Comes Again	4:51
5 – Some Summer Day	3:25
6 – Spanish Dance	2:05
7 – Take A Look At That Baby	1:24
8 – I'm Going To Do All I Can For My Lord	1:23
9 – The Last Steam Engine Train	2:15
10 – In Christ There Is No East Or West	2:44
11 – Give Me Cornbread When I'm Hungry	3:09
12 – Dance Of The Inhabitants Of The Palace Of King Philip XIV Of Spain	3:16
13 – Revolt Of The Dyke Brigade	3:00
14 – On The Sunny Side Of The Ocean	3:51
15 – Spanish Two-Step	2:19
16 – America	7:40
17 – Fare Forward Voyagers	23:35
18 – Desperate Man Blues	3:59

Recording Dates: same as Takoma LP #1. Bonus tracks are: track 16 from *America* TAKCD-8903-2 (1971), track 17 from *Fare Forward Voyagers* (1973), & track 18 from *Blind Joe Death*, 3rd version (1967).
Booklet: by Henry Kaiser, Leo Kottke, Peter Lang, Michael Gulezian, Jim O'Rourke, Terry Robb, and George Winston.
Remastering: Joe Tarantino, Fantasy Studios, Berkeley.
Reissue Producer: Henry Kaiser
Of note: (1) The UPC code on the back cover is: 025218891523.

#4

Release date: 2002 (UK)
Catalog number: CDTAK 8915
Format: CD
Cover: Fahey with Martin guitar.   **Disc label**: white

Original Cover credit: Steven J. Cahill
Songs: version #2 (18)
Recording Dates: same as Takoma LP #1. Bonus tracks are: track 16 from *America* TAKCD-8903-2 (1971), track 17 from *Fare Forward Voyagers* (1973), & track 18 from *Blind Joe Death*, 3rd version (1967).
Booklet: by Henry Kaiser, Leo Kottke, Peter Lang, Michael Gulezian, Jim O'Rourke, Terry Robb, and George Winston)
Remastering: Joe Tarantino, Fantasy Studios, Berkeley.
Reissue Producer: Henry Kaiser
Of note: (1) Marketed and distributed by ACE Records. (2) The UPC code on the back cover is: 029667981521.

#5

Release date: 2003 (Japan)
Record company: P-Vine Records
Catalog number: PCD-3277
Format: CD
Of note: (1) The CD, its tray card and booklet are the same as the ACE Records edition from the UK (CDTAK 8915). This is packaged with an obi strip and an attached booklet that contains the translation of the original CD booklet in Japanese. (2) The EAN-13 code on the obi strip is: 4995879032770.

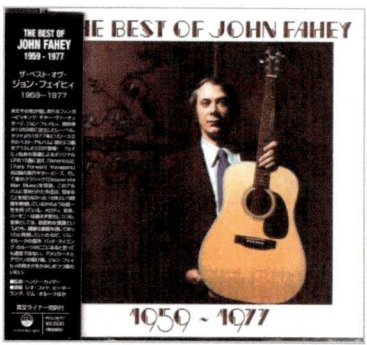

JOHN FAHEY VISITS WASHINGTON, D.C.

#1
Release date: 1979
Edition: 1st issue (label #1, jacket #1, songs #1)
Catalog number: TAK-7069
Format: 12" LP, 33⅓ rpm, stereo
Jacket cover: 1st
  - **Front cover**: Two Arabs and Washington, D.C.
  - **Spine**: TAK 7069   JOHN FAHEY   JOHN FAHEY VISITS WASHINGTON, D.C. TAKOMA RECORDS PRINTED IN U.S.A.
  - **Back cover**: dragon logo; bar code.
Cover credit: John Van Hamersveld
Label: Do[1]

 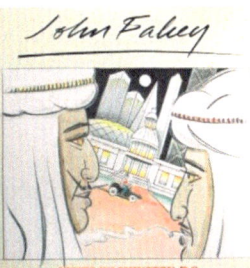 

Matrix #: T1   TAK-7069-A- (1)   *or*   T1   TAK-7069-A (2)
       T1   TAK-7069-B - (2)
Songs: version 1-a (3+3)
A1 – Medley: Silver Bell / Cheyenne	4:27
A2 – Ann Arbor / Death By Reputation	8:04
A3 – The Discovery Of The Sylvia Scott	7:43
B1 – Guitar Lamento	5:30
B2 – Melody McBad	10:08
B3 – The Grand Finale	6:30

Recording Dates:
Liner notes: yes
Producer:
Of note: (1) The prefix T1 in the matrix # stands for: T=Terre Haute, Indiana, pressing plant used by Columbia; "1"=denotes the 1st metal mother used. (2) The suffix circle-1 or circle-2 in the matrix # may signify that two different mixes or equalizations were used. (3) This LP comes with a 3-page Takoma newsletter with John Fahey's biography up until 1979. (4) This is the first Fahey album produced after Takoma was sold to Chrysalis. (5) The 2nd guitar on track A1 is by Richard Ruskin. (6) **Variant 1a** (label #1, jacket #3, songs #1) from 1983 has the trapezoidal Allegiance sticker.

#2

Release date: 1979 (Australia)
Edition: 2nd issue (label #2, jacket #2, songs #2)
Catalog number: Takoma L37168
Format: 12" LP, 33⅓ rpm, stereo
Jacket cover: 2nd
  - Front cover: Two Arabs and Washington, D.C.
  - Spine: L37168   JOHN FAHEY VISITS WASHINGTON, D.C.
  - Back cover: L 37168; FESTIVAL logo on bottom right.
Cover credit: John Van Hamersveld
Label: Do^AUS

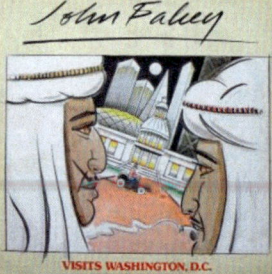

Matrix #: SMX 55651   P2A
         SMX 55652   P2A
Songs: version 1-b (7+8)
Recording Dates:
Liner Notes: yes
Producer:
Of note: (1) Manufactured and distributed under license by Festival Records Pty. Limited, Australia.

John Van Hamersveld mixed facts with fantasy when he designed the album cover of *John Fahey Visits Washington, D.C.* He was influenced by occurrences in the news. In 1979, the Shah of Iran fled his country amid massive protests, and the Ayatollah Khomeini came to power. Protests and strikes severely disrupted Iran's oil production. Due to the decreased oil output in the wake of the Iranian Revolution, the 1979 (or second) oil crisis occurred in the United States.

Hamersveld's illustration depicts two Arabs in Washington with the Capitol off balance. In the image is the fantasy of John Fahey riding his guitar into Washington during the turmoil.

> Dear Joe:
>
> Here's $10.00 down. Can you send me a list of what you have on the Wheeling label — anything by Doc Williams + the border riders?
>
> How much for a list of bluegrass & related up to 1950?
>
> yrs John Fahey
>
> _____ Box 5369
> PLUS CREDIT. SM, CA, 90405

John Fahey relied on Joe Bussard for many of his blues and bluegrass tunes that he would use for inspiration. In the letter above he asks Joe for songs on the Wheeling label. This was a label from West Virginia (named after the town of Wheeling, WV) issued by the bluegrass master Doc Williams himself (a/k/a Andrew John Smik, Jr; 1914-2011). Williams' rendition of "Silver Bell" (on Wheeling 1002 from 1947) was familiar to Fahey ever since his childhood and it was used as a source for the first medley track on this album.

#3

Release date: 1987
Edition: 3rd issue (label #3, jacket #3, songs #3)
Catalog number: ST-72769
Format: 12" LP, 33⅓ rpm, stereo
Jacket cover: 3rd
  - *Front cover*: Two Arabs and Washington, D.C.
  - *Spine*: TAK 7069   JOHN FAHEY   JOHN FAHEY VISITS WASHINGTON, D.C.   TAKOMA RECORDS PRINTED IN U.S.A.
  - *Back cover*: dragon logo; ST-72769 sticker.
Cover credit: John Van Hamersveld
Label: Do^3

 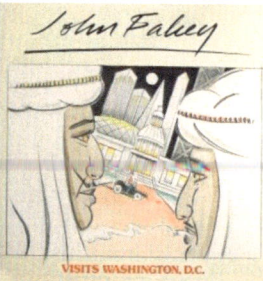 

Matrix #: ST-1-72769 G-1   Q B-28571-G1   Δ 17646 1-1 MASTERED BY CAPITOL
             ST-2-72769 G-1   Q B-28572-G1   Δ 17646-X 1-1 MASTERED BY CAPITOL
Songs: version 1-c (3+3)

A1 – Medley: Silver Bell / Cheyenne		4:27
A2 – Ann Arbor / Death By Reputation		8:04
A3 – The Discovery Of The Sylvia Scott		7:43
B1 – Guitar Lamento		5:30
B2 – Melody McBad		10:08
B3 – The Grand Finale		6:30

Recording Dates:
Liner notes: yes
Producer:
Of note: (1) This record's matrix # contains the following components:
  ST-1-72769 = record company prefix code, side, and catalogue number;
  G = Neumann lathe used by Capitol Mastering in Hollywood, California;
  Q (or 0) = pressed at the Jacksonville, Illinois plant
  B-28571 = pressing plant's matrix number
  Δ number = the delta sign and 5-digit number (an X is added for the B-side) was originally used by Monarch pressing plant in L.A., and then adopted by others.
  MASTERED BY CAPITOL = the record company that mastered the album.

Non-Takoma LP re-issue

#1

Release date: 1979 (Canada)
Record company: Chrysalis Records
Catalog number: TAK-7069
Format: 12" LP, 33⅓ rpm, stereo
Jacket cover:
 - Front cover: Two Arabs and Washington, D.C.
 - Spine: TAK 7069   JOHN FAHEY   JOHN FAHEY VISITS WASHINGTON, D.C.   TAKOMA RECORDS PRINTED IN CANADA
 - Back cover: dragon logo; *no* bar code; "Manufactured and distributed in Canada by Capitol Records-EMI of Canada Limited".
Cover credit: John Van Hamersveld
Label: blue-white

 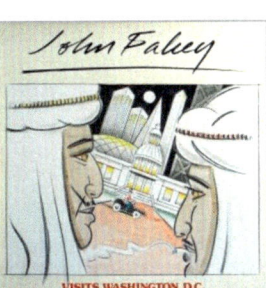 

Matrix #: TAK 7069-A   TLC-A
           TAK 7069 B   TLC .T
Songs: version 1-d (3+3)
A1 – Medley: Silver Bell / Cheyenne   4:27
A2 – Ann Arbor / Death By Reputation   8:04
A3 – The Discovery Of The Sylvia Scott   7:43
   B1 – Guitar Lamento   5:30
   B2 – Melody McBad   10:08
   B3 – The Grand Finale   6:30
Recording Dates:
Liner notes: yes
Producer:
Of note: (1) This is technically a Takoma release in Canada since Takoma Records had just been bought by Chrysalis. It retains the catalogue number TAK-7069.

8-Track re-issue

#1

Release date: 1979
Record company: Takoma Records
Catalog number: 8TA-7069
Format: 8-track stereo
Cover: Two Arabs and Washington, D.C.

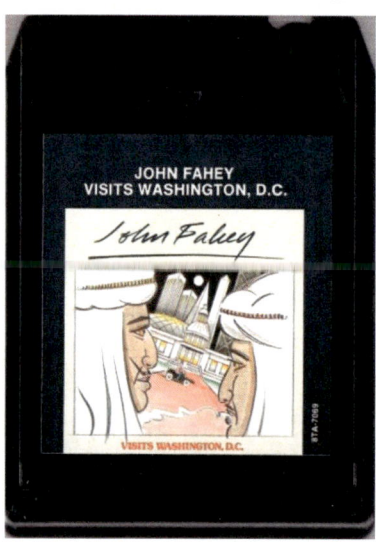 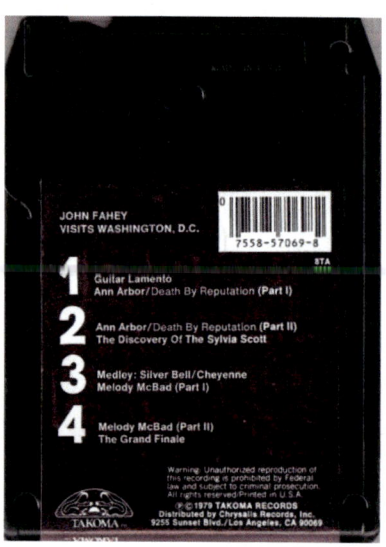

Original Cover credit: John Van Hamersveld
Songs: version #1 (6)
A1 – Guitar Lamento
A2 – Ann Arbor / Death By Reputation (Part I)
  B1 – Ann Arbor / Death By Reputation (Part II)
  B2 – The Discovery Of The Sylvia Scott
    C1 – Medley: Silver Bell / Cheyenne
    C2 – Melody McBad (Part I)
      D1 – Melody McBad (Part II)
      D2 – The Grand Finale
Recording Dates:
Liner notes: no
Of note: (1) This is one of the only two Fahey 8-tracks to have a UPC barcode.
(2) The UPC code on the back cover is: 07558570698.

Tape re-issue

#1

Release date: 1979
Record company: Takoma Records
Catalog number: CTA 7069
Format: cassette tape
Cover: Two Arabs and Washington, D.C.
Original Cover credit: John Van Hamersveld
Songs: version #1 (3+3)
A1 – Medley: Silver Bell / Cheyenne
A2 – Ann Arbor / Death By Reputation
A3 – The Discovery Of The Sylvia Scott
  B1 – Guitar Lamento
  B2 – Melody McBad
  B3 – The Grand Finale
Recording Dates:
Of note: (1) The UPC code on the front cover is: 07558570694.

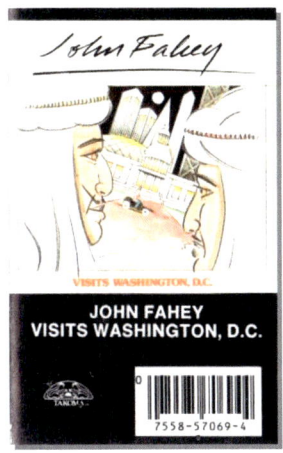

#2

Release date: 1987
Record company: Takoma Records
Catalog number: D41G 72769
Format: cassette tape
Cover: Two Arabs and Washington, D.C.
Original Cover credit: John Van Hamersveld
Songs: version #1 (3+3)
A1 – Medley: Silver Bell / Cheyenne
A2 – Ann Arbor / Death By Reputation
A3 – The Discovery Of The Sylvia Scott
  B1 – Guitar Lamento
  B2 – Melody McBad
  B3 – The Grand Finale
Recording Dates:
Of note: (1) The UPC code on the back cover is: 022397276943.

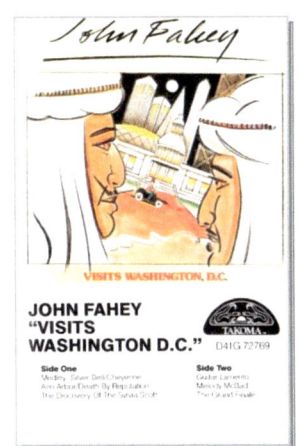

CD re-issue

#1

Release date: 1987
Catalog number: TAKCD-7069 or CDP-72769
Format: CD
Cover: Two Arabs and Washington, D.C.   **Disc label**: silver

Original Cover credit: John Van Hamersveld
Songs: version #1 (6)

1 – Medley: Silver Bell / Cheyenne	4:29
2 – Ann Arbor / Death By Reputation	8:10
3 – The Discovery Of The Sylvia Scott	7:45
4 – Guitar Lamento	5:47
5 – Melody McBad	10:11
6 – The Grand Finale	6:55

Recording Dates:
Liner notes: none
Remastering: Michael Boshears
Reissue Producer: none given
Of note: (1) Made in Japan for Allegiance Records.
(2) The CD label has the early 1987 catalog number TAKCD-7069, while the cover has the late 1987 catalog number CDP-72769.
(3) The UPC code on the back cover is: 022397276929.
(4) Some of the CDs came in a generic Allegiance Records 5 ½" x 12" CD longbox.

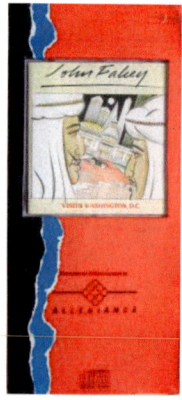

#2

Release date: 2008 (UK)
Catalog number: CDTAK-1069
Format: CD
Cover: Two Arabs and Wash,. D.C; dragon logo   Disc label: white

Original Cover credit: John Van Hamersveld
Songs: version #1 (6)
1 – Medley: Silver Bell / Cheyenne	4:27
2 – Ann Arbor / Death By Reputation	8:04
3 – The Discovery Of The Sylvia Scott	7:42
4 – Guitar Lamento	5:30
5 – Melody McBad	10:08
6 – The Grand Finale	6:30

Recording Dates:
Original Liner notes: yes
New Liner notes: by Kris Needs
Remastering: Rob Shread (Sound Mastering Ltd)
Reissue Producer: none given
Of note: (1) Interesting to see the catalog number being reverted from the 7000 series back to the 1000 series. (2) Made in the UK by ACE Records. (3) The UPC code on the back cover is: 029667033220.

JOHN FAHEY RE-VISITS HIS HOMETOWN

The liner notes to *John Fahey Visits Washington, D.C.* describe a trip through Fahey's childhood stomping grounds, especially Takoma Park in suburban Washington, D.C. Fahey had come to the East Coast many times over the past decade and occasionally visited his hometown and some of his old acquaintances. The notes begin with a list of people to whom the album is dedicated. This resembles the *Voice of the Turtle* notes wherein Fahey listed the names of many of his friends and acquaintances.

The dedication list includes (1) musicians that he heard over the radio while growing up in Takoma Park; (2) neighborhood friends; and (3) priests from the Episcopal Church that he attended.

Mac Weisman = Mac Wiseman (b. 1925) the famous bluegrass and country singer from Virginia.

Kenneth Fisher = Kenneth Frank Fisher, one of the Fisher brothers who lived on Baltimore Avenue. He was one year senior to Fahey in junior high school.

Joey Srour = Joseph Ralph Srour (b. 1941) was a neighborhood friend of Fahey. Joe lived in Takoma Park on Baltimore Avenue, next door to the Fisher brothers (Kenneth, Richard, David and James). Their backyard fences bordered the house on Cleveland Avenue where Patti (a junior high schoolmate of John Fahey) and her younger sister, the future actress Goldie Hawn, lived. Joe, John and the Fisher brothers belonged to the same neighborhood gang, and they would often play on the nearby railroad tracks, a fact that would explain Fahey's fascination with trains. Since turtles could be found all over the place in their neighborhood in those days, and the Fisher boys had a turtle pen in their backyard, it was not surprising that Fahey would develop a lifelong passion for these creatures.

John Fahey (called "Johnnie" by his childhood friends) was two years older than Joe Srour and he would take him under his wing, so much so that every time John changed his newspaper delivery, he would transfer the paper route to Joey. Joe remembers that Fahey first delivered the *Washington Daily News*, then the *Washington Evening Star*, and finally the *Washington Post*.

The last time Joe saw Fahey on the East Coast was around 1958 when he pulled into Martin's Esso gas station late one night to deliver some newspapers. As he walked in, he saw to his surprise John sitting on a chair and playing his guitar. It was then that he found out that Fahey was the gas station's night manager. They would meet up again in 1968 when, after moving to Los Angeles, Joe went to see Fahey at a gig in the Ash Grove. It was at one of these shows that Joe asked why Fahey had never put his name in any liner notes, especially after having included many other childhood friends. When the next album *Visits Washington, D.C.* came out, it would have Joe's name on it. The two would intermittently see each other over the following years whenever Fahey was playing in town.

After graduating from Catholic University of America in Washington, DC, as an electrical engineer, Joe Srour became a successful aerospace engineer. When Joe married in 1994, his wedding was also attended by the two Hawn sisters, a fact that emphasizes how the childhood friends of this special neighborhood would keep in touch throughout their lives. Fahey will talk about the Hawn sisters in his book *How Bluegrass Music Destroyed My Life*.

Joe still recalls the time when Fahey bought his first guitar and how he carried it strapped around his shoulder everywhere he went, never being seen without it. Joe collected all of Fahey's albums, and is still today ever more fascinated by all things Fahey.

Gilbert Purvis =

Louise Livings = Louise Maybelle Livings (see *The John Fahey Handbook* - volume I).

Anna Caluzzi =

Caroll Mc---- = supposedly Carole McClay, a Northwestern High School classmate of Fahey and whose picture is depicted in the *Voice of the Turtle* photo album.

Wilma Lee and Stoney Cooper = Wilma Lee Leary (1921-2011) and her husband Dale Troy "Stoney" Cooper (1918-1977) were bluegrass / country entertainers from West Virginia. After marrying, the duo formed their own group called "Wilma Lee and Stoney Cooper with the Clinch Mountain Clan." Fahey heard Stoney Cooper in the 1950s on a radio show hosted by the dee-jay Don Owens who broadcast over WARL (Arlington, Virginia). Fahey credits Owens for introducing his ear to bluegrass music.

Greg Eldridge = In the video *John Fahey in Concert* from 1996, Fahey said "Me and a guy named Greg Eldridge, we were sitting around drinking beer one night and I was trying to find a catchy name, and he was helping me – we were going 'round and 'round and finally said *Blind Joe Death* – hmmm, That's it!"

Jim Hensen = James Maury Henson (1936-1990), creator of The Muppets. Born in Mississippi, his family moved to Maryland in the 1940s and Jim attended Northwestern High School in Hyattsville, the same school that John Fahey attended. Henson was two years senior to Fahey and graduated in 1954.

Tim Wright =

Sylvia Scott =

Carl Storey = Carl Story (1916-1995), a gospel bluegrass musician. His band was called "Carl Story and his Rambling Mountaineers." Fahey heard him, too, on Don Owen's radio show.

George Kerrick = George Alfred Kerrick (b. 1938), a classmate of Fahey at NWHS. He was band president and his goal was to become a professional musician. He graduated from University of Maryland and became a trombone instructor.

Fr. Don Seaton = Rev. Donald Wylie Seaton Jr (1928 -1992). See next section.

Fr. Dick Gary =

Fr. Don Shaw = Rev. Donald Coulter Shaw (see *The John Fahey Handbook* - volume I).

Several other persons that Fahey encounters or remembers are mentioned in the notes as he travels through the Takoma Park area:

Don Catudell/Katudell/Katudall = Donald Bruce Catudal,

Dorothy Gooch = (see *The John Fahey Handbook* - volume I).

Elmer Williams = (see *The John Fahey Handbook* - volume I).

Tommy Flynn = Thomas J. Flynn, a classmate of John Fahey in 10th grade at Northwestern High School. The following year Tommy transferred to St. Anthony's High School in Washington, DC. Fahey's narrative suggests that he met with an untimely "death." In the manuscript *Admiral Kelvinator: Clockworks Factory* he states that Tommy died in the summer of 1955 after shooting himself in the head. This incident actually occurred on November 15, 1955, in the boy's home and, though the parents' story suggested a possible accident, his death by his own .22-caliber rifle was ruled a suicide. Sadly, the grieving mother of the 17-year-old boy committed suicide by hanging herself in the same home five months later.

This is just one of several gruesome incidents that occurred in the area during the summer of 1955. These obviously left indelible memories in John Fahey's mind, and he would refer to them a number of times in his writings.

In the manuscript *Admiral Kelvinator: Clockworks Factory*, Fahey recalls the death of his 11th grade geometry teacher, Thorman A. Nelson. He was murdered by suffocation on August 15, 1955, while staying at the Sloan House YMCA hotel in New York City. The following month, two men were charged with homicide in the death of the well-liked 50-year-old teacher.

In his article "Vignettes, Digressions, and Screens" (*Grinning Idiot*, 1984), John Fahey wrote about two girls (aged 14 and 16) who were murdered near Sligo Creek while walking to Northwestern High School in Hyattsville on June 15, 1955. He said "Nobody ever found out who did it." However, in 1996, a man confessed on his deathbed to the double murder. When he was 17, he apparently shot the girls with his .22-caliber rifle after having being rebuffed by one of them.

One story that Fahey would repeat at least twice in his writings is the exorcism by a priest of a boy said to be possessed by the devil when living in nearby Mt. Ranier in 1949. That story would go on to furnish the plot to the famous horror movie *The Exorcist* (1973).

Miss Hardy = Miss Caroline Hardy, Fahey's English teacher at Northwestern High School.

FATHER DON SEATON

Rev. Donald Wylie Seaton Jr (1928 -1992) grew up in Hancock, Michigan. He attended the University of Chicago from which he graduated in 1953. While there he worked during the summers in a Michigan copper mine. He later served in the Navy where he was also trained as an explosive ordnance disposal officer.

Donald Seaton became layman-in-charge for five months at St. John's Episcopal Church in Washington, DC. He then entered the Virginia Theological Seminary in Alexandria, Virginia, and graduated in 1959. He was a deacon at St. Michael's and All Angels Church in Adelphi, Maryland, and was ordained an Episcopal priest in December of 1959. Seaton then continued as assistant rector at St. Michael's. A year later, after the departure of the Rev. Don Shaw, rector of St. Michael's, Seaton became its new rector. Under their rectorship, the church had acquired the reputation as "a swinging parish."

In May of 1965, Seaton accepted the rectorship of Christ Church in Washington, DC. Here he gained notoriety for opening the church to local African-Americans, as well as reaching out to the hippies, some of whom began living in the rectory. The old congregation did not welcome this happily and, in January 1968, the *Washington Post* reported on these events, as well as the use of marijuana and LSD by the young people who considered them as "lanterns along the path towards spiritual truth." In the wake of the scandal, Rev. Donald Seaton handed in his resignation one month later.

Seaton then moved to California. In the summer of 1969 he ran the Hospitality House for youth in the X-rated Tenderloin district of San Francisco. He eventually was asked to be the rector of St. Aidan's Church in Oakland. He organized folk music concerts at the church. It was at one of these concerts held in November 1971 that the guest artist was none other than John Fahey himself. A newspaper article advertised this event by stating:

> *"John Fahey began his career with thanks to the rector of an Episcopal church in Maryland. The church provided some needed financial backing for his first disc. Fahey will do a benefit concert at St. Aidan's church, San Francisco. The rector there today is the same person who had such faith in Fahey long ago."*

This statement implies that Seaton was Fahey's benefactor who had lent him $300 to press his 1959 *Blind Joe Death* album. Other accounts credit Rev. Don Shaw for this. In fact, Shaw was rector at St. Michael's during all of 1959, while Seaton was just a deacon and would only become its rector after the departure of Shaw in 1960. In a 1996 interview, Fahey said that it actually cost him $500 to press the album, and $300 of these were borrowed from an Episcopalian minister. He ended by saying under his breath, "I never paid him back." Some friends also helped, such as Thomas Curtis and Flea who each gave $10.

Rev. Donald Seaton would go on to become the rector of St. Paul's Church in San Francisco in 1974 and remained there until he retired in 1991. In 1989 he was diagnosed with lung cancer and died on November 23, 1992.

YES! JESUS LOVES ME

#1

Release date: 1980
Edition: 1st issue (label #1, jacket #1, songs #1)
Catalog number: TAK-7085
Format: 12" LP, 33⅓ rpm, stereo
Jacket cover: 1st
  - **Front cover**: Jesus on the Cross
  - **Spine**: TAK 7085   JOHN FAHEY / YES! JESUS LOVES ME
    TAKOMA RECORDS   PRINTED IN U.S.A.
  - **Back cover**: dragon logo; bar code.
Cover credit: Melody Brennan Fahey
Label: Do[1]

 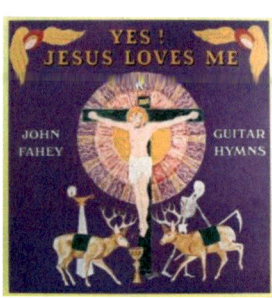 

Matrix #: T1   TAK-7085-A-RE-1-1
        T1   TAK-7085-B-RE-1-1
Songs: version 1 (10+10)

A1 – Yes, Jesus Loves Me	1:43
A2 – Stand Up, Stand Up For Jesus	1:06
A3 – Medley: Lord Of All Hopefullness / All Through The Night	3:33
A4 – Oh Come, Oh Come Emmanuel	2:28
A5 – Two American Folk Hymns	2:20
A6 – For All The Beauty Of The Earth	1:33
A7 – St. Patrick's	1:46
A8 – Holy, Holy, Holy	1:54
A9 – Come Labor On	1:33
A10 – St. Clement's	1:40
B1 – For All The Saints	1:28
B2 – At The Name Of Jesus	1:18
B3 – Medley: Come Thou Almighty King / Wild Western Hero	1:40
B4 – Praise To The Lord	1:37
B5 – Lord, I Want To Be A Christian In My Heart	1:48

B6 – Faith Of Our Fathers 1:10
B7 – Just As I Am 1:15
B8 – Let All Mortal Flesh Keep Silence 3:24
B9 – Jesus Christ Is Risen Today 3:10
B10 – Yes, Jesus Loves Me (reprise) 0:33
Recording Dates: 1980
Liner notes: none
Producer:
Of note: (1) The sound quality is suboptimal due to out-of-phase mastering; one will notice the sound cancellation when playback is converted to mono. (2) Fahey said he approved the test pressing without actually listening to it as he was in a hurry to get the album out. Because of the defective pressing, the album was returned in huge amounts. Fahey said it was his poorest selling album, which is why Takoma never issued a second pressing.

Tape re-issue

#1

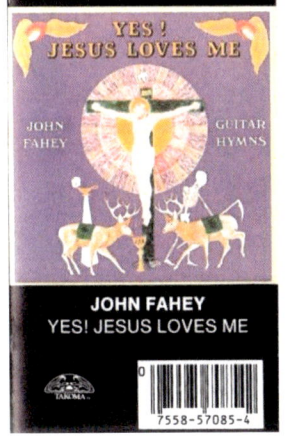

Release date: 1980
Catalog number: CTA 7085
Format: cassette tape
Cover: Jesus on the Cross
Original Cover credit: Melody Brennan Fahey
Songs: version #1 (10+10)
Recording Dates: same as LP #1
Liner notes: none
Of note: (1) Later issues (from 1987) may have the 4XT-72785 sticker on the back. (2) The UPC code on the front cover is: 07558570854.

CD re-issue

#1

Release date: 1987
Catalog number: TAKCD-7120 or CDP-72820
Format: CD
Cover: 2 albums in one CD.

Disc label: silver

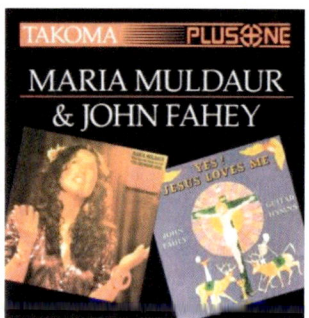

Original Cover credit:
Songs: version #1 (14)
12 – Yes, Jesus Loves Me
13 – Stand Up, Stand Up For Jesus
14 – Medley: Lord Of All Hopefullness / All Through The Night
15 – Oh Come, Oh Come Emmanuel
16 – Two American Folk Hymns
17 – St. Patrick's
18 – Holy, Holy, Holy
19 – St. Clement's
20 – For All The Saints
21 – At The Name Of Jesus
22 – Medley: Come Thou Almighty King / Wild Western Hero
23 – Praise To The Lord
24 – Lord, I Want To Be A Christian In My Heart
25 – Let All Mortal Flesh Keep Silence
Recording Dates: same as LP #1
Remastering: Michael Boshears
Reissue Producer: none given
Liner notes: none
Of note: (1) This is a combined CD called *PLUS ONE* where tracks 1-11 are from Maria Muldaur's 1980 Takoma album *Gospel Nights*, TAK 7084. (2) Only fourteen of the twenty tracks from *Yes! Jesus Loves Me* are present on this CD. (3) Made in Japan for Allegiance Records. (4) The CD has the early 1987 catalog # TAKCD-7120, but the cover has the later 1987 catalog # CDP-72820. (5) The sound quality has been restored. (6) The UPC code on the back cover is: 022397282029.

#2

Release date: 2007 (England)
Catalog number: CDTAK 7085
Format: CD
Cover: Jesus on the Cross.   **Disc label**: yellow

Original Cover credit: Melody Brennan Fahey
Songs: version #2 (20)

1 – Yes, Jesus Loves Me	1:45
2 – Stand Up, Stand Up For Jesus	1:07
3 – Medley: Lord Of All Hopefullness / All Through The Night	3:36
4 – Oh Come, Oh Come Emmanuel	2:31
5 – Two American Folk Hymns	2:20
6 – For All The Beauty Of The Earth	1:34
7 – St. Patrick's	1:47
8 – Holy, Holy, Holy	1:55
9 – Come Labor On	1:35
10 – St. Clement's	1:42
11 – For All The Saints	1:29
12 – At The Name Of Jesus	1:19
13 – Medley: Come Thou Almighty King / Wild Western Hero	1:40
14 – Praise To The Lord	1:37
15 – Lord, I Want To Be A Christian In My Heart	1:49
16 – Faith Of Our Fathers	1:11
17 – Just As I Am	1:16
18 – Let All Mortal Flesh Keep Silence	3:24
19 – Jesus Christ Is Risen Today	2:58
20 – Yes, Jesus Loves Me (reprise)	0:38

Recording Dates: same as LP #1
Remastering: Rob Shread at Sound Mastering Ltd.
Reissue Producer: none given
Liner notes: Kris Needs
Of note: (1) The sound quality has been restored. (2) The UPC code on the back cover is: 029667030625.

LIVE IN TASMANIA

#1

Release date: 1981
Edition: 1st issue (label #1, jacket #1, songs #1)
Catalog number: TAK-7089
Format: 12" LP, 33⅓ rpm, stereo
Jacket cover: 1st
  - **Front cover**: Two kangaroos
  - **Spine**: TAK 7089   LIVE IN TASMANIA / JOHN FAHEY
       TAKOMA RECORDS   Printed in U.S.A.
  - **Back cover**: dragon logo; bar code & TAK 7089 in upper right corner.
Cover credit: John Van Hamersveld
Label: Do[1]

Matrix #: SX TS1 TAK-7089 AS- Sm2 MASTERED BT CAPITOL J. LEMAY
       S1 SXT TAK-7089 BS Sm2 MASTERED BT CAPITOL J. LEMAY
Songs: version 1-a (2+4)
A1 – Introduction by Stefan Markovitch: 13:54
       On The Sunny Side Of The Ocean
       Tasmanian Two-Step
       Tiger
A2 – The Approaching of the Disco Void   6:33
  B1 – Waltzing Matilda   2:34
  B2 – Fahey Establishes Rapport With The Tasmanians;   8:58
       A Disertation On "Obscurity" (spoken)
       The Return Of The Tasmanian Tiger
       Funeral Song For Mississippi John Hurt
  B3 – Steamboat Gwine 'Round De Bend   4:57
  B4 – Indian-Pacific R. R. Blues   5:03
Recording Dates: 1980 in Hobart, Island of Tasmania (Australia) – see page 262.
Liner notes: by Peter Noble
Producer: Peter Noble
Of note: (1) Track B4 is the studio recording "Beverly" from *After The Ball*.

(2) Four songs are actually re-titled versions of previously recorded tunes:
- o Tasmanian Two-Step = Hawaiian Two-Step = Spanish Two-Step
- o Tiger = Lion
- o Return of the Tasmanian Tiger = Revolt of the Dyke Brigade
- o Indian-Pacific R.R. Blues = Beverly

As for "The Approaching of the Disco Void," it is a reworking of "Wine and Roses." Charles M. Young said: "Fahey can get away with cannibalizing his previous work because there's so much of it and because it's as beautiful and hypnotic as almost any music ever made."

#2

Release date: 1981 (England)
Edition: 2nd issue (label #2, jacket #2, songs #2)
Catalog number: Sonet SNTF 861
Format: 12" LP, 33⅓ rpm, stereo
Jacket cover: 2nd
  - **Front cover**: Two kangaroos
  - **Spine**: JOHN FAHEY   LIVE IN TASMANIA   SNTF 861
  - **Back cover**: dragon logo; *no* bar code; Sonet logo; London address
Cover credit: John Van Hamersveld
Label: Do^{EU}

Matrix #: SNTF 861-A.
               SNTF 861.B.1.
Songs: version 1-b (2+4)
Recording Dates: 1980 in Hobart, Island of Tasmania (Australia)
Liner notes: by Peter Noble
Producer: Peter Noble
Of note: (1) Sonet now begins issuing Takoma Records with a modified Takoma label.

#3

Release date: 1981   (Australia)
Edition: 3rd issue (label #3, jacket #3, songs #3)
Catalog number: L-37559
Format: 12" LP, 33⅓ rpm, stereo
Jacket cover: 3rd
  - **Front cover**: Two kangaroos
  - **Spine**: L 37559   LIVE IN TASMANIA   JOHN FAHEY
  - **Back cover**: dragon logo; *no* bar code; L-37559 in upper right corner.
Cover credit: John Van Hamersveld
Label: Do^{AUS}

Matrix #: SMX·57299
              SMX 57300   G2A 2   3
Songs: version 1-c (2+4)
Recording Dates: 1980 in Hobart, Island of Tasmania (Australia)
Liner notes: by Peter Noble
Producer: Peter Noble
Of note: (1) Issued by Festival Records of Australia.

Non-Takoma LP re-issue

#1

Release date: 1981   (Italy)
Record company: Sonet
Catalog number: Sonet   SNTL 2861
Format: 12" LP, 33⅓ rpm, stereo
Jacket cover:
  - **Front cover**: Two kangaroos
  - **Spine**: SNTL 2861   LIVE IN TASMANIA - JOHN FAHEY   SONET
  - **Back cover**: dragon logo; *no* bar code; Sonet logo; Dischi Ricordi.
Cover credit: John Van Hamersveld
Label: pyramid

Matrix #: SNTL • 2861 - 1   ΛΛ
              SNTL • 2861 • 2
Songs: version 1-d (2+4)
Recording Dates: 1980 in Hobart, Island of Tasmania (Australia)
Liner notes: by Peter Noble
Producer: Peter Noble
Of note: (1) This record was distributed by Dischi Ricordi S.P.A.

8-Track re-issue

#1

Release date: 1981
Catalog number: 8TA-7089
Format: 8-track stereo
Cover: Two kangaroos

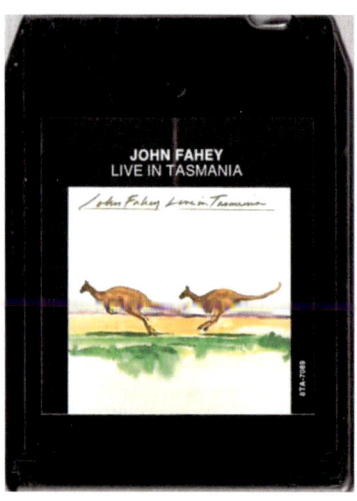 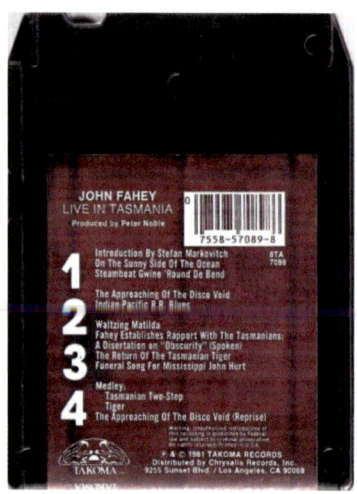

Original Cover credit: John Van Hamersveld
Songs: version #1 (2+2+2+2)
A1 – Introduction by Stefan Markovitch
    On The Sunny Side Of The Ocean
A2 – Steamboat Gwine 'Round De Bend
    B1 – The Approaching of the Disco Void
    B2 – Indian-Pacific R. R. Blues
        C1 – Waltzing Matilda
        C2 – Fahey Establishes Rapport With The Tasmanians;
            A Disertation On "Obscurity" (spoken)
            The Return Of The Tasmanian Tiger
            Funeral Song For Mississippi John Hurt
            D1 – Medley:
                Tasmanian Two-Step
                Tiger
            D2 – The Approaching of the Disco Void (Reprise)
Recording Dates: same as LP #1
Manufacturer: Takoma Records
Of note: (1) One of only two Fahey 8-track to have a UPC barcode. (2) The UPC code on the back cover is: 07558570898.

Tape re-issue

#1

Release date: 1981
Catalog number: CTA 7089
Format: cassette tape
Cover: Two kangaroos
Original Cover credit: John Van Hamersveld
Songs: version #1 (5+6)
A1 – Introduction by Stefan Markovitch
A2 – On The Sunny Side Of The Ocean
A3 – Tasmanian Two-Step
A4 – Tiger
A5 – The Approaching of the Disco Void
    B1 – Waltzing Matilda
    B2 – Fahey Establishes Rapport With The Tasmanians; A Disertation On "Obscurity" (spoken)
    B3 – The Return Of The Tasmanian Tiger
    B4 – Funeral Song For Mississippi John Hurt
    B5 – Steamboat Gwine 'Round De Bend
    B6 – Indian-Pacific R. R. Blues
Recording Dates: same as LP #1
Of note: (1) Distributed by Chrysalis. (2) The UPC code on the front cover is: 07558570894.

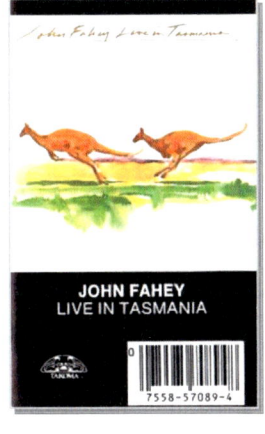

CD re-issue

#1

Release date: 1987
Catalog number: Takoma CDP-72789
Format: CD
Cover: Two kangaroos & catalog number.   **Disc label**: silver

Original Cover credit: John Van Hamersveld
Songs: version #1-a (6)
1 – Introduction by Stefan Markovitch: 13:54
      On The Sunny Side Of The Ocean
      Tasmania Two-Step
      Tiger
2 – The Approaching of the Disco Void   6:33
3 – Waltzing Matilda   2:34
4 – Fahey Established Rapport With The Tasmanians;   8:58
      A Disertation On "Obscurity" (spoken)
      The Return Of The Tasmanian Tiger
      Funeral Song For Mississippi John Hurt
5 – Steamboat Gwine 'Round The Bend   4:57
6 – Indian-Pacific R. R. Blues   5:03
Recording Dates: same as LP #1
Remastering: Michael Boshears
Liner Notes: none
Original Producer: Peter Noble
Reissue Producer: none given
Of note: (1) The UPC code on the back cover is: 022397278923.
(2) Some of the CDs came in a generic Allegiance Records 5 ½" x 12" CD longbox.
(3) The tray cover mispells track #1-c as "Tasmania Two-Step," and track #4 as "Fahey Established . . ."

#2

Release date: 2004
Catalog number: TAKCD-6513-2
Format: CD
Cover: Two kangaroos.   **Disc label**: yellow-green

Original Cover credit: John Van Hamersveld
Songs: version #1-b (6)
1 – Introduction by Stefan Markovitch:	13:34
On The Sunny Side Of The Ocean	
Tasmanian Two-Step	
Tiger	
2 – The Approaching of the Disco Void	6:48
3 – Waltzing Matilda	2:27
4 – Fahey Establishes Rapport With The Tasmanians;	8:53
A Dissertation On "Obscurity" (spoken)	
The Return Of The Tasmanian Tiger	
Funeral Song For Mississippi John Hurt	
5 – Steamboat Gwine 'Round de Bend	4:54
6 – Indian-Pacific R. R. Blues	4:57

Recording Dates: same as LP #1
Remastering: Joe Tarantino (Fantasy Studios, Berkeley)
Liner Notes: by Peter Noble and Jim O'Rourke
Original Producer: Peter Noble
Reissue Producer: none given
Of note: (1) The titles finally have the correct spelling of all their words.
(2) The UPC code on the back cover is: 025218651325.

#3

Release date: 2004 (UK)
Catalog number: CDTAK 6513
Format: CD
Cover: 2 kangaroos; Takoma dragon logo.   **Disc label**: silver-kangaroos

Original Cover credit: John Van Hamersveld
Songs: version #1-b (6)

1 – Introduction by Stefan Markovitch:	13:34
On the Sunny Side of the Ocean	
Tasmanian Two-Step	
Tiger	
2 – The Approaching of the Disco Void	6:48
3 – Waltzing Matilda	2:27
4 – Fahey Establishes Rapport with the Tasmanians;	8:53
A Dissertation on "Obscurity" (spoken)	
The Return of the Tasmanian Tiger	
Funeral Song for Mississippi John Hurt	
5 – Steamboat Gwine 'Round de Bend	4:54
6 – Indian-Pacific R. R. Blues	4:57

Recording Dates: same as LP #1
Remastering: Joe Tarantino (Fantasy Studios, Berkeley)
Liner Notes: by Peter Noble and Jim O'Rourke
Original Producer: Peter Noble
Reissue Producer: none given
Of note: (1) The titles have the correct spelling of all their words. (2) Marketed and produced by ACE Records. (3) The UPC code on the back cover is: 029667002929.

CHRISTMAS GUITAR, VOLUME ONE

#1

Release date: 1982
Edition: 1st issue (label #1, jacket #1, songs #1)
Catalog number: Varrick VR-002
Format: 12" LP, 33⅓ rpm, stereo
Jacket cover: 1st
  - Front cover: green
  - Spine: VR-002   JOHN FAHEY   CHRISTMAS GUITAR
       VARRICK RECORDS 002
  - Back cover: green.
Cover credit: Susan Marsh
Label: green

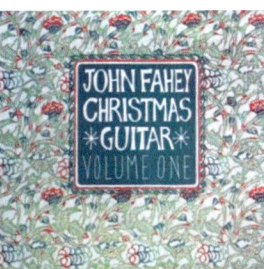

Matrix #: VR 002-A   41019.A #7
          VR 002-B   41019.B MO#2
Songs: version 1-a (9+9)

A1 – Joy to the World	1:34
A2 – What Child Is This?	3:15
A3 – Medley: Hark, the Herald Angels Sing / O Come All Ye Faithful	4:22
A4 – Auld Lang Syne	2:00
A5 – Bells of St. Mary's	2:15
A6 – Good Christian Men Rejoice	1:13
A7 – We Three Kings	1:45
A8 – Away in the Manger #1	1:19
A9 – God Rest Ye Merry Gentlemen Fantasy	2:52
B1 – The First Noel	3:48
B2 – Good King Wenceslas	1:02
B3 – Evermore and Evermore (of the Father's Love Begotten)	1:20
B4 – Away in the Manger #2	2:27
B5 – In the Bleak Midwinter	1:46
B6 – It Came Upon a Midnight Clear	2:54
B7 – Medley: Jesus Won't You Come By Here? / Go Tell it on the Mountain	3:22

B8 – Lo How a Rose E'er Blooming 1:48
B9 – Silent Night, Holy Night 3:10
Recording Dates: High Tech Recorders, Portland, Oregon, October 1982.
Liner notes: none
Producer: John Fahey and Terry Robb
Of note: (1) The arrangement of track A8 is credited to Ralph C. Johnston a/k/a Ragtime Ralph. (2) Tracks A8 and B4 are called "Away In A Manger" on the label. (3) For this album, John Fahey re-recorded 12 of the 14 songs originally issued on the 1968 album *The New Possibility*.

#2

Release date: 1984
Edition: 2nd issue (label #2, jacket #1, songs #2)
Catalog number: Varrick VR-002
Format: 12" LP, 33⅓ rpm, stereo
Jacket cover: 1st
  - **Front cover**: green
  - **Spine**: VR-002   JOHN FAHEY   CHRISTMAS GUITAR
      VARRICK RECORDS   002
  - **Back cover**: green.
Cover credit: Susan Marsh
Label: blue

Matrix #: VR 002-A   41019.A   MO#3
     VR 002-B-RE1   41019.B^{RE1} MO#2 32
Songs: version 1-b (9+9)
Recording Dates: High Tech Recorders, Portland, Oregon, October 1982.
Liner notes: none
Producer: John Fahey and Terry Robb

Tape re-issue

#1

Release date: 1982
Catalog number: VR-C-002
Format: cassette tape
Cover: green
Original Cover credit: Susan Marsh
Songs: version #1 (9+9)
Recording Dates: same as LP #1
Of note: (1) Tracks A8 and B4 are called "Away In The Manger" on the cover, but are called "Away In A Manger" on the cassette.

#2

Release date: 1989
Catalog number: C-VR-002
Format: cassette tape
Cover: green
Original Cover credit: Susan Marsh
Songs: version #1 (9+9)
Recording Dates: same as LP #1
Of note: (1) Tracks A8 and B4 are called "Away In The Manger" on the cover, but are called "Away In A Manger" on the cassette. (2) The UPC code on the back cover is: 011671000244.

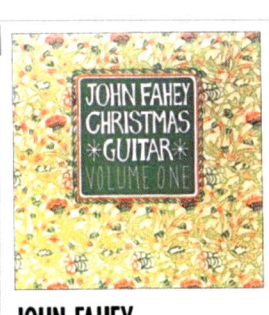

CD re-issue

#1

Release date: 1994
Record company: Varrick Records
Catalog number: CD VR 002
Format: CD
Cover: snow and sleigh   **Disc label**: white

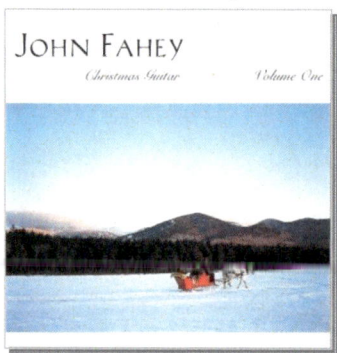
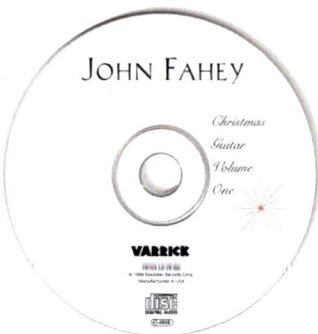

Cover credit: Jean Hangarter
Songs: version #1 (18)
Recording Dates: same as LP #1
Remastering:
Reissue Producer:
Of note: (1) The UPC code on the back cover is: 011671000220.

THE GUITAR OF JOHN FAHEY

#1
Release date: 1983
Edition: 1st issue
Record company: Stefan Grossman Guitar Workshop
Catalog number:
Format: cassette tape (x6)
Cover: photograph of Fahey

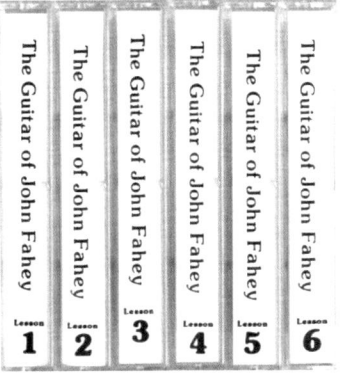

Songs: version #1 (3+4+2+4+2+5)
A1 – In Christ There Is No East Or West
A2 – Take A Look At That Baby
A3 – Some Summer Day
  B1 – On The Sunny Side Of The Ocean
  B2 – Spanish Two Step
  B3 – It Came Upon A Midnight Clear
  B4 – St. Louis Blues
    C1 – Indian Pacific Railroad Blues (Beverley)
    C2 – The Last Steam Engine Train
      D1 – The Union Pacific (The Revolt Of The Dyke Brigade)
      D2 – Requiem For John Hurt
      D3 – Auld Lang Syne
      D4 – Joy To The World / Bells of St. Mary
        E1 – When The Springtime Comes Again
        E2 – The Approaching Of The Disco Void
          F1 – Steamboat Gwine 'Round The Bend
          F2 – Silent Night
          F3 – Poor Boy A Long Way From Home
          F4 – Imitation Train Whistles
          F5 – Steel Guitar Rag
Recording Dates: 1982 in Rome, Italy
Of note: (1) This tape set was in print for many years; the issue pictured here is from 1994. (2) A companion tablature book was also released in 1985.

#2

Release date: 1995
Edition: 2nd issue
Record company: Mel Bay
Catalog number: MB95399CD
Format: CD
Cover: painting of Fahey   **Disc label**: silver

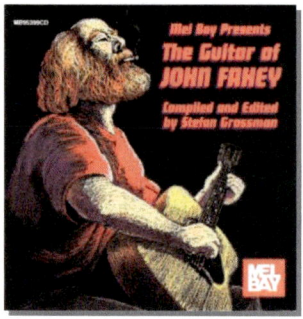

Songs: version #2 (17)
1	– In Christ There Is No East Or West	1:55
2	– Take A Look At That Baby	0:51
3	– Some Summer Day	2:49
4	– On The Sunny Side Of The Ocean	3:39
5	– Spanish Two Step	1:00
6	– It Came Upon The Midnight Clear	2:02
7	– St. Louis Blues	3:16
8	– Indian Pacific Railroad	5:23
9	– The Last Steam Engine Train	2:20
10	– The Union Pacific	2:45
11	– Requiem For John Hurt	3:41
12	– Auld Lang Syne	1:07
13	– When The Springtime Comes	4:59
14	– The Approaching Of The Disco Void	3:30
15	– Steamboat Gwine Round The Bend	3:32
16	– Silent Night	3:16
17	– Poor Boy Long Way From Home	1:41

Recording Dates: 1982 in Rome, Italy
Of note: (1) This CD issue includes excerpts from the 1983 taped guitar lessons by Fahey, and includes only the sections where he performs the tunes he teaches. (2) A companion tablature book (#MB95399) was also released. It contains an introduction by Stefan Grossman and a reprint of an article by Mark Humphrey. (3) The ISBN code on the back cover is: 0786605162.

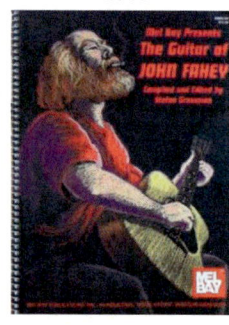

#3

Release date: 2002
Edition: 3rd issue (first part)
Record company: Mel Bay / Stefan Grossman's Guitar Workshop
Catalog number: MB 99801 BCD
Format: book and CD (x3)
Cover: photograph of Fahey on slide guitar   **Disc label**: black

Songs: version #2 (4+4+5)
A1 – On The Sunny Side Of The Ocean	3:39
A2 – Spanish Two Step	1:00
A3 – It Came Upon A Midnight Clear	2:02
A4 – St. Louis Blues	3:16
B1– The Union Pacific	2:45
B2 – Requiem For John Hurt	3:41
B3 – Auld Lang Syne	1:07
B4 – Joy To The World / Bells of St. Mary	2:03
C1 – Steamboat Gwine 'Round The Bend	3:32
C2 – Silent Night, Holy Night	3:16
C3 – Poor Boy A Long Way From Home	1:41
C4 – Imitation Train Whistles	1:29
C5 – Steel Guitar Rag	0:54

Recording Dates: 1982 in Rome, Italy
Of note: (1) This CD set includes the lessons and performances of the songs played in open tuning that were included in the six taped lessons by Fahey from 1983. (2) It comes with a companion tablature book that contains an interview with John Fahey by Stefan Grossman and an article by Mark Humphrey.

#4

Release date: 2002
Edition: 3rd issue (second part)
Record company: Mel Bay / Stefan Grossman's Guitar Workshop
Catalog number: MB 99802 BCD
Format: book and CD (x3)
Cover: photograph of Fahey with acoustic guitars   **Disc label**: tri-color

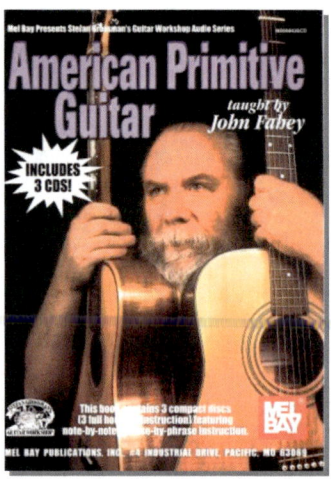

Songs: version #3 (3+2+2)
A1 – In Christ There Is No East Or West	1:55
A2 – Take A Look At That Baby	0:51
A3 – Some Summer Day	2:49
B1 – Indian Pacific Railroad Blues	5:23
B2 – The Last Steam Engine Train	2:20
C1 – When The Springtime Comes Again	4:59
C2 – The Approaching Of The Disco Void	3:30

Recording Dates: 1982 in Rome, Italy
Of note: (1) This CD set includes the remaining songs and lessons (not in open tuning) included in the 6 taped lessons by Fahey from 1983.
(2) It comes with a companion tablature book that contains the article "Blood On The Frets" by Edwin Pouncey.

RAILROAD I

#1

Release date: 1983
Edition: 1st issue (label #1, jacket #1, songs #1)
Catalog number: TAK-7102
Format: 12" LP, 33⅓ rpm, stereo
Jacket cover: 1st
  - **Front cover**: Fahey on railroad tracks
  - **Spine**: TAK 7102   JOHN FAHEY•RAILROAD I   TAKOMA RECORDS
  - **Back cover**: dragon logo.
Cover credit: Melody Fahey
Label: Do²

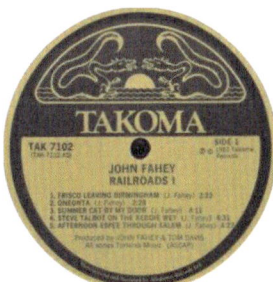  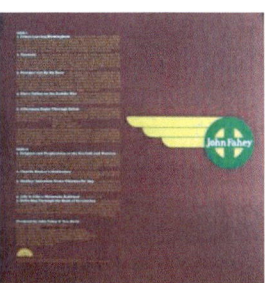

Matrix #: TAK-7102-1   G1   PRC-C 1-1-1   gene   MASTERED BY CAPITOL
             TAK-7102-2   G1   PRC-C 1-1-1   gene   MASTERED BY CAPITOL
Songs: version 1-a (5+5)
A1 – Frisco Leaving Birmingham   3:23
A2 – Oneonta   2:28
A3 – Summer Cat By My Door   4:11
A4 – Steve Talbot on the Keddie Wye   4:31
A5 – Afternoon Espee Through Salem   4:27
   B1 – Enigmas and Perplexities of the Norfolk and Western   3:10
   B2 – Charlie Becker's Meditation   3:20
   B3 – Medley: Imitation Train Whistles / Po' Boy   4:53
   B4 – Life Is Like a Mountain Railroad   2:13
   B5 – Delta Dog Through the Book of Revelation   4:50
Recording Dates: at Dirk Dalton Studios, Los Angeles, California
Liner notes: by John Fahey
Producer: John Fahey and Tom Davis
Of note: (1) This matrix # contains the following components:
  • TAK-7102-1 = record company prefix code, catalogue number, and side;
  • G1 = Neumann lathe used by Capitol Mastering in Hollywood, California;
  • PRC-C = Philips Recording Company pressing plant in Compton, California;
  • gene = name of the mastering engineer.

#2

Release date: 1984   (England)
Edition: 2nd issue (label #2, jacket #2, songs #2)
Catalog number: TKMLP 6005
Format: 12" LP, 33⅓ rpm, stereo
Jacket cover: 2nd
  - **Front cover**: Fahey on railroad tracks
  - **Spine**: TKMLP 6005   JOHN FAHEY•RAILROAD I
  - **Back cover**: Takoma dragon logo; bar code; TKMLP 6005
        Marketed & Distributed by Precision Records & Tapes, Ltd.
Cover credit: Melody Fahey
Label: Do^{UK}

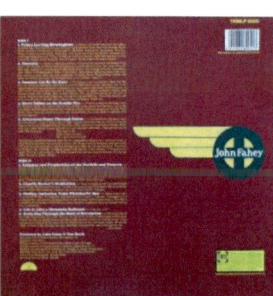

Matrix #: TKMLP 6005 A1   PAG   A
            TKMLP-6005 B1   PAG   B
Songs: version 1-b (5+5)
A1 – Frisco Leaving Birmingham   3:23
A2 – Oneonta   2:28
A3 – Summer Cat By My Door   4:11
A4 – Steve Talbot on the Keddie   4:31
A5 – Afternoon Espee Through Salem   4:27
  B1 – Enigmas and Perplexities of the Norfolk and Western 3:10
  B2 – Charlie Backer's Meditation   3:20
  B3 – Medley: Imitation Train Whistle / Po' Boy   4:53
  B4 – Life Is Like a Mountain Railroad   2:13
  B5 – Delta Dog Through the Book of Revelation   4:50
Recording Dates: at Dirk Dalton Studios, Los Angeles, California
Liner notes: by John Fahey
Producer: John Fahey and Tom Davis
Of note: (1) On the label, the title of track A4 is incomplete and that of B2 is misspelled. (2) The picture on the front cover shows John Fahey holding his Kona Hawaiian lap steel guitar.

#3

Release date: 1987
Edition: 3rd issue (label #3, jacket #3, songs #3)
Catalog number: ST-72802
Format: 12" LP, 33⅓ rpm, stereo
Jacket cover: 3rd
 - **Front cover**: Fahey on railroad tracks
 - **Spine**: TAK 7102   JOHN FAHEY•RAILROAD I   TAKOMA RECORDS
 - **Back cover**: dragon logo; ST-72802 sticker.
Cover credit: Melody Fahey
Label: Do³

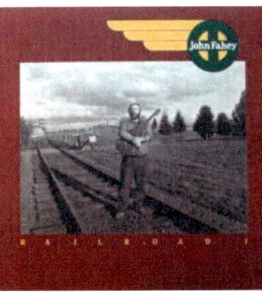

Matrix #: ST-1-72802 – G2   QB-28863-G2   Δ17954 1-1
ST-2-72802   G-1   QB-28864-G1   Δ17954-X 1-1   MASTERED BY CAPITOL
Songs: version 1-c (5+5)
A1 – Frisco Leaving Birmingham	3:23
A2 – Oneonta	2:28
A3 – Summer Cat By My Door	4:11
A4 – Steve Talbot on the Keddie Wye	4:31
A5 – Afternoon Espee Through Salem	4:27
B1 – Enigmas and Perplexities of the Norfolk and Western	3:10
B2 – Charlie Becker's Meditation	3:20
B3 – Medley: Imitation Train Whistles / Po' Boy	4:53
B4 – Life Is Like a Mountain Railroad	2:13
B5 – Delta Dog Through the Book of Revelation	4:50

Recording Dates: at Dirk Dalton Studios, Los Angeles, California.
Liner notes: by John Fahey
Producer: John Fahey and Tom Davis

Tape re-issue

#1

Release date: 1983
Catalog number: Takoma CTA 7102
Format: cassette tape
Cover: Fahey on railroad tracks
Original Cover credit: Melody Fahey
Songs: version #1 (5+5)
Recording Dates: same as LP #1
Liner notes: by John Fahey
Of note: (1) No UPC code on the cover.

#2

Release date: 1984   (England)
Catalog number: Takoma ZCTKM 6005
Format: cassette tape
Cover:
Original Cover credit:
Songs:
Recording Dates:
Liner notes:
Of note:

#3

Release date: 1987
Catalog number: Takoma 4XT-72802
Format: cassette tape
Cover: Fahey on railroad tracks
Original Cover credit: Melody Fahey
Songs: version #1 (5+5)
Recording Dates: same as LP #1
Liner notes: by John Fahey

Of note: (1) This later edition is identical to cassette #1, but has a sticker on the back with the catalog # 4XT-72802. The UPC code on the sticker is: 022397280247.

#4

Release date: 1992
Catalog number: Shanachie SH-99003
Format: cassette tape
Cover: Fahey on railroad tracks
Original Cover credit: Melody Fahey
Songs: version #1 (5+5)
Recording Dates: same as LP #1
Liner notes: by John Fahey
Of note: (1) The UPC code on the back cover is: 016351990341.

CD re-issue

#1

Release date: 1992
Catalog number: Shanachie 99003
Format: CD
Cover: Fahey on railroad tracks   **Disc label**: silver

Original Cover credit: Melody Fahey
Songs: version #1 (10)

1 – Frisco Leaving Birmingham	3:23
2 – Oneonta	2:28
3 – Summer Cat By My Door	4:11
4 – Steve Talbot on the Keddie Wye	4:31
5 – Afternoon Espee Through Salem	4:27
6 – Enigmas and Perplexities of the Norfolk and Western	3:10
7 – Charlie Becker's Meditation	3:20
8 – Medley: Imitation Train Whistles / Po' Boy	4:53
9 – Life Is Like a Mountain Railroad	2:13
10 – Delta Dog Through the Book of Revelation	4:50

Recording Dates: same as LP #1

Liner notes: by John Fahey
Remastering: Robert Vosgien
Reissue Producer:
Of note: (1) The UPC code on the back cover is: 016351990327.

#2

Release date: 2007 (UK)
Record company: Takoma / ACE
Catalog number: CDTAK 7102
Format: CD
Cover: Fahey on railroad tracks   **Disc label**: yellow/black

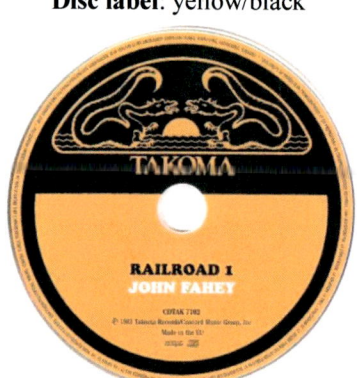

Original Cover credit: Melody Fahey
Songs: version #1 (10)
1 – Frisco Leaving Birmingham	3:25
2 – Oneonta	2:29
3 – Summer Cat By My Door	4:15
4 – Steve Talbot on the Keddie Wye	4:32
5 – Afternoon Espee Through Salem	4:27
6 – Enigmas and Perplexities of the Norfolk and Western	3:10
7 – Charlie Becker's Meditation	3:22
8 – Medley: Imitation Train Whistles / Po' Boy	4:54
9 – Life Is Like a Mountain Railroad	2:14
10 – Delta Dog Through the Book of Revelation	4:54

Recording Dates: same as LP #1
Liner notes: by John Fahey and Kris Needs
Remastering: Rob Shread at Sound Mastering Ltd.
Reissue Producer:
Of note: (1) The UPC code on the back cover is: 029667029223.

TRAIN & RAILROAD REFERENCES

Almost every song on this album makes a reference to a train or railroad, reflecting a passion that possessed John Fahey throughout his life.

Frisco Leaving Birmingham = The *Frisco* is the Saint Louis-San Francisco Railway Company (SLSF). It was established in 1876 and had two main lines: St. Louis–Tulsa–Oklahoma City and Kansas City–Memphis–Birmingham. The junction of the two lines was in Springfield, Missouri. It was originally intended to reach the West Coast, but this never materialized. In 1980 it merged with the Burlington Northern Railroad. The title comes from the song "Frisco Leaving Birmingham" by the harmonica player by George "Bullet" Williams recorded in Chicago in May 1928 (Paramount 12651).

Oneonta = A city in New York State. Oneonta became a major railroad center when the Delaware and Hudson Railroad reached it in 1885. The D & H roundhouse was once the largest in the world.

Summer Cat By My Door = This title refers to the Chessie, a company that owned the Chesapeake and Ohio Railway (C&O), the Baltimore and Ohio Railroad (B&O), the Western Maryland Railway (WM). Its logo was an emblem with the outline of a kitten, and was placed on the front and flanks of its locomotives. In 1980, the Chessie System merged with Seaboard Coast Line Industries to form CSX Corporation.

Steve Talbot on the Keddie Wye = The Keddie Wye is where the Western Pacific Railroad makes a wye at Keddie, California. A *wye* is a triangular junction (i.e., a triangular-shaped arrangement of rail tracks). In 1931, the Keddie Wye along the Feather River Canyon was created to join the Western Pacific Railroad to the Oakland-Salt Lake City mainline of the Great Northern Railway in northern California. Two sides of the Keddie Wye are on trestles above a river, and the third is a tunnel bored through a mountain. The Western Pacific is now part of the Union Pacific Railroad. Steve Talbot was the train operator.

The *Keddie Wye* with two of its legs suspended on trestles over Spanish Creek. The mountain in the background contains the third leg in a tunnel.

Afternoon Espee Through Salem = The Espee or SP is the Southern Pacific Railroad which runs through Salem, Oregon, where Fahey had been living since 1981. The Union Pacific Railroad absorbed the Southern Pacific in 1996. In the album notes, Fahey makes reference to the lyrics of "The Panama Limited" by Bukka White (recorded 26 May 1930, Vocalion 23295).

Enigmas and Perplexities of the Norfolk and Western = Norfolk and Western Railway (N&W) was formed by more than 200 railroad mergers between 1838 and 1982, and had headquarters in Roanoke, Virginia.

Charlie Becker's Meditation = a conductor for the Mount Hood Railway. This is a 21-mile long excursion passenger and freight railroad located in Hood River, east of Portland, Oregon.

Medley: Imitation Train Whistles / Po' Boy = no reference to any specific railway here.

Life Is Like a Mountain Railroad = This is the title of a hymn originally called "Life's Railway to Heaven" and written in 1891 by M. E. Abbey and Charlie D. Tillman. It is sometimes titled as "Life Is Like a Mountain Railroad" which corresponds to the first verse of the hymn.

"Life Is Like A Mountain Railroad" (Victor 23350, recorded on October 25, 1929) by the Pace Jubilee Singers. This is the earliest recorded version with this title.

Delta Dog Through the Book of Revelation = The Delta Dog refers to the *Yellow Dog*, a nickname from the initials Y.D. on the freight cars of the Yazoo-Delta Railroad. This is the area where Charley Patton lived, and the *Book of Revelation* was Patton's favorite book of the Bible.

POPULAR SONGS OF CHRISTMAS & NEW YEAR'S

#1

Release date: 1983
Edition: 1st issue (label #1, jacket #1, songs #1)
Catalog number: Varrick VR-012
Format: 12" LP, 33⅓ rpm, stereo
Jacket cover: 1st
  - **Front cover**: red
  - **Spine**: VR-012   JOHN FAHEY   "POPULAR SONGS OF CHRISTMAS AND NEW YEAR'S"   VARRICK RECORDS VR-012
  - **Back cover**: red.
Cover credit: Susan Marsh
Label: green

 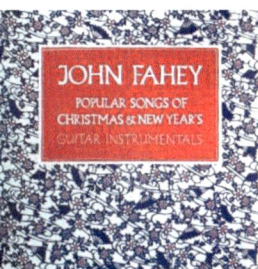 

Matrix #: VR-012-A   MASTERDISK BK   42020-A   #6 (or #9)
            VR-012-B   MASTERDISK BK   42020-B   #2 (or #8)
Songs: version 1-a (8+7)

A1 – Jolly Old Saint Nicholas	1:45
A2 – Santa Claus Is Coming To Town	2:53
A3 – The Skater's Waltz	3:52
A4 – The Christmas Song	2:18
A5 – Medley: Christmas Time's A-Coming / Rudolph The Red-Nosed Reindeer	4:02
A6 – Medley: The Holly And The Ivy / The Cherry Tree Carol	2:00
A7 – Apple Blossom Time	1:30
A8 – White Christmas	1:34
B1 – Medley: Let It Snow, Let It Snow, Let It Snow / Winter Wonderland	3:43
B2 – Remember	2:00
B3 – Christmas Time Is Here	1:15
B4 – Do You Hear What I Hear	2:23

B5 – I'll Be Home For Christmas 1:53
B6 – The Waltz You Saved For Me 3:16
B7 – Medley: Deck The Halls With Boughs Of Holly / We Wish
    You A Merry Christmas 3:40
Recording Dates: High Tech Recorders, Portland, OR, 1983
Liner notes: (only song list and recording details)
Producer: Terry Robb
Of note: (1) Terry Robb accompanies John Fahey on the following tracks: A2, A3, A4, A5, A8, B1, B3, B4, B5 and B7.

#2

Release date: 1984
Edition: 2nd issue (label #2, jacket #1, songs #1)
Catalog number: Varrick VR-012
Format: 12" LP, 33⅓ rpm, stereo
Jacket cover: 1st
  - **Front cover**: red
  - **Spine**: VR-012   JOHN FAHEY   "POPULAR SONGS OF
      CHRISTMAS AND NEW YEAR'S"   VARRICK RECORDS   VR-012
  - **Back cover**: red.
Cover credit: Susan Marsh
Label: blue

Matrix #: VR-012-A   MASTERDISK   BK   42020-A   MO#2   #10
              VR-012-B   MASTERDISK   BK   42020-B   MO#3   #10
Songs: version 1-a (8+7)
Recording Dates: High Tech Recorders, Portland, OR, 1983
Liner notes: (only song list and recording details)
Producer: Terry Robb

Tape re-issue

#1

Release date: 1983
Catalog number: C-VR-012
Format: cassette tape
Cover: print design & black background
Original Cover credit: Susan Marsh
Songs: version #1 (8+7)
Recording Dates: same as LP #1
Liner notes: none

#2

Release date: 1990
Catalog number: C-VR-012
Format: cassette tape
Cover: print design & white background
Original Cover credit: Susan Marsh
Songs: version #1 (8+7)
Recording Dates: same as LP #1
Liner notes: (only song list and recording details)
Of note: (1) The UPC code on the back cover is: 011671001241.

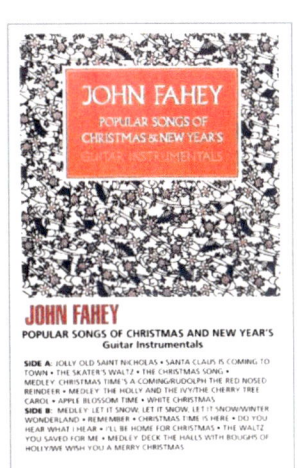

CD re-issue

#1

Release date: 1994
Catalog number: Varrick CD VR 012
Format: CD
Cover: Winter landscape   **Disc label**: white

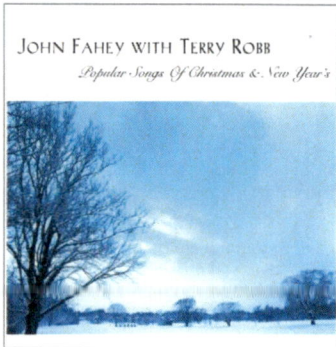 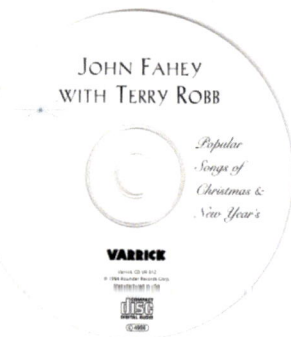

Cover credit: Jean Hangarter
Songs: version #1 (15)
Recording Dates: same as LP #1
Liner notes: (only song list and recording details)
Remastering:
Reissue Producer:
Of note: (1) The UPC code on the back cover is: 011671001227.

LET GO

#1
Release date: 1984
Edition: 1st issue (label #1, jacket #1, songs #1)
Catalog number: Varrick VR-008
Format: 12" LP, 33⅓ rpm, stereo
Jacket cover: 1st
  - **Front cover**: green
  - **Spine**: 008   JOHN FAHEY   LET GO   VARRICK RECORDS 008
  - **Back cover**: blue
Cover credit: Melody Fahey
Label: blue

Matrix #: VR-008-A   MASTERDISK BK   43134-A   #3
           VR-008-B   MASTERDISK BK   43134-B   #3   MO#2
Songs: version 1 (4+6)

A1 – Let Go	6:34
A2 – Lost Lake	- - - -
A3 – Black Mommy	8:04
A4 – Dvorak	4:04
A5 – The World Is Waiting For The Sunrise	2:30
B1 – River Medley	4:53
B2 – Lights Out	2:44
B3 – Pretty Afternoon	3:05
B4 – Sunset On Prince George's County	4:13
B5 – Layla	5:15
B6 – Old Country Rock	1:20

Recording Dates: High Tech Recorders, Portland, OR, February-March, 1983
Liner notes: yes   **Producer**: Terry Robb
Of note: (1) Even though mentioned in the back cover notes, track A2 is neither listed on the label nor present on the disc -- see page 194. (2) Track B1 is listed on the label as "Medley: Deep River / Old Man River." (3) Terry Robb accompanies Fahey on tracks A1, A4, B1, B2, B3, B5 and B6. (4) This LP has an issue number that is lower than the previous Fahey album on Varrick because Fahey was reluctant to release it too soon after the previous 1983 Takoma issue, *Railroad I*, and thus delayed it.

"BOLA SETE DRIVES ME INSANE."

John Fahey uttered this phrase when speaking of Bola Sete (1923-1987), a jazz guitarist born in Rio de Janeiro, whose real name was Djalma de Andrade. The term "bola sete" in Portuguese means "7-ball," the black-colored ball worth seven points in Brazilian snooker (sinuca brasileira). Bola got his name when he played in a small jazz combo in which he was the only black member. After touring Europe and South America, he moved to the U.S. in 1959, eventually settling in Sausalito, California.

In the early 1970s, Bola Sete saw Fahey perform, and thereafter decided to play solo instead of in a group. In 1972, John Fahey saw Sete performing solo in the Boarding House club in San Francisco (February 28-March 5, 1972); Stefan Grossman was on the same bill those nights. Fahey was greatly impressed and asked Sete if he would be interested in recording for Takoma. Sete instead offered Fahey tapes that he had recorded on March 9 and 10, 1972, for Fantasy Records, just a week after his Boarding House concerts. The music was a mixture of Brazilian folk music, classical guitar, and jazz standards. Considering Sete's daring move of recording solo, Fantasy had not known what to make of it and so Bola Sete ended up buying the session tapes back from the label. Fahey released a selection of them on Bola's 1975 album *Ocean* (Takoma C-1049).

> ●Bola Sete, Stefan Grossman. The Boarding House 960 Bush SF 441-4333 dinner fr 6, show 9:30 $2

Ad in the **Berkeley Barb** for a Bola Sete show on March 3, 1972

If Charlie Patton was the inspiration for many of Fahey's early pieces, Bola Sete was a strong influence in his middle period. After hearing Bola Sete during his week-long engagement at the Boarding House, Fahey's life and work took a turn that lasted more than a decade.

Sete also introduced Fahey to the benefits of meditation which Sete practiced. Fahey was also introduced to yoga and spirituality by Takoma manager Charlie Mitchell. He soon joined Yogaville West and during the next year was participating in several benefit concerts sponsored by the Integral Yoga Institute (one of which led to his meeting his future second wife). By the following year, all this began to transpire in his new works starting with *After The Ball* ("Om Shanthi Norris"), then *Fare Forward Voyagers*, and *Old Fashioned Love* ("Jaya Shiva Shankara").

Thereafter, the music of Bola Sete began to sink in and would inspire several new guitar pieces by Fahey. "It's nice to find someone I want to learn to play" said Fahey in 1983. The first was Fahey's rendition of Bola Sete's "Guitar

Lamento" on *Visits Washington, DC*, a tune from Sete's *Ocean*. Then, in the mid 1980s, Fahey dug deeper into Bola's repertoire and recorded "Let Go" and "Black Mommy" (both from the *Ocean* album) as well as "Pretty Afternoon" (originally issued on Bola Sete's *Goin' To Rio* album from 1973 [Columbia KC 32375]). These were issued on Fahey's *Let Go*. Then, on *Rain Forests* he played "Ocean Waves" (from the *Ocean* album again), and on *I Remember Blind Joe Death* he played "Gaucho" (originally titled "The Lonely Gaucho in the Pampas Awaiting the Advent of Christmas," also on Sete's *Ocean* LP) and "Unknown Tango" (originally titled "Jongada," an outtake of Sete, later issued on *Ocean Memories* on CD in 1999).

Tape re-issue

#1

Release date: 1984
Catalog number: VR-008
Format: cassette tape
Cover: green
Original Cover credit: Melody Fahey
Songs: version #1 (4+6)
A1 – Let Go
A2 – Black Mommy
A3 – Dvorak
A4 – The World Is Waiting For The Sunrise
    B1 – River Medley
    B2 – Lights Out
    B3 – Pretty Afternoon
    B4 – Sunset On Prince George's County
    B5 – Layla
    B6 – Old Country Rock
Recording Dates: same as LP #1
Liner notes: none
Of note: (1) There is no mention of the track "Lost Lake."

It is in this album's liner notes that John Fahey penned one of his most memorable and telling phrases:

> "I mean, I got an M.A. in Folklore from UCLA. I know what volkmuisic is. I'm not a volk; I'm from the suburbs."

This was his response to those who continuously pigeonholed him as a folk musician and, consequently, his albums were regularly placed in the "FOLK" bins in record stores.

The Case of the Missing "Lost Lake" Track

In a typed manuscript to his record label, Fahey had included the notes to the album's songs. The notes for the first track "Let Go" analyze the structure of the piece in greater depth than would appear in the final version.

Notes to the Song "Let Go" (Unabridged Version)

LET GO: This is a literal translation of Baden Powell's composition "Canto de Ossanha." In Portuguese this expression has the following connotations: "Let it go. There's nothing you can do so why continue fighting it. The battle is already over, only you don't know it and YOU LOSE. Forget it. Give in. Relax. Resignation."

The 4 descending notes played relentlessly throughout the entire piece (except for the bridge) suggest the <u>Dies Irae</u>, and thus death. The melodic and harmonic structure follows these bass notes very closely like a flea or some other parasite on the back of a dog --- although this is not immediately apparent to the listener. The Improvisation (by Terry Robb) is developed from a careful analysis of all known recordings of this song by the composer. The conclusion however suggests the Bola Sete version (on Takoma C-1049, OP, reissued minus one song on Lost Lake.

The major key bridge suggests a backward look at a pleasant time in life during which the petty pace, the clock-like descending notes, the latin fatalism perhaps abated for a short period. But the piece ends the same way it began, expressing the inexorable goose steps of time and mixed metaphors.

Bola Sete's *Ocean* album was indeed re-issued in 1981 on the Lost Lake Arts label (LL-0082). Interestingly, it appears that the words "Lost Lake" at the end of the second paragraph were misconstrued as the heading for the next paragraph, and thus were transcribed as if they were the title of the subsequent Fahey track. And the following paragraph, despite belonging to the "Let Go" track, became the descriptive notes for the non-existent "Lost Lake."

CD re-issue

#1

Release date: 1997
Catalog number: Varrick CD VR 008
Format: CD
Cover: green   **Disc label**: blue

Cover credit: Melody Fahey
Songs: version #1 (10)

1 – Let Go	6:34
2 – Black Mommy	8:04
3 – Dvorak	4:04
4 – The World Is Waiting For The Sunrise	2:30
5 – River Medley	4:53
6 – Lights Out	2:44
7 – Pretty Afternoon	3:05
8 – Sunset On Prince George's County	4:13
9 – Layla	5:15
10 – Old Country Rock	1:20

Recording Dates: same as LP #1
Liner notes: yes
Remastering: David Glasser
Reissue Producer:
Of note: (1) Even though the CD and booklet title list do not include it, the song "Lost Lake" is still mentioned in the notes. (2) The UPC code on the back cover is: 011671000824.

ALBUM COVER OF *LET GO*

When planning the album, Fahey toyed with several ideas for the album's cover. In an earlier concept, the title *Let Go* was intended as a response to "Windhamhillism." Inspired by the graphics of ECM Records, Windham Hill Records used minimalist cover artwork, nothing too striking, which fit in with the conservative times. Fahey's intent was to use a painting that suggested serenity, while the title would be written in a strident manner, thus creating a visual tension between the painting and the title.

The paintings that Fahey initially considered are shown below. They were painted by two masters of the American Luminist School, Fitz Hugh Lane and John F. Kensett.

"Marine off Big Rock" by John F. Kensett (1864).

"Brace's Rock, Brace's Cove" Fitz Hugh Lane (1864).

Ultimately, the cover employed photographs of John Fahey shot by his wife Melody. The front cover shows a brooding and stern-faced Fahey behind a fence, as if he were a wild animal imprisoned, while the surrounding artwork displays drifting pastel-colored party confetti -- the contrast that Fahey had alluded to.

The back cover shows him more laid-back, even smiling, possibly implying the final outcome of "letting go."

FONOTONE 6809

Release date: 1985
Artist name: John Fahey
Catalog number: 6809
Format: cassette tape

GUITAR SOLO'S by JOHN FAHEY
Fonotone 6809   Frederick, Md.
John Fahey recorded for Fonotone Records from 1950's To 1962 These Are some of His Early Guitar Work's. Titles Have Been Lost To Many Of These Sole's.

Songs: (15+11)

A1 – Brenda's Blues	1:49
A2 – St. Patrick's Hymn	1:52
A3 – Bicycle Built For Two	1:24
A4 – The Blues You Saved For Me	1:35
A5 – House Carpenter	1:30
A6 – How Long	2:25
A7 – The Portland Cement Factory at Monolith, California	4:32
A8 – You Take the E Train	2:33
A9 – I Sing a Song of the Saints of God	3:14
A10 – Goodbye Old Paint #1 / Whoopi Ti-Yi-Yo	1:26
A11 – Goodbye Old Paint #2	1:01
A12 – Simple Gifts	0:53
A13 – Untitled #3	1:38
A15 – Bottleneck Blues (*aka* Rainy Days Down Metzerott Road)	2:59
B1 – Western Medley	6:01
B2 – Bury Me Not On The Lone Prairie	1:42
B3 – Goodbye Old Paint #3	1:16
B4 – Durgan Park	2:07
B5 – The Bitter Lemon	2:46
B6 – O Jesus I Have Promised	3:07
B7 – Untitled #1	1:09
B8 – Untitled #2 / O Jesus I Have Promised	3:24
B9 – I Am a Rake and Rambling Boy	1:46
B10 – Train	2:34
B11 – Texas & Pacific Blues	2:12

FONOTONE 6810

Release date: 1985
Artist name: John Fahey
Catalog number: 6810
Format: cassette tape
Songs: 9+9

EARLY RECORDINGS of JOHN FAHEY
Fonotone 6810   Frederick, Md.
John Fahey First Recordings Were Made At Frederick, Md. From 1959 To 1962. The Last Fonotone Records Were Issued In 1970 Now After More Than 20 Years, These Recordings Can Be Hear Again.

Side A   Issued as BLIND THOMAS
1. BLIND BLUES   Nov. 15, 1959
2. POOR BOY BLUES   "
3. LONG TOWN TOWN BLUES   "
4. GULF PORT INLAND BLUES   "
5. BLIND THOMAS BLUES - PART 1   "
6. BLIND THOMAS BLUES - PART 2   "
7. WANDA RUSSELL'S BLUES   April 15, 1960
8. GOING AWAY TO LEAVE YOU BLUES "
9. LAY MY BURDEN DOWN   "

Side B
1. HILL HIGH BLUES   "
2. JOHN HENRY   "
3. PAINT BRUSH BLUES   "
4. BLIND THOMAS BLUES - PART 3 Oct. 11, 1960
5. BLIND THOMAS BLUES - PART 4   "
6. YOU GONNA NEED SOMEONE ON YOUR BOND "
7. JESUS GONNA MAKE UP MY DYIN' BED "
8. BANTY ROOSTER BLUES   "
9. TOM RUSHIN BLUES   "

Note: (1) For additional information, see *Your Past Comes Back To Haunt You* (DTD-21).

FONOTONE 6811

Release date: 1985
Artist name: John Fahey
Catalog number: 6811
Format: cassette tape
Songs: 9+9

```
EARLY Recordings Of JOHN FAHEY No. 2
Fonotone 6811   Frederick, Md.
Early Recordings of John Fahey Recorded
for Fonotone Records - 1960 1961
Side A
1.  YOU GONNA MISS ME          Oct. 11, 1960
2.  WISSEN SCHAETLICH RIVER BLUES - PART 1
3.  WISSEN SCHAETLICH RIVER BLUES - PART 2
4.  TITLE UNKNOWN    - 1961
5.  WEISSMAN BLUES    -    March 24, 1961
6.  DASEIN RIVER BLUES          "
7.  ICKWEISSNKT RIVER BLUES     "
8.  DYING DEATH BLUES           "
9.  SMOKY ORDINARY BLUES        "
Side B
The last Recordings By Fahey Were Made
In June 15, 1962 with B. SAM FIRK
1.  BLACK SWAMPER'S BLUES - PART 1
2.  BLACK SWAMPER'S BLUES - PART 2
3.  GREEN BLUES
4.  STONE PONEY
5.  SOME SUMMER DAY No. 2
6.  DARK AND LONEY NIGHT BLUES
Recordings by B. SAM FIRK
7.  MONEY GREEN No. 2
8.  DELTA MOODISH BLUES
9.  OLD COUNTRY ROCK
```

Note: (1) Track A4 is a version of "Night Train to Valhalla." (2) Track A7 "Ickweissnkt River Blues" is actually "Racemic Tartrate River Blues, Part 1." (3) Track A8 "Dying Death Blues" is actually "Racemic Tartrate River Blues, Part 2." (4) For additional information, see *Your Past Comes Back To Haunt You* (DTD-21).

RAIN FORESTS, OCEANS, AND OTHER THEMES

#1
Release date: 1985
Edition: 1st issue (label #1, jacket #1, songs #1)
Catalog number: Varrick VR-019
Format: 12" LP, 33⅓ rpm, stereo
Jacket cover: 1st
  - **Front cover**: waves
  - **Spine**: VR-019   JOHN FAHEY   "RAIN FORESTS, OCEANS, AND OTHER THEMES"   VARRICK RECORDS 019
  - **Back cover**: leaves
Cover credit: Susan Marsh / DeeAnn Hall
Label: blue

 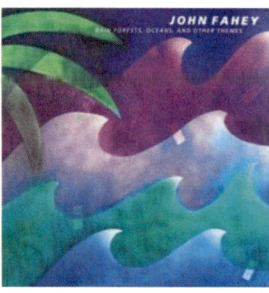 

Matrix #: VR-019-A   44536   #1
            VR-019-B   44536   #4
Songs: version #1 (5+5)

A1 – Melody McOcean	6:38
A2 – Rain Forest	6:44
A3 – Lullaby and Finale from the Firebird	4:16
A4 – Atlantic High	2:06
A5 – Samba de Orfeo	3:11
B1 – Themes and Variations	2:58
B2 – May This Be Love / Casey Jones	3:25
B3 – Intro to Ocean Waves / Ocean Waves	6:20
B4 – Juroscho Ascopi	5:28
B5 – St. Patrick's Hymn	2:37

Recording Studio Dates: Cascade Recording Studios, Portland, Oregon.
            in November-December, 1984 and February, 1985.
Liner notes: yes
Producer: Terry Robb
Note: (1) Terry Robb accompanies Fahey on guitar on tracks A3, A5, B1, B2 and B4. (2) Due to the continuing Brazilian theme, this album might be considered a sequel to *Let Go*. It is Fahey's first digitally recorded album.

Tape re-issue

#1
Release date: 1985
Catalog number: VR-019
Format: cassette tape
Cover: waves
Original Cover credit: Susan Marsh / DeeAnn Hall
Songs: version #1 (5+5)
Recording Dates: same as LP #1
Liner notes: none

CD re-issue

#1
Release date: 1986
Catalog number: Varrick CD 019
Format: CD
Cover: waves (purple sky)   **Disc label**: silver + blue

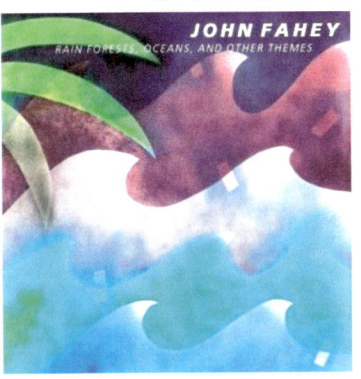 

Cover credit: Susan Marsh / DeeAnn Hall
Songs: version #2 (12)
1 – Melody McOcean   6:38
2 – Layla   5:15
3 – Rain Forest   6:44
4 – The World Is Waiting for the Sunrise   2:30
5 – Lullaby and Finale from the Firebird   4:16
6 – Atlantic High   2:06
7 – Samba de Orfeo   3:11

8 – Themes and Variations   2:58
9 – May This Be Love / Casey Jones   3:25
10 – Intro to Ocean Waves / Ocean Waves   6:20
11 – Juroscho Ascopi   5:28
12 – St. Patrick's Hymn   2:37
Recording Studio Dates: same as LP #1; except tracks A2 and A4 at High Tech
              Recorders, Portland, Oregon, in February-March, 1983
Liner notes: yes
Remastering:
Reissue Producer:
Note: (1) The two additional tracks A2 and A4 are taken from the album *Let Go* (Varrick 008). (2) Manufactured in Japan. (3) No UPC code on the back cover.

#2

Release date: 1988
Catalog number: Varrick VR-019
Format: CD
Cover: waves (blue sky)   **Disc label**: dark blue + silver

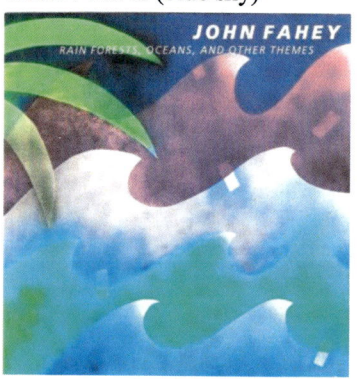

Cover credit: Susan Marsh / DeeAnn Hall
Songs: version #2 (12): same as CD #1
Recording Dates: same as LP #1; except tracks A2 and A4 at High Tech
              Recorders, Portland, Oregon, in February-March, 1983
Liner notes: yes
Remastering:
Reissue Producer:
Note: (1) The two additional tracks A2 and A4 are taken from the album *Let Go* (Varrick 008). (2) The tray notes have the issue number "Varrick CD 019." (3) The UPC code on the back cover is: 11671001920.

CHRISTMAS GUITAR

#1

Release date: 1986
Edition: 1st issue
Record company: Varrick / Rounder
Catalog number: CD VR 11503
Format: CD
Cover: green; similar to *Christmas Guitar, Volume 1* (see page 171)
Cover credit: Susan Marsh   **Disc label**: green + silver

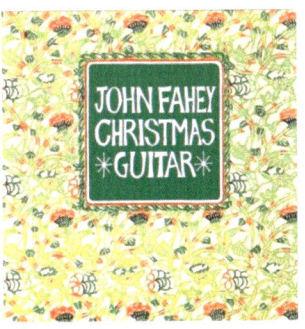 

Songs: version #1 (26)
1 – Joy to the World	1:34
2 – What Child Is This?	3:15
3 – Medley: Hark, the Herald Angels Sing / O Come All Ye Faithful	4:22
4 – Auld Lang Syne	2:00
5 – The Bells of St. Mary's	2:15
6 – Good Christian Men Rejoice	1:13
7 – We Three Kings Of Orient Are	1:45
8 – Away in the Manger #1	1:19
9 – God Rest Ye Merry Gentlemen Fantasy	2:52
10 – Jolly Old Saint Nicholas	1:45
11 – Santa Claus Is Coming To Town	2:53
12 – The Skater's Waltz	3:52
13 – The Christmas Song	2:18
14 – Medley: Christmas Time's A–Coming / Rudolph The Red-Nosed Reindeer	4:02
15 – Medley: The Holly And The Ivy / The Cherry Tree Carol	2:00
16 – Apple Blossom Time	1:30
17 – White Christmas	1:34
18 – The First Noel	3:48
19 – Good King Wenceslas	1:02
20 – Of the Father's Love Begotten	1:20
21 – Away in the Manger #2	2:27

22 – In the Bleak Midwinter 1:46
23 – It Came Upon a Midnight Clear 2:54
24 – Medley: Jesus Won't You Come By Here? / Go Tell It on the 3:22
   Mountain
25 – Lo How a Rose E'er Blooming 1:48
26 – Silent Night, Holy Night 3:10
Recording Dates: High Tech Recorders, Portland, Oregon, 1982-1983
Liner notes: none
Mastering:
Producer: John Fahey and Terry Robb
Note: (1) Terry Robb is on guitar on selections 11-14 and 17. (2) This CD compilation includes all of *Christmas Guitar, Volume 1*, and Side 1 of *Popular Songs of Christmas & New Year's*. (2) The UPC code on the back cover is: 011661150324.

#2

Release date: 1989 (Japan)
Edition: 2nd issue
Record company: Better Days
Catalog number: CA-4196
Format: CD
Cover: blue
Cover credit: Ken Done **Disc label**: silver

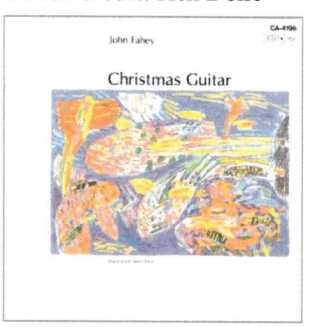

Songs: version #1 (26)
Recording Dates: High Tech Recorders, Portland, Oregon, 1982-1983
Booklet: yes (in Japanese)
Mastering:
Producer: John Fahey and Terry Robb
Note: (1) Terry Robb is on guitar on selections 11-14 and 17.
(2) The EAN-13 code on the back cover is: 4988001353737.

I REMEMBER BLIND JOE DEATH

#1

Release date: 1987
Edition: 1st issue (label #1, jacket #1, songs #1)
Catalog number: Varrick VR-028
Format: 12" LP, 33⅓ rpm, stereo
Jacket cover: 1st
 - **Front cover**: two skeletons
 - **Spine**: VR-028   JOHN FAHEY   "I REMEMBER BLIND JOE DEATH"
       VARRICK RECORDS 028
 - **Back cover**: Varrick – Rounder logo; bar code.
Cover credit: Susan Marsh
Label: blue

 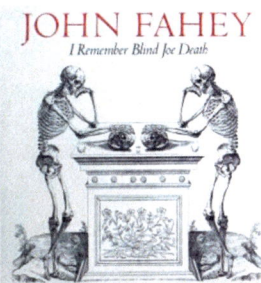 

Matrix #: Side 1:   VAR-028 - A̶ B   46044 – A̶ B   #1 F/w ¢
         Side 2:   VAR-028 - B̶ A   46044 – B̶ A   #1
         or VAR-028 - B A̶ B   46044 – B A̶ B   #2

Songs: version 1-a (6+6)
A1 – The Evening Mysteries of Ferry Street   3:25
A2 – You'll Find Her Name Written There   1:33
A3 – The Minutes Seem Like Hours, The Hours Seem Like Days 3:59
A4 – Are You From Dixie?   2:42
A5 – A Minor Blues   4:39
A6 – Steel Guitar Rag   2:22
  B1 – Nightmare / Summertime   5:22
  B2 – Let Me Call You Sweetheart   2:10
  B3 – Unknown Tango   3:50
  B4 – Improv In E Minor   7:27
  B5 – Lava On Waikiki   2:16
  B6 – Gaucho   5:56
Recording Dates: 1986 at Spectrum Studios, Portland, Oregon.
Liner notes: yes
Producer: Tinh Mahoney

The front cover image of this album is an illustration "adapted from Vesalius-Kalkar," as credited on the LP's back cover. Indeed, it corresponds to an adaptation of a woodcut image from the book *De Humani Corporis Fabrica, Libri Septem*, printed in 1543 by **Andreas Vesalius** (1514-1564). On page 164 of this book is the depiction of a skeleton studying a skull:

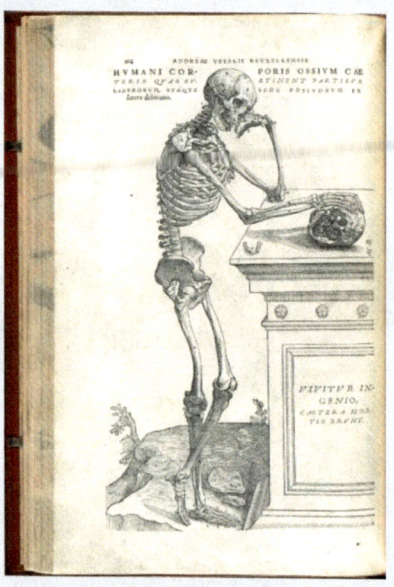

Vesalius was a Flemish anatomist at the University of Padua in Italy whose sketches were the basis for these anatomic illustrations. These are attributed to the Flemish artist **Jan Stefan van Kalkar** (1499-1545), a pupil of Titian in Venice. They were engraved on blocks of pear wood, and then transported to Basel in Switzerland where they were used by the printer Johannes Oporinus to publish the book in seven volumes. In this drawing, a skeleton ponders mortality while resting his bony hand on a skull in a *memento mori* style (i.e., "Remember that you will die"). The tomb carries the inscription *Vivitus ingenio, caetera mortis erunt* ("Genius lives on, all else is mortal").

#2

Release date: 1987 (Europe)
Edition: 2nd issue (label #2, jacket #2, songs #2)
Record Company: Demon Records / Rounder Europa
Catalog number: REU 1025
Format: 12" LP, 33⅓ rpm, stereo
Jacket cover: 2nd
  - **Front cover**: two skeletons
  - **Spine**: JOHN FAHEY   "I REMEMBER BLIND JOE DEATH"
    ROUNDER EUROPA   REU 1025
  - **Back cover**: Demon – Rounder Europa logo; bar code; REU 1025.
Cover credit: Susan Marsh
Label: red

 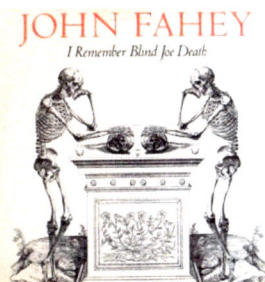 

Matrix #: REU 1025 A   A Resmi Prime Cut   CED
             REU 1025 B   A Resmi Prime Cut   CED
Songs: version 1-b (6+6)

A1 – The Evening Mysteries of Ferry Street	3:25
A2 – You'll Find Her Name Written There	1:33
A3 – The Minutes Seem Like Hours, The Hours Seem Like Days	3:59
A4 – Are You From Dixie?	2:42
A5 – A Minor Blues	4:39
A6 – Steel Guitar Rag	2:22
B1 – Nightmare / Summertime	5:22
B2 – Let Me Call You Sweetheart	2:10
B3 – Unknown Tango	3:50
B4 – Improv In E Minor	7:27
B5 – Lava On Waikiki	2:16
B6 – Gaucho	5:56

Recording Dates: 1986 at Spectrum Studios, Portland, Oregon.
Liner notes: yes
Producer: Tinh Mahoney

> Glenn Jones found the Vesalius illustration in an old book and showed it to Fahey at one of his Boston shows. Fahey had Jones give it to one of the label owners with instructions to use it as the album cover for *I Remember Blind Joe Death* which he had just completed.

Tape re-issue

#1
Release date: 1987
Catalog number: Varrick C-VR-028
Format: cassette tape
Cover: two skeletons
Original Cover credit: Susan Marsh
Songs: version #1 (6+6)
Recording Dates: same as LP #1
Liner notes: none
Of note: (1) The UPC code on the back cover is: 011671002842.

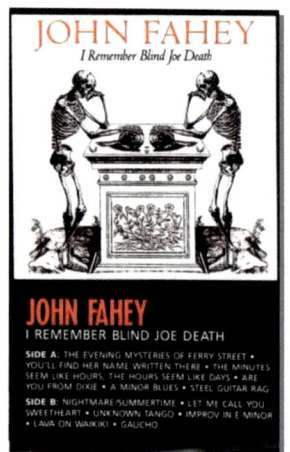

THE EVENING MYSTERIES OF FERRY STREET

In 1986 Fahey said, "This is a street in Salem, Oregon, where I live. I like to take my bicycle out at ten or ten-thirty at night, and it's very quiet and spooky. Sort of like the *Twilight Zone*, but with no plot."

(B.A. Nilsson, "Fahey 'Original' at Caffe Lena"; Schenectady Gazette, Nov 25, 1986).

LAVA ON WAIKIKI

Fahey lived in Hawaii for three months in 1962 where he had a job as a teaching assistant. He left before his contract expired and never felt good about it, so much so that he kept his visit to the island a guarded secret. "I didn't like Hawaii" he said in a 1987 interview. "I really couldn't stand it. I was going nuts." Fahey's composition "Lava on Waikiki" is his reflection on that period of his life.

(A. Greenblatt. "Guitarist 'steels' the show"; *The Cavalier Daily*, Mar 22, 1988).

CD re-issue

#1

Release date: 1987
Catalog number: Varrick CD VR-028
Format: CD
Cover: two skeletons   **Disc label**: red + silver

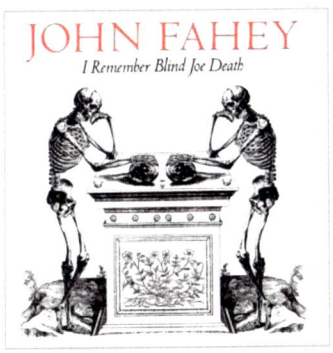

Cover credit: Susan Marsh
Songs: version #1 (12)

1 – The Evening Mysteries of Ferry Street	3:25
2 – You'll Find Her Name Written There	1:33
3 – The Minutes Seem Like Hours, The Hours Seem Like Days	3:59
4 – Are You From Dixie?	2:42
5 – A Minor Blues	4:39
6 – Steel Guitar Rag	2:22
7 – Nightmare / Summertime	5:22
8 – Let Me Call You Sweetheart	2:10
9 – Unknown Tango	3:50
10 – Improv In E Minor	7:27
11 – Lava On Waikiki	2:16
12 – Gaucho	5:56

Recording Dates: 1986 at Spectrum Studios, Portland, Oregon.
Liner notes: yes (reproduced)
Remastering:
Reissue Producer:
Of note: (1) The UPC code on the back cover is: 011671002828.

#2

Release date: 1987   (Europe)
Record company: Demon Records
Catalog number: Fiend CD 207
Format: CD
Cover: two skeletons; black border   **Disc label**: white

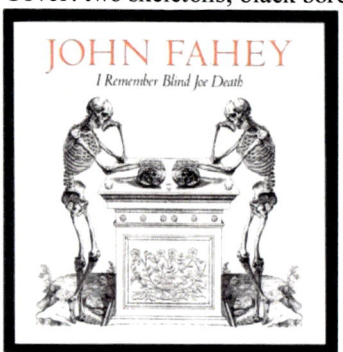
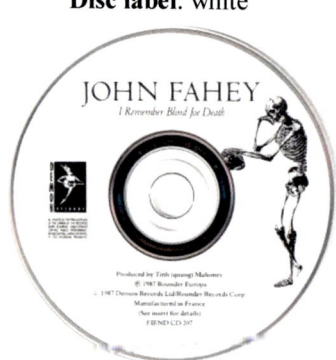

Cover credit: Susan Marsh
Songs: version #1 (12)

#	Title	Time
1	The Evening Mysteries of Ferry Street	3:25
2	You'll Find Her Name Written There	1:33
3	The Minutes Seem Like Hours, The Hours Seem Like Days	3:59
4	Are You From Dixie?	2:42
5	A Minor Blues	4:39
6	Steel Guitar Rag	2:22
7	Nightmare / Summertime	5:22
8	Let Me Call You Sweetheart	2:10
9	Unknown Tango	3:50
10	Improv In E Minor	7:27
11	Lava On Waikiki	2:16
12	Gaucho	5:56

Recording Dates: 1986 at Spectrum Studios, Portland, Oregon.
Liner notes: yes (reproduced)
Remastering:
Reissue Producer:
Of note: (1) The EAN-13 code on the back cover is: 5014757072079.

GOD, TIME AND CAUSALITY

#1

Release date: 1989
Edition: 1st issue (label #1, jacket #1, songs #1)
Catalog number: Shanachie 97006
Format: 12" LP, 33⅓ rpm, stereo
Jacket cover: 1st
  - **Front cover**: Fahey on guitar
  - **Spine**: JOHN FAHEY   GOD, TIME AND CAUSALITY   SHANACHIE 97006
  - **Back cover**: Shanachie logo.
Cover credit: Melody Fahey (photo); Frederick Carlson (design)
Label: tan

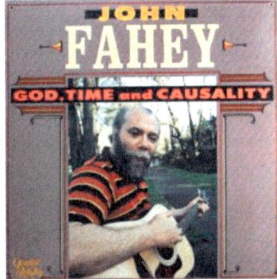

Matrix #: SH-97006-A   9-89   Emw   #05464   63K2914   595-11
             SH-97006 B   Emw   #05464 X
Songs: version 1 (4+2)
A1 – Revelation   3:47
A2 – The Red Pony   6:28
A3 – Lion   6:38
A4 – Medley: Interlude / The Portland Cement Factory / Requiem For
       Mississippi John Hurt   11:37
   B1 – Medley: Snowflakes / Steamboat 'Gwine Around The Bend /
       Death of the Clayton Peacock / How Green Was My Valley   11:46
   B2 – Medley: Sandy On Earth / I'll See You In My Dreams   16:29
Recording Dates: September 1989 at Spectrum Studios, Portland, Oregon.*
Liner notes: yes (by Mark Humphrey)
Booklet: yes (with guitar tab)
Producer: Terry Robb and John Fahey
Of note: (1) * The album was actually recorded for Takoma in 1977 but was rejected. When in 1989 Fahey got an advance from Shanachie for a new album, he gave them the old tape with one newly recorded piece (probably track B2), and pocketed the savings from studio costs. (2) The insert booklet has the guitar tablature for two songs: "Requiem For John Hurt" and "Steamboat Gwine 'Round The Bend." (3) The tab booklet correctly spells the "Steamboat" title, since the label and back cover add an apostrophe to the word "Gwine."

Tape re-issue

#1
Release date: 1989
Catalog number: Shanachie SH-97006
Format: cassette tape
Cover: Fahey on guitar
Cover credit: Melody Fahey (photo);
Frederick Carlson (design)
Songs: version #1 (4+2)
Recording Dates: same as LP #1
Liner notes: yes

CD re-issue

#1
Release date: 1989
Catalog number: Shanachie SH-97006
Format: CD
Cover: Fahey on guitar

Disc label: silver

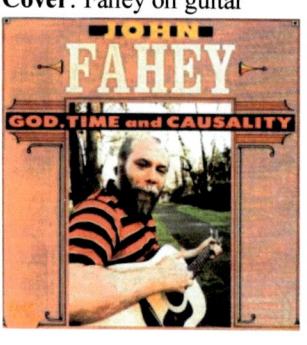

Cover credit: Melody Fahey (photo); Frederick Carlson (design)
Songs: version #1 (6)
1 – Revelation   3:47
2 – The Red Pony   6:28
3 – Lion   6:38
4 – Medley: Interlude / The Portland Cement Factory / Requiem For
         Mississippi John Hurt   11:37
5 – Medley: Snowflakes / Steamboat 'Gwine Around The Bend / Death
         of the Clayton Peacock / How Green Was My Valley   11:46
6 – Medley: Sandy On Earth / I'll See You In My Dreams   16:29
Recording Dates: same as LP #1
Liner notes: yes (reproduced)
Remastering: Robert Vosgien at CMS Digital, CA

JOULUYÖ, JUHLAYÖ

#1

Release date: 1989   (Finland)
Edition: 1st issue (label #1, songs #1)
Catalog number: Ää ÄS241289
Format: split 7", 45 rpm, stereo
Jacket cover: no
Label: Ää

Matrix #: AS-241289 A   FINNVOX mj
               AS-241289 B   FINNVOX mj
Songs: version #1 (1+1)
A1 – "Jouluyö, Juhlayö (Silent Night)" by John Fahey   3:47
  B1 – "Porot Ja Kulkuset" by Antero Jakoila   3:06
Recording Dates:
Of note: (1) The record was issued as a limited edition on red translucent vinyl. It was given as a Christmas gift to those associated with the Martinus concert hall in Helsinki where Fahey had recently played. The Ää record label is obscure. (2) This is a new version by Fahey of "Silent Night, Holy Night." (3) Side B is by Antero Jakoila, a Finnish guitarist born in 1945, who has worked as a studio musician and performer and is known for his tango guitar playing.

THE JOHN FAHEY CHRISTMAS ALBUM

#1
Release date: 1991
Catalog number: Burnside BCD 0004-2
Format: CD
Cover: purple   **Disc label**: silver + purple

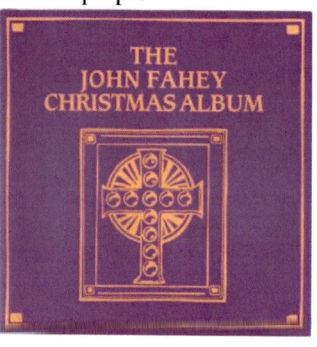 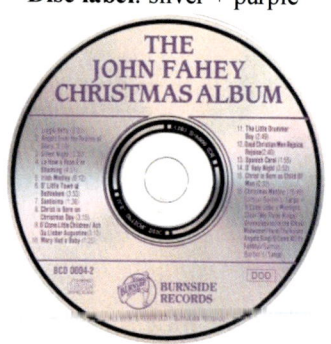

Cover credit: Tom Weller
Songs: version #1 (16)

#	Song	on cover	on disc	actual
1	Jingle Bells	3:02	3:20	3:04
2	Angels from the Realms of Glory	2:02	2:10	2:05
3	Silent Night	3:13	3:30	3:16
4	Lo How a Rose E'er Blooming	4:28	4:51	4:31
5	Irish Medley	5:42	6:12	5:45
6	O' Little Town of Bethlehem	3:06	3:33	3:19
7	Santisima	1:32	1:38	1:34
8	Christ is Born on Christmas Day	3:01	3:15	3:05
9	O' Come Little Children / Ach Du Lieber Augustine	2:57	3:13	2:59
10	Mary Had a Baby	1:18	1:25	1:20
11	The Little Drummer Boy	2:34	2:49	2:35
12	Good Christian Men, Rejoice, Rejoice	1:32	2:40	1:33
13	Spanish Carol	1:58	1:55	2:00
14	O' Holy Night	3:34	3:52	3:35
15	Christ is Born as Child of Man	2:22	2:32	2:24
16	Christmas Medley: Samuel Barber's "Largo" / It Came Upon a Midnight Clear / We Three Kings / Greensleeves / In the Bleak Midwinter / Hark! The Herald Angels Sing / O Come All Ye Faithful / Samuel Barber's "Largo"	14:22	15:46	14:23

Recording Dates: 1991 at Spectrum Sound Studios, Portland, Oregon.
Liner notes: by Dan Lissy

Producer: Terry Robb and Don MacLeod
Of note: (1) Notice the discrepancy in the duration for the songs when comparing those written on the back cover and those written on the disc label. The actual times are given on the 3rd column. (2) This is the first Fahey album not to be released on vinyl. (3) The UPC code on the back cover is: 008781000424.

#2
Release date: 1992 (Canada)
Catalog number: Attic ACD 1362
Format: CD
Cover: purple   **Disc label**: silver + black

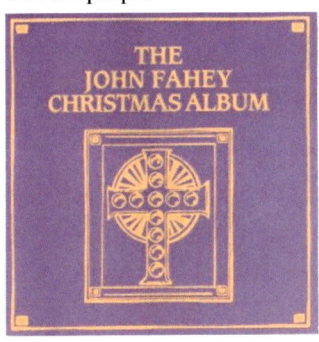 

Cover credit: Tom Weller
Songs: version #1 (16)

	on cover	on disc
1 – Jingle Bells	3:02	3:03
2 – Angels from the Realms of Glory	2:02	2:05
3 – Silent Night	3:13	3:17
4 – Lo How a Rose E'er Blooming	4:28	4:30
5 – Irish Medley	5:42	5:45
6 – O' Little Town of Bethlehem	3:06	3:19
7 – Santisima	1:32	1:34
8 – Christ is Born on Christmas Day	3:01	3:04
9 – O' Come Little Children / Ach Du Lieber Augustine	2:57	2:59
10 – Mary Had a Baby	1:18	1:20
11 – The Little Drummer Boy	2:34	2:35
12 – Good Christian Men, Rejoice, Rejoice	1:32	1:32
13 – Spanish Carol	1:58	2:01
14 – O' Holy Night	3:34	3:34
15 – Christ is Born as Child Of Man	2:22	2:25
16 – Christmas Medley: (see CD #1)	14:22	14:23

Recording Dates: same as CD #1
Liner notes: by Dan Lissy
Producer: Terry Robb and Don MacLeod
Of note: (1) On the disc label, we now have a third series of song durations. (2) The UPC code on the back cover is: 057362136229.

#3

Release date: 2008
Catalog number: Burnside BCD 4
Format: CD
Cover: purple   **Disc label**: silver + purple

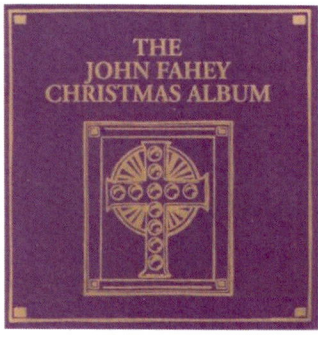

Cover credit: Tom Weller
Songs: version #1 (16)

	on cover	on disc
1 – Jingle Bells	3:20	3:20
2 – Angels from the Realms of Glory	2:10	2:10
3 – Silent Night	3:30	3:30
4 – Lo How a Rose E'er Blooming	4:51	4:51
5 – Irish Medley	6:12	6:12
6 – O' Little Town of Bethlehem	3:16	3:33
7 – Santisima	1:38	1:38
8 – Christ is Born on Christmas Day	3:15	3:15
9 – O' Come Little Children / Ach Du Lieber Augustine	3:13	3:13
10 – Mary Had a Baby	1:25	1:25
11 – The Little Drummer Boy	2:49	2:49
12 – Good Christian Men, Rejoice, Rejoice	2:40	2:40
13 – Spanish Carol	1:55	1:55
14 – O' Holy Night	3:52	3:52
15 – Christ is Born as Child Of Man	2:32	2:32
16 – Christmas Medley: (see CD #1)	15:46	15:46

Recording Dates: same as CD #1
Liner notes: by Dan Lissy
Producer: Terry Robb and Don MacLeod
Of note: (1) On the back cover, we now have a fourth series of song durations, while the disc label replicates the song durations on the disc label of the first Burnside issue. (2) The UPC code on the back cover is: 008781000424; this is the same UPC code as #1.

Tape issue

#1

Release date: 1991
Catalog number: Burnside BCA 0004-4
Format: cassette tape
Cover: purple
Cover credit: Tom Weller
Songs: version #1 (10+6)

A1 – Jingle Bells	3:02
A2 – Angels from the Realms of Glory	2:02
A3 – Silent Night	3:13
A4 – Lo How a Rose E'er Blooming	4:28
A5 – Irish Medley	5:42
A6 – O' Little Town of Bethlehem	3:06
A7 – Santisima	1:32
A8 – Christ is Born on Christmas Day	3:01
A9 – O' Come Little Children / Ach Du Lieber Augustine	2:57
A10 – Mary Had a Baby	1:18
B1 – The Little Drummer Boy	2:34
B2 – Good Christian Men, Rejoice, Rejoice	1:32
B3 – Spanish Carol	1:58
B4 – O' Holy Night	3:34
B5 – Christ is Born as Child Of Man	2:22
B6 – Christmas Medley: (see CD #1)	14:22

Recording Dates: same as CD #1
Liner notes: by Dan Lissy
Of note: (1) The song durations are now the same on the cover and tape.
(2) The UPC code on the back cover is: 008781000448.

#2

Release date: 1992   (Canada)
Catalog number: Attic CAT 1362
Format: CD
Cover: purple
Cover credit: Tom Weller
Songs: version #1 (10+6)
Recording Dates: same as CD #1
Liner notes: by Dan Lissy
Of note: (1) This cassette has the same discrepancy in song duration as seen on the CD version by Attic.

OLD GIRLFRIENDS AND OTHER HORRIBLE MEMORIES

CD issue

#1

Release date: 1992
Catalog number: Varrick CD VR 031
Format: CD
Cover: purple-red Vodou spirit   **Disc label**: white + purple

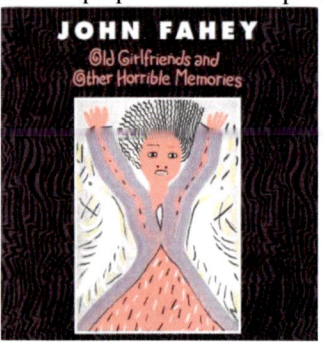
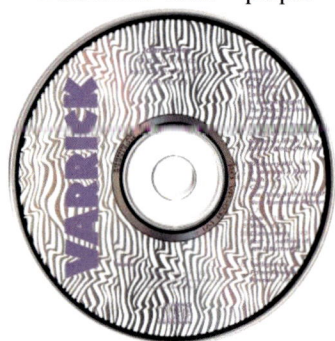

Cover credit: Levoy Exil
Songs: version #1 (12)

1 – Twilight Time	2:30
2 – The Sea Of Love	2:04
3 – In Darkest Night: The Objectification and Recurrent Sightings Of Bizarre and Cathected Screen Memories (From Below) Along the Sligo	4:00
4 – Blueberry Hill	2:40
5 – A Rose and a Baby Ruth	2:02
6 – Claire	3:13
7 – The Thing at the End of New Hampshire Avenue	3:29
8 – Don't	3:07
9 – View	4:13
10 – Dianne Kelly	7:40
11 – Fear & Loathing at 4th & Butternut	3:29
12 – Twilight on Prince Georges Avenue	4:06

Recording Dates: 1988 ("Dianne Kelly") & 1990 at Spectrum Sound Studios, Portland, Oregon
Mastering: Randy Kling at Disc Mastering
Liner notes: by Elijah P. Lovejoy – i.e., John Fahey
Producer: Terry Robb

Of note: (1) Track 1 with Terry Robb on guitar; track 5 with Melody Fahey on ukulele. (2) Track 11 is a non-Fahey piece. It is purported to be Al Wilson on harmonica, and is an excerpt from the session that produced the song "Raga Kafi" of the "Parthenogenesis" medley on the Canned Heat album *Living The Blues*. (3) Levoy Exil is a Haitain artist (b. 1944) whose paintings are mystic and abstract, and often depict Haitian Vodou spirits (or Loas). (4) The UPC code on the back cover is: 011671003122.

Tape issue

#1

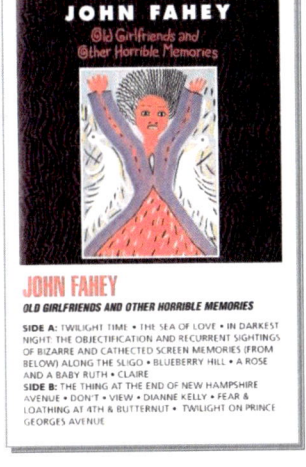

Release date: 1992
Catalog number: Varrick C VR 031
Format: cassette tape
Cover: purple-red Vodou spirit
Cover credit: Levoy Exil
Songs: version #1 (6+6)
A1 – Twilight Time
A2 – The Sea Of Love
A3 – In Darkest Night: The Objectification and Recurrent Sightings Of Bizarre and Cathected Screen Memories (From Below) Along the Sligo
A4 – Blueberry Hill
A5 – A Rose and a Baby Ruth
A6 – Claire
   B1 – The Thing at the End of New Hampshire Avenue
   B2 – Don't
   B3 – View
   B4 – Dianne Kelly
   B5 – Fear & Loathing at 4th & Butternut
   B6 – Twilight on Prince Georges Avenue
Recording Dates: same as CD #1
Liner notes: yes
Of note: (1) The UPC code on the back cover is: 011671003146.

THE NEW POSSIBILITY:
JOHN FAHEY'S GUITAR SOLI CHRISTMAS ALBUM / CHRISTMAS WITH JOHN FAHEY VOL II

#1

Release date: 1993
Catalog number: Rhino   R2 71437
Format: CD
Cover: cream.   **Disc label**: yellow + red

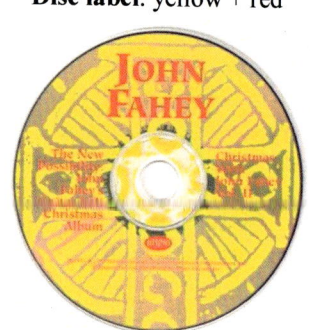

Original Cover credit: Tom Weller
Songs: version #1 (20)
1 – Joy To The World	1:52
2 – What Child Is This?	3:02
3 – Medley: Hark, The Herald Angels Sing / O Come All Ye Faithful	3:10
4 – Auld Lang Syne	2:01
5 – The Bells Of Saint Mary's	2:10
6 – Good King Wenceslas	1:10
7 – We Three Kings Of Orient Are	1:50
8 – God Rest Ye Merry Gentlemen Fantasy	3:00
9 – The First Noel	2:12
10 – Christ's Saints Of God Fantasy	10:12
11 – It Came Upon A Midnight Clear	1:28
12 – Go I Will Send Thee	3:00
13 – Lo How A Rose E'er Blooming	3:45
14 – Silent Night, Holy Night	1:14
15 – Oh Holy Night	3:26
16 – Christmas Medley: Oh Tannenbaum / Angels We Have Heard On High / Jingle Bells	3:28
17 – Russian Christmas Overture	6:45
18 – White Christmas	4:55
19 – Carol Of The Bells	2:34
20 – Christmas Fantasy – Part II	12:20

Recording Dates: 1968 and 1975
Remastering: Bill Inglot & Phil Brown
Original liner notes: none
New liner notes: by Barry Hansen
Of note: (1) This is a CD containing all tracks from the 1968 album *The New Possibility* (Takoma C-1020), as well as 6 out of 7 tracks from the 1975 album *Christmas with John Fahey Vol II* (Takoma C-1045).
(2) The UPC code on the back cover is: 081227143725.

#2

Release date: 2000
Catalog number: Takoma   TAKCD-8912-2
Format: CD
Cover: cream.   **Disc label**: yellow + black

Original Cover credit: Tom Weller
Songs: version #1 (20)
Recording Dates: same as CD #1
Remastering: Bill Inglot and Phil Brown
Original liner notes: none
New liner notes: by Barry Hansen
Of note: (1) This is a CD containing all tracks from the 1968 album *The New Possibility* (Takoma C-1020), as well as 6 out of 7 tracks from the 1975 album *Christmas with John Fahey Vol II* (Takoma C-1045).
(2) The UPC code on the back cover is: 025218891226.

#3

Release date: 2000 (UK)
Catalog number: Takoma CDTAK 8912
Format: CD
Cover: cream.

Disc label: yellow + black

Original Cover credit: Tom Weller
Songs: version #1 (20)
Recording Dates: same as CD #1
Remastering: Bill Inglot and Phil Brown
Original liner notes: none
New liner notes: by Barry Hansen
Of note: (1) This is a CD containing all tracks from the 1968 album *The New Possibility* (Takoma C-1020), as well as 6 out of 7 tracks from the 1975 album *Christmas with John Fahey Vol II* (Takoma C-1045).
(2) Marketed and distributed by ACE Records.
(3) The UPC code on the back cover is: 029667981224.

Tape issue

#1

Release date: 1993
Catalog number: Rhino R4 71437
Format: cassette tape
Cover: cream; *no* Takoma logo.
Original Cover credit: Tom Weller
Songs: version #2 (14+5)
Recording Dates: same as CD #1
New liner notes: by Barry Hansen
Of note: (1) This is a cassette containing all tracks from the 1968 album *The New Possibility* (Takoma C-1020) on side 1, as well as 6 out of 7 tracks from the 1975 album *Christmas with John Fahey Vol II* (Takoma C-1045) on side 2.
(2) The UPC code on the back cover is: 081227143749.

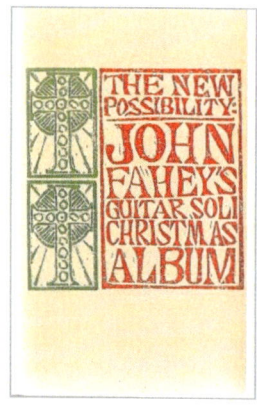

RETURN OF THE REPRESSED

#1

Release date: 1994
Edition: 1st issue
Record company: Rhino
Catalog number: R2 71737
Format: CD (x2)
Cover: desert landscape   **Disc label**: blue

Cover credit: James Austin
Songs: version #1 (22+20)

A1 – Desperate Man Blues	4:01
A2 – Dance of the Inhabitants of the Palace of King Phillip XIV of Spain	2:33
A3 – Sligo River Blues	2:37
A4 – Sun Gonna Shine In My Back Door Someday Blues	4:39
A5 – On Doing An Evil Deed Blues	4:00
A6 – I'm Gonna Do All I Can For My Lord	1:26
A7 – Some Summer Day	3:28
A8 – Worried Blues	2:30
A9 – Tell Her To Come Back Home	2:43
A10 – Poor Boy	3:21
A11 – Orinda-Moraga	3:57
A12 – The Death Of The Clayton Peacock	2:57
A13 – Brenda's Blues	1:50
A14 – On The Sunny Side Of The Ocean	3:16
A15 – Revelation On The Banks Of The Pawtuxent	2:37
A16 – Night Train To Valhalla	2:19
A17 – Knott's Berry Farm Molly	4:35
A18 – Bill Cheatum	1:56
A19 – Knoxville Blues	3:10
A20 – Sunflower River Blues	6:03
A21 – A Raga Called Pat – Part One	6:26
A22 – In Christ There Is No East Or West	2:45

B1 – The Yellow Princess 4:52
B2 – Lion 5:11
B3 – The Revolt Of The Dyke Brigade 2:43
B4 – The Portland Cement Factory At Monolith California 4:28
B5 – Steamboat Gwine 'Round De Bend 4:19
B6 – Lord Have Mercy 2:32
B7 – Beverly 4:51
B8 – Hawaiian Two-Step 2:44
B9 – Candy Man 1:28
B10 – Jaya Shiva Shankarah 5:03
B11 – Medley: Silver Bell/Cheyenne 4:32
B12 – The Approaching Of The Disco Void 6:34
B13 – Summer Cat By My Door 4:18
B14 – Theme and Variations 3:01
B15 – Lava On Waikiki 2:19
B16 – Samba De Orfeo 3:13
B17 – Rain Forest 6:48
B18 – Twilight Time 2:33
B19 – The Sea Of Love 2:08
B20 – Yes, Jesus Loves Me 1:46

Recording Dates: 1963-1992.
Booklet: by Barry Hansen, as well as John Fahey and James Austin
Mastering: Bill Inglot and Ken Perry
Producer: Barry Hansen and James Austin
Of note: (1) This is an excellent compilation of songs selected from the *Blind Joe Death* LP up to *Old Girlfriends and Other Horrible Memories*. (2) Barry Hansen's notes are exceptionally informative and well written. (3) The UPC code on the back cover is: 081227173722.

225

MORNING / EVENING

#1

Release date: 1996
Edition: 1st issue (label #1, jacket #1, songs #1)
Catalog number: Perfect 14404
Format: double 10", 78 rpm, stereo
Jacket cover: 1st (gatefold)
Label: red

Matrix #: ARC-1002-A
ARC-1002-B
ARC-1003-A
ARC-1003-B
Songs: version #1 (1+1+1+1)

A1 – Morning (Pt. 1)	4:11
B1 – Morning (Pt. 2)	4:24
C1 – Evening, Not Night (Pt. 1)	5:15
D1 – Evening, Not Night (Pt. 2)	4:31

Recording Dates: 1996 in a hotel room in Salem, Oregon, by Scott Colburn.
Liner notes: none
Producer: Dean Blackwood
Of note: (1) The labels are difficult to read due to insufficient contrast between the dark gold lettering and the burgundy-red background.
(2) "Morning" is described as Solo Guitar Alap, while "Evening, Not Night" as Solo Guitar Cathexis.
(3) A 10" 78 rpm by Perfect with same catalogue # 14404 was issued in 1925. It had "Yearning" by Lou Gold and His Orchestra b/w "Cheatin' On Me" by Bill Wirgis and His Orchestra.

CITY OF REFUGE

#1

Release date: 1997
Catalog number: Tim/Kerr Records 644 380 127-2
Format: CD
Cover: white – promo   **Disc label**: silver

Songs: version #1 (7)
1 – Fanfare	5:13
2 – The Mill Pond	3:53
3 – Chelsey Silver, Please Come Home	4:32
4 – City Of Refuge I	20:35
5 – City Of Refuge III	6:31
6 – Hope Slumbers Eternal	5:05
7 – On The Death and Disembowelment of the New Age	19:26

Mastering: Scott Colburn
Liner notes: none

#2

Release date: 1997
Catalog number: Tim/Kerr Records 644 380 127-2 AD
Format: CD
Cover: vertical stripes   **Disc label**: silver

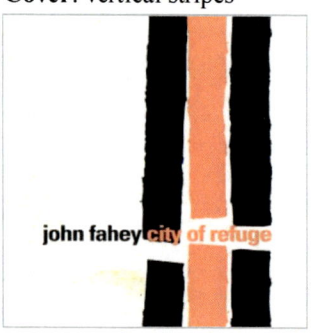

Songs: version #1 (7)
1 – Fanfare	5:13
2 – The Mill Pond	3:53
3 – Chelsey Silver, Please Come Home	4:32
4 – City Of Refuge I	20:35
5 – City Of Refuge III	6:31
6 – Hope Slumbers Eternal	5:05
7 – On The Death and Disembowelment of the New Age	19:26

Mastering: Scott Colburn
Liner notes: yes

#3

Release date: 1997
Catalog number: Tim/Kerr Records 644 830 127-2
Format: CD
Cover: vertical stripes   **Disc label**: black

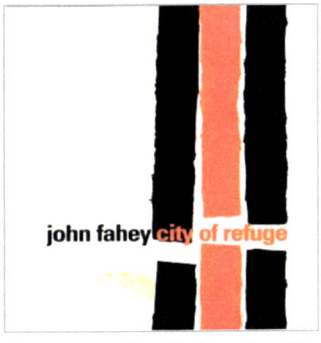
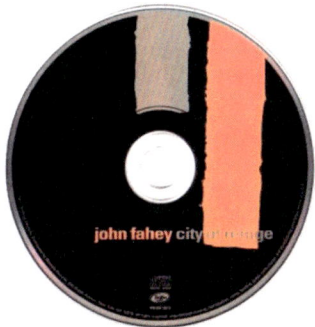

Cover credit: Christopher Douglas
Songs: version #1 (7)
Mastering: Scott Colburn
Liner notes: yes (letter from John Fahey to Bill Belmont)
Of note: (1) The UPC code on the back cover is: 764483012720.

The title of the album is derived from the song "I'm Gonna Run To The City Of Refuge" by Blind Willie Johnson, recorded in Dallas, Texas on Dec 5, 1928 (Blind Willie Johnson on vocal and guitar; Willie B. Richardson on vocal) and issued on Columbia 14391-D.

In biblical times, a *City of Refuge* was a sanctuary in which someone accused of manslaughter could find asylum, and thus avoid blood-revenge.

THE MILL POND

#1 a

Release date: 1997
Edition: 1st issue (label #1, jacket #1, songs #1)
Catalog number: Little Brother lb-009
Format: double 7", 33⅓ rpm, stereo
Jacket cover: 1st
  - **Front cover**: Mill - red
  - **Back cover**: screen print
Cover credit: Paula Gilovich
Label: red + black

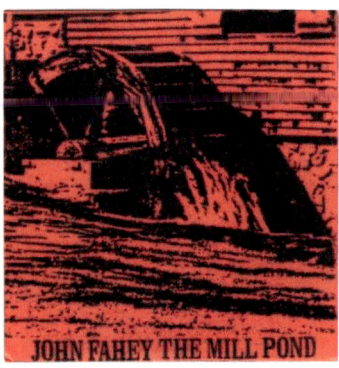 

Matrix #: LB-009-A
          LB-009-B
          LB-009-C
          LB-009-D
Songs: version 1 (1+1+1+1)
1-1 – Ghosts   5:48
1-2 – Garbage   10:40
2-1 – You Can't Cool Off In The Mill Pond, You Can Only Die   3:37
2-2 – The Mill Pond Drowns Hope   7:05
Recording Dates:
Booklet: no
Producer: Scott Colburn
Of note: (1) #1a and #1b were issued in 1000 copies. (2) Record 1, side 1 consistently skips at 3'25". (3) John Fahey on guitar and vocals; Jeff Allman on electronics. (4) One record has the side numbers on the label printed in red, the other has them printed in black.

#1 b

Release date: 1997
Edition: 1st issue - variant (label #2, jacket #2, songs #1)
Catalog number: Little Brother   lb-009
Format: double 7", 33⅓ rpm, stereo
Jacket cover: 2nd
  - **Front cover**: Mill - grey
  - **Back cover**: screen print
Cover credit: Paula Gilovich
Label: black + black

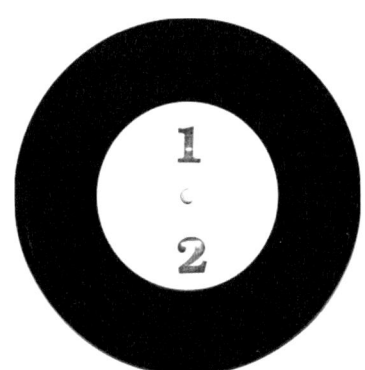

Matrix #: LB-009-A
      LB-009-B
      LB-009-C
      LB-009-D
Songs: version 1 (1+1+1+1)
1-1 – Ghosts   5:48
1-2 – Garbage   10:40
2-1 – You Can't Cool Off In The Mill Pond, You Can Only Die   3:37
2-2 – The Mill Pond Drowns Hope   7:05
Recording Dates:
Booklet: no
Producer: Scott Colburn
Of note: (1) Both records have the label numbers printed in black.

CD re-issue

#1 a

Release date: 2009
Catalog number: Important Records   Imprec 183
Format: CD
Cover: Mill – white   **Disc label**: silver

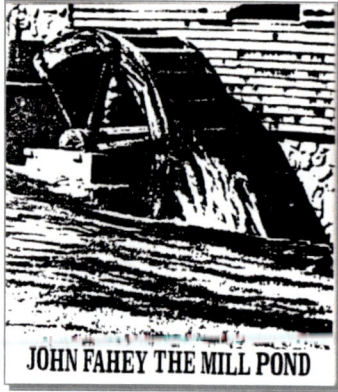
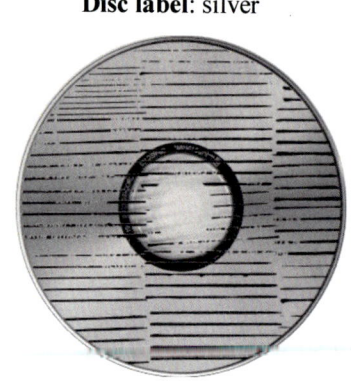

Cover credit:
Songs: version #1 (4)
1 – Ghosts	5:48
2 – Garbage	10:40
3 – You Can't Cool Off In The Mill Pond, You Can Only Die	3:37
4 – The Mill Pond Drowns Hope	7:05

Recording Dates:
Mastering: Scott Colburn
Booklet: yes (with photographs of 28 paintings and collages by John Fahey)
Producer:
Of note: (1) Limited edition of 3000 copies. (2) The UPC code on the plastic wrapping is: 793447518329.

#1 b

Release date: 2009
Catalog number: Important Records Imprec 183
Format: CD
Cover: Mill - brown
Songs: version #1 (4)
Mastering: Scott Colburn
Booklet: yes (with photographs of 28 paintings and collages by John Fahey)
Of note: (1) Same as CD #1a except for the jacket.

The Mill Pond

A mill pond is a body of water used as a reservoir for a water-powered mill. It is usually a quiet, smooth and flat body of water, a tranquil setting for fishing, and ideal for cooling off in the summer.

John Fahey slashes this serene image by setting off an aural storm. Titles such as "You Can't Cool Off In The Mill Pond, You Can Only Die" and "The Mill Pond Drowns Hope," coupled with mechanical drones and de-tuned tones, symbolize Fahey's break from the past and from that New Age conservative tranquility of which he had become the loath grandfather.

"The Mill Pool" by Edward Fahey
A photogravure in *The Encyclopaedia of Sport*, Vol. 1; 1897.

WOMBLIFE

#1

Release date: 1997
Record company: Table of the Elements
Catalog number: Rb37
Format: CD
Cover: Fahey in car   **Disc label**: white + green

Cover credit: Bettina Herzner
Songs: version #1 (5)

1 – Sharks	9:20
2 – Planaria	9:54
3 – Eels	6:13
4 – Coelacanths	7:28
5 – Juana	12:34

Recording Dates: November 1996 at Steam Room Studios, Chicago, Illinois.
Mastering: Scott Colburn
Liner notes: none
Producer: Jim O'Rourke
Of note: (1) Tracks 1 and 2 re-introduce gamelan music as a background to Fahey's guitar playing. (2) "Juana" is actually played by guitarist Jim O'Rourke, a fact revealed in Fahey's biography *Dance of Death* by Steve Lowenthal.

#2

Release date: 1999
Record company: P-Vine Records
Catalog number: PCD-23014
Format: CD
Cover: Fahey in car   **Disc label**: white + silver

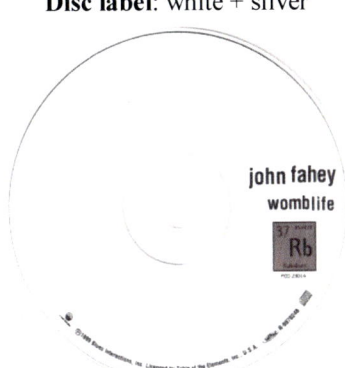

Cover credit: Bettina Herzner
Songs: version #1 (5)
1 – Sharks   9:20
2 – Planaria   9:54
3 – Eels   6:13
4 – Coelacanths   7:28
5 – Juana   12:34
Recording Dates: November 1996 at Steam Room Studios, Chicago, Illinois.
Mastering: Scott Colburn
Liner notes: yes (in Japanese).
Producer: Jim O'Rourke
Of note: (1) The UPC code on the obi strip is: 4995879230145.

THE EPIPHANY OF GLENN JONES

#1

Release date: 1997
Record company: Thirsty Ear Recordings
Catalog number: thi 57037.2
Format: CD
Cover: Frog painting   **Disc label**: frog + fruit

Cover credit: Laurie Hogin
Songs: version #1 (10)
1 – Tuff	5:06
2 – Gamelan Collage	10:11
3 – The New Red Pony	5:52
4 – Maggie Campbell Blues	3:17
5 – Our Puppet Selves	8:20
6 – Gamelan Guitar	5:28
7 – Come On In My Kitchen	4:07
8 – Magic Mountain	9:00
9 – More Nothing	6:37
10 – Nothing	15:49

Recording Dates: November 1996 at Normandy Studios, Warren, Rhode Island.
Mastering: Jon Williams
Liner notes: by Glenn Jones
Producer: Jon Williams
Of note: (1) The UPC code on the back cover is: 700435703728.

OF RIVERS AND REVISION: JOHN FAHEY AND CUL DE SAC

(written by Glenn Jones in 1998 - excerpt)

What a year it has been, and what a curious and (occasionally) amusing series of reactions we've seen in response to the album John Fahey and Cul de Sac released last year. The album *(The Epiphany of Glenn Jones)* has received nearly as much attention for the "psychodramatic" aspects surrounding its creation as for the music it contains.

True, much of the album's success (if, indeed, it can be considered successful) stems from the friction between the players involved. Trials and tribulations aside, I've begun to make peace with the album. Finally I can hear it for itself and not for the ordeal it was to create. In spite of (or because of) Cul de Sac's and John Fahey's musical antagonism, the record is a true collaboration in every sense, and to my ears, it's also the most flattering recent portrait of Fahey's present-day abilities.

The songs we'd planned to include that actually made it onto the album were "Our Puppet Selves" (a Cul de Sac number which Fahey really liked -- he barely plays on it though; the day he was to do his part, he decided to stay at his hotel to flirt with the woman who cleaned his room -- listen for a snatch of Fahey on lapsteel at the very end of the piece, which we cut-and-pasted from an earlier rehearsal); "New Red Pony" (Fahey tried to talk us out of recording it, but eventually relented; then was enthusiastic about the version we did); and "Gamelan Collage."

Songs we rehearsed but which were axed by John in his "I refuse to be associated with this" meeting with me a few days into the project, were "K" (which appeared on the next Cul de Sac album, *Crashes to Light, Minutes to its Fall*); Fahey had written a nice longish introduction to the piece, but had trouble executing it properly when it came time to record, which may have contributed to his reason for nixing this song; and "Immortality Lessons," another CdS number which we've never rerecorded.

John had considered covering Ace Cannon's "Tuff" from the beginning, but I was unimpressed with it when he played it for me fingerstyle and he dropped it. In the studio he got the idea of playing it lapsteel style instead -- REALLY slow -- and that worked beautifully. In fact the version on the CD is the first take of the very first time he tried it this way. He also wanted to record the Del Vikings' "Come Go with Me," and even though we never got a complete take, you can hear John segue into it at the end of "Maggie Campbell Blues."

The album, generally, has been received enthusiastically. Reviews, unfortunately, don't sell records. The European labels approached to license the album were scared of it ("too dark," "too difficult"), which pretty much killed its chances overseas.

I still haven't been able to bring myself to listen to the many rehearsal tapes we made with John in our space prior to recording the album, or to the album's out-takes. I'm sure there are things I've forgotten (or repressed!), that will come joltingly back into focus when I do.

THINGS TO COME

#1

Release date: 1997
Catalog number: -
Format: Cassette tape
Cover: Fahey & brick wall

Cover credit: Jason Carter
Songs: version #1 (1)
A1 – Things To Come   20:50
Recording Dates: mastered at Wavelength
Mastering: Tom Nunes and T. Revell
Liner notes: none
Producer:
Of note: (1) This one-sided tape was self made and distributed at the few shows that the John Fahey Trio played around the Northwest. There is no catalogue number or song listing.
The John Fahey Trio is: John Fahey: guitars
                          Tim Knight: keyboards, bass
                          Rob Scrivner: guitars, EFX
(2) The front cover photograph appears to be from the same photo session as seen on the back cover of *KBOO Radio Live Session*.
(3) It ends with over three minutes of circus sounds and calliope music, excerpts of which were used for the 'noise' sequence associated with Fahey's Beatles pop song segment in "Requiem for Molly, part 2" from 1967.

GEORGIA STOMPS, ATLANTA STRUTS, AND OTHER CONTEMPORARY DANCE FAVORITES

#1

Release date: 1998
Edition: 1st issue (label #1, jacket #1, songs #1)
Catalog number: Table of the Elements TOE-LP-38   Sr38
Format: double 12" LP, 33⅓ rpm, stereo
Jacket cover: 1st
  - **Front cover:** woodcut image
  - **Spine**: JOHN FAHEY   GEORGIA STOMPS, ATLANTA STRUTS, AND
       OTHER CONTEMPORARY DANCE FAVORITES
       TABLE OF THE ELEMENTS   TOE-LP-38
  - **Back cover**: Fahey photo
Cover credit: Jeff Hunt
Label: Sr 38

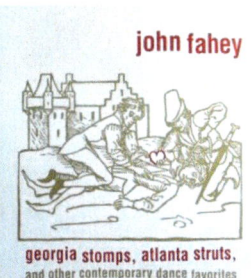

Matrix #: TOE-LP-38-A   KRG@ATM 2701.1(2)
         TOE LP-38-B   KRG@ATM 2701.2(2)
         TOE-LP-38-C   KRG@ATM 2701.3(2)
         TOE LP-38-D   KRG@ATM 2701.4(2)
Songs: version #1 (1+1+2+1)
  A1 – House of the Rising Sun / Nightmare   19:09
    B1 – Juana / Guitar Lamento   17:06
      C1 – Red Rocking Chair   9:26
      C2 – Song for Sara   6:20
        D1 – Son House / Marilyn / My Prayer / Moon Indigo   21:05
Recording Dates: August 9, 1997 - live at the Horizon Theater, Atlanta, Georgia
Liner notes: none
Producer: Kristina Johnson and Jeff Hunt

Of note: (1) Issued as a limited edition on audiophile high-quality 150 gram vinyl. (2) The remaining labels for sides B to D show more wood carving images. Side D has the image "Four winds from four directions."

CD issue
#1

Release date: 1998
Catalog number: TOF-CD-38   Sr38
Format: CD
Cover: woodcut image.

Disc label: gold & red on white

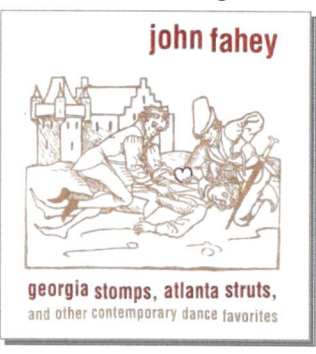

Original Cover credit: Jeff Hunt
Songs: version #1 (5)

1 – House of the Rising Sun / Nightmare	19:09
2 – Juana / Guitar Lamento	17:06
3 – Red Rocking Chair	9:26
4 – Song for Sara	6:20
5 – Son House / Marilyn / My Prayer / Moon Indigo	21:05

Recording Dates: same as LP #1
Remastering:
Liner notes: none
Producer: Kristina Johnson and Jeff Hunt
Of note: (1) The UPC code on the back cover is: 600401038123.

#2

Release date: 1999 (Japan)
Record company: P-Vine Records
Catalog number: PCD-23015
Format: CD
Cover: woodcut image.   **Disc label**: black on white

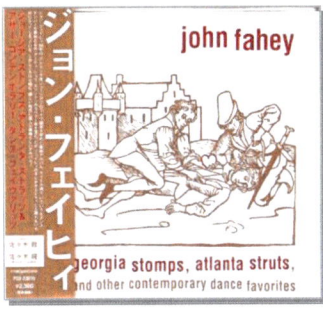

Original Cover credit: Jeff Hunt
Songs: version #1 (5)
1 – House of the Rising Sun / Nightmare   19:09
2 – Juana / Guitar Lamento   17:06
3 – Red Rocking Chair   9:26
4 – Song for Sara   6:20
5 – Son House / Marilyn / My Prayer / Moon Indigo   21:05
Recording Dates: same as LP #1
Remastering:
Liner Notes: yes (in Japanese)
Producer: Kristina Johnson and Jeff Hunt
Of note: (1) The EAN-13 code on the obi strip is: 4995879230152.

BEST OF THE VANGUARD YEARS

#1
Release date: 1999
Edition: 1st issue
Record company: Vanguard
Catalog number: 79532-2
Format: CD
Cover: blue; Fahey with guitar
Cover credit: Jeff Lovelace   **Disc label**: black

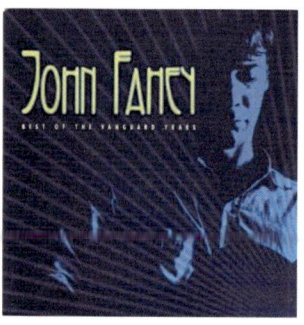

Songs: version #1 (15)
1 – The Yellow Princess	4:48
2 – View (East From The Top Of The Riggs Road/B & O Trestle)	4:53
3 – Lion	5:06
4 – March! For Martin Luther King	3:39
5 – The Singing Bridge Of Memphis, Tennessee	2:49
6 – Dance Of The Inhabitants Of The Invisible City Of Bladensburg	4:06
7 – Charles A. Lee: In Memoriam	3:58
8 – Irish Setter	7:13
9 – Commemorative Transfiguration and Communion at Magruder Park	5:57
10 – Requiem For John Hurt	5:05
11 – Requiem For Russell Blaine Cooper	8:51
12 – When The Catfish Is In Bloom	7:36
13 – Fight On Christians, Fight On	1:54
14 – Requiem For Molly (Part 3)	2:28
15 – Requiem For Molly (Part 4)	2:55

Recording Dates: 1967-1968
Liner notes: by Ed Ward
Mastering: Jeff Zaraya
Producer: Vince Hans
Of note: (1) This compilation includes all the songs from *The Yellow Princess* (tracks 1-9) and selected songs from *Requia* (tracks 10-15). "Requiem For Molly" parts 1 and 2 are not included. (1) The UPC code on the back cover is: 015707952323.

HITOMI

CD issue

#1

Release date: 2000 (Europe)
Record company: Liverpool House Records
Catalog number: 70334 90001 2
Format: CD
Cover: a painting by John Fahey   **Disc label**: silver

Cover credit: John Fahey
Songs: version #1 (9)
1 – Delta Flight 53	3:50
2 – Despair	2:47
3 – Hitomi	9:43
4 – Tanaka Jun	5:33
5 – East Meets West	7:43
6 – Hitomi Smiles	5:10
7 – The Dance of the Cat People	10:31
8 – A History of Tokyo Rail Traction	7:06
9 – Delta Flight 54	11:30

Recording Dates:
Liner notes: none
Mastering:
Producer: John Fahey
Of note: (1) Track 8 corresponds to the 39'30" to 46'35" section of the *KBOO Radio Live Session*. (2) Hitomi is the name of a would-be girlfriend that Fahey met during his 1999 tour of Japan. (3) Delta Flights 53 and 54 were the flight numbers of the Delta Airlines route between Los Angeles and Tokyo. (4) The front and rear cover paintings are by John Fahey. (5) The UPC code on the back cover is: 703349000189.

LP issue

#1

Release date: 2003
Edition: 1st issue (label #1, jacket #1, songs #1)
Record company: Important Records
Catalog number: imprec 030
Format: 12" LP, 33⅓ rpm, stereo
Jacket cover: 1st
  - **Front cover**: John Fahey painting
  - **Spine**: bar code   John Fahey   Hitomi   Important
  - **Back cover**: John Fahey on electric guitar
Cover credit: John Fahey
Label: white

  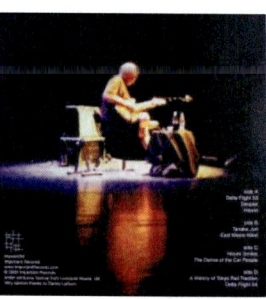

Matrix #: L-13707 M-A   IMPREC-030 A   WWW.IMPORTANTRECORDS.COM
             L-13707 M-B   IMPREC-030 B   WWW.IMPORTANTRECORDS.COM
             L-13709 M-C   IMPREC-030 C   WWW.IMPORTANTRECORDS.COM
             L-13709 M-D   IMPREC-030 D   WWW.IMPORTANTRECORDS.COM

Songs: version #1 (3+2+2+2)

A1 – Delta Flight 53	3:50
A2 – Despair	2:47
A3 – Hitomi	9:43
B1 – Tanaka Jun	5:33
B2 – East Meets West	7:43
C1 – Hitomi Smiles	5:10
C2 – The Dance of the Cat People	10:31
D1 – A History of Tokyo Rail Traction	7:06
D2 – Delta Flight 54	11:30

Recording Dates:
Liner notes: none
Producer: John Fahey
Of note: (1) The record was issued in a limited number of 1000; 100 on clear vinyl and 900 on black vinyl.

GOOD LUCK

#1
Release date: 2001
Catalog number: One Hit Records 0002
Format: CD
Cover: John Fahey Trio

Cover credit: Corey Winslow
Songs: version #1 (7)
1 – Things Fall Apart	3:31
2 – The Center Will Not Hold	6:10
3 – Like Being Reborn Again	4:56
4 – Slouching Toward Jerusalem	7:56
5 – A Drunken Tale To Hide	2:24
6 – Scherzo	6:33
7 – Tina In The Rain	7:42

Recording Dates: at Jazzoo Studio. "Tina In The Rain" recorded live at Guitar Castle, Salem, Oregon.
Mastering: Lastra Studio & Sound in Motion
Liner notes: none
Producer:
Of note: (1) The back cover has a die cut symbol that means *Good Luck* in Japanese.
(2) The John Fahey Trio is:
- John Fahey: guitar
- Tim Knight: organ, bass, guitar
- Rob Scrivener: guitar

John Fahey plays organ on track 2.
(3) On track 7, John Fahey recites two paragraphs from the notes to *Death Chants, Breakdowns & Military Waltzes*. Within this he mentions two books: *Myth of the Negro Past* (1941) by Melville J. Herskovits; and *Fear and Trembling* (1843) by Søren Kierkegaard.

The title of three songs in *Good Luck* are derived from a poem written in 1919 by William Butler Yeats (1865-1939):

THE SECOND COMING

Turning and turning in the widening gyre
The falcon cannot hear the falconer;
Things fall apart; the centre cannot hold;
Mere anarchy is loosed upon the world,
The blood-dimmed tide is loosed, and everywhere
The ceremony of innocence is drowned;
The best lack all conviction, while the worst
Are full of passionate intensity.

Surely some revelation is at hand;
Surely the Second Coming is at hand.
The Second Coming! Hardly are those words out
When a vast image out of Spiritus Mundi
Troubles my sight: a waste of desert sand;
A shape with lion body and the head of a man,
A gaze blank and pitiless as the sun,
Is moving its slow thighs, while all about it
Wind shadows of the indignant desert birds.
The darkness drops again but now I know
That twenty centuries of stony sleep
Were vexed to nightmare by a rocking cradle,
And what rough beast, its hour come round at last,
Slouches towards Bethlehem to be born?

KBOO RADIO LIVE SESSION

#1

Release date: 2001
Catalog number: One Hit Records 0004
Format: CD
Cover: dinosaur

Cover credit: Corey Winslow
Songs: version #1 (1)
1 – KBOO Radio Live Recording   52:43
Recording Dates: at KBOO 90.7 fm studio, Portland, Oregon.
Mastering: Tom Nunes
Liner notes: none
Producer:
Of note: (1) The John Fahey Trio is:
- John Fahey: guitar, lap steel
- Tim Knight: guitar, organ, toys
- Rob Scrivener: guitar, EFX

(2) From 24:00 to 37:00 are 13 minutes of classic Fahey on solo guitar.

JOHN FAHEY TRIO – VOL. ONE

#1

Release date: 2002
Catalog number: Jazzoo Records
Format: CD
Cover: a painting by John Fahey

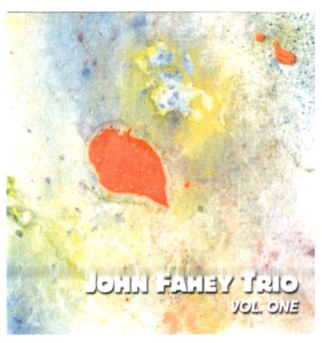 

Cover credit: John Fahey
Songs: version #1 (8)

1	Intro / She / Things Fall Apart	14:13
2	Hitomi Cries	11:03
3	The Center Will Not Hold	6:08
4	Scherzo / Oregon Capitol Inn	17:30
5	A Drunken Tale To Hide	2:11
6	Like Being Reborn Again	4:53
7	Final Song Live	9:02
8	Tina In The Rain	7:31

Recording Dates: Tracks 1c, 3, 4a, 5, and 6 at Jazzoo Studio. Track 8 recorded live at Guitar Castle, Salem OR.
Mastering: Lastra Studio & Sound in Motion
Liner notes: none
Producer:
Of note: (1) The John Fahey Trio is:
- John Fahey: guitar, organ, EFX, story
- Tim Knight: organ, piano, bass, guitar, horn, melowbar, bells and seagulls, EFX
- Rob Scrivener: guitar, EFX

(2) John Flaming plays alto sax on track 7.
(3) On track 8, John Fahey recites the notes to *Death Chants, Breakdowns & Military Waltzes*. (4) Tracks 1c, 3, 4a, 5, 6 and 8 are from the CD *Good Luck*.
(5) The UPC code on the back cover is: 821997000121.

RED CROSS

CD issue

#1

Release date: 2002
Edition: 1st / promo issue (label #1, jacket #1, songs #1)
Catalog number: Revenant Promo CD #104
Format: CD
Jacket cover: 1st (promo)   **Disc Label**: red cross on white

Songs: version #1 (8)	on cover	on disc
1 – Remember	4:46	4:41
2 – Red Cross, Disciple of Christ Today	4:10	4:06
3 – Summertime	5:45	5:40
4 – Ananaias	7:35	7:32
5 – Motherless Child	8:26	8:22
6 – Charley Bradley's Ten Sixty-Six Blues	3:27	3:24
7 – Untitled with Rain	6:56	24:00
8 – Untitled (hidden track)	-	2:14

Recording Dates: 2000-2001
Booklet: none
Producer: Dean Blackwood
Of note: (1) Track #7 has 6'56" of music; the rest consists of silence that eventually leads into the "hidden" track.

#2

Release date: Feb 11, 2003
Edition: 2nd issue (label #1, jacket #2, songs #1)
Catalog number: Revenant No. 104
Format: CD
Jacket cover: 2nd   **Disc Label**: red cross on white

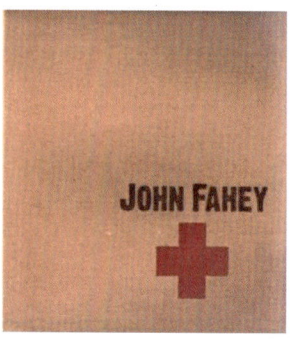 

Songs: version #1 (8)

1 – Remember	4:41
2 – Red Cross, Disciple of Christ Today	4:06
3 – Summertime	5:40
4 – Ananaias	7:32
5 – Motherless Child	8:22
6 – Charley Bradley's Ten Sixty-Six Blues	3:24
7 – Untitled with Rain	24:00
8 – Untitled (hidden track)	2:14

Recording Dates: 2000-2001
Booklet: by Glenn Jones
Producer: Dean Blackwood
Of note: (1) The UPC code on the packaging is: 630814010423.

#3

Release date: 2003 (Japan)
Edition: 3rd issue (label #1, jacket #2, songs #1)
Catalog number: P-Vine Records PCD-3276
Format: CD
Of note: (1) The CD and its case and booklet are actually the Revenant Records edition [No. 104]. This is packaged with an obi strip and attached booklet that contains the Japanese translation of the original CD booklet.
(2) The EAN-13 code on the obi strip is: 4995879032763.

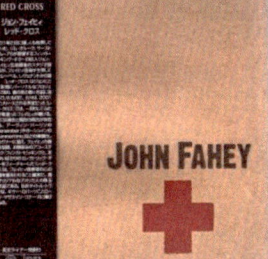

The title of this record is derived from the sermon "Red Cross The Disciple of Christ Today" by Rev. Moses Mason (Paramount 12601, recorded in Chicago in January 1928). It was inspired by the Red Cross relief effort during the great Mississippi flood of April 1927. The flood inspired such songs as Charlie Patton's "High Water Everywhere" which was recorded in 1929, and many others.

LP issue

#1

Release date: 2003
Edition: 1st issue (label #1, jacket #1, songs #1)
Catalog number: Revenant
Format: 12" LP, 33⅓ rpm, stereo
Jacket cover: 1st (fold-out)
  - **Front cover**: John Fahey and red cross
  - **Spine**: no spine
  - **Back cover**: numbered edition (# of 1000) on bottom left
Cover credit: Noel Waggener
Label: red cross on white; side number

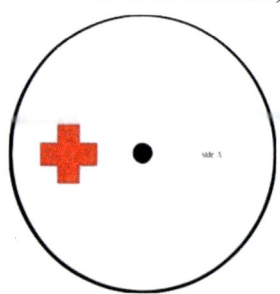

Matrix #: AE 48741 / A   www.gzvinyl.com
              AE 48742 / A
Songs: version #1 (4+4)

A1 – Remember	4:41
A2 – Red Cross, Disciple Of Christ Today	4:06
A3 – Summertime	5:40
A4 – Ananaias	7:32
B1 – Motherless Child	8:22
B2 – Charley Bradley's Ten Sixty-Six Blues	3:24
B3 – Untitled with Rain	6:56
B4 – Untitled (hidden track)	2:14

Recording Dates: 2000-2001
Booklet: by Glenn Jones
Producer: Dean Blackwood
Of note: (1) The record was issued as a limited numbered edition of 1000.
(2) The record is 180 gram HQ vinyl.

#2

Release date: 2004
Edition: 2nd issue (label #1, jacket #2, songs #1)
Catalog number: Revenant 6001
Format: 12" LP, 33⅓ rpm, stereo
Jacket cover: 2nd (regular)
  - **Front cover**: John Fahey and red cross
  - **Spine**: JOHN FAHEY +   6001
  - **Back cover**: *no* numbered edition
Cover credit: Noel Waggener
Label: red cross on white; side number

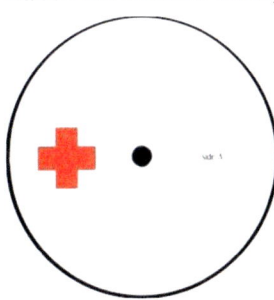 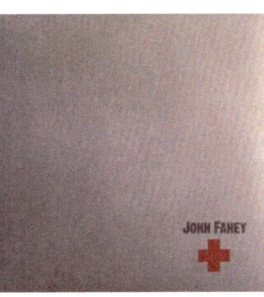 

Matrix #: AE 48741 / A   www.gzvinyl.com
                AE 48742 / A
Songs: version #1 (4+4)

A1	– Remember	4:41
A2	– Red Cross, Disciple Of Christ Today	4:06
A3	– Summertime	5:40
A4	– Ananaias	7:32
	B1 – Motherless Child	8:22
	B2 – Charley Bradley's Ten Sixty-Six Blues	3:24
	B3 – Untitled with Rain	6:56
	B4 – Untitled (hidden track)	2:14

Recording Dates: 2000-2001
Booklet: by Glenn Jones
Producer: Dean Blackwood
Of note: (1) The record is 180 gram HQ vinyl.

HARD TIME EMPTY BOTTLE BLUES

#1

Release date: 2003
Edition: 1st issue (label #1, jacket #1, songs #1)
Catalog number: Table of the Elements   Nd 60
Format: 12" LP, 33⅓ rpm, stereo, one-sided
Jacket cover: none
Label: Nd 60

Matrix #: TOE-LP-60   "NEODYMIUM"   "1993-2003"   KRG@ATM   10217(2)
Songs: version #1 (4)

1 – Hard Time Empty Bottle Blues 1	2:18
2 – Hard Time Empty Bottle Blues 2	3:05
3 – Hard Time Empty Bottle Blues 3	1:34
4 – Hard Time Empty Bottle Blues 4	2:24

Recording Dates: November 8, 1996, at the Table of the Elements "Yttrium" festival, held at the *Empty Bottle*, 1035 N. Western Ave., Chicago, Illinois.
Liner notes: none
Producer: Kristina Johnson and Jeff Hunt.
Of note: (1) The record was issued as a limited edition of 2000 copies on clear, light green vinyl. A woodcut image was screen-printed in purple on side B depicting "The Fall of Icarus" adapted from a woodcut print (attributed to Albrecht Dürer) in the book *Spiegel der wahren Rhetorik* by Friedrich Riedrer from 1493.

OF RIVERS AND RELIGION & AFTER THE BALL

#1
Release date: 2003 (Germany)
Edition: 1st issue
Catalog number: Warner Bros Records   8122-73663-2
Format: CD
Cover: **Disc Label**: green

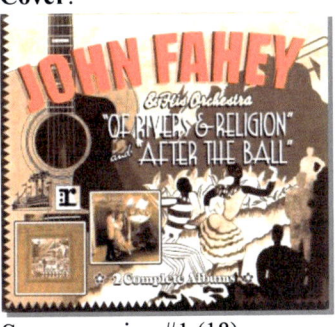

Songs: version #1 (18)
1 – Steamboat Gwine 'Round De Bend	4:16
2 – Medley: Deep River / Ol' Man River	5:45
3 – Dixie Pig Bar-B-Q Blues	4:00
4 – Texas And Pacific Blues	4:32
5 – Funeral Song For Mississippi John Hurt	4:23
6 – Medley: By The Side Of The Road / I Come, I Come	6:05
7 – Lord Have Mercy	2:32
8 – Song	5:24
9 – Horses	2:11
10 – New Orleans Shuffle	3:17
11 – Beverly	4:51
12 – Om Shanthi Norris	5:52
13 – I Wish I Knew How It Would Feel To Be Free	2:36
14 – When You Wore A Tulip (And I Wore A Big Red Rose)	2:37
15 – Hawaiian Two-Step	2:42
16 – Bucktown Stomp	2:15
17 – Candy Man	1:26
18 – After The Ball	3:43

Recording Dates: 1972-1973
Liner notes: by Sid Griffin and Nat Hentoff
Mastering: Dan Hersh and Bill Inglot at Digiprep, Los Angeles, California.
Producer: Rick Conrad
Of note: (1) The jewel-cased CD comes with a card dust jacket. (2) This is a compilation with all the songs from *Of Rivers and Religion* and *After The Ball*. (3) The EAN-13 code on the back cover is: 0081227366322.

#2

Release date: 2011 (Japan)
Edition: 2nd issue
Catalog number: Reprise   WQCP-1167
Format: CD
Cover: **Disc Label**: tan-green

Songs: version #1 (18)
1	– Steamboat Gwine 'Round De Bend	4:16
2	– Medley: Deep River / Ol' Man River	5:45
3	– Dixie Pig Bar-B-Q Blues	4:00
4	– Texas And Pacific Blues	4:32
5	– Funeral Song For Mississippi John Hurt	4:23
6	– Medley: By The Side Of The Road / I Come, I Come	6:05
7	– Lord Have Mercy	2:32
8	– Song	5:24
9	– Horses	2:11
10	– New Orleans Shuffle	3:17
11	– Beverly	4:51
12	– Om Shanthi Norris	5:52
13	– I Wish I Knew How It Would Feel To Be Free	2:36
14	– When You Wore A Tulip (And I Wore A Big Red Rose)	2:37
15	– Hawaiian Two-Step	2:42
16	– Bucktown Stomp	2:15
17	– Candy Man	1:26
18	– After The Ball	3:43

Recording Dates: 1972-1973
Liner notes: by Kazuhiro Uda (in Japanese)
Mastering: Dan Hersh and Bill Inglot at Digiprep, Los Angeles, California.
Producer: Rick Conrad
Of note: (1) The CD is issued on SHM-CD (Super High Material CD).
(2) This is a compilation with all the songs from *Of Rivers and Religion* and *After The Ball*.
(3) The EAN-13 code on the obi strip is: 4943674114306.

THE BEST OF JOHN FAHEY
VOL. 2: 1964-1983

#1

Release date: 2004
Edition: 1st issue
Record company: Takoma
Catalog number: TAKCD-8916-2
Format: CD
Cover: Fahey playing guitar
Cover credit: Jo Ayres   **Disc label**: black (white writing)

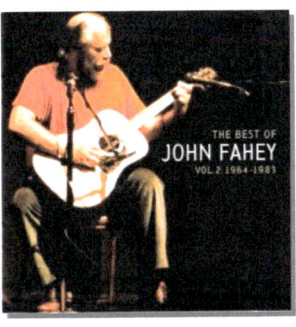

Songs: version #1 (15)
1 – Twilight On Prince George's Avenue	5:43
2 – Frisco Leaving Birmingham	3:27
3 – Sligo Mud	5:59
4 – Orinda-Moraga	3:58
5 – On The Beach At Waikiki	2:39
6 – Oneonta	2:33
7 – Dance Of Death	7:36
8 – The Assassination Of Stephan Grossman	2:12
9 – Tuff	5:05
10 – Ann Arbor/Death By Reputation	8:11
11 – Medley: Hark The Herald Angels Sing/O Come All Ye Faithful	3:12
12 – The Approaching Of The Disco Void	6:43
13 – Steamboat Gwine 'Round De Bend	4:51
14 – The Fahey Sampler	13:20
15 – Let All Mortal Flesh Keep Silence	3:26

Recording Dates: see below
Booklet: by Henry Kaiser
Mastering: Joe Tarantino at Fantasy Studios, Berkeley, California.
Producer: Henry Kaiser
Of note: (1) The songs were previously released on the following albums:

Track 2 and 6: *Railroad 1*
Track 4: *Transfiguration Of Blind Joe Death*
Track 5: *Death Chants, Breakdowns and Military Waltzes*
Track 7: *Dance of Death*
Track 8: *Old Fashioned Love*
Track 10: *Visits Washington, D.C.*
Track 11: *The New Possibility: John Fahey's Christmas Guitar Soli*
Track 12 & 13: *Live in Tasmania*
Track 14: *Contemporary Guitar*
Track 15: *Yes! Jesus Loves Me*
(2) Regarding tracks 1, 3 & 9, the notes specify that they are unissued Fahey tunes from 1991, recorded for a never-issued Shanachie (or Takoma) album called *Azalea City Memories*. However, they are not performed by Fahey at all, but instead by his friend and fellow guitarist Charlie Schmidt. For the full story, read: "Sheep In Wolf's Clothing" by Bob Mehr, *Chicago Reader*, Aug 11, 2005. Intuitively, the album's title does say "Vol. 2: 1964-1983", and not "1964-1991." (3) The UPC code on the back cover is: 025218891660, then changed to 025218891622.

#2
Release date: 2004 (UK)
Edition: 2nd issue
Catalog number: CDTAK 8916
Format: CD
Cover: Fahey playing guitar
Cover credit: Jo Ayres   **Disc label**: black (silver writing)

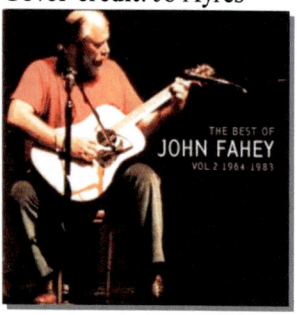

Songs: version #1 (15)
Recording Dates: see CD #1
Booklet: by Henry Kaiser
Mastering: Joe Tarantino at Fantasy Studios, Berkeley, California.
Producer: Henry Kaiser
Of note: (1) Marketed by ACE Records. (1) The UPC code on the back cover is: 029667001625.

#3

Release date: 2008 (Japan)
Edition: 3rd issue
Record company: P-Vine
Catalog number: PCD-3300
Format: CD
Cover: Fahey playing guitar
Cover credit: Jo Ayres
Disc label: black (silver writing)

Songs: version #1 (15)
Recording Dates: see CD #1
Booklet: by Henry Kaiser
Mastering: Joe Tarantino at Fantasy Studios, Berkeley, California.
Producer: Henry Kaiser
Of note: (1) The CD and its case and booklet are actually the ACE Records edition from the UK (CDTAK 8916). This is packaged with an obi strip and attached booklet that contains the Japanese translation of the original CD booklet. (2) The EAN-13 code on the obi strip is: 4995879033005.

THE GREAT SANTA BARBARA OIL SLICK

#1

Release date: 2004
Edition: 1st issue (label #1, jacket #1, songs #1)
Catalog number: Water 139
Format: CD
Jacket cover: John Fahey in concert   **Disc label**: white

Cover credit: Jim Anderson
Songs: version #1 (17)

1 – Introduction	0:12
2 – When The Springtime Comes Again	9:48
3 – Joe Kirby Blues	3:45
4 – Requiem for Mississippi John Hurt	4:14
5 – When the Catfish is in Bloom	7:56
6 – Fahey Blows His Nose	0:46
7 – Intro to "Lion" / Challenges to Quitting Cigarettes	1:02
8 – Lion	5:15
9 – Dance of the Inhabitants of the Palace of King Philip XIV of Spain	5:31
10 – View East From the B&O Railroad Viaduct and the Riggs Road Intersection	5:36
11 – On the Sunny Side of the Ocean	3:31
12 – The Great Santa Barbara Oil Slick	6:36
13 – In Christ There Is No East or West	2:48
14 – Announcement	0:36
15 – The Death of the Clayton Peacock	4:35
16 – The Revolt of the Dyke Brigade	4:01
17 – Magruder Park	9:52

Recording Dates: Tracks 1-14: Feb 14, 1968 at the Matrix, San Francisco, CA. Tracks 15-17: probably Feb 20, 1969 at the Matrix, San Francisco, CA.
Liner notes: by Glenn Jones
Producer: Glenn Jones

Mastering: Matt Azevedo, M-Works, Cambridge, Massachusetts.

Of note: (1) The "Live in Concert" photographs on the front cover and page 1 of the booklet are from a concert that Fahey gave at the Washington Square Methodist Church in Greenwich Village, New York City, on October 26, 1970. This was one of a series of folk concerts organized by Izzy Young of the Folklore Center in New York.

(2) The photographs within the booklet were taken in September 1970 while traveling in the Mojave Desert. They should have the captions:

"Giant tortoise's burrow" – page 4
"Tally Ho!" – page 12
"Tortoise hiding in bush" – page 15
"Me and my army of tortoises" – page 21

These are closely linked to Patrick Finnerty's drawings for the *America* booklet.

(3) The UPC code on the plastic wrapping is: 646315713923.

AMERICANA MASTERS

#1

Release date: 2004
Edition: 1st issue
Record company: Digital Masterworks International
Format: mp3 digital files
Cover image: Recording King guitar & Fahey from *Days Have Gone By*
Label: n/a

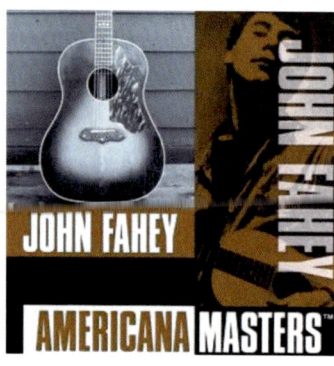

Songs: version #1 (16)
1 – Introduction by Stefan Markovitch / On The Sunny Side of the Ocean (live)	14:47
2 – Tasmanian Two-Step (live)	5:11
3 – Tiger (live)	1:45
4 – The Approaching of the Disco Void (live)	9:45
5 – Sunflower River Blues	3:19
6 – St. Louis Blues	3:16
7 – Poor Boy a Long Way From Home	2:24
8 – When The Spring Time Comes Again	4:52
9 – Some Summer Day	3:25
10 – Spanish Dancer	2:06
11 – Take a Look at That Baby	1:27
12 – The Assassination of Stephan Grossman	2:13
13 – Old Fashioned Love	3:31
14 – Boodle Am Shake	3:18
15 – Keep Your Lamp Trimmed and Burning	3:06
16 – Dry Bones in the Valley	8:52

Recording Dates: see below
Liner notes: none
Producer:

Of note: (1) This appears to be the first Fahey album made available only for digital download from the internet. (2) It is a compilation that includes side 1 of *Best of John Fahey: 1959-1977*, side 2 of *Old Fashioned Love*, as well as *Live in Tasmania* with alternate takes.

Unfortunately, the sound is muffled and of poor fidelity.

Track 10 is spelled "Dancer" instead of "Dance."

The first four tracks are mistitled. They should read:

1 – Introduction by Stefan Markovitch & John Fahey /	0:50
On the Sunny Side Of The Ocean /	3:57
Tasmanian Two-Step /	1:50
Tiger	6:46
2 – Steamboat Gwine 'Round The Bend	5:11
3 – How Green Was My Valley	1:45
4 – Steve Talbot On The Keddie Wye /	4:15
The Approaching Of The Disco Void (truncated version)	5:29

These songs differ somewhat from those on the official Takoma album *Live in Tasmania*.

Curiously, the first track starts off with the introduction by Stefan Markovitch, in the same way as on the album *Live in Tasmania,* and then we have Fahey saying:

> "Thank you very much. Let me get my guitar out here and . . . This is a strange situation. I mean, they make the smallest Guinesses in the world here; it's like medicine bottles or something. Well, it's a great pleasure to be here again in Auckland, and . . ."

Auckland? New Zealand?

On his Australian tour, Fahey did not visit New Zealand.

This begs the telling of the interesting background story of this record. The following narrative of the events is drawn from the recollections of Steve Gadd, a Tasmanian guitarist who attended this particular concert, as well as from tour promoter and producer Peter Noble (see next page).

LIVE IN TASMANIA . . . TWO TIMES

The idea to come and record in Tasmania was hatched while John Fahey was travelling with tour promoter Peter Noble between concert venues on his Australian tour in September 1980. John was brought to the remote city of Hobart, capital of the island of Tasmania (Australia), and with the aid of Stefan Markovitch, a guitar music enthusiast and the owner of the local Discurio record store, a concert was organized.

Once news got out that Fahey was coming, every finger-picking guitar player in Hobart showed up at the Stanley Burbury Theatre on Churchill Avenue at the University of Tasmania. This venue seats up to 345 persons. A good-sized crowd turned up for the concert held during that second week of September 1980.

After the introduction of John Fahey, the audience was asked to clap loudly for the live recording. John came out and the tapes began rolling. Fahey's opening remarks included his disappointment that, apart from being required to drive on the opposite side of the road, Tasmania did not seem so esoteric. But he liked the local beer, which was then brought to him on stage with ample generosity.

Fahey gave a solid performance. And when it was over and as the audience began to shuffle towards the exit, an announcement was made. Since John wanted to do a few more takes where he thought he could do a better performance, the remaining audience was invited to stay for a repeat of several tunes. The twenty or so audience members were asked to get close to the front and make as much noise and clapping as possible so as to give the impression that the house was still full.

Fahey took the stage and proceeded to play. The small group of enthusiasts cheered loudly, the pile of beer cans grew, though never to a major drinking affair, at least by Fahey's standards. And the music flowed magnificently. In the end, the evening had metamorphosed into what Fahey had been seeking . . . a surreal and otherworldly experience!

As for the recording, Noble delivered a master that included a 100% live performance to the Chrysalis / Takoma headquarters in the USA.

Stefan Markovitch would go on to set up the Tasmanian record importing company Another Record Distribution. In 1991 he obtained a B.A. in political sciences at the University of Tasmania.

Peter Noble is currently a music promoter and runs the annual BluesFest in Australia.

AMERICANA MASTERS, VOL 2

#1
Release date: 2004
Edition: 1st issue
Record company: Digital Masterworks International
Format: mp3 digital files
Cover image: Recording King guitar & Fahey from *Days Have Gone By*
Label: n/a

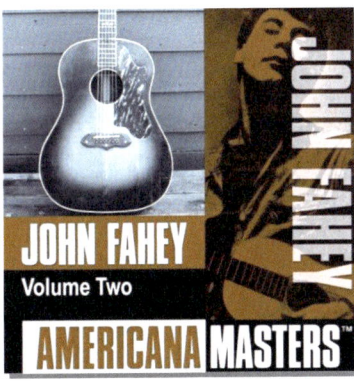

Songs: version #1 (11)
1 – I'm Going To Do All I Can For My Lord	1:25
2 – The Last Steam Engine Train	2:17
3 – In Christ There Is No East Or West	2:44
4 – Give Me Corn Bread When I'm Hungry	3:11
5 – Dance Of The Inhabitants Of The Place	3:16
6 – Revolt Of The Dyke Brigade	2:59
7 – On The Sunny Side Of The Ocean	3:49
8 – Spanish Two-Step	2:19
9 – In A Persian Market / Chinatown	7:42
10 – Jaya Shiva Shankarah	4:59
11 – Marilyn	6:31

Recording Dates: see below
Liner notes: none
Of note: (1) This album is available for digital download from the internet. (2) This compilation includes side 2 of *Best of John Fahey: 1959-1977*, and side 1 of *Old Fashioned Love*. (3) The shortened title of track 5 has the word "Palace" misspelled as "Place." (4) Track 9 includes the word "Chinatown" because the piece "In a Persian Market" incorporates the 1910 tune "Chinatown, My Chinatown," which can be heard at 5'20" into the song.

AMERICANA MASTERS, VOL 3

#1

Release date: 2004
Edition: 1st issue
Record company: Digital Masterworks International
Format: mp3 digital files
Jacket cover: Recording King guitar & Fahey from *Days Have Gone By*
Label: n/a

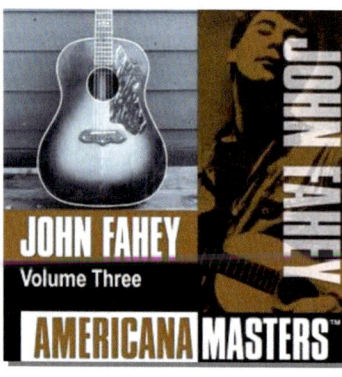

Songs: version #1 (21)
1	Frisco Leaving Birmingham, take 1	0:31
2	Frisco Leaving Birmingham, take 2	2:17
3	Frisco Leaving Birmingham, take 3	2:18
4	Life Is Like a Mountain Railroad	2:18
5	Frisco Leaving Birmingham (longer version)	3:42
6	Fix Me a Pallet on the Floor	1:33
7	Love Song	5:18
8	The Cat, take 1	4:08
9	The Cat, take 2	2:47
10	Steve Talbot	5:09
11	New York Central, take 1	4:25
12	New York Central, take 2	3:28
13	Bottle Neck No. 1, take 1	4:36
14	Bottle Neck No. 1, take 2	2:39
15	Bottle Neck No. 2, Illinois Central	2:49
16	Bottle Neck No. 1, The Virginian	3:18
17	Bottle Neck No. 3 (in open D)	5:02
18	Bottle Neck No. 4 (in open D)	4:32
19	Damned If I Know the Dog	4:55
20	Dvorsack	2:44
21	Chessie	4:18

Recording Dates: 1983
Liner notes: none
Producer:
Of note: (1) The album was made available for digital download from the internet.
(2) The songs are out-takes from the *Railroad 1* recording session. The out-take tracks that correspond to the official tracks on *Railroad* are as follows:

Tracks 1-3, 5	"Frisco Leaving Birmingham"
Track 15	"Oneonta"
Tracks 8, 9, 21	"Summer Cat By My Door"
Track 10	"Steve Talbot On The Keddie Wye"
Track 18	"Afternoon Espee Through Salem"
Track 13, 14, 16	"Enigmas & Perplexities of the Norfolk and Western"
Track 11, 12	"Charlie Becker's Meditation"
Track 17	"Medley: Imitation Train Whistles / Po' Boy"
Track 4	"Life Is Like A Mountain Railroad"
Track 19	"Delta Dog Through The Book Of Revelation"
Track 6	(new): Fahey played this live in Houston in March 1984. Bob Claypool of *The Houston Post* said: ". . . [Fahey] cut short a masterful 'Make Me a Pallet On Your Floor' by saying, "That song doesn't go anywhere! Just round and round in circles!' "
Track 7	This would evolve to "Sandy on Earth" on the 1989 album *God, Time and Causality*.
Track 20	This would become "Dvořák" on the 1984 album *Let Go*.

ON AIR

#1

Release date: 2005 (Germany)
Edition: 1st issue (label #1, jacket #1, songs #1)
Catalog number: Tradition & Moderne GmbH   T&M 034
Format: CD
CD cover: orange and black   **Disc label**: orange & black

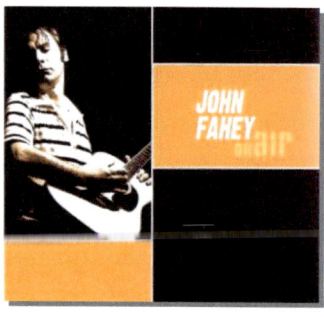 

Songs: version #1 (13)
1 – On The Sunny Side Of The Ocean	3:52
2 – Spanish Two-Step	2:09
3 – Lion	6:28
4 – Poor Boy A Long Way From Home	5:02
5 – Wine & Roses	4:17
6 – Steamboat Gwine 'Round De Bend	4:07
7 – Worried Blues	2:11
8 – Some Summer Day	3:26
9 – Candy Man	4:05
10 – Stomping Tonight On The Pennsylvania / Alabama Border	8:16
11 – In Christ There Is No East Or West	8:05
12 – Beverly	11:42
13 – Requiem For John Hurt	4:12

Recording Dates: March 20, 1978, at Bürgerzentrum Neue Vahr, Bremen, Germany.
Liner notes: by Henry Kaiser
Producer:
Of note: (1) Track 11 is actually a medley of *In Christ There Is No East Or West* and *Beverly*. (2) Track 12 is a medley of *Dance of the Inhabitants of the Palace of King Philip XIV of Spain* and an un-named tune. (3) The EAN-13 code on the back cover is: 4015698544022.

SOME SUMMER DAY

#1

Release date: 2005
Edition: 1st issue
Catalog number: Intergroove   20728   00027
Format: CD
CD cover: castle and lake   **Disc label**: guitar

Songs: version #1 (8)
1 – Stomping Tonight On The Pennsylvania-Alabama Border   9:19
2 – In Christ There Is No East Or West   1:54
3 – Beverly   5:13
4 – The Dance of the Inhabitants of the Palace of King Philip XIV
  of Spain   12:03
5 – tuning and talking   5:41
6 – Thus Krishna On The Battlefield   27:11
7 – Some Summer Day   3:17
8 – Brenda's Blues / When You Wore A Tulip   3:27
Recording Dates: July 15, 1972, recorded live in concert at the Jabberwocky Club, Syracuse, New York.
Liner notes: none
Producer:
Of note: (1) The UPC code on the back cover is: 620728000278.

THE SUNNY SIDE OF THE OCEAN

#1

Release date: 2005   (Ireland)
Edition: 1st issue
Record Company: Brook
Catalog number: Brook 1045
Format: CD
Jacket cover: Fahey playing guitar   **Disc Label**: Fahey playing guitar

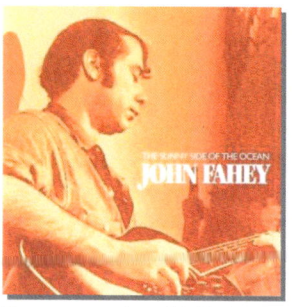 

Songs: version #1 (15)
1 – On The Sunny Side Of The Ocean	3:17
2 – When The Springtime Comes Again	2:43
3 – St. Louis Blues	2:24
4 – Give Me Cornbread When I'm Hungry	3:53
5 – Spanish Two Step	3:01
6 – Spanish Dance	3:26
7 – Dance Of The Inhabitants Of The Palace Of King Phillip XIV Of Spain	1:26
8 – I'm Gonna Do All I Can For My Lord	2:19
9 – The Last Steam Engine Train	4:52
10 – Poor Boy A Long Way From Home	2:17
11 – Some Summer Day	3:16
12 – In Christ There Is No East Or West	2:06
13 – Sunflower River Blues	3:18
14 – Revolt Of The Dyke Brigade	3:11
15 – Take A Look At That Baby	1:26

Recording Dates: see page 130.
Liner notes: by Chris White
Producer:
Of note: (1) This is a compilation including all tracks from *The Best of John Fahey 1959-1977*. (2) Bizarrely, the sequence of the songs on the CD disc is actually: 7, 12, 10, 1, 14, 11, 8, 5, 2, 9, 3, 6, 13, 4, 15.
(2) The CD comes with a card dust jacket. (3) The UPC code on the back cover is: 883717700278.

SEA CHANGES AND COELACANTHS

#1
Release date: 2006
Edition: 1st issue (label #1, jacket #1, songs #1)
Catalog number: Table of Elements   TOE-85
Format: 12" LP (x4), 33⅓ rpm, stereo
Box cover: 1st
- **Front cover**: coelacanth, mermaid
- **Spine**: TOE-LP-85   SEA CHANGES & COELACANTHS
       A Young Person's Guide to JOHN FAHEY   4xLPs
       At85   TABLE OF THE ELEMENTS
- **Back cover**: song titles and excerpts
Cover credit: Jon Brouchoud
Label: white

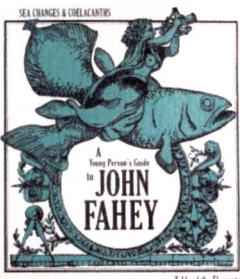
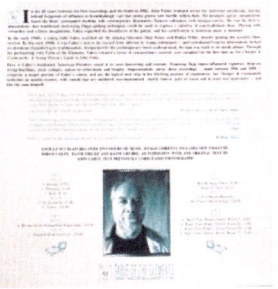

Matrix #: TOE-LP-85-A   KRG@ATm   14621.1 (2)
        TOE-LP-85-B   KRG@ATm   14621.2 (2)
        TOE-LP-38-A   KRG@ATm   2701.1 (2)
        TOE-LP-38-B   KRG@ATm   2701.2 (2)
        TOE-LP-38-C   KRG@ATm   2701.3 (2)
        TOE LP 38-D   KRG@ATm   2701.4 (2)
        TOE-LP-60 "NEODYMIUM"   "1993-2003" KRG@ATm   10217(2)

Songs: version #1   (3+2+1+1+2+1+4)
A1 – Sharks   9:20
A2 – Planaria   9:54
A3 – Eels   6:13
B1 – Coelacanths   7:38
B2 – Juana   12:34
C1 – House of the Rising Sun / Nightmare   19:09
D1 – Juana / Guitar Lamento   17:06
E1 – Red Rocking Chair   9:26
E2 – Song for Sara   6:20
F1 – Son House/Marilyn/My Prayer/Mood Indigo   21:05
G1 – Hard-Time Empty-Bottle Blues Part 1   2:18

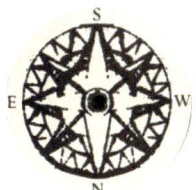

G2 – Hard-Time Empty-Bottle Blues Part 2   3:05
G3 – Hard-Time Empty-Bottle Blues Part 3   1:34
G4 – Hard-Time Empty-Bottle Blues Part 4   2:23
Recording Dates: 1996-1998
Liner notes: by David Fricke, Byron Coley, David Grubbs, Jason Gross, and John Fahey.
Producer: Jeff Hunt, Kris Johnson
Of note: (1) LP #1 corresponds to *Womblife* with newly mastered sides. (2) LPs #2 & #3 are a re-issue with same masters of *Georgia Stomps, Atlanta Struts, and Other Contemporary Dance Favorites*. (3) LP #4 corresponds to *Hard Times Empty Bottle Blues* with the same master.

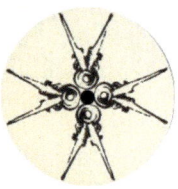

CD issue

#1
Release date: 2006
Catalog number: TOE-CD-85
Format: CD – promo sampler
Cover: none
Label: white with coelacanths

Songs: version #0 (10)
1 – Juana   12:34
2 – Hard-Time Empty-Bottle Blues Part 1   2:18
3 – Song for Sarah   6:19
4 – Sharks   9:20
5 – Eels (edit)   4:02
6 – Hard-Time Empty-Bottle Blues Part 2   3:05
7 – Hard-Time Empty-Bottle Blues Part 3   1:34
8 – Hard-Time Empty-Bottle Blues Part 4   2:33
9 – Son House/Marilyn/My Prayer/Mood Indigo   21:04
10 – Intro to Juana / Guitar Lamento   0:18
Recording Dates: same as LP #1
Liner Notes: none
Of note: (1) Track 10 is a hidden track. It is the intro to "Juana / Guitar Lamento" where Fahey talks about his sunglasses.

#2

Release date: 2006
Catalog number: TOE-CD-85
Format: CD (x2)
Cover: green with coelacanth
Cover credit: Jon Brouchoud
Disc label: green compass & green coelacanths

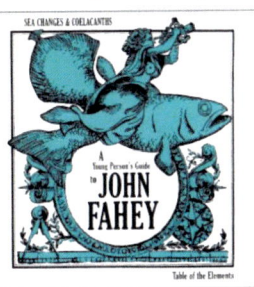

Songs: version #1 (9+5)

A1 – Sharks	9:20
A2 – Planaria	9:54
A3 – Eels	6:13
A4 – Coelacanths	7:38
A5 – Juana	12:34
A6 – Hard-Time Empty-Bottle Blues Part 1	2:18
A7 – Hard-Time Empty-Bottle Blues Part 2	3:05
A8 – Hard-Time Empty-Bottle Blues Part 3	1:34
A9 – Hard-Time Empty-Bottle Blues Part 4	2:23
B1 – House of the Rising Sun / Nightmare	19:09
B2 – Juana / Guitar Lamento	17:06
B3 – Red Rocking Chair	9:26
B4 – Song for Sara	6:20
B5 – Son House/Marilyn/My Prayer/Mood Indigo	21:05

Recording Dates: same as LP #1
Booklet: (x2) by David Fricke, Byron Coley, David Grubbs, Jason Gross, and John Fahey.
Producer: Jeff Hunt, Kris Johnson
Of note: (1) The jewel-cased CDs come in a card dust jacket. (2) The UPC code on the card dust jacket is: 600401018521.

ADDENDUM

#1

Release date: 2006
Edition: 1st issue
Record company: Vanguard
Catalog number: 942-2
Format: promo CD
Cover: white
Cover credit: **Disc label**: black

Songs: version #1 (5)
1 – Commemorative Transfiguration & Communion at Magruder Park 6:04
2 – When the Catfish is in Bloom   7:43
3 – Requiem for John Hurt   5:10
4 – The Singing Bridge of Memphis, Tennessee   2:54
Recording Dates: Tracks 2 and 3 are from *Requia* (1967); tracks 1 and 4 are from *The Yellow Princess* (1968).
Liner notes: none
Mastering:
Producer:
Of note: (1) This promotional CD contains the original Fahey recordings of four of the songs that appear on the Vanguard tribute album *I Am The Resurrection* from 2006. (2) Track 5 is "Night Train of Valhalla" played by Immerglück, Kaphan, Krummenacher, & Hanes.

VANGUARD VISIONARIES:
JOHN FAHEY

#1

Release date: 2007
Edition: 1st issue
Record company: Vanguard
Catalog number: 73160-2
Format: CD
Cover: Fahey with guitar
Cover credit: Melvin Lyons   Disc label: green

Songs: version #1 (10)
1 – Lion	5:10
2 – March! For Martin Luther King	3:43
3 – Requiem For John Hurt	5:08
4 – Dance of the Inhabitants of the Invisible City of Bladensburg	4:10
5 – The Yellow Princess	4:53
6 – Irish Setter	7:17
7 – Requiem For Molly (Part 1)	7:40
8 – Requiem For Molly (Part 2)	7:46
9 – Requiem For Molly (Part 3)	2:32
10 – Requiem For Molly (Part 4)	2:56

Recording Dates: 1967-1968
Liner notes: none
Mastering:
Producer: Vince Hans
Of note: (1) This is a sampler compilation including selected songs from *Requia* [tracks 3, 7-10] and *The Yellow Princess* [tracks 1, 2, 4-6].
(2) The UPC code on the back cover is: 015707316026.

TWILIGHT ON PRINCE GEORGES AVENUE

#1

Release date: 2009
Edition: 1st issue
Record company: Rounder
Catalog number: 11661-9093-2
Format: CD
Cover: Fahey in green
Cover credit: DeeAnn Hall and Martin Spreafico.

Disc label: blue

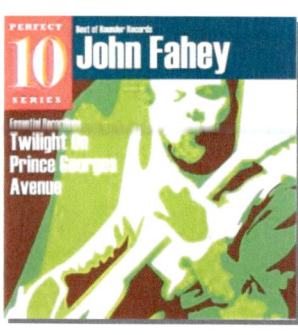

Songs: version #1 (10)
1 – The Thing At The End Of New Hampshire Avenue	3:29
2 – Atlantic High	2:06
3 – Dianne Kelly	7:40
4 – A Minor Blues	4:39
5 – Black Mommy	8:04
6 – Sunset On Prince George's County	4:13
7 – Twilight On Prince Georges Avenue	4:06
8 – Rain Forest	6:44
9 – Improv In E Minor	7:27
10 – Love On Waikiki	2:16

Recording Dates: 1983-1990
Liner notes: none
Mastering: Matt Azevedo at M-Works.
Producer: Dave Godowsky
Of note: (1) This is a selection of tunes previously released on Varrick Records:
- Tracks 5 and 6 are from *Let Go*.
- Tracks 2 and 8 are from *Rain Forests, Oceans and Other Themes*.
- Tracks 4, 9 and 10 are from *I Remember Blind Joe Death*.
- Tracks 1, 3 and 7 are from *Old Girlfriends and Other Horrible Memories*.
(2) The UPC code on the back cover is: 011661909328.

LIVE AT STUDIO KAFE

#1

Release date: 2010
Edition: 1st issue
Label: Jackalope Records
Format: mp3 digital download
Jacket cover: n/a

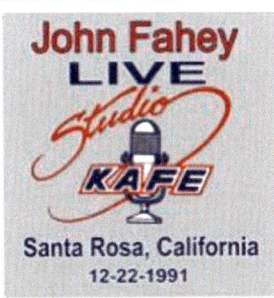

Songs: version #1 (14)

1 – O' Holy Night	5:49
2 – Twilight On Prince George Avenue	7:43
3 – Steamboat Gwine 'Round De Bend	3:07
4 – Silent Night	2:23
5 – Blues Medley	3:32
6 – Poor Boy Long Ways From Home	6:45
7 – O Little Town Of Bethlehem / Jingle Bells	4:42
8 – The Great Eight	6:19
9 – 1950's Medley: Blueberry Hill / Sea Of Love	15:55
10 – Dorothy (part two)	7:25
11 – It Came Upon The Midnight Clear / What Child Is This	5:14
12 – Irish Christmas Medley	4:40
13 – Dorothy	3:35
14 – Auld Lang Syne	8:01

Recording Dates: December 22, 1991, Studio KAFE, Santa Rosa, California.
Liner notes: none
Producer:
Of note: (1) The album was made available for digital download from the internet.

SOME SUNNY DAY

#1

Release date: 2010
Edition: 1st issue
Record company: One Media Publishing / Vanilla OMP
Format: mp3 digital download

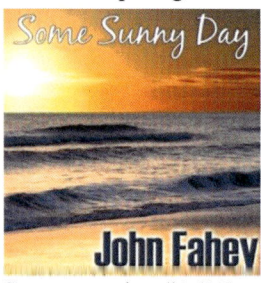

Songs: version #1 (15)
1 – Some Summer Day	3:18
2 – Dance Of The Inhabitants Of The Palace Of King Philip XIV Of Spain	1:26
3 – I'm Gonna Do All I Can For My Lord	1:25
4 – When the Spring Comes Again	2:46
5 – In Christ There Is No East Or West	2:44
6 – Spanish Two Step	2:18
7 – On the Sunny Side of the Ocean	3:49
8 – Poor Boy a Long Way from Home	2:19
9 – Spanish Dance	3:30
10 – Give Me Corn Bread When I'm Hungry	3:09
11 – St Louis Blues	2:28
12 – Sunflower Blues	3:22
13 – Revolt of the Dyke Brigade	3:00
14 – Take a Look at That Baby	1:35
15 – The Last Steam Engine Train	2:17

Recording Dates: see page 130
Liner notes: none
Producer:
Of note: (1) The album was made available for digital download from the internet. (2) It is a compilation with, allegedly, all the tracks from *The Best of John Fahey 1959-1977*. However, the sequence of the songs is: 11, 3, 3, 5, 5, 6, 7, 15, 1, 10, 8, 12, 13, 14, 15. Thus, songs 2, 4 and 9 are missing.

THE GUITAR MASTERS COLLECTION: JOHN FAHEY

#1

Release date: 2011
Edition: 1st issue
Record company: One Media Publishing / Vanilla OMP
Format: mp3 digital download

Songs: version #1 (15)

1 – Dance Of The Inhabitants Of The Palace Of King Philip XIV Of Spain	1:26
2 – Sunflower Blues	3:22
3 – Poor Boy a Long Way from Home	2:19
4 – On the Sunny Side of the Ocean	3:49
5 – Some Summer Day	3:18
6 – In Christ There Is No East Or West	2:44
7 – The Last Steam Engine Train	2:17
8 – I'm Gonna Do All I Can For My Lord	1:25
9 – Spanish Two Step	2:18
10 – St Louis Blues	2:28
11 – Take a Look at That Baby	1:35
12 – Revolt of the Dyke Brigade	3:00
13 – Give Me Corn Bread When I'm Hungry	3:09
14 – Spanish Dance	3:30
15 – When the Spring Comes Again	2:46

Recording Dates: see page 130.
Liner notes: none
Producer:
Of note: (1) The album is available for digital download from the internet. (2) This is another compilation with, allegedly, all the tracks from *The Best of John Fahey 1959-1977*. The sequence of the songs is actually: 8, 2, 7, 4, 10, 6, 7, 8, 9, 3, 11, 12, 13, 5, 6. Thus, songs 1, 14 and 15 are missing.

PICK IT BABY
(THE DAVE CASH COLLECTION)

#1

Release date: 2011
Edition: 1st issue
Record company: One Media Publishing / Vanilla OMP
Format: mp3 digital download

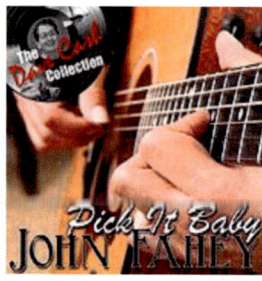

Songs: version #1 (15)
1 – Dance Of The Inhabitants Of The Palace Of King Philip XIV Of Spain	1:26
2 – Give Me Corn Bread When I'm Hungry	3:09
3 – I'm Gonna Do All I Can For My Lord	1:25
4 – In Christ There Is No East Or West	2:44
5 – On the Sunny Side of the Ocean	3:49
6 – Poor Boy a Long Way from Home	2:19
7 – Revolt of the Dyke Brigade	3:00
8 – Some Summer Day	3:18
9 – Spanish Dance	3:30
10 – Spanish Two Step	2:18
11 – St Louis Blues	2:28
12 – Sunflower Blues	3:22
13 – Take a Look at That Baby	1:35
14 – The Last Steam Engine Train	2:17
15 – When the Spring Comes Again	2:46

Recording Dates: see page 130.
Liner notes: none
Producer:
Of note: (1) The album is available for digital download from the internet. (2) This is yet another compilation with, allegedly, all the tracks from *The Best of John Fahey 1959-1977*. The sequence of the songs is actually: 3, 2, 3, 4, 5, 14, 7, 11, 8, 10, 6, 12, 13, 14, 4. Thus, titles 1, 9 and 15 are missing.

JOHN FAHEY CONCERT
THE GREAT AMERICAN MUSIC HALL

#1

Release date: 2011
Edition: 1st issue
Record company: Wolfgang's Vault
Format: mp3 or FLAC digital download

Songs: version #1 (11)
1 – Tuning	0:58
2 – Christ's Saints of God Fantasy / Stomping Tonight on the Pennsylvania/Alabama Border / In Christ There Is No East Or West / Beverly	17:04
3 – Death of the Clayton Peacock / Steamboat Gwine 'Round De Bend / How Green Was My Valley	9:31
4 – tuning	0:52
5 – Revolt of the Dyke Brigade / Requiem for Mississippi John Hurt	8:24
6 – Tuning	1:13
7 – Red Pony	4:32
8 – tuning	0:26
9 – Knoxville Blues	3:18
10 – tuning / ambience	1:33
11 – Lion	7:23

Recording Dates: August 8, 1975, at *The Great American Music Hall*, San Francisco, California.
Liner notes: none
Producer:
Of note: (1) The album was made available for digital download from the internet. (2) It was later added to the Wolfgang Concert Vault series.

YOUR PAST COMES BACK TO HAUNT YOU
(THE FONOTONE YEARS 1958-1965)

#1
Release date: 2011
Edition: 1st issue (label #1, jacket #1, songs #1)
Catalog number: Dust-to-Digital   DTD-21
Format: CD (x5) + book
Box cover: 1st
   - **Front cover**: John Fahey with Bacon & Day guitar
Cover credit: **Disc labels**: pictures of Fahey

Songs: version #1 (22+21+22+20+30)
DISC ONE
1 – Interview with John Fahey on Fonotone Records and Joe Bussard   2:59
2 – Franklin Blues   3:16
3 – Smoketown Strut   3:15
4 – Steel Guitar Rag   3:25
5 – Takoma Park Pool Hall Blues   3:32
6 – Buck Dancer's Choice   3:19
7 – Medley: Pretty Polly / Shortnin' Bread   3:41
8 – Barbara Namkin Blues   3:13
9 – In Christ There Is No East or West   3:57
10 – Stak 'o Lee Blues [Louis Collins]   3:25
11 – The Transcendental Waterfall   3:02
12 – John Henry   3:10
13 – Over The Hill Blues   3:57
14 – St. Louis Blues   4:06
15 – On Doing an Evil Deed Blues   3:29
16 – Reinumeration Blues   2:08
17 – The Transcendental Waterfall   5:10
18 – Mississippi Boweavil Blues   2:47
19 – Green River Blues   2:59

20 – Over the Hill Blues 2:45
21 – Libba's Rag 3:08
22 – Chris's Rag 3:15

DISC TWO
1 – St. Louis Tickle 3:12
2 – Pat Sullivan's Blues 3:25
3 – Blind Blues [Martin's Esso Blues] 2:42
4 – Poor Boy Blues 3:37
5 – Long Time Town Blues 3:29
6 – Gulf Port Island Blues 3:32
7 – Blind Thomas Blues Part 1 3:21
8 – Blind Thomas Blues Part 2 3:24
9 – New Newport News Blues #2 2:56
10 – Wanda Russell's Blues 3:21
11 – Going Away to Leave You Blues 3:14
12 – Lay My Burden Down 2:28
13 – Hill High Blues 3:07
14 – John Henry 2:55
15 – Paint Brush Blues 3:19
16 – Blind Thomas Blues Part 3 3:12
17 – Blind Thomas Blues Part 4 3:30
18 – You Gonna Need Somebody on Your Bond 3:01
19 – Jesus Gonna Make Up My Dyin' Bed 3:11
20 – Banty Rooster Blues 3:14
21 – Tom Rushen Blues 3:36

DISC THREE
1 – Yallaboosha River Blues 3:43
2 – You Gonna Miss Me 3:21
3 – Wissenschaftlich River Blues Part 1 3:17
4 – Wissenschaftlich River Blues Part 2 3:29
5 – Zekiah Swamp Blues 3:25
6 – Nobody's Business 3:12
7 – Going Crabbing Talking Blues Part 1 3:09
8 – Going Crabbing Talking Blues Part 2 3:16
9 – You Better Get Right So God Can Use You 3:28
10 – Weissman Blues 3:06
11 – Dasein River Blues 3:13
12 – Racemic Tartrate River Blues Part 1 3:11
13 – Racemic Tartrate River Blues Part 2 3:13
14 – Smoky Ordinary Blues [Dance of the Inhabitants] 3:01
15 – I Shall Not Be Moved 3:07
16 – Old Country Rock 3:12
17 – Little Hat Blues 3:19

18 – Guitar Solo Title Unknown [Revelation on the Banks of the Pawtuxent]   2:57
19 – Guitar Solo Title Unknown [Night Train to Valhalla]   3:27
20 – Some Summer Day   5:45
21 – The Langley Two-Step   1:37
22 – Dream of the Origin of the French Broad River   2:53

DISC FOUR
1 – Saint John's Hornpipe   1:12
2 – Sail Away Ladies   1:17
3 – Dreaming Under the B & O Trestle   3:20
4 – 900 Miles   4:37
5 – Prince George's Dance   3:00
6 – Improvisation for Flute and Guitar   3:34
7 – Dorothy / Calvert Street Blues [Brenda's Blues]   1:41
8 – Brenda's Blues   0:47
9 – Buck Dancer's Choice   1:29
10 – Night Train to Valhalla   4:22
11 – In the Pines   2:49
12 – Pretty Polly   3:31
13 – Take This Hammer   4:10
14 – Yazoo Basin Blues   6:38
15 – Stomping Tonight on the (Old) Pennsylvania / Alabama Border   3:47
16 – Smoky Ordinary Blues [Dance of the Inhabitants]   2:22
17 – Revelation on the Banks of the Pawtuxent   3:17
18 – Bean Vine Blues [Pea Vine Blues]   2:18
19 – Green Blues   2:47
20 – Stone Pony   2:50

DISC FIVE
1 – Dorothy / Calvert Street Blues [Brenda's Blues]   0:57
2 – Days Have Gone By   3:11
3 – Some Summer Day   3:47
4 – Texas & Pacific Blues [My Bucket's Got a Hole In It]   2:10
5 – John Henry Blues   2:38
6 – Brenda's Blues   1:50
7 – St. Patrick's Hymn   1:52
8 – Bicycle Built for Two   1:24
9 – The Blues You Saved For Me   1:35
10 – House Carpenter   1:31
11 – How Long   2:26
12 – The Portland Cement Factory at Monolith, California   4:33
13 – You Take The E Train [The Last Steam Engine Train]   2:34
14 – I Sing a Song of the Saints of God   3:14
15 – How Long   2:11
16 – O Jesus I Have Promised   3:07

17 – Untitled	1:09
18 – Medley: Untitled / O Jesus I Have Promised	3:24
19 – I Am a Rake and Rambling Boy	1:46
20 – Medley: Goodbye Old Paint / Whoopee Ti-Yi-Yo, Git Along Little Doggies	1:26
21 – Goodbye Old Paint	1:01
22 – Simple Gifts	0:53
23 – Untitled	1:38
24 – Bury Me Not On the Lone Prairie	1:42
25 – Goodbye Old Paint	1:16
26 – Western Medley	6:01
27 – Durgan Park	2:07
28 – The Bitter Lemon	2:46
29 – Old Southern Medley (Fragment)	0:13
30 – Bottleneck Blues	2:59

Recording Dates: 1958-1965
Liner notes: (12" x 12" hardcover book with 88 pages), by Glenn Jones, Malcolm Kirton, Claudio Guerrieri, R. Anthony Lee, Douglas Blazek, Byron Coley, and Eddie Dean.
Producer: Dean Blackwood, Glenn Jones, and Steven Lance Ledbetter.
Of note: (1) Issued as a limited 1st edition of 2500. (2) Tracks CD3 #20 and CD4 #15 are switched. Tracks CD4 #15 and CD5 #3 are identical. (3) The UPC code on the sticker is: 880226002121.

#2

Release date: 2011 (Japan)
Edition: 1st issue (label #1, jacket #1, songs #1)
Record company: P-Vine
Catalog number: PCD-17510
Format: CD (x5) + book

#3

Release date: 2012
Edition: 2nd issue (label #1, jacket #2, songs #2)
Catalog number: Dust-to-Digital   DTD-21
Format: CD (x5) + book
Box cover: 2nd
  - **Front cover:**
Cover credit:
Disc labels: pictures of Fahey

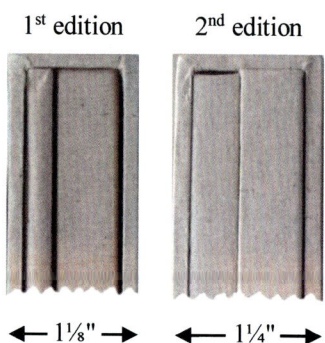

1st edition   2nd edition

← 1⅛" →   ← 1¼" →

Songs: version #1 (22+21+22+20+30)
Recording Dates: 1958-1965
Liner notes: (12" x 12" hardcover book with 88 pages), by Glenn Jones, Malcolm Kirton, Claudio Guerrieri, R. Anthony Lee, Douglas Blazek, Byron Coley, and Eddie Dean.
Producer: Dean Blackwood, Glenn Jones, and Steven Lance Ledbetter.
Of note: (1) This 2nd edition can be recognized by the flat spine of the CD holder as opposed to the rounded and thinner spine of the 1st edition, and the overall width of the slipcase is wider at 1¼" instead of 1⅛" (see image above). (2) The minor inaccuracies present in the 1st edition of the book have been corrected, and the CD track mixups have been fixed.

THE DEFINITIVE JOHN FAHEY

#1

Release date: 2012
Edition: 1st issue
Record company: One Media Publishing / Vanilla OMP
Format: mp3 digital download

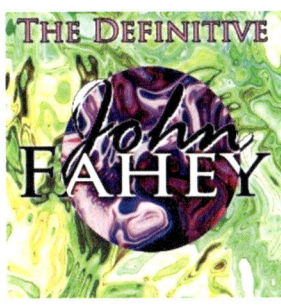

Songs: version #1 (15)
1 – On the Sunny Side of the Ocean	3:49
2 – Spanish Dance	3:30
3 – When the Spring Comes Again	2:46
4 – Dance Of The Inhabitants Of The Palace Of King Philip XIV Of Spain	1:26
5 – In Christ There Is No East Or West	2:44
6 – St Louis Blues	2:28
7 – Some Summer Day	3:18
8 – Revolt of the Dyke Brigade	3:00
9 – Take a Look at That Baby	1:35
10 – Give Me Corn Bread When I'm Hungry	3:09
11 – Sunflower Blues	3:22
12 – Poor Boy a Long Way from Home	2:19
13 – I'm Gonna Do All I Can For My Lord	1:25
14 – The Last Steam Engine Train	2:17
15 – Spanish Two Step	2:18

Recording Dates:
Liner notes: none
Producer:
Of note: (1) The album is available for digital download from the internet. (2) This is yet another compilation with, allegedly, all the tracks from *The Best of John Fahey 1959-1977*. The sequence of the songs is actually: 1, 11, 5, 9, 5, 12, 6, 8, 13, 10, 6, 14, 9, 14, 15. Thus, titles 2, 3 and 4 are missing. (3) Notice the curious titles of tracks 3 and 11.

THE TRANSCENDENTAL WATERFALL
GUITAR EXCURSIONS (1962-1967)

#1

Release date: 2012
Edition: 1st issue
Record company: 4 Men With Beards
Format: 12" LP (x6), 33⅓ rpm, box set
Jacket cover: Fahey with guitar

Songs: version #1 (11+12+11+7+15+11)
Recording Dates:
Liner notes: Samuel Charters
Producer:
Of note: (1) This 6-LP box set is a re-issue of John Fahey's first six albums *Blind Joe Death, Death Chants, Dance of Death, The Great San Bernardino Birthday Party, The Transfiguration of Blind Joe Death* and *Days Have Gone By*. It is a limited edition of 2000 numbered copies. The records are made of 180 gm vinyl and are accompanied by facsimiles of the original booklets. The set also includes a T-shirt, a poster, liner notes, and a postcard. (2) The S-##### matrix number of the six records suggests that they were mastered in 2010 and pressed by Rainbo Records in Canoga Park, California. (3) Note that the record labels all have a small stamper ring measuring 1¼" in diameter. (4) The details of the six records are as follows:

TW #1

Album Title: Blind Joe Death
Release date: 2012
Catalog number: 4m201
Format: 12" LP, 33⅓ rpm, stereo
Jacket cover: *replica* of Blue with woodcut design
  - **Front cover**: blue, woodcut design, red lettering
  - **Spine**: JOHN FAHEY • BLIND JOE DEATH   4m201
  - **Back cover**: *no* Takoma catalogue;
            4 Men with Beards logo on bottom left;
            black lettering on grey background in left upper corner.
Cover credit: Tom Weller
Label: *replica* of a Da^{2S} label

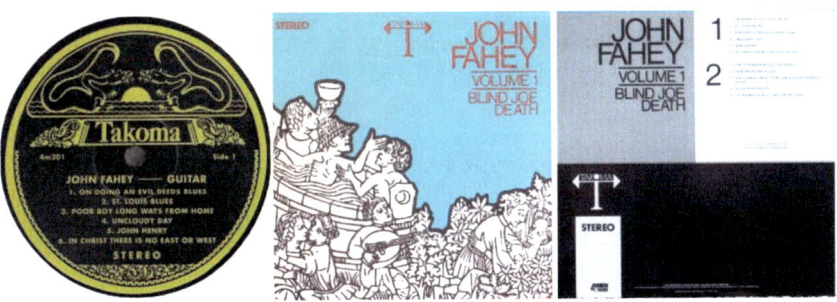

Matrix #: 4M-201 A1 RE2   S-74291 RE-1
         4M-201 B1 RE2   S-74292 RE-1
Songs: version BJD-3b (6+5)

A1 – On Doing An Evil Deeds Blues	3:56
A2 – St. Louis Blues	3:15
A3 – Poor Boy Long Ways From Home	2:23
A4 – Uncloudy Day	2:22
A5 – John Henry	2:05
A6 – In Christ There Is No East Or West	2:43
B1 – The Transcendental Waterfall	6:30
B2 – Desperate Man Blues	3:58
B3 – Sun Gonna Shine In My Back Door Some Day Blues	4:36
B4 – Sligo River Blues	2:33
B5 – I'm Gonna Do All I Can For My Lord	1:24

Recording Dates: same as BJD #7.
Booklet: yes (a 6" x 9" replica of the original 2nd version; but without the printer's union logo on the last page).
Of note: (1) The label resembles a Da^{2S} type of Takoma label. (2) "On Doing An Evil Deed Blues" contains the word <u>Deeds</u> instead of <u>Deed</u> in the title.

TW #2

Album Title: Death Chants, Breakdowns and Military Waltzes
Release date: 2012
Catalog number: 4m202
Format: 12" LP, 33⅓ rpm, mono
Jacket cover: *replica* of 1st B&W version (BW)
  - **Front cover**: title in black script lettering on white background
  - **Spine**: JOHN FAHEY • DEATH CHANTS BREAKDOWNS AND MILITARY WALTZES   4m202
  - **Back cover**: blank, except for "4 Men with Beards" logo on bottom center.
Cover credit: none given
Label: *replica* of a BL label

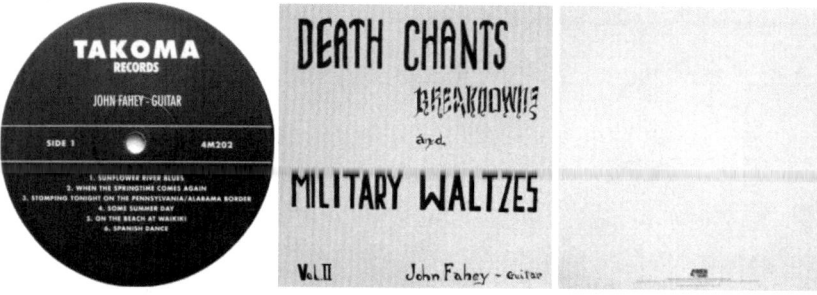

Matrix #: 4M-202 A   S-74293
             4M-202 B   S-74294
Songs: version DC-1a

A1 – Sunflower River Blues	2:33
A2 – When the Springtime Comes Again	3:50
A3 – Stomping Tonight on the Pennsylvania/Alabama Border	6:58
A4 – Some Summer Day	3:20
A5 – On the Beach at Waikiki	2:55
A6 – Spanish Dance	1:53
B1 – John Henry Variations	5:40
B2 – The Downfall of the Adelphi Rolling Grist Mill	3:35
B3 – Take A Look At That Baby	1:25
B4 – Dance of the Inhabitants of the Palace of King Phillip XIV of Spain	2:28
B5 – America	7:52
B6 – Episcopal Hymn	1:10

Recording Dates: same as DC #1
Booklet: yes (a 6¾" x 10½" replica of the original 1st version).

TW #3

Album Title: Dance of Death & Other Plantation Favorites
Catalog number: 4m203
Format: 12" LP, 33⅓ rpm, mono
Jacket cover: *replica* of B&W version
 - **Front cover**: black letters on white background.
 - **Spine**: JOHN FAHEY•DANCE OF DEATH & PLANTATION FAVORITES   4m203
 - **Back cover**: Produced by Ed Denson;
       no union logo;
       "4 Men with Beards" logo in upper right corner.
Cover credit: none given
Label: *replica* of a BS label

 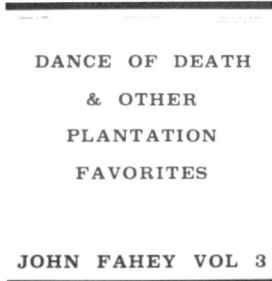 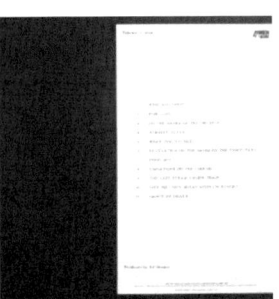

Matrix #: 4M-203 A1   S-74295
          4M-203 B1   S-74296
Songs: version DOD-2 (5+6)
A1 – Wine and Roses   3:24
A2 – How Long   2:52
A3 – On The Banks of the Owchita   3:48
A4 – Worried Blues   2:20
A5 – What The Sun Said   10:08
    B1 – Revelation on the Banks of the Pawtuxent   2:31
    B2 – Poor Boy   3:14
    B3 – Variations on the Coocoo   3:56
    B4 – The Last Steam Engine Train   2:14
    B5 – Give Me Corn Bread When I'm Hungry (*short version*) 3:08
    B6 – Dance of Death   7:35
Recording Dates: same as DOD #1.
Booklet: yes (a 7" x 10" replica of the original 3rd version; but without the two pages of the "Notes on the Songs").

TW #4

Album Title: The Great San Bernardino Birthday Party and Other Excursions
Catalog number: 4m204
Format: 12" LP, 33⅓ rpm, mono
Jacket cover: *replica* of 4th version
  - **Front cover**: red, "T" logo, <u>no</u> black border.
  - **Spine**: JOHN FAHEY • THE GREAT SAN BERNADINO BIRTHDAY PARTY AND OTHER EXCURSIONS   4m204
  - **Back cover**: Map, dark yellow; "4 Men with Beards" logo in lower left corner.
Cover credit: David Goines
Label: *replica* of a BL label

 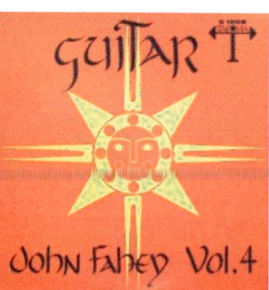 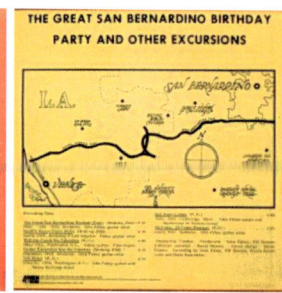

Matrix #: 4M-204 A1 RE2   S-74297
          4M-204 B1   S-74298
Songs: version #1 (2+5)

A1 – The Great San Bernardino Birthday Party	19:00
A2 – Knott's Berry Farm Molly	4:30
B1 – Will The Circle Be Unbroken	5:40
B2 – Guitar Excursion into the Unknown	3:30
B3 – 900 Miles	4:00
B4 – Sail Away Ladies	6:00
B5 – Oh Come. Oh Come Emmanuel	1:55

Recording Dates: same as GSBBP #1
Booklet: yes (a 6½" x 8½" replica of the original version; but without the printer's union logo on the last page).
Of note: (1) "Oh Come. Oh Come Emmanuel" contains a period instead of a comma in the title. On the jacket spine, the word "Bernardino" is lacking the second "r."

TW #5

Album Title: The Transfiguration of Blind Joe Death
Catalog number: 4m205
Format: 12" LP, 33⅓ rpm, mono
Jacket cover: *replica* of the 7th version
 - **Front cover**: green, Takoma dragon logo
 - **Spine**: JOHN FAHEY • THE TRANSFIGURATION OF BLIND JOE DEATH   4m205
 - **Back cover**: "4 Men with Beards" logo in upper right corner; Takoma dragon logo in bottom center.
Cover credit: David Omar White
Label: *replica* of a Do[1] label, but with a white instead of gold background

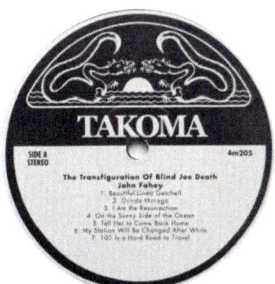 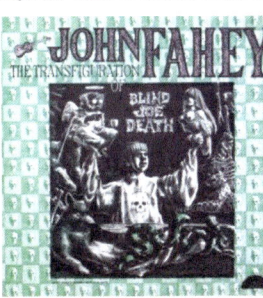 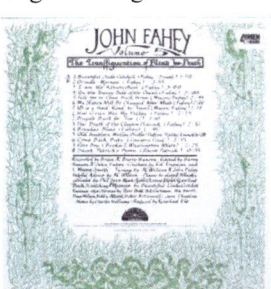

Matrix #: 4M-205 A   S-74361
    4M-205 B1   S-74362
Songs: version #1 (7+8)

A1	Beautiful Linda Getchell	1:50
A2	Orinda-Moraga	3:55
A3	I Am The Resurrection	3:00
A4	On The Sunny Side Of The Ocean	3:00
A5	Tell Her To Come Back Home	2:45
A6	My Station Will Be Changed After While	2:02
A7	101 Is A Hard Road To Travel	2:17
B1	How Green Was My Valley	2:15
B2	Bicycle Built For Two	1:10
B3	The Death Of The Clayton Peacock	2:52
B4	Brenda's Blues	1:45
B5	Old Southern Medley	6:08
B6	Come Back Baby	2:15
B7	Poor Boy	2:25
B8	Saint Patrick's Hymn	0:55

Recording Dates: same as TOBJD #1
Booklet: yes (a 8½" x 11" replica of the original version)
Of note: (1) The label says "stereo," but the record is monaural.

TW #6

Album Title: Days Have Gone By
Catalog number: 4m206
Format: 12" LP, 33⅓ rpm, stereo
Jacket cover: *replica* of the 5th version
  - **Front cover**: red-brown lettering; brown-tinted photograph; <u>no</u> black border.
  - **Spine**: JOHN FAHEY • DAYS HAVE GONE BY   4m206
  - **Back cover**: "4 Men with Beards" logo in upper left corner; Jeff Lovelace; <u>no</u> black border.
Cover credit: Tom Weller / Jeff Lovelace / Paul Kagan
Label: *replica* of a Da^{3S} label

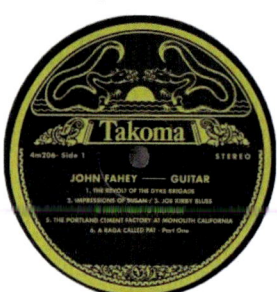  

Matrix #: 4M-206 A1   S-74363
             4M-206 B2   S-74364 RE-1
Songs: version #1 (6+5)

A1 – The Revolt Of The Dyke Brigade	2:38
A2 – Impressions Of Susan	5:05
A3 – Joe Kirby Blues	3:08
A4 – Night Train To Valhalla	2:14
A5 – The Portland Cement Factory At Monolith California	4:23
A6 – A Raga Called Pat - part one	6:22
B1 – A Raga Called Pat - part two	8:06
B2 – My Sheperd Will Supply My Needs	8:48
B3 – My Grandfather's Clock	1:27
B4 – Days Have Gone By	2:51
B5 – We Would Be Building	1:57

Recording Dates: same as DHGB #1
Booklet: yes (a 9¼" x 10½" replica of the original 1st version; but with black lettering).
Of note: (1) On the label, the word "Factory" of track A5 is correctly spelled, but the word "Shepherd" of track B2 is lacking the second "h."

CHRISTMAS SOLI

#1

Release date: 2013
Edition: 1st issue
Catalog number: FAN-34805
Record company: Fantasy
Format: CD
Cover: three camels   **Disc label**: red

Cover credit: Tom Weller
Songs: version #1 (14)
1 – Joy To The World	1:55
2 – Medley: Hark, The Herald Angels Sing / O, Come All Ye Faithful	3:15
3 – We Three Kings Of Orient Are	1:53
4 – God Rest Ye Merry Gentlemen Fantasy	2:48
5 – Auld Lang Syne	2:06
6 – Oh Holy Night	3:31
7 – Christmas Medley: Oh, Tannenbaum / Angels We Have Heard On High / Jingle Bells	3:34
8 – Carol Of The Bells	2:41
9 – The First Noel	3:54
10 – It Came Upon A Midnight Clear	3:00
11 – Silent Night, Holy Night	3:14
12 – Santa Claus Is Coming To Town	2:42
13 – Medley: Deck The Halls With Boughs Of Holly / We Wish You A Merry Christmas	3:19
14 – The Christmas Song	2:25

Recording Dates: see below
Liner notes: no
Producer: Chris Clough
Of note: (1) Tracks 1-5 are from *The New Possibility* (reissued on TAKCD-8912-2); tracks 6-8 from *Christmas with John Fahey, Volume II* (reissued on TAKCD-8912-2); tracks 9-11 from *John Fahey Christmas Guitar, Volume One* (Varrick CD VR 002); and tracks 12-14 from *Popular Songs of Christmas & New Year's* (Varrick CD VR 012).

JOHN FAHEY CONCERT
AMAZINGRACE: 8/24/1974

Release date: 2013
Record company: Wolfgang's Vault
Format: mp3 or FLAC digital download
Songs: version #1 (4)

1 – Melody McBad / Fare Forward Voyagers	33:00
2 – Dance of the Inhabitants of the Palace of King Phillip XIV	17:00
3 – On the Sunny Side of the Ocean	4:30
4 – Spanish Two Step	2:40

Recording Dates: August 24, 1974, at the *Amazingrace Coffeehouse*, Evanston, Illinois.
Of note: (1) The album was made available for digital streaming from the internet at www.concertvault.com.

JOHN FAHEY CONCERT
THE GREAT AMERICAN MUSIC HALL
10/10/1974 – SET 1

Release date: 2013
Record company: Wolfgang's Vault
Format: mp3 or FLAC digital download
Songs: version #1 (6)

1 – Thus Krishna On The Battlefield	9:23
2 – Fare Forward Voyagers	17:15
3 – Dance of the Inhabitants of the Palace of King Phillip XIV	14:26
4 – Christmas Fantasy - Part 2	4:40
5 – On the Sunny Side of the Ocean / Lion / Hawaiian Two-Step	13:30
6 – Revolt of the Dyke Brigade	6:50

Recording Dates: October 10, 1974, at *The Great American Music Hall*, San Francisco, California.
Of note: (1) The album was made available for digital streaming from the internet at www.concertvault.com.

JOHN FAHEY CONCERT
THE GREAT AMERICAN MUSIC HALL
10/10/1974 - SET 2

Release date: 2013
Record company: Wolfgang's Vault
Format: mp3 or FLAC digital download
Songs: version #1 (6)
1 – Some Summer Day / Candy Man / Stomping Tonight On The Pennsylvania-Alabama Border / In Christ There Is No East Or West / Beverly   20:42
2 – Dance of the Inhabitants of the Palace of King Phillip XIV   13:59
3 – On the Sunny Side of the Ocean / Hawaiian Two-Step   7:11
4 – Thus Krishna On The Battlefield   5:34
5 – Melody McBad   5:00
6 – Revolt of the Dyke Brigade / Funeral Song For Mississippi John Hurt   6:30

Recording Dates: October 10, 1974, at *The Great American Music Hall*, San Francisco, California.
Of note: (1) The album can be heard at www.concertvault.com on the internet.

JOHN FAHEY CONCERT
AMAZINGRACE: 8/15/1975

Release date: 2013
Record company: Wolfgang's Vault
Format: mp3 or FLAC digital download
Songs: version #1 (4)
1 – Thus Krishna On The Battlefield / Fare Forward Voyagers   29:00
2 – Dance of the Inhabitants of the Palace of King Phillip XIV   15:00
3 – On the Sunny Side of the Ocean   6:05
4 – Revolt of the Dyke Brigade   4:00

Recording Dates: August 15, 1975, at the *Amazingrace Coffeehouse*, Evanston Illinois.
Of note: (1) The album was made available for digital streaming from the internet at www.concertvault.com.

JOHN FAHEY CONCERT
AMAZINGRACE: 8/16/1975

Release date: 2013
Record company: Wolfgang's Vault
Format: mp3 or FLAC digital download
Songs: version #1 (5)
1 – Some Summer Day / Candy Man / Stomping Tonight On The Pennsylvania-Alabama Border / In Christ There Is No East Or West / Beverly   23:25
2 – Dance of the Inhabitants of the Palace of King Phillip XIV   17:30
3 – Guitar Lamento ?   4:30
4 – On the Sunny Side of the Ocean / Hawaiian Two-Step / Lion   14:40
5 – Revolt of the Dyke Brigade / Requiem for Mississippi John Hurt   8:19
Recording Dates: August 16, 1975, at the *Amazingrace Coffeehouse*, Evanston Illinois.
Of note: (1) The album was made available for digital streaming from the internet at www.concertvault.com.

JOHN FAHEY CONCERT
THE GREAT AMERICAN MUSIC HALL 7/14/1976 – SET 1

Release date: 2013
Record company: Wolfgang's Vault
Format: mp3 or FLAC digital download
Songs: version #1 (6)
1 – Thus Krishna On The Battlefield / Fare Forward Voyagers   31:00
2 – Steamboat Gwine 'Round De Bend / The Death of the Clayton Peacock   17:04
3 – Mark 1:15   14:30
4 – Give Me Cornbread When I'm Hungry / On the Sunny Side of the Ocean / Spanish Two-Step (*guitar string breaks*)   6:00
5 – Spanish Two-Step (*reprise*)   3:00
6 – Lion   6:00
Recording Dates: September 14, 1976, at *The Great American Music Hall*, San Francisco, California.
Of note: (1) The album was made available for digital streaming from the internet at www.concertvault.com.

JOHN FAHEY CONCERT
THE GREAT AMERICAN MUSIC HALL
7/14/1976 - SET 2

Release date: 2013
Record company: Wolfgang's Vault
Format: mp3 or FLAC digital download
Songs: version #1 (6)
1 – I'll See You In My Dreams 0:43
2 – Stomping Tonight On The Pennsylvania-Alabama Border / In Christ
   There Is No East Or West / Beverly 17:40
3 – Dance of the Inhabitants of the Palace of King Phillip XIV 15:10
4 – Candy Man / Some Summer Day / Candy Man 6:00
5 – Sunflower River Blues / ? / Revolt of the Dyke Brigade / Funeral Song
   For Mississippi John Hurt 18:00
6 – ? 5:45

Recording Dates: September 14, 1976, at *The Great American Music Hall*, San Francisco, California.
Of note: (1) The album was made available for digital streaming from the internet at www.concertvault.com.

JOHN FAHEY CONCERT
THE GREAT AMERICAN MUSIC HALL
11/2/1976 - SET 2

Release date: 2013
Record company: Wolfgang's Vault
Format: mp3 or FLAC digital download
Songs: version #1 (7)
1 – Stomping Tonight on the Pennsylvania-Alabama Border / In Christ There Is
   No East Or West / Beverly 14:20
2 – Dance of the Inhabitants of the Palace of King Phillip XIV 13:20
3 – Some Summer Day 3:00
4 – Spanish Dance 2:40
5 – On the Sunny Side of the Ocean / Spanish Two-Step / Lion 11:00
6 – Sunflower River Blues / Revolt of the Dyke Brigade / Funeral Song
   For Mississippi John Hurt 9:00
7 – Melody McBad / Grand Finale 12:30

Recording Dates: November 2, 1976, at *The Great American Music Hall*, San Francisco, California.
Of note: (1) The album was made available for digital streaming from the internet at www.concertvault.com.

JOHN FAHEY CONCERT
THE GREAT AMERICAN MUSIC HALL
10/31/1979

Release date: 2013
Record company: Wolfgang's Vault
Format: mp3 or FLAC digital download
Songs: version #1 (8)

1 – On the Sunny Side of the Ocean / Spanish Two-Step	7:00
2 – Lion	6:00
3 – Steamboat Gwine 'Round De Bend / ?	5:55
4 – Poor Boy Long Ways From Home	4:00
5 – Approaching of the Disco Void	6:00
6 – Guitar Lamento	13:00
7 – ?	3:00
8 – ? / Stomping Tonight On The Pennsylvania-Alabama Border / In Christ There Is No East Or West	15:20

Recording Dates: October 31, 1979, at *The Great American Music Hall*, San Francisco, California.
Of note: (1) The album was made available for digital streaming from the internet at www.concertvault.com.

Several additional compilations of John Fahey songs have been issued in the last few years, all as internet downloads. These are anthologies containing material from various previously issued albums.

RAW COUNTRY BLUES 1958 / 1960 (78 RPMS)
Record company: Git It Records   **Format**: *mp3*   **Songs**: 21   **Release date**: 2010

JOY TO THE WORLD
Record company: Cugate ltd   **Format**: *mp3*   **Songs**: 14   **Release date**: 2012

OH HOLY NIGHT
Record company: Cugate ltd   **Format**: *mp3*   **Songs**: 7   **Release date**: 2012

THE LAST STEAM ENGINE TRAIN
Record company: Cugate ltd   **Format**: *mp3*   **Songs**: 11   **Release date**: 2012

NEW YORK CENTRAL
Record company: Cugate ltd   **Format**: *mp3*   **Songs**: 13   **Release date**: 2012

MASTERS OF THE LAST CENTURY: BEST OF JOHN FAHEY
Record company: Sinostate   **Format**: *mp3*   **Songs**: 24   **Release date**: 2014

Chapter 6
JOHN FAHEY DISCOGRAPHY
— COLLABORATIONS & COMPILATIONS WITH ORIGINAL MUSIC —

This section lists records where Fahey accompanies another artist with his guitar. It also includes records or tapes that include one or more tracks of original and never-before-issued compositions played by John Fahey.

CONTEMPORARY GUITAR

#1
Release date: 1967
Edition: 1st issue (label #1, jacket #1, songs #1)
Catalog number: C-1006
Format: 12" LP, 33⅓ rpm, stereo
Jacket cover: 1st
  - Front cover: purple; SPRING '67
  - Spine: CONTEMPORARY GUITAR   TAKOMA C-1006
  - Back cover: Takoma catalogue list up to C-1015
Cover credit: Tom Weller
Label: BL[6]

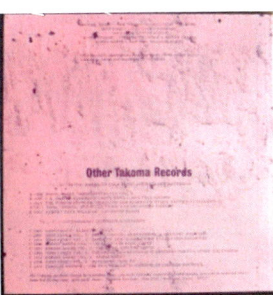

Matrix #: TAKOMA C 1006-A   4-66
         TAKOMA C 1006-B   SSL
Songs: version #1 (3+4)
A1 – Max Ochs: Raga
A2 – **John Fahey**: The Fahey Sampler   13:20
A3 – Bukka White: Old Man Walking Blues
  B1 – Max Ochs: Raga
  B2 – Harry Taussig: Water Verses
  B3 – Harry Taussig: Children's Dance
  B4 – Robbie Basho: The Thousand Incarnations of the Rose

Recording Dates: mastered in April 1966
Of note: (1) **Variant 1a** (label #1, jacket #2, songs #1) is a later issue with the 2nd jacket cover. (2) "The Fahey Sampler" would later be re-issued on CD in 2004 on *The Best of John Fahey, Vol 2:1964-1983*.

> The purple version of this album cover was an idea of Tom Weller. He had photographs of pebbles and stuff, and thought it would be cool to inlay one photo into another.

#2

Release date: 1968
Edition: 2nd issue (label #2, jacket #2, songs #1)
Catalog number: C-1006
Format: 12" LP, 33⅓ rpm, stereo
Jacket cover: 2nd
   - **Front cover**: Guitar missile launch center
   - **Spine**: CONTEMPORARY GUITAR   TAKOMA C-1006
   - **Back cover**: Takoma catalogue list up to C-1020.
Cover credit: Tom Weller
Label: BD[1]

Matrix #: TAKOMA C 1006-A   4-66
            TAKOMA C 1006-B   SSL
Songs: version #1 (3+4)
A1 – Max Ochs: Raga
A2 – **John Fahey**: The Fahey Sampler   13:20
A3 – Bukka White: Old Man Walking Blues
  B1 – Max Ochs: Raga
  B2 – Harry Taussig: Water Verses
  B3 – Harry Taussig: Children's Dance
  B4 – Robbie Basho: The Thousand Incarnations of the Rose
Recording Dates: mastered in April 1966
Of note: (1) The catalogue list on the back cover is correct up to C-1019 (released in 1968), but lists C-1020 as Jones & Hazleton's *One String Blues* which was actually released as C-1023 in 1969.

The front cover of the 2nd jacket of *Contemporaray Guitar* is a collage of images sampled and cropped from various sources.

The images, as numbered in the outline above, represent:
1. Harmony Sovereign Jumbo H1260 (acoustic flat-top guitar).
2. The refueling floor of the reactor at the country's first nuclear power plant located at Indian Point, NY.
3. Lunar Orbiter spacecraft built by Boeing for NASA.
4. Celestron 16 Schmidt-Cassegrain Telescope.
5. Bendix Laser/TOF Microprobe Mass Spectrometer.
6. Apparatus for the automatic synthesis of peptide chains: the programming unit (right) & glass vessels with amino acids (left and sideways).
7. Du Pont 900 Differential Thermal Analyzer.
8. Fluke 885 DC Differential Voltmeter.
9. LSSM (Local Scientific Survey Module) or "moon car" by Bendix.
10. same as 9.
11. Gaertner Ellipsometer.

The back cover shows a guitar with its arm substituted by an Apollo/Saturn V space rocket and its launch tower. The guitar's body is actually the same image of the guitar that Robbie Basho is holding as depicted on the back cover of his album *Basho Sings!* (Takoma C-1012) from 1967.

#3

Release date: 1969
Edition: 3rd issue (label #3, jacket #2, songs #1)
Catalog number: C-1006
Format: 12" LP, 33⅓ rpm, stereo
Jacket cover: 2nd
  - **Front cover**: Guitar missile launch center
  - **Spine**: CONTEMPORARY GUITAR   TAKOMA C-1006
  - **Back cover**: Takoma catalogue list up to C-1020.
Cover credit: Tom Weller
Label: O

Matrix #: TAKOMA C 1006-A   4-66
            TAKOMA C 1006-B   SSL
Songs: version #1 (3+4)
Recording Dates: mastered in April 1966

#4

Release date: 1977
Edition: 4th issue (label #4, jacket #2, songs #1)
Catalog number: C-1006
Format: 12" LP, 33⅓ rpm, stereo
Jacket cover: 2nd
  - **Front cover**: Guitar missile launch center
  - **Spine**: CONTEMPORARY GUITAR   TAKOMA C-1006
  - **Back cover**: Takoma catalogue list up to C-1020.
Cover credit: Tom Weller
Label: Da^{3S}

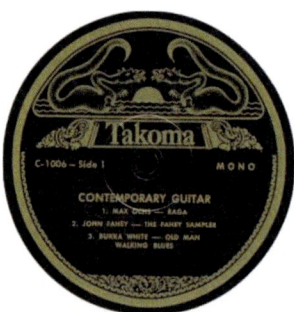

Matrix #: TAKOMA C 1006-A   4-66
            TAKOMA C 1006-B   SSL
Songs: version #1 (3+4)
Recording Dates: mastered in April 1966

Non-Takoma LP re-issue

#1
Release date: 2012
Record company: 4 Men With Beards
Catalog number: 4m226
Format: 12" LP, 33 1/3 rpm, stereo
Jacket cover: 2nd simile
- **Front cover**: Guitar missile launch center
- **Spine**: CONTEMPORARY GUITAR   4m226
- **Back cover**: *no* Takoma catalogue list;
    "4 Men with Beards" logo on bottom center.
Cover credit: Tom Weller
Label: Da^{S-G} simile

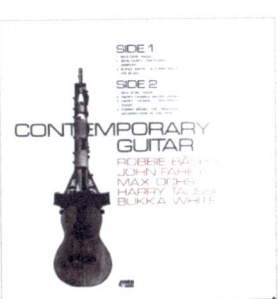

Matrix #: S-82821   4M-226 A1
             S-82822   4M-226 B1
Songs: version #1 (3+4)
A1 – Max Ochs: Raga
A2 – **John Fahey**: The Fahey Sampler   13:20
A3 – Bukka White: Old Man Walking Blues
   B1 – Max Ochs: Raga
   B2 – Harry Taussig: Water Verses
   B3 – Harry Taussig: Children's Dance
   B4 – Robbie Basho: The Thousand Incarnations of the Rose
Recording Dates: mastered in April 1966
Producer: none given
Of note: (1) This is a 180 gm issue. (2) The matrix number suggests that this album was mastered and pressed in 2012 by Rainbo Records in Canoga Park, California.
(3) The Da^{S-G}-variant label is a replica of a Dragon-Black Takoma label, except that it has the 4m226 catalogue number.
(4) The jacket is similar to the original jacket #2. However, the catalogue list on the back cover is no longer present.
(5) The UPC code on the sticker is: 646315122619.

TONY THOMAS:
OLD STYLE TEXAS & OKLAHOMA FIDDLIN'

#1
Release date: 1967
Edition: 1st issue (label #1, jacket #1, songs #1)
Catalog number: A-1013
Format: 12" LP, 33⅓ rpm, mono
Jacket cover: 1st
  - **Front cover**: Tony Thomas with guitar and horse.
  - **Spine**: TONY THOMAS   OLD-STYLE TEXAS AND OKLAHOMA FIDDLIN'   TAKOMA A 1013
  - **Back cover**: song listing.
Label: BL[8]

  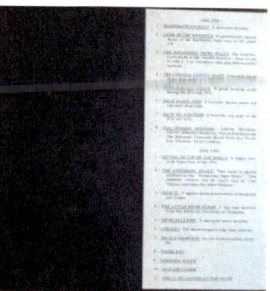

Matrix #: 1013-A
             1013-B
Songs: version #1 (15+11)

A4 – Carroll County Blues		1:30
A7 – Back Up And Push		1:35
B1 – Sitting On Top Of The World		2:17
B4 – The Little River Stomp		1:42
B6 – Chicken		0:59
B10 – Old Joe Clark		1:24

Recording Dates: December 18-19, 1966, in Hugo, Oklahoma
Booklet: by Graham Wickham and John Fahey
Producer: John Fahey and ED Denson
Of note: (1) John Fahey and Rod Thomas accompany Tony Thomas on fiddle as follows:

	Guitar	Hawaiian Guitar
Track A4:	John Fahey	Rod Thomas
" A7:	John Fahey	Rod Thomas
" B1:	Rod Thomas	John Fahey
" B4:	John Fahey	Rod Thomas
" B6:	John Fahey	Rod Thomas
" B10:	John Fahey	Rod Thomas

(2) The front cover photograph of Tony Thomas and his horse Comanche is not just a pose for the photographer. In fact, when the two would entertain a crowd, Tony would make his horse rear on his hind legs and then lie down. Taking his guitar, he would place one foot on the side of the resting animal and start to play the guitar and sing. (3) The front cover picture was reversed compared to the original in Tony's brochure.

#2
Release date: 1969
Edition: 2nd issue (label #2, jacket #1, songs #1)
Catalog number: A-1013
Format: 12" LP, 33⅓ rpm, mono
Jacket cover: 1st
  - **Front cover**: Tony Thomas with guitar and horse.
  - **Spine**: TONY THOMAS   OLD-STYLE TEXAS AND OKLAHOMA
         FIDDLIN'   TAKOMA A 1013
  - **Back cover**: song listing.
Label: O

Matrix #: 1013-A
         1013-B
Songs: version #1 (15+11)
A4 – Carroll County Blues   1:30
A7 – Back Up And Push   1:35
  B1 – Sitting On Top Of The World   2:17
  B4 – The Little River Stomp   1:42
  B6 – Chicken   0:59
  B10 – Old Joe Clark   1:24
Recording Dates: December 18-19, 1966, in Hugo, Oklahoma
Booklet: ?
Producer: John Fahey and ED Denson

#3
Release date: 1971
Edition: 3rd issue (label #3, jacket #1, songs #1)
Catalog number: A-1013
Format: 12" LP, 33⅓ rpm, mono
Jacket cover: 1st
  - **Front cover**: Tony Thomas with guitar and horse.
  - **Spine**: TONY THOMAS   OLD-STYLE TEXAS AND OKLAHOMA FIDDLIN'   TAKOMA A 1013
  - **Back cover**: song listing.
Label: Da²

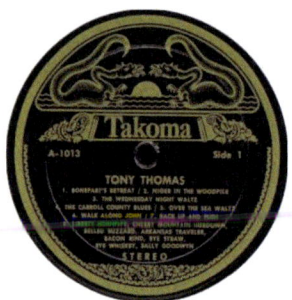

Matrix #: 1013-A
              1013-B
Songs: version #1 (15+11)

A4 – Carroll County Blues	1:30
A7 – Back Up And Push	1:35
B1 – Sitting On Top Of The World	2:17
B4 – The Little River Stomp	1:42
B6 – Chicken	0:59
B10 – Old Joe Clark	1:24

Recording Dates: December 18-19, 1966, in Hugo, Oklahoma
Booklet: by Graham Wickham and John Fahey
Producer: John Fahey and ED Denson

```
--#2   Sale Price   $5.00
Takoma 12" Lp of Oklahoma/Texas old-time fiddler Tony Thomas,
accomp. by Rod Thomas (Hawaiian acoustic guitar) & John Fahey,
straight acoustic guitar. An easy rival to the Clark Kessinger
records.  More than 20 selections, with lengthy notes.
```

Ad in a *Fahey & Fahey* auction list from 1967.

TONY THOMAS

Carrel "Tony" Thomas (1911-1997), a descendant from an old Virginia family dating back to Jamestown in 1610, was born near Afton in the northeast corner of Oklahoma and was the only son of five siblings. When he was six years old, his family moved to Hugo in two covered wagons. He was reared on a farm and completed 8th grade, after which he had to work on the farm to help support the family. His father, Emerson Baynard "Bert" Thomas (1881-1928) was a country fiddler who taught his son how to play the fiddle. Later, Tony also learned to fingerpick the guitar.

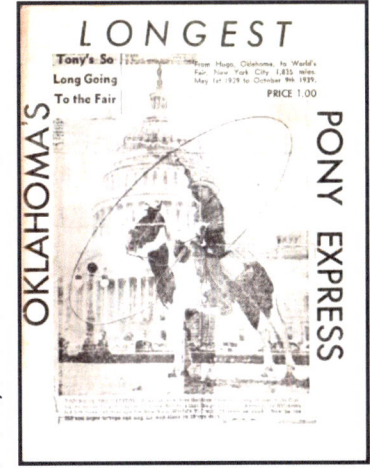

At age 29, the lanky, Gary Cooperish cowboy set off with 28 cents in his pocket on a 1,835 mile trek on horseback from Hugo, Oklahoma, to New York to participate in the 1939 World's Fair. The journey took him five months and nine days (May 1, 1939 to October 9, 1939). He rode his six-year-old, brown and white Pinto cow-pony Comanche. His guitar case was strapped to the right side of his saddle and a light suitcase on the other. Their road was the shoulder of various highways and on the way they stopped in every town to rest. Wearing a denim outfit, neckerchief, and cowboy boots made of kangaroo leather with jingling spurs, Tony would spin ropes, play the guitar and sing before a crowd, and then pass his broad-brimmed hat for contributions. He even taught his horse to pick up the hat and pass it around. Comanche lived to the venerable age of 29. In 1962 Tony published a 20-page illustrated brochure narrating this feat entitled *Oklahoma's Longest Pony Express*. Of his journey he said, "I've met with nothing but the best of treatment all the way along." The long trip had one setback in West Virginia when Tony received a letter from home informing him that his girlfriend had married somebody else.

Tony's dream was to capitalize on his accomplishment and hit it big in show business. All this ended with the beginning of World War II. On March 12, 1941, Thomas enlisted in the army, hoping to employ his horse-riding skills in a cavalry troop. He spent almost five years as a sergeant in the army. As a member of the U.S. Third Army, he went overseas for 16 months where he participated with his tank destroyer battalion in the Normandy campaign. He saw action in Northern France, the Ardennes, Rhineland and Central Europe. He was released from duty on November 20, 1945.

On his return to Hugo, the ex-GI turned to chicken farming, after absorbing logistic lessons from his military life. He later operated a saw-mill.

Besides playing fiddle Tony Thomas was renowned for his story-telling: folk tales, cowboy lore, jokes, etc. And dubbed as "The Fiddling Sawmiller," he contributed to a quarterly magazine column called "Old Timer's Tales."

When John Fahey was travelling in the South during the summer of 1966 with Nick Perls, he met Tony Thomas in Hugo, Oklahoma, in late July. He saw Tony practicing for Bob Bickett's radio show "Little Dixie Hayride" which was broadcast over local radio station KIHN. In September, Fahey returned to Hugo, this time to record Tony Thomas and the radio show for the UCLA Folklore Department with support from D. K. Wilgus. The recordings took place on September 22-24 and consisted of three days worth of tapes with playing by Tony, his nephew Rod, and others, including Fahey himself. Indeed, certain tracks listed on the tapes appear to be Fahey-related tunes:

<pre>
    John Henry
    Old Country Rock
    Uncloudy Day
    Take This Hammer
    The Last Steam Engine Train
</pre>

Some or all of these may well be Fahey guitar pieces, as yet to be heard. The recordings are on eight reels of tape and held in the UCLA Ethnomusicology Archives.

Tony Thomas & Rod Thomas

In December 1966, John Fahey and Barry Hansen went back to the area and, in addition to recording two other fiddlers, they spent two days (December 18-19) recording Tony Thomas on fiddle, his nephew Rod Thomas on Hawaiian guitar, and John Fahey on guitar. These tunes would be issued on Takoma as *Old Time Texas and Oklahoma Fiddlin'* (Takoma A-1013, 1967). The liner notes for this album were written by Fahey and Graham Wickham, and are remarkably thorough.

In 1967, Tony participated in the 10th Annual Berkeley Folk Music Festival. He played an evening concert on June 30; and afternoon and evening sets on July 2.

In the 1970s and '80s, Thomas continued to play the fiddle at family reunions, barn dances, honkytonks, contests, and nursing homes. By that time he could play up to 645 songs by memory. In 1971, Thomas also began to repair and construct fiddles. Each fiddle took about six weeks to make, and by 1985 he had completed 29 of them (one made from an apricot tree in his yard).

Tony Thomas passed away at the age of 85 on April 6, 1997, and was buried in Sawyer Cemetery (Sawyer, Oklahoma).

In addition to his record on Takoma, Thomas has another recording of fiddle music to his credit from the late 1970s: *Bring Two And Hurry* issued by the Prairiland Record Co. of Hugo, Oklahoma.

Sources for some Tony Thomas songs

"**Carroll County Blues**" is a fiddle blues tune by the fiddle and guitar duo Willie T. Narmour and Shell W. Smith (OKeh 45317) recorded on March 11, 1929, in Atlanta, Georgia. It is titled after Narmour's home county, Carroll County, located in the heart of the Mississippi River delta.

"**Back Up And Push**" is an old time fiddle tune by the famous band Gid Tanner and his Skillet Lickers from Georgia (Bluebird B-5562) recorded on March 24, 1934, in San Antonio, Texas.

"**Old Joe Clark**" is a Southern dance tune. One version was recorded by the fiddler Tommy Jackson (Mercury 6280) in February of 1950 in Cincinnati, Ohio.

CANNED HEAT
"LIVING THE BLUES"

#1
Release date: 1968
Edition: 1st issue
Record company: Liberty Records
Catalog number: LST-27200
Format: double 12" LP, 33⅓ rpm, stereo
Jacket cover: 1st - gatefold
  - Front cover: Canned Heat group
  - Spine: LST-27200   LIVING THE BLUES • CANNED HEAT   LIBERTY
  - Back cover: song titles
Cover credit: Peter Bernuth
Label: black

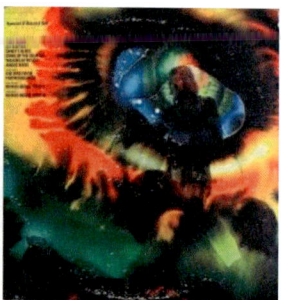

Matrix #: LST 27200-1   114
         LST 27200-2   14
         LST 27200-3
         LST 27200-4   9-5-68
Songs: version #1 (6+2+1+1)
  B2.I – Parthenogenesis: Nebulosity   2:20
Recording Dates: I. D. Sound Recorders, Hollywood, California
Producer: Canned Heat and Skip Taylor
Of note: (1) On track B2.I, "Owl" (i.e., Al Wilson) is credited on Jaw-Harp and John Fahey on guitar. Fahey plays only five guitar strum notes at the beginning of the piece. (2) This album also contains the B2.VII track called "Raga Kafi" as part of the suite "Parthogenesis." It is credited to "Owl" playing the chromatic harp. This is reportedly a portion of a much longer piece, another snippet of which would eventually be included in Fahey's *Old Girlfriends and Other Horrible Memories* under the name of "Fear and Loathing at 4th and Butternut." Al Wilson's "Raga Kafi" is based on the 20-minute piece called "Raga Palas Kafi" on the 1964 album *The Master Musicians of India – Ravi Shankar and Ali Akbar-Kahn* (Prestige PR 7537). This was a favorite album of Wilson and his roommate Phil Spiro.

#2

Release date: 1971
Edition: 2nd issue
Record company: United Artists Records
Catalog number: UAS-9955
Format: double 12" LP, 33⅓ rpm, stereo
Jacket cover: 2nd - gatefold
  - **Front cover**: open mouth
  - **Spine**: STEREO   UAS-9955   UNITED ARTISTS   LIVING THE BLUES   CANNED HEAT
  - **Back cover**: head
Cover credit: Robert Lockhart
Label: cream

Matrix #: UAS   9955-A-1   1T
             UAS   9955-B-1   1T
             UAS   9955-C-1   1T
             UAS   9955-D-2   1T
Songs: version #2 (6+2+1+1)
Side 2, track 2.I – Parthenogenesis: Nebulosity   2:20
Recording Dates: I. D. Sound Recorders, Hollywood, California
Producer: Canned Heat and Skip Taylor

MEMPHIS SWAMP JAM

#1
Release date: 1969
Edition: 1st issue (label #1, jacket #1, songs #1)
Record company: Blue Thumb
Catalog number: BTS 6000
Format: double 12" LP, 33⅓ rpm, stereo
Jacket cover: 1st - gatefold
  - **Front cover**: six blues singers
  - **Spine**: MEMPHIS SWAMP JAM / BTS 6000
  - **Back cover**: song titles
Cover credit: Jim Marshall
Label: cream with blue thumbprint logo

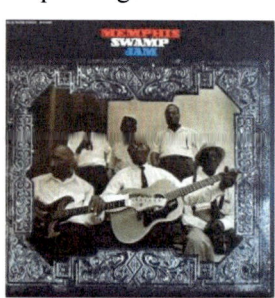
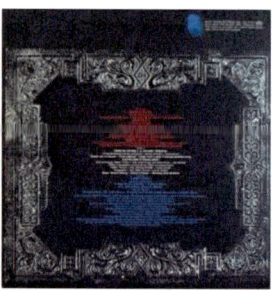

Matrix #: 5035 BTS-6000- 1D
  5036 BTS 6000 B – 1B
  5037 BTS 6000 C – 1B
  5038 BTS 6000 D – 1B
or
  5035 BTS-6000 1E
  5036 BTS-6000 1D
  5037 BTS 6000-1C
  5038 BTS 6000-1C

Songs: version 1 (5+4+6+5)
  D3 – Memphis Rag   2:00
  D4 – St. Louis Blues   3:00
  D5 – Praying On The Old Camp Ground & Lonesome Blues   2:20

Recording Dates: June 12, 1969, at Royal Recording Studios in Memphis, TN.
Liner notes: by Pete Welding (on the record sleeves)
Producer: Chris Strachwitz
Of note: (1) Deluxe two album set issued at a price of $6.98. (2) R. L. Watson and Josiah Jones, who perform the guitar duets on tracks D3-D5, are pseudonyms for John Fahey and Bill Barth. (3) Track D5 is an edited version. The complete version (over one minute longer) will later appear on the Arhoolie reissue.

#2

Release date: 1969 (Canada)
Edition: 2nd issue (label #2, jacket #2, songs #2)
Record company: Blue Thumb
Catalog number: BTS 6000 X
Format: double 12" LP, 33⅓ rpm, stereo
Jacket cover: 2nd - gatefold
  - **Front cover**: six blues singers; red Polydor logo
  - **Spine**: MEMPHIS SWAMP JAM   BLUE THUMB STEREO BTS 6000X
  - **Back cover**: song titles; "MANUFACTURED ... BY POLYDOR RECORDS CANADA LIMITED"
Cover credit: Jim Marshall
Label: black with blue thumbprint logo

Matrix #: BTS-6000X A -2   PK   M
　　　　　　BTS-6000X B -2   PK   M
　　　　　　BTS-6000X C -2   PKZ   M
　　　　　　BTS-6000X D -2   PK   M
Songs: version 1 (5+4+6+5)
　D3 – Memphis Rag   2:00
　D4 – St. Louis Blues   3:00
　D5 – Praying On The Old Camp Ground & Lonesome Blues   2:20
Recording Dates: June 12, 1969, at Royal Recording Studios in Memphis, TN.
Liner notes: none
Producer: Chris Strachwitz
Of note: (1) Track D5 is an edited version. The complete version (over one minute longer) will later appear on the Arhoolie reissue.

#3

Release date: 1973 (France)
Edition: 3rd issue (label #3, jacket #3, songs #3)
Record company: Blue Thumb
Catalog number: BT 10.018
Format: double 12" LP, 33⅓ rpm, stereo
Jacket cover: 3rd - gatefold
  - **Front cover**: six blues singers; "For Blues Collectors Only".
  - **Spine**: MEMPHIS SWAMP JAM / BT 10.018
  - **Back cover**: song titles; "Distribution VOGUE P.I.P."
Cover credit: Jim Marshall
Label: cream with blue thumbprint logo

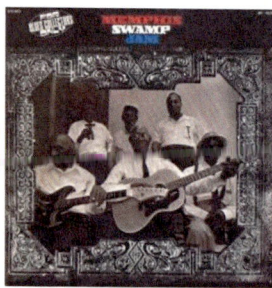

Matrix #: BT 10018   A1
             BT 10018   A2
             BT 10018   B1
             BT 10.018   B2
Songs: version 1 (5+4+6+5)
  D3 – Memphis Rag   1:58
  D4 – St. Louis Blues   3:03
  D5 – Praying On The Old Camp Ground & Lonesome Blues   2:20
Recording Dates: June 12, 1969, at Royal Recording Studios in Memphis, TN.
Liner notes: none
Producer: Chris Strachwitz
Of note: (1) Track D5 is an edited version. The complete version (over one minute longer) will later appear on the Arhoolie reissue.

#4

Release date: 1981
Edition: 4th issue (label #4, jacket #4, songs #4)
Record company: Arhoolie
Catalog number: 1085
Title: KINGS OF COUNTRY BLUES, VOL. 2
Format: 12" LP, 33⅓ rpm, stereo
Jacket cover: 4th
  - **Front cover**: six blues singers
  - **Spine**: ARHOOLIE 1085   KINGS OF COUNTRY BLUES • VOLUME 2
    ARHOOLIE 1085
  - **Back cover**: song titles and biographies
Cover credit: Jim Marshall
Label: red and black

 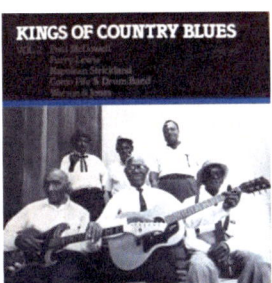 

Matrix #: ARHOOLIE 1085 A
             ARHOOLIE 1085 B
Songs: version 1 (6+5)
  B3 – Memphis Rag   2:00
  B4 – St. Louis Blues   3:00
  B5 – Praying On The Old Camp Ground & Lonesome Blues   3:30
Recording Dates: June 12, 1969, at Royal Recording Studios in Memphis, TN.
Liner notes: by Pete Welding
Producer: Chris Strachwitz
Of note: (1) This re-issue is on Chris Strachwitz's Arhoolie Records. He was the producer for the original 1969 record. (2) Track B5 is now issued in its full version which is 3:30 long, even though the label states 2:20.

CD re-issue

#1

Release date: 1993
Edition: 1st issue
Record company: Arhoolie
Catalog number: CD-385
Title: MISSISSIPPI DELTA BLUES JAM IN MEMPHIS, VOLUME 1
Format: CD
Cover: Fred McDowell
Cover credit: Jim Marshall   **Disc label**: silver & red

Songs: version 1 (16)
12 – Memphis Rag   2:00
13 – St. Louis Blues   3:00
14 – Praying On The Old Camp Ground & Lonesome Blues   3:30
Recording Dates: June 12, 1969, at Royal Recording Studios in Memphis, TN.
Liner notes: by Pete Welding
Producer: Chris Strachwitz
Of note: (1) R. L. Watson is spelled out as Rosa Lee Watson on the CD disc's digital playlist. This happens to be the name of Doc Watson's wife. (2) Actual times for tracks B3-B5 are 2:02, 3:10 and 3:40, respectively. (3) The UPC code on the back cover is: 096297038529.

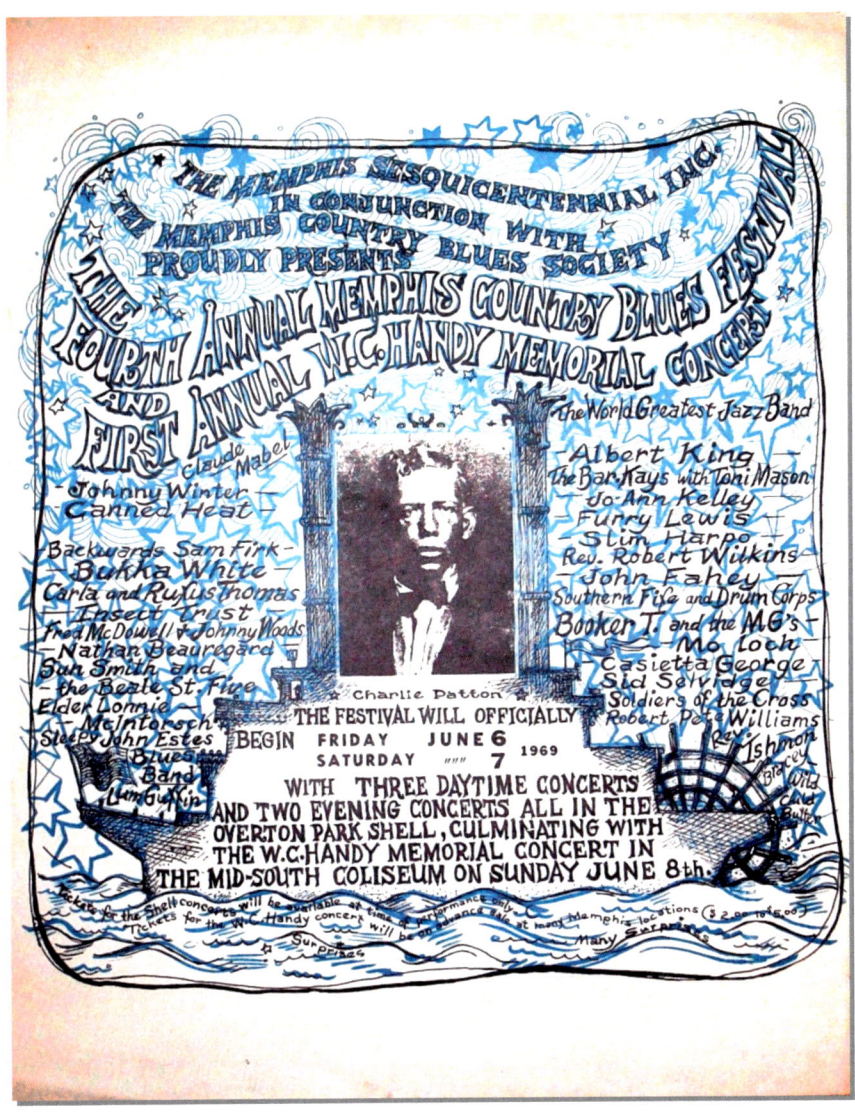

Poster for the 4th Annual Memphis Country Blues Festival in 1969 (Design by Claude Mabel)

This two-record anthology was issued by Blue Thumb records, which had just recently become associated with Arhoolie Records in a joint effort to promote grassroots blues music. Bob Krasnow and Don Graham of Blue Thumb flew Chris Strachwitz of Arhoolie to Memphis for the festival. Strachwitz selected the artists for the LP project. Blue Thumb then rented the Ardent Recording Studios in Memphis and in three days recorded the blues performers. Fahey and Barth were recorded the following day, June 12, at Royal Recording Studios in Memphis.

LEO KOTTKE - PETER LANG - JOHN FAHEY

#1

Release date: 1974
Edition: 1st issue (label #1, jacket #1, songs #1)
Catalog number: C-1040
Format: 12" LP, 33⅓ rpm, stereo
Jacket cover: 1st
  - **Front cover**: two sea dragons; names in a circle
  - **Spine**: LEO KOTTKE/PETER LANG/JOHN FAHEY
       TAKOMA C-1040   STEREO
  - **Back cover**: *no* writing on white bottom border
Cover credit: Eric Monson and John Cabalka
Label: Da^{3K}

Matrix #: C 1040-A Re-1   ⊚NC
           C 1040-B Re-1   ⊚NC
Songs: version 1-a (6+6)
  B3 – On The Sunny Side Of The Ocean   3:51
  B4 – Sunflower River Blues   4:26
  B5 – Revolt Of The Dyke Brigade   2:59
  B6 – In Christ There Is No East Or West   2:27
Recording Dates: Mastered at United Sound, Burbank, California.
Booklet: none
Producer: none given
Of note: (1) The album has four compositions contributed by each of three guitarists: Leo Kottke, Peter Lang and John Fahey – all Takoma Records artists.
(2) The tunes by Fahey [B3-B6] are new renditions of previously issued pieces.
(3) Track B4 is only 4:26 long since it lacks the reprise section present on later editions.

#2

Release date: 1975
Edition: 2nd issue (label #2, jacket #1, songs #2)
Catalog number: C-1040
Format: 12" LP, 33⅓ rpm, stereo
Jacket cover: 1st
  - **Front cover**: two sea dragons; names in a circle
  - **Spine**: LEO KOTTKE/PETER LANG/JOHN FAHEY
        TAKOMA C-1040   STEREO
  - **Back cover**: *no* writing on white bottom border
Cover credit: Eric Monson and John Cabalka
Label: Da^{3G}

Matrix #: C 1040-A Re-1 ⓒNC
         C 1040-B Re-2
Songs: version 1-b (6+6)
  B3 – On The Sunny Side Of The Ocean   3:51
  B4 – Sunflower River Blues   5:57
  B5 – Revolt Of The Dyke Brigade   2:59
  B6 – In Christ There Is No East Or West   2:27
Recording Dates: Mastered at United Sound, Burbank, California.
Booklet: none
Producer: none given
Of note: (1) On track B4, a reprise section is now added. The track's total duration is now 5:57, and this *long* version will be present on all future issues of this album. The added reprise section will be a source of confusion on some later editions.

#3

Release date: 1977
Edition: 3rd issue (label #3, jacket #1, songs #2)
Catalog number: C-1040
Format: 12" LP, 33⅓ rpm, stereo
Jacket cover: 1st
  - **Front cover**: two sea dragons; names in a circle
  - **Spine**: LEO KOTTKE/PETER LANG/JOHN FAHEY
        TAKOMA C-1040   STEREO
  - **Back cover**: *no* writing on white bottom border
Cover credit: Eric Monson and John Cabalka
Label: Da$^{3S\text{-}K}$

Matrix #: C 1040-A Re-1   ⓝNC
         C 1040-B Re-2
Songs: version 1-b (6+6)
   B3 – On The Sunny Side Of The Ocean   3:51
   B4 – Sunflower River Blues   5:57
   B5 – Revolt Of The Dyke Brigade   2:59
   B6 – In Christ There Is No East Or West   2:27
Recording Dates: Mastered at United Sound, Burbank, California.
Booklet: none
Producer: none given

KOTTKE-LANG-FAHEY vs FAHEY-KOTTKE-LANG

The 1974 European release of Leo Kottke's first Takoma album *6 and 12-String Guitar* was a big seller in Europe. Due to the attention he was garnering at this time, Takoma decided to give Kottke's name top billing on the new album's title in the hope that it would be bought by his fans. On later editions Kottke and Fahey would alternate as top-billed artist, supposedly in accordance with how their respective popularity changed. This would be evident on the album jacket spine, cassettes, 8-tracks and CD labels.

#4

Release date: 1978
Edition: 4th issue (label #4, jacket #1, songs #2)
Catalog number: C-1040
Format: 12" LP, 33⅓ rpm, stereo
Jacket cover: 1st
  - **Front cover**: two sea dragons; names in a circle
  - **Spine**: LEO KOTTKE/PETER LANG/JOHN FAHEY
          TAKOMA C-1040   STEREO
  - **Back cover**: *no* writing on white bottom border
Cover credit: Eric Monson and John Cabalka
Label: Da^{3S-G}

Matrix #: C 1040-A Re-1   ⓒNC
         C 1040-B Re-2
Songs: version 1-b (6+6)
  B3 – On The Sunny Side Of The Ocean   3:51
  B4 – Sunflower River Blues   5:57
  B5 – Revolt Of The Dyke Brigade   2:59
  B6 – In Christ There Is No East Or West   2:27
Recording Dates: Mastered at United Sound, Burbank, California.
Booklet: none
Producer: none given

#5

Release date: 1979
Edition: 5th issue (label #5, jacket #2, songs #3)
Catalog number: TAK-7040
Format: 12" LP, 33⅓ rpm, stereo
Jacket cover: 2nd
  - **Front cover**: two sea dragons; names in a circle
  - **Spine**: TAK 7040   LEO KOTTKE/PETER LANG/JOHN FAHEY   TAKOMA RECORDS   PRINTED IN U.S.A.
  - **Back cover**: "Distributed by Chrysalis Records" on white bottom border.
Cover credit: Eric Monson and John Cabalka
Label: Do[1]

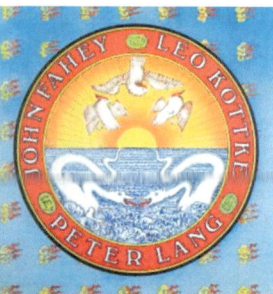

Matrix #: T1   TAK-7040-A   (1)   >
              T1   TAK-7040-B   (2)   >
Songs: version 1-c (6+6)

B3 – On The Sunny Side Of The Ocean	3:51
B4 – Sunflower River Blues	5:57
B5 – Revolt Of The Dyke Brigade	2:59
B6 – In Christ There Is No East Or West	2:27

Recording Dates: Mastered at United Sound, Burbank, California.
Booklet: none
Producer: none given

#6

Release date: 1979-1980   (Australia)
Edition: 6th issue (label #6, jacket #3, songs #4)
Catalog number: L 37284
Format: 12" LP, 33⅓ rpm, stereo
Jacket cover: 3rd
  - **Front cover**: two sea dragons; names in a circle
  - **Spine**: L 37284   JOHN FAHEY – LEO KOTTKE – PETER LANG
  - **Back cover**: *no* record company on white bar;
        L 37284 in upper right corner;
        "... distributed under license by Festival Records Pty ..." on bottom left;
        no writing on white bottom border.
Cover credit: Eric Monson and John Cabalka
Label: Do^{AUS}

Matrix #: 1   SMX 56073   P2A
            3   SMX 56074   P2A
Songs: version 1-d (6+6)

	actual	on label
B3 – On The Sunny Side Of The Ocean	3:51	3:49
B4 – Sunflower River Blues	5:57	4:27*
B5 – Revolt Of The Dyke Brigade	2:59	1:28*
B6 – In Christ There Is No East Or West	2:27	5:24*

Recording Dates: Mastered at United Sound, Burbank, California.
Booklet: none
Producer: none given
Of note: (1) *The label has the wrong times for tracks B4-B6. The confusion probably occurred because track B4 was thought to end at 4'27" and, consequently, its reprise (which lasts an additional 1'28") was thought to represent track B5. As a result, the duration of track B6 became the sum of the next two tracks "Revolt of the Dyke Brigade" and "In Christ There Is No East Or West" (i.e., 2'59" + 2'27" = 5'26").

#7

Release date: 1983
Edition: 7th issue (label #7, jacket #4, songs #5)
Catalog number: TAK-7040
Format: 12" LP, 33⅓ rpm, stereo
Jacket cover: 4th
  - **Front cover**: glossy; two sea dragons; names in a circle
  - **Spine**: LEO KOTTKE/PETER LANG/JOHN FAHEY
      TAKOMA C-1040   STEREO
  - **Back cover** *no* writing on white bottom border;
      TAK-7040 sticker;
      Allegiance trapezoidal sticker;
      Chrysalis butterfly imprint.
Cover credit: Eric Monson and John Cabalka
Label: Do²

Matrix #: TAK-7040 ~~C-1040~~ – A Re-1 -1-1-8 ⊚NC PRC ~~C~~
           TAK-7040 ~~C-1040~~ – B Re-2 -1-2-1 PRC ~~C~~
Songs: version 1-b (6+6)
  B3 – On The Sunny Side Of The Ocean   3:51
  B4 – Sunflower River Blues   5:57
  B5 – Revolt Of The Dyke Brigade   2:59
  B6 – In Christ There Is No East Or West   2:27
Recording Dates: Mastered at United Sound, Burbank, California.
Booklet: none
Producer: none given
Of note: (1) The matrix number implies that this is the same master as LP #2, but a new mother or stamper was pressed at PRC (Philips Recording Company). (2) The jacket is the same as the 1st jacket version except that it has the Chrysalis and Allegiance stickers on the back.

#8

Release date: 1985
Edition: 8th issue (label #8, jacket #5, songs #6)
Catalog number: ST-72740
Format: 12" LP, 33⅓ rpm, stereo
Jacket cover: 5th
  - **Front cover**: glossy; two sea dragons; names in a circle
  - **Spine**: TAK 7040   LEO KOTTKE/PETER LANG/JOHN FAHEY
    TAKOMA RECORDS   PRINTED IN U.S.A.
  - **Back cover**: "Distributed by Chrysalis Records" on
    the white bottom border;
    ST-72740 sticker.
Cover credit: Eric Monson and John Cabalka
Label: Do³

Matrix #: ST-1-72740 Q B-28247-G1 Δ 17307   1-1 MASTERED BY CAPITOL
         ST-2-72740 Q B-28248-G1 Δ 17307-X 1-1 MASTERED BY CAPITOL
Songs: version 1-e (6+6)
  B3 – On The Sunny Side Of The Ocean   3:51
  B4 – Sunflower River Blues   5:57
  B5 – Revolt Of The Dyke Brigade   2:59
  B6 – In Christ There Is No East Or West   2:27
Recording Dates: Mastered at United Sound, Burbank, California.
Booklet: none
Producer: none given

Non-Takoma LP re-issue

#1

Release date: 1974 (England)
Record Company: Sonet Records
Catalog number: SNTF 675
Format: 12" LP, 33⅓ rpm, stereo
Jacket cover:
  - **Front cover**: glossy; two sea dragons; names in a circle
  - **Spine**: LEO KOTTKE/PETER LANG/JOHN FAHEY   SNTF 675
  - **Back cover**: SONET on white bar; SNTF 675 in upper right corner; "Sonet Records Ltd" on the white bottom border.
Cover credit: Eric Monson and John Cabalka
Label: Sonet orange-pink

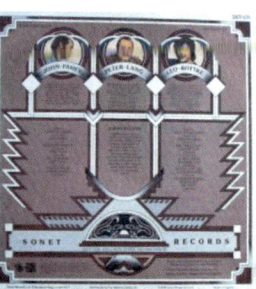

Matrix #: SNTF 675 A-1◊X
          SNTF 675 B-1◊X
Songs: version 1-b (6+6)
  B3 – On The Sunny Side Of The Ocean   3:51
  B4 – Sunflower River Blues   5:57
  B5 – Revolt Of The Dyke Brigade   2:59
  B6 – In Christ There Is No East Or West   2:27
Recording Dates: Mastered at United Sound, Burbank, California.
Booklet: none
Producer: none given

#2

Release date: 1976   (Germany)
Record Company: Metronome Records
Catalog number: 60.017
Format: 12" LP, 33⅓ rpm, stereo
Jacket cover:
- **Front cover**: glossy; two sea dragons; names in a circle
- **Spine**: LEO KOTTKE/PETER LANG/JOHN FAHEY
- **Back cover**: SONET on white bar; 60.017 in upper right corner; "METRONOME RECORDS GmbH" on white bottom border.

Cover credit: Eric Monson and John Cabalka
Label: black

Matrix #: 60017-A   0701.037 S1   PF
               60.017-B   PF   0701.037 S2

Songs: version 1 (6+6)

	actual	on label
B3 – On The Sunny Side Of The Ocean	3:51	3:49
B4 – Sunflower River Blues	5:57	4:25*
B5 – Revolt Of The Dyke Brigade	2:59	1:26*
B6 – In Christ There Is No East Or West	2:27	2:19

Recording Dates: Mastered at United Sound, Burbank, California.
Booklet: none
Producer: none given
Of note: (1) *The label has the wrong times for tracks B4-B5. The confusion probably occurred because track B4 was thought to end at 4'25" and, consequently, its reprise (which lasts an additional 1'26") was thought to be track B5.

#3

Release date: 1977   (Italy)
Record Company: Sonet Records
Catalog number: SNTL 2675
Format: 12" LP, 33⅓ rpm, stereo
Jacket cover:
- **Front cover**: two sea dragons; names in a circle
- **Spine**: SNTL 2675   LEO KOTTKE, PETER LANG & JOHN FAHEY   SONET
- **Back cover**: SONET on white bar;   SNTL 2675 in upper right corner; "DISTRIBUZIONE DISCHI RICORDI S.P.A." on white bottom border.

Cover credit: Eric Monson and John Cabalka
Label: Sonet with mountains

 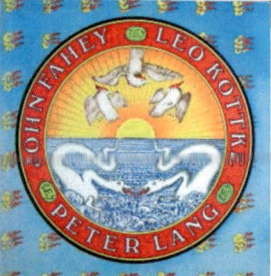 

Matrix #: SNTL . 2675 . 1   4.5.77
                   SNTL . 2675 . 2
Songs: version 1-b (6+6)

B3 – On The Sunny Side Of The Ocean		3:51
B4 – Sunflower River Blues		5:57
B5 – Revolt Of The Dyke Brigade		2:59
B6 – In Christ There Is No East Or West		2:27

Recording Dates: Mastered at United Sound, Burbank, California.
Booklet: none
Producer: none given
Of note: (1) The label has "STEREO 33 ⅓ GIRI" stamped *over* the mountains.

#4

Release date: 1977 (Italy)
Record Company: Sonet Records
Catalog number: SNTL 2675
Format: 12" LP, 33⅓ rpm, stereo
Jacket cover:
  - **Front cover**: two sea dragons; names in a circle
  - **Spine**: SNTL 2675   LEO KOTTKE, PETER LANG & JOHN FAHEY   SONET
  - **Back cover**: SONET on white bar;   SNTL 2675 in upper right corner; "Printed in Italy by La Grafica Cremonese" on lower right corner; "DISTRIBUZIONE DISCHI RICORDI S.P.A." on white bottom border.
Cover credit: Eric Monson and John Cabalka
Label: Sonet with mountains

  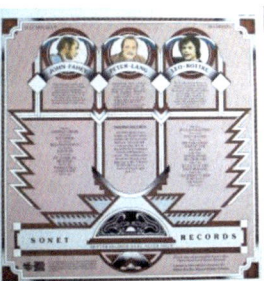

Matrix #: SNTL . 2675 . 1   4.5.77
            SNTL . 2675 . 2
Songs: version 1-b (6+6)
  B3 – On The Sunny Side Of The Ocean   3:51
  B4 – Sunflower River Blues   5:57
  B5 – Revolt Of The Dyke Brigade   2:59
  B6 – In Christ There Is No East Or West   2:27
Recording Dates: Mastered at United Sound, Burbank, California.
Booklet: none
Producer: none given
Of note: (1) The label now has "STEREO   33 ⅓ GIRI   LATO 1" stamped *below* the mountains.

8-Track re-issue

#1

Release date: 1974
Catalog number: 1040-8
Format: 8-track stereo
Cover: two sea dragons; names in a circle; Takoma 'T' logo.
Original Cover credit: Eric Monson and John Cabalka
Songs: version #1 (4+3+3+2)
C2 – On The Sunny Side Of The Ocean 3:51
C3 – In Christ There Is No East Or West 2:27
D1 – Sunflower River Blues 5:57
D2 – Revolt Of The Dyke Brigade 2:59
Recording Dates: same as LP #1
Manufacturer: Takoma Records
Of note: (1) Notice how the order of the artists is reversed, with Fahey as the first name of the trio.

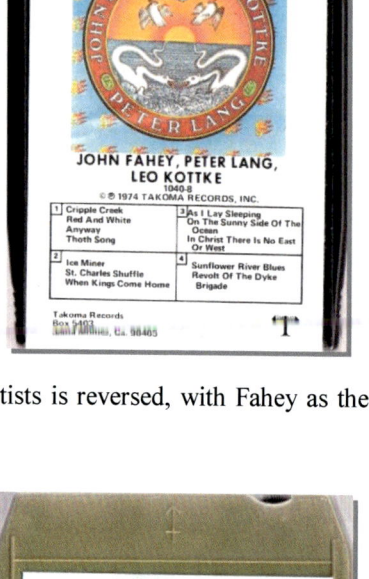

#2

Release date: 1974
Catalog number: Y8 SN 675
Format: 8-track stereo
Cover: two sea dragons; names in a circle; Sonet logo.
Original Cover credit: Eric Monson and John Cabalka
Songs: version #2 (3+3+2+4)
B2 – Revolt Of The Dyke Brigade 2:59
C1 – On The Sunny Side Of The Ocean 3:51
C2 – Sunflower River Blues 5:57
D1 – In Christ There Is No East Or West 2:27
Recording Dates: same as LP #1
Manufacturer: Sonet Records
Of note: (1) The order of the artists is reversed, with Fahey as the first name of the trio.

Tape re-issue

#1
Release date: 1979
Catalog number: CTA 7040
Format: cassette tape
Cover: two sea dragons; names in a circle; Takoma dragon logo; black bottom.
Cover credit: Eric Monson and John Cabalka
Songs: version #1 (7+5)
B2 – On The Sunny Side Of The Ocean
B3 – In Christ There Is No East Or West
B4 – Sunflower River Blues
B5 – Revolt Of The Dyke Brigade
Recording Dates: same as LP #1
Of note: (1) Distributed by Chrysalis.

#2
Release date: 1979-1980   (Australia)
Catalog number: C 37284
Format: cassette tape
Cover: two sea dragons; names in a circle; artists' names in color.
Cover credit: Eric Monson and John Cabalka
Songs: version #2 (6+6)
B3 – On The Sunny Side Of The Ocean
B4 – Sun Flower River Blues
B5 – Revolt Of The Dyke Brigade
B6 – In Christ There Is No East Or West
Recording Dates: same as LP #1
Of note: (1) The order of the artists is now reversed, with Fahey as the first name of the trio.
(2) Manufactured and distributed under license by Festival Records Pty.

#3
Release date: 1987
Catalog number: DA 72740 *or* 4XT-72740
Format: cassette tape
Cover: two sea dragons; names in a circle; Takoma dragon logo
Cover credit: Eric Monson and John Cabalka
Songs: version #2 (6+6)
B3 – On The Sunny Side Of The Ocean
B4 – Sunflower River Blues
B5 – Revolt Of The Dyke Brigade
B6 – In Christ There Is No East Or West
Recording Dates: same as LP #1
Of note: (1) The UPC code on the back cover is: 022397274048.

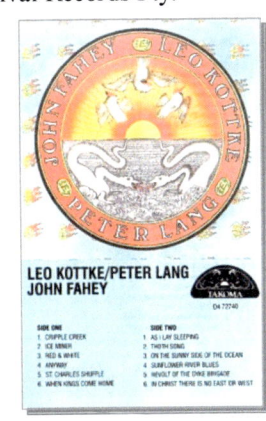

CD re-issue

#1
Release date: 1987
Catalog number: CDP-72740
Format: CD
Cover: two sea dragons; names in a circle.   **Disc label**: silver

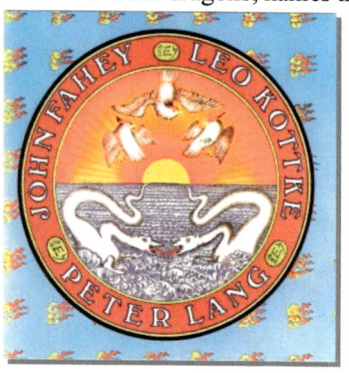

Cover credit: Eric Monson and John Cabalka
Songs: version #1 (12)

	on cover	on disc
9 – On The Sunny Side Of The Ocean	3:50	3:57
10 – In Christ There Is No East Or West	3:06	2:31
11 – Sunflower River Blues	6:39	6:00
12 – Revolt Of The Dyke Brigade	3:02	3:04

Recording Dates: same as LP #1
Remastering: Michael Boshears at David Pell Digital
Of note: (1) The duration of tracks 10 and 11 mentioned on the back cover are incorrect. (2) The UPC code on the back cover is: 022397274024.

#2
Release date: 1996
Catalog number: TAKCD-6502-2
Format: CD
Cover: two sea dragons; names in a circle.   **Disc label**: brown

Cover credit: Eric Monson and John Cabalka
Songs: version #1 (12)

9 – On The Sunny Side Of The Ocean	3:51
10 – Sunflower River Blues	5:57
11 – Revolt Of The Dyke Brigade	2:59
12 – In Christ There Is No East Or West	2:27

Recording Dates: same as LP #1
New Liner Notes: yes (by Dale Miller)
Remastering: Joe Tarantino (Fantasy Studios, Berkeley, CA)
Reissue Producer: none given
Of note: (1) The order of the artists is now reversed on the spine insert and in the liner notes, with Fahey as the first name of the trio (i.e., Fahey / Lang / Kottke). (2) The UPC code on the back cover is: 025218650229.

#3

Release date: 1996 (UK)
Catalog number: CDTAK 1040
Format: CD
Cover: two sea dragons; names in a circle.
Cover credit: Eric Monson and John Cabalka   **Disc label**: red

Songs: version #1 (12)

9 – On The Sunny Side Of The Ocean	3:51
10 – Sunflower River Blues	5:57
11 – Revolt Of The Dyke Brigade	2:59
12 – In Christ There Is No East Or West	2:27

Recording Dates: same as LP #1
New Liner Notes: yes (by Dale Miller)
Remastering: Joe Tarantino (Fantasy Studios, Berkeley, CA)
Reissue Producer: none given
Of note: (1) The order of the artists is now reversed on the spine insert, liner notes, and CD label, with Fahey as the first name of the trio (i.e., Fahey / Lang / Kottke). (2) Licensed to ACE Records. (3) The UPC code on the back cover is: 029667984027.

JO ANN KELLY
WITH JOHN FAHEY, WOODY MANN, JOHN MILLER, ALAN SIEDLER

#1

Release date: 1972
Edition: 1st issue
Record company: Blue Goose
Catalog number: BG 2009
Format: 12" LP, 33⅓ rpm, stereo
Jacket cover: 1st
  - **Front cover**: Jo Ann Kelly
  - **Spine**: JO ANN KELLY   BLUE GOOSE   2009
  - **Back cover**: biographies and pictures; 9 West 20th Street address.
Cover credit: Valerie Wilmer
Label: gold goose

Matrix #: BG 2009 A-2
                BG 2009 B
Songs: version #1 (7+6)
A2 – Stocking Feet Blues   2:59
A6 – High Sheriff Blues   2:55
  B5 – New Mind Reader Blues   4:34
Recording Dates:
Back liner notes: yes
Producer: Nick Perls
Of note: (1) John Fahey on guitar accompanies Jo Ann Kelly on vocals.
o   Track A2 resembles "Beverly" from *After The Ball*.
o   Track A6: Fahey plays slide guitar.
o   Track B5 resembles the mid-section of "Lion" from *The Yellow Princess*.
(2) The back cover has a picture of Fahey with Jo Ann Kelly, and the inner sleeve has another picture of Fahey.

#2

Release date: 1974
Edition: 2nd issue
Record company: Blue Goose
Catalog number: BG 2009
Format: 12" LP, 33⅓ rpm, stereo
Jacket cover: 2nd
  - **Front cover**: Jo Ann Kelly
  - **Spine**: JO ANN KELLY   BLUE GOOSE   2009
  - **Back cover**: biographies and pictures; 245 Waverly Place address.
Cover credit: Valerie Wilmer
Label: blue goose on orange

Matrix #: BG 2009 A-2
            BG 2009 B
Songs: version #1 (7+6)
A2 – Stocking Feet Blues   2:59
A6 – High Sheriff Blues   2:55
   B5 – New Mind Reader Blues   4:34
Recording Dates:
Back liner notes: yes
Producer: Nick Perls
Of note: (1) John Fahey accompanies Jo Ann Kelly on guitar.

CD re-issue

#1

Release date: 2002 (Japan)
Record company: Air Mail Recordings
Catalog number: AIRAC-1022
Format: CD
Cover: Jo Ann Kelly   **Disc label**: blue goose on orange

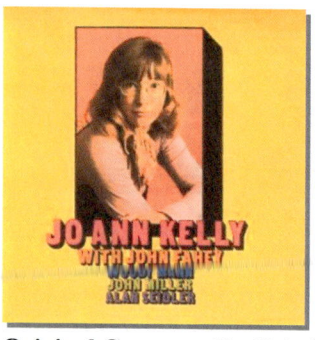

Original Cover credit: Valerie Wilmer
Songs: version #1 (13)
2 – Stocking Feet Blues	2:59
6 – High Sheriff Blues	2:55
13 – New Mind Reader Blues	4:34

Recording Dates:
Remastering:
Original Liner Notes: yes (reproduced)
Booklet: yes (in Japanese)
Original Producer: Nick Perls
Reissue Producer:
Of note: (1) John Fahey on guitar accompanies Jo Ann Kelly on vocals.
(2) The EAN-13 code on the obi strip is: 4571136370023.

GIVE ME WINGS
MUSIC FOR THE NEW AGE

#1
Release date: 1977
Edition: 1st issue
Record company: Unity Records
Catalog number: UR 1000
Format: 12" LP, 33⅓ rpm, stereo
Jacket cover: 1st
  - **Front cover**: "Visitation" painting – white border
  - **Spine**: UR 1000   ANTHOLOGY: VOLUME ONE   GIVE ME WINGS   MUSIC FOR THE NEW AGE   UNITY RECORDS
  - **Back cover**: "Return to the Source" painting
Cover credit: Gilbert Williams
Label: gold

  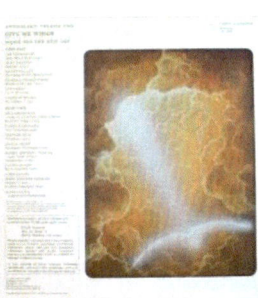

Matrix #: UR 1000 A   L-6167
              UR 1000 B   L-6167-X
Songs: version #1 (6+6)
  B5 – Gopinatha   3:00
Recording Dates: B5: at United Western Recording Studio, Los Angeles, CA
Booklet: none
Producer: Peter Georgi
Of note: (1) "Gopinatha" is by the Radha Krishna Temple with John Fahey on lead guitar.

'[Fahey] has even played background music for a Krishna record out West. Of the sect, he says: "I don't believe in their theology but their temples create a beautiful atmosphere. It's a different world, a fairytale." '

Excerpt from an article in the *Boston Globe*; July 10, 1977; by Steve Morse.

#2
Release date: 1977 or later
Edition: 2nd issue
Record company: Unity Records
Catalog number: UR 1000
Format: 12" LP, 33⅓ rpm, stereo
Jacket cover: 2nd
  - **Front cover**: "Visitation" painting – tan border
  - **Spine**: UR 1000   ANTHOLOGY: VOLUME ONE   GIVE ME WINGS   MUSIC FOR THE NEW AGE   UNITY RECORDS
  - **Back cover**: "Return to the Source" painting
Cover credit: Gilbert Williams
Label: silver

 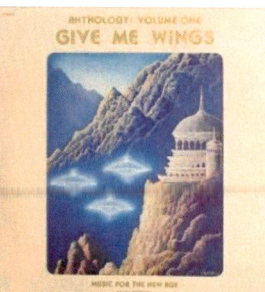 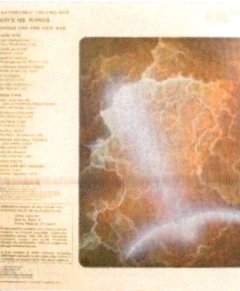

Matrix #: UR-1000-A-RE-2-1A S1   B3
            UR-1000-B-RE-2-1A S2   A1
Songs: version #1 (6+6)
    B5 – Gopinatha   3:00
Recording Dates: B5: at United Western Recording Studio, Los Angeles, California.
Booklet: yes   **Producer**: Peter Georgi
Of note: (1) This edition includes a 20-page booklet and a bonus 7" record UR 101 by *Hope And Her Friends*.

Tape re-issue

#1
Release date: 1978
Catalog number: Unity UR 1000
Format: cassette tape
Cover: "Visitation" – white border
Original Cover credit: Gilbert Williams
Songs: version 1 (6+6)
    B5 – Gopinatha   3:00
Recording Dates: same as LP #1

GUITAR HEAVEN

#1

Release date: 1978 (Germany)
Edition: 1st issue (label #1, jacket #1, songs #1)
Record company: Happy Bird
Catalog number: F 90073
Format: 12" LP, 33⅓ rpm, stereo
Jacket cover: 1st
  - **Front cover**: orange with guitar and birds
  - **Spine**: GUITAR HEAVEN VOL. II   F 90073
  - **Back cover**: song titles
Cover credit: Fessel & Hoffmann
Label: orange

Matrix #: 90073-A
          90073-B
Songs: version 1 (7+6)
   A1 – Delta Blues   7:31
Recording Dates: 1978
Liner notes: none
Producer: none given

Delta Blues

This is a new composition by John Fahey. It was issued in the same year that Fahey did a concert tour in Germany, from which two live shows were recorded and issued on DVD and CD: *Rockpalast* and *On Air*. When Fahey toured in a foreign country it was not unusual for him to be invited to record songs at a local recording studio, and "Delta Blues" may have been one such recording. This tune is played on slide guitar and consists of three segments, each played faster than the previous.

JO ANN KELLY
"RETROSPECT 1964-72"

#1

Release date: 1990 (England)
Edition: 1st issue
Record company: Document
Catalog number: CSAP LP 101
Format: 12" LP, 33⅓ rpm, stereo
Jacket cover: 1st
  - **Front cover**: Jo Ann Kelly
  - **Spine**: DOCUMENT   JO ANN KELLY - RETROSPECT 1964-72
    CSAP LP 101
  - **Back cover**: pictures.
Cover credit:
Label: white

Matrix #: CSAPLP-101-A-1   EW
           CSAPLP-101-B-1   EW
Songs: version #1 (7+7)
A5 – Shave 'Em Dry   2:15
  B2 – Try Me One More Time   3:49
Recording Dates: 1972 in New York.
Back liner notes: by Paul Jones
Producer:
Of note: (1) John Fahey on guitar accompanies Jo Ann Kelly on vocals. The two songs come from the Nick Perls session in New York from 1972.

CD issue

#1

Release date: 1990 (England)
Record company: Document
Catalog number: CSAP CD 101
Format: CD
Cover: Jo Ann Kelly   **Disc label**: gold

Original Cover credit:
Songs: version #1 (14)
5 – Shave 'Em Dry   2:15
9 – Try Me One More Time   3:49
Recording Dates: 1972 in New York.
Back liner notes: yes
Producer:
Remastering:
Liner Notes: yes
Of note: (1) John Fahey on guitar accompanies Jo Ann Kelly on vocals.
(2) The EAN-13 code on the back cover is: 5015773911298.

Tape issue

#1

Release date: 1990 (England)
Record company: Document
Catalog number: CSAP MC 101
Format: cassette tape
Songs: version #1 (7+7)
A5 – Shave 'Em Dry   2:15
  B2 – Try Me One More Time   3:49
Recording Dates: 1972 in New York.
Liner Notes: yes
Of note: (1) The EAN-13 code on the back cover is: 5015773911281.

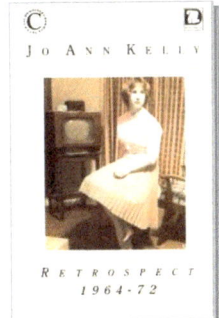

LORI CARSON
"SHELTER"

#1

Release date: 1990
Edition: 1st issue
Record company: DGC Records
Catalog number: DGC 24256
Format: 12" LP, 33⅓ rpm, stereo
Jacket cover: 1st
  - **Front cover**: Lori Carson
  - **Spine**: DGC 24256   LORI CARSON   SHELTER   DGC
  - **Back cover**: song titles
Cover credit: Matt Mahurin
Label: black

Matrix #: GHS 24256-A-SR1 DMM   SP1-1   STERLING   DMM gr
              GHS 24256-B-SR1 DMM   SP1-1   STERLING   DMM gr
Songs: version #1 (6+6)
  B4 – Which Way Be Broadway   4:49
Recording Dates:
Producer: Hal Willner
Of note: (1) On track B4, Lori Carson is on vocals, John Fahey on guitar, Paul Pimsler on guitar, and Sharon Freeman on French horn.

CD issue

#1

Release date: 1990
Edition: 1st issue
Record company: DGC Records
Catalog number: 9 24256-D2
Format: CD
Cover: Lori Carson   **Disc label**: silver

Songs: version #1 (12)
    10 – Which Way Be Broadway   4:49
Recording Dates:
Mastering:
Producer: Hal Willner
Of note: (1) John Fahey plays guitar on track 10. (2) A promotional copy was distributed inside a 5" x 7" booklet. Its catalog number is: D2-24256-DJ.

Tape issue

#1

Release date: 1990
Edition: 1st issue
Record company: DGC Records
Catalog number: D5G 24256
Format: cassette tape
Cover: Lori Carson
Songs: version #1 (6+6)
    B4 – Which Way Be Broadway   4:49
Recording Dates:
Producer: Hal Willner
Of note: (1) John Fahey plays guitar on track B4.

STORIES FROM THE HEARTH
WORLD FOLK STORIES – VOLUME 1

#1
Release date: 1994
Publisher: Glasswing Media
Format: CD
Cover:

Catalog number: SH-401-2

Disc label: silver-purple

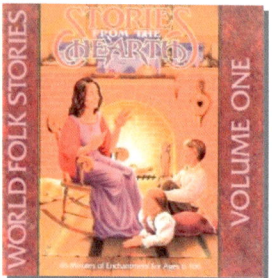

Cover credit: Raphael Schnepf
Stories: version #1 (6)
    2 – Jack The Miller's Son   13:41
    5 – Finn & The Salmon Of Knowledge   7:22
Recording Dates: at Glasswing Productions, Portland, Oregon.
Producer: Joanna Hussman and Richard Sales
Of note: (1) John Fahey on guitar accompanies two Celtic folk stories narrated by Meghan O'Flaherty.

#2
Release date: 1994
Publisher: Glasswing Media
Format: cassette tape (x2)

Catalog number: SH-401-4

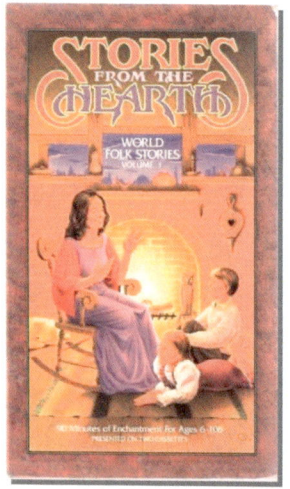

Cover credit: Raphael Schnepf
Stories: version #1 (4+4)
Cassette 2, side A, #1 – Finn & The Salmon Of Knowledge   7:22
Cassette 2, side A, #2 – Jack The Miller's Son   13:41
Recording Dates: at Glasswing Productions, Portland, Oregon.
Producer: Joanna Hussman and Richard Sales
Of note: (1) John Fahey on guitar accompanies two Celtic folk stories narrated by Meghan O'Flaherty.

MISS MURGATROID:
"MYOCLONIC MELODIES"

Release date: 1996
Edition: 1st issue
Record Company: W.I.N. Records
Catalog number: WIN 018
Format: CD
CD cover: red translucent case; Miss Murgatroid with accordion
                                     Disc label: black

Songs: version #1 (9)
2 – Dolls Inside the Walls   3:19
Recording Dates: Skunkworks, PDX, Oregon.
Liner notes:
Producer: Miss Murgatroid, Peter Drake, and Scott Colburn.
Of note: (1) John Fahey plays Hawaiian slide guitar on track 2.

HALANA
VOLUME 1, NUMBER 3 – WINTER 1997

Release date: 1997
Record company: Halana magazine   **Catalog number**: N/A
Format: CD
Cover: Halana logo   **Disc label**: fern pattern

Songs: version #1 (6)
3 – HS2   7:53
Recording Dates: May 16, 1996
Of note: (1) The piece by John Fahey is a detuned guitar piece from the Lastra Sessions of May 16, 1996.

THE RED CRAYOLA: "LIVE 1967"

Release date: 1998
Record company: Drag City   **Catalog number**: DC92CD
Format: CD (x2)
Cover: The Red Crayola band   **Disc label**: silver

Songs: version #1 (3+3)
B2 – 7/3, afternoon: Red Crayola with John Fahey   22:54
Recording Dates: July 3, 1967, at the Pauley Ballroom of the University of California at Berkeley.
Booklet: yes
Of note: (1) John Fahey plays guitar with The Red Crayola band at the 10th annual Berkeley Folk Music Festival held on June 30-July 4, 1967.

MISS MURGATROID:
"DRILL: WHAT'S THE CURSE?"

#1

Release date: 1999   (France)
Record Company: FBWL (From Belgium With Love *or* Fat Butt Without Love) in collaboration with TOW Records.
Catalog number: FBWL 73
Format: split 7" single, 45 rpm
Jacket cover: yes   **Disc label**: woman feeding child

Matrix #: FWBL 73-A1
              FBWL 73-B1
Songs: 1+1
A1 – VOODOO MUZAK: NNZZ   4:07
     B1 – MISS MURGATROID: Drill: What's Your Curse?   4:02*
Recording Dates: *September 1997 (but Fahey's part is most likely from 1996 – see below).
Insert: yes
Of note: (1) Issued as a limited edition of 500.

(2) Track B1 "Drill: What's Your Curse?" is by Miss Murgatroid on accordion with John Fahey on slide guitar. This is from the sessions that produced "Dolls Inside The Walls" by Miss Murgatroid. Some of the outtakes from these sessions were cut up, turned inside out, and used on "Drill," with Fahey's approval. Miss Murgatroid a/k/a Alicia J. Rose said: "It's not as normal and awesome as his playing on 'Dolls' – but it's still him. Interpreted liberally of course!"

(3) The song "Drill: What's Your Curse?" is inspired by the album "Drill" by the group *Wire*, wherein one of the songs is called "What's Your Desire?"

KIM'S BEDROOM

#1

Release date: 2000 (Netherlands)
Edition: 1st issue
Publisher: Purple Book
Catalog number: MU 1408
Format: book and CD   **Disc label**: silver

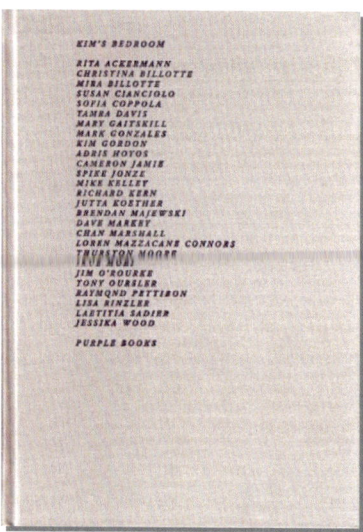

Songs: version 1 (11)
    3 – John Fahey Recorded in Chicago May '98   6:37
Recording Dates: Chicago, 1998
Producer: Kim Gordon (curator)
Of note: (1) The book and accompanying CD were published for the exhibition *Kim's Bedroom* curated by Kim Gordon, which took place on March 17-April 24, 2000, at the art institute MU – De Witte Dame in Eindhoven, Netherlands. (2) The digital information on the CD mistakenly corresponds to the CD *Syr 5: Olive's Horn* by Kim Gordon / Ikeu Mori / DJ Olive (2000). This was recorded at the Tribeca Recording Studio in NYC, the same place where Kim Gordon's CD was mastered.

MORE MUSIC, LESS PARKING: WFMU LIVE FROM JERSEY CITY

#1

Release date: 2000
Edition: 1st issue
Record company: WFMU
Catalog number:
Format: CD (x2)
Cover: parking lot
Cover credit: Brian Turner

Disc label: white

Songs: version #1 (18+13)
   A8 – Manicure   1:42
Recording Dates: live on the "Stork Club" show at WFMU studio, Jersey City, New Jersey, on July 19, 1998.
Booklet: by Lee Ranaldo and Brian Turner
Mastering: Irene Trudel
Producer: Brian Turner, Irene Trudel
Of note: (1) The piece by John Fahey is a short break during the show when he clips his fingernails.

JACK NITZSCHE
THREE PIECE SUITE: THE REPRISE RECORDINGS 1971-1974

#1

Release date: 2001
Edition: 1st issue
Record company: Warner Bros – Rhino Handmade
Catalog number: RHM2 7787
Format: CD
Cover: Jack Nitzsche
Cover credit: Joel Bernstein

Disc label: white

Songs: version #1 (21)
   A16 – Marie   2:44 (a)
   A21 – Reno   2:10 (b)
Recording Dates: (a) April 1971. (b) February 7, 1972
Booklet: by Elliot Mazer and Denny Bruce
Mastering: Bob Fisher
Original Producer: Elliot Mazer, Denny Bruce, Robert Downey
Compilation Producer: Roland Worthington Hand
Of note: (1) John Fahey plays slide guitar on "Marie." This song was made for a never-released Reprise album MS 2189 *Jack Nitzsche*. Notice that Denny Bruce was also the co-producer of John Fahey's albums on Reprise around the same time. (2) Fahey plays fingerstyle on "Reno."

JEFF FUCCILLO
"DISTURBED STRINGS"

#1
Release date: 2004
Edition: 1st issue
Record company: Roaratorio
Catalog number: roar 07
Format: 12" LP, 33⅓ rpm, stereo
Jacket cover: 1st
   - **Front cover**: ink on paper.
   - **Spine**: JEFF FUCCILLO   DISTURBED STRINGS   roar 07
   - **Back cover**: artwork by John Fahey.
Cover credit: Judith Lindbloom
Label: white

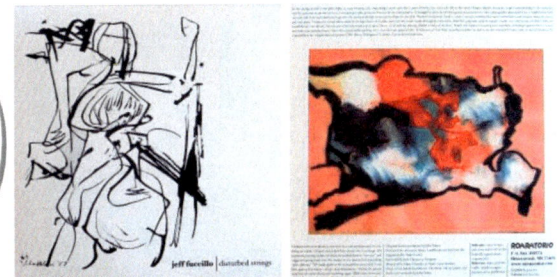

Matrix #: ROAR 07-A   11217.1
              ROAR 07-B   11217.2
Songs: version #1 (6+5)

A1 – Sazar	4:27
A2 – Heroes And Zeros	3:00
A3 – Birth	2:11
A4 – Lilt Of The Butterfly	4:51
A5 – Repeat Clearly	3:04
A6 – Nogawa River	3:24
B1 – Dance With Me	3:29
B2 – Traffic	4:09
B3 – Death	3:57
B4 – Setagaya Shimmy	3:01
B5 – Zeros And Heroes	2:17

Recording Dates: April 11, 1998, at Smegma, Portland, Oregon.
Back liner notes: by Jeff Fuccillo
Producer: John Fahey, James Lindbloom and Jeff Fuccillo
Of note: (1) Jeff Fuccillo, guitar; John Fahey, sound effects.

LOREN CONNORS
"SAILS"

Release date: 2005
Publisher: Table of the Elements
Format: CD (x2)
Cover: white-blue

Catalog number: Ac 89

Label: white + blue

Songs: version 1 (15+2)
    CD #2, track 1 – Dark Is the Night, Cold Is the Ground   6:49
Recording Dates:
Of note: (1) John Fahey accompanies Loren Mazzacane Connors on this guitar duet.

FRIENDS OF FAHEY TRIBUTE

Release date: 2006
Record company: Slackertone
Format: CD
Cover: Fahey in blue

Catalog number: ST-021

Label: black + title

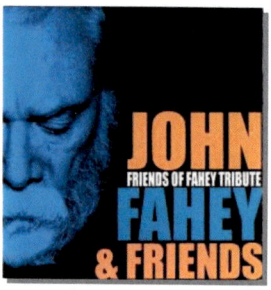

Songs: version #1 (15)
    14 – Why Haven't I Heard From You   5:43
Booklet: yes (by Tinh)
Mastering: Jason Carter at Wavelength.   **Producer**: Tinh Mahoney
Of note: (1) John Fahey leaves a message on someone's answering machine and then plays electric guitar with echo.

THE GREAT KOONAKLASTER SPEAKS
A JOHN FAHEY CELEBRATION

#1

Release date: 2007
Edition: 1st issue
Publisher: Table of the Elements
Catalog number: TOE-CD-91
Format: CD
Cover: Fahey-fish-tree   **Disc label**: white + green

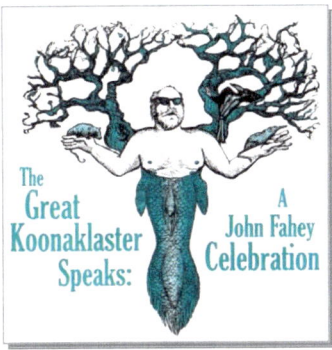
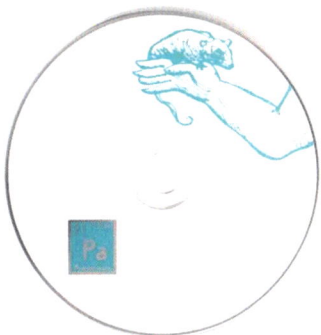

Cover credit: Stacey Earley
Stories: version 1 (11)
   6 – Overcome   3:46
Recording Dates: live at the The Tractor Tavern, Seattle, Washington, in 1998.
Producer: Regina Greene and Jeff Hunt
Liner Notes: by Rabbi Sky
Of note: (1) John Fahey accompanies the No Neck Blues Band and Coach Fingers.

CHAPTER 7

JOHN FAHEY DISCOGRAPHY
– COMPILATIONS –

This section lists albums or tapes that include one or more tracks of previously-issued compositions played by John Fahey. The source of the Fahey piece is given for each item.

THE CONTEMPORARY GUITAR SAMPLER

Release date: 1969 (England)
Record company: Transatlantic
Catalog number: TRASAM 14
Format: LP
Songs: 7+8
A5 – The Death Of Clayton Peacock 2:51
B5 – I Am The Resurrection 2:50
Source: *The Transfiguration of Blind Joe Death* – Transatlantic TRA 173
Of note: (1) The error in the title of track A5 gives it a different meaning. It should be "The Death of The Clayton Peacock."

ZABRISKIE POINT

Release date: 1970
Record company: MGM
Catalog number: SE-4668ST
Format: LP
Songs: 6+5
B4 – Dance Of Death 2:39
Source: *Dance Of Death* – Takoma 1004
Of note: (1) The film's soundtrack only includes the first segment of the song "Dance of Death". The tune appears 1h30m into the film, in the scene when Daria learns of the shooting death of the main character played by Mark Frechette. After the radio announcer says: "We return you now to John Fahey . . . ," Fahey's song is played on her car radio as Daria sways mournfully in the desert breeze. It actually lasts only 1'50" in the movie itself.

ZABRISKIE POINT

The title of Michelangelo Antonioni's film from 1970 is named after "Zabriskie Point," an elevated overlook with sweeping views of the colorful landscape situated on the eastern fringe of Death Valley. It was named after Christian Brevoort Zabrinskie (1864-1936), a former vice-president and general manager of the Pacific Coast Borax Company. Borax, a mineral with a wide variety of uses, was extensively mined in this region. The Pacific Coast Borax Company is now called Rio Tinto Borax and still operates the largest open-pit mine in California next to the company town of Boron, in the Mojave Desert.

Boron!

The name of this mining town, as a matter of fact, was featured in plate #2 on the third page of Patrick Finnerty's drawings in the booklet to Fahey's 1971 album *America*.

John Fahey hated *Zabriskie Point*, and gloated in the knowledge that it was once included in a list of the 50 worst movies of all time.

THE TRANSATLANTIC CONTEMPORARY GUITAR ALBUM, VOLUME 1

Release date: 1972 ?   (England)
Record company: Transatlantic
Catalog number: TRS 5001
Format: LP
Songs: 7+8
A5 – The Death Of Clayton Peacock   2:51
B5 – I Am The Resurrection   2:50
Source: *The Transfiguration of Blind Joe Death* – Transatlantic TRA 173
Of note: (1) A re-issue of *The Contemporary Guitar Sampler* from 1969.

BURBANK

Release date: 1972
Record company: Warner Brothers
Catalog number: PRO 529
Format: double LP
Songs: 7+6+6+6
Side #3, track 5 – Steamboat Gwine 'Round De Bend   4:15
Source: *Of Rivers and Religion* – Reprise MS 2089

DISPLAY CASE #8

Release date: 1972
Record company: Reprise / Warner Brothers
Catalog number: PRO 532
Format: double LP
Songs: 5+6+6+5
Side #3, track 1 – Steamboat Gwine 'Round De Bend   4:15
Side #3, track 2 – Dixie Pig Bar-B-Q Blues   3:55
Side #3, track 3 – Funeral Song For Mississippi John Hurt   4:20
Source: *Of Rivers and Religion* – Reprise MS 2089

SUPERB SUPER GUITAR SESSION

Release date: 1972 ?   (France)
Record company: Transatlantic
Catalog number: TRA/SAM 14/15
Format: double LP
Songs: 7+8+7+7
LP #1, A5 – The Death Of Clayton Peacock   2:51
LP #1, B5 – I Am The Resurrection   2:50
Source: *The Transfiguration of Blind Joe Death* – Transatlantic TRA 173
Of note: (1) The error in the title of track A5 gives it a different meaning.

CONTEMPORARY GUITAR

Release date: 1973   (France)
Record company: Transatlantic
Catalog number: TRA 89505/6
Format: double LP
Songs: 7+8+7+7
LP #1, A5 – The Death Of Clayton Peacock   2:51
LP #1, B5 – I Am The Resurrection   2:50
Source: *The Transfiguration of Blind Joe Death* – Transatlantic TRA 173
Of note: (1) The error in the title of track A5 gives it a different meaning.

ACOUSTIC GUITAR SOUNDS

Release date: 1977   (Germany)
Record company: Metronome
Catalog number: 80.011-2
Format: double LP
Songs: 6+6+6+5
LP #1, A4 – In Christ There Is No East Or West   2:19
LP #2, B5 – On The Sunny Side Of The Ocean   3:48
Source: *Leo Kottke/Peter Lang/John Fahey* – Metronome 60.017

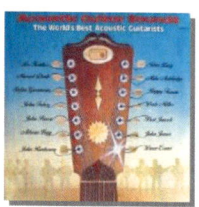

HOME FOR CHRISTMAS

Release date: 1982
Record company: Book-of-the-Month Records
Catalog number: 91-6561
Format: triple LP
Songs: 7+8+10+8+8+9
Side 2, track 4 – Go I Will Send Thee   3:00
Side 6, track 2 – Carol Of The Bells   2:41
Source: *The New Possibility* – Takoma 1020 & *Christmas with John Fahey, Vol II* – Takoma 1045

FONOTONE GUITAR CLASSICS

Release date: 1985
Record company: Fonotone
Catalog number: 6812
Format: cassette tape
Songs: 10+10
B4 – Weissman Blues   3:06
Source: Fonotone 6148

ROUNDER FOLK 1

Release date: 1985
Record company: Rounder Records
Catalog number: AN-04
Format: LP
Songs: 7+7
A3 – The Firebird   2:00
Source: *Rain Forests, Oceans and Other Themes* – Varrick 019

Release date: 1985
Record company: Rounder Records
Catalog number: AN-04
Format: cassette tape
Songs: 7+7
A3 – The Firebird   2:00
Source: *Rain Forests, Oceans and Other Themes* – Varrick 019

ROUNDER FOLK

Release date: 1986
Record company: RykoDisc
Catalog number: RCD 20018
Format: CD
Songs: 21
4 – Atlantic High   2:06
Source: *Rain Forests, Oceans and Other Themes* – Varrick 019

FINGERPICKING GUITAR SOLOS FOR THE ADVANCED GUITARIST

Release date: 1986
Record company: Mel Bay
Catalog number: MB94083
Format: book + cassette tape
Songs: 4+9
B5 – When The Springtime Comes Again 4:49
B6 – On The Sunny Side Of The Ocean 3:45
Source: *Death Chants, Breakdowns & Military Waltzes* – Takoma 1003 & *Leo Kottke, Peter Lang, John Fahey* – Takoma 1040
Of note: (1) The book includes the guitar tablature for Fahey's two songs. It also reprints the *Guitar Player* interview with John Fahey by Michael Brooks. (2) This was re-issued in 1992 as a book + CD with a different title: *Folk, Blues, Jazz & Beyond* (see below).

ROCK GOES TO THE MOVIES 1

Release date: 1990
Record company: CBS
Catalog number: AK 46806
Format: CD
Songs: 12
4 – Dance of Death   2:39
Source: *Zabriskie Point* soundtrack
Of note: The digital information on the CD corresponds to a different CD called *Rock Goes to the Movies #3*.

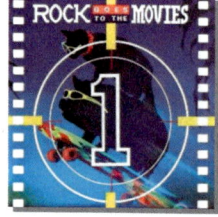

USA WEST COAST TRIP

Release date: 1990   (England)
Record company: Psychedelic Archives
Catalog number: #6
Format: cassette tape (x2)
Songs: 15+16+13+16
Tape #1, Side B, track 16 – Sail Away Ladies   1:20
Source: *The Great San Bernardino Birthday Party* – Takoma 1008
Of note: (1) Two tapes housed in a 5" x 7" black box issued by Strange Things magazine for its subscribers.

LIFE IN THE FOLK LANE

Release date: 1992   (England)
Record company: Demon
Catalog number: FIENDCD722
Format: CD
Songs: 20
6 – Are You From Dixie?   2:42
Source: *I Remember Blind Joe Death* – Demon FIENDCD207

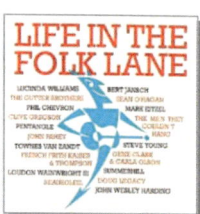

FINGERSTYLE GUITAR SOLOS IN OPEN TUNINGS

Release date: 1992
Record company: Mel Bay
Catalog number: MB94025BCD
Format: book + CD
Songs: 25
22 – Spanish Two Step   2:19
23 – Poor Boy A Long Way From Home   2:26
24 – Joy To The World   1:40
25 – Auld Lang Syne   2:05
Source: *The Best of John Fahey 1959-1977* – Takoma 1058; *Blind Joe Death* – Takoma 1002; & *The New Possibility* – Takoma 1020
Of note: (1) The book has the guitar tablature for Fahey's four songs.
(2) This is a re-issue of the 1984 book + tape: *The Art of Fingerstyle Guitar: Solos in Open Tunings*. The tape, however, did not feature the Fahey tunes.

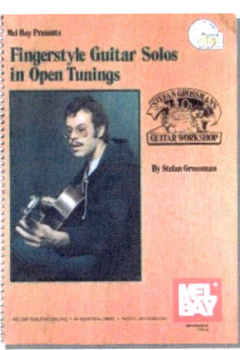

FOLK, BLUES, JAZZ & BEYOND

Release date: 1992
Record company: Mel Bay
Catalog number: MB94637BCD
Format: book + CD
Songs: 13
9 – When The Springtime Comes Again   4:49
10 – On The Sunny Side Of The Ocean   3:45
Source: *Death Chants, Breakdowns & Military Waltzes* – Takoma 1003 & *Leo Kottke, Peter Lang, John Fahey* – Takoma 1040
Of note: (1) The book has the guitar tablature for Fahey's two songs. It also reprints the *Guitar Player* interview with John Fahey by Michael Brooks.
(2) It is a re-issue of the 1986 book + tape with a different title: *Fingerpicking Guitar Solos for the Advanced Guitarist* (see page 358).

THE ART OF FINGERSTYLE GUITAR

Release date: 1992
Record company: Mel Bay
Catalog number: MB94638BCD
Format: book + CD
Songs: 14
2 – The Last Steam Engine Train   2:18
3 – Some Summer Day   3:24
4 – Beverly (Indian Pacific Railroad Blues)   4:38
Source: *Dance Of Death* - Takoma 1004; *Death Chants, Breakdowns & Military Waltzes* - Takoma 1003; & *Live In Tasmania* - Takoma 7089
Of note: (1) The book has the guitar tablature for Fahey's three songs. It also reprints the interview with John Fahey by Mark Humphrey.
(2) This is a re-issue of the 1986 book + tape with a different title: *Fingerpicking Guitar Solos for the Intermediate Guitarist*.

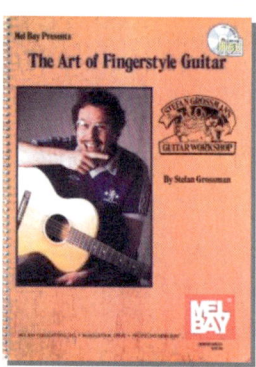

RHINO PRESENTS HOME FOR CHRISTMAS

Release date: 1992
Record company: Rhino
Catalog number: R2 71316
Format: CD (x2)
Songs: 20+20
Disc A, #12 – Joy To The World   1:52
Source: *The New Possibility* – Takoma 1020

TOYS FROM THE ATTIC

Release date: 1992   (Canada)
Record company: Attic
Catalog number: ACDP 030
Format: CD
Songs: 20
8 – Little Drummer Boy   2:35
18 – O' Little Town of Bethlehem   3:17
Source: *The John Fahey Christmas Album* – Attic CAT/ACD 1362

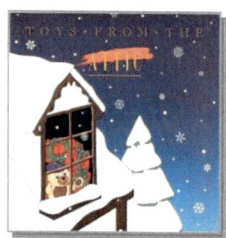

ROCK GOES TO THE MOVIES / BLUE FEELING

Release date: 1992
Record company: Sony Music
Catalog number: A 22676
Format: CD
Songs: 10
4 – Dance of Death   2:40
Source: *Zabriskie Point* soundtrack
Of note: The digital information on the CD corresponds to a different CD called *Jazz Ballads with a Blue Feeling*.

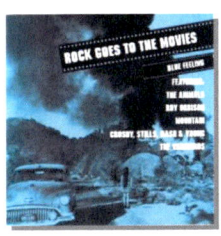

Release date: 1992
Record company: Sony Music
Catalog number: BT 22676
Format: cassette tape
Songs: 5+5
A4 – Dance of Death   2:40
Source: *Zabriskie Point* soundtrack

TOYS FROM THE ATTIC 2

Release date: 1994   (Canada)
Record company: Attic
Catalog number: ACDP 050
Format: CD
Songs: 19
4 – O Holy Night   3:34
Source: *The John Fahey Christmas Album* – Attic CAT/ACD 1362

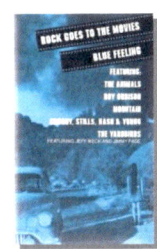

THE BEST OF CHRISTMAS CHEER

Release date: 1994
Record company: Excelsior
Catalog number: EXL-2-5304
Format: CD
Songs: 12
11 – Medley: Hark The Herald Angels Sing / O Come All Ye Faithful   3:12
Source: *The New Possibility* – Takoma 1020
Of note: (1) The digital information on the CD states a completely different album: *Joy To The World* by the Royal Philharmonic Orchestra (1988).

THE GREAT SONGS OF CHRISTMAS

Release date: 1994
Record company: GSC
Catalog number: #18118
Format: CD (x5)
Songs: 20+25+17+13+25
CD #4, track 11 – Medley: Hark The Herald Angels Sing / O Come All Ye Faithful   3:12
Source: *The New Possibility* – Takoma 1020

THE GREAT SONGS OF CHRISTMAS

Release date: 1994
Record company: GSC / Timeless Media Group
Catalog number: #18656
Format: CD
Songs: 13
11 – Medley: Hark The Herald Angels Sing / O Come All Ye Faithful   3:12
Source: *The New Possibility* – Takoma 1020

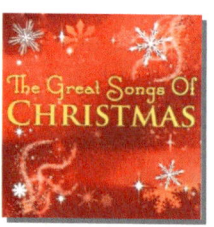

THE ROUNDER CHRISTMAS ALBUM: MUST BE SANTA!

Release date: 1995
Record company: Rounder
Catalog number: CD 3118
Format: CD
Songs: 19
16 – The Holly & The Ivy / The Cherry Tree Carol   2:13
Source: *Popular Songs of Christmas & New Year's* – Varrick 012

THE GREATEST HITS OF CHRISTMAS

Release date: 1996
Record company: ESX / Special Music Co.
Catalog number: SCD-5122
Format: CD
Songs: 12
11 – Medley: Hark The Herald Angels Sing / O Come All Ye Faithful   3:12
Source: *The New Possibility* – Takoma 1020

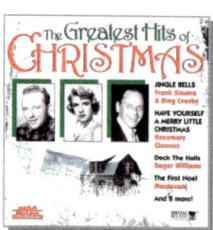

THE BEST OF REQUEST – VOL. 4

Release date: 1996
Record company: Request Media
Catalog number: -
Format: CD
Songs: 17
17 – Chelsea Silver, Please Come Home   4:33
Source: *City Of Refuge* – Tim/Kerr Records 644 830 127-2

MONTECARLO CHRISTMAS NIGHTS

Release date: 1996 (Italy)
Record company: MCA
Catalog number: MCD 77023
Format: CD
Songs: 21
8 – Silent Night, Holy Night   1:13
Source: *The New Possibility* – Takoma TAKCD-8912
Of note: (1) From the Radio Montecarlo show (10 pm to midnight).

MONTECARLO CHRISTMAS NIGHTS

Release date: 1996 (Italy)
Record company: MCA
Catalog number: MCC 77023
Format: cassette tape
Songs: 11+10
A8 – Silent Night, Holy Night   1:13
Source: *The New Possibility* – Takoma TAKCD-8912
Of note: (1) From the Radio Montecarlo show (10 pm to midnight).

BEGINNERS' FINGERPICKING GUITAR

Release date: 1996
Record company: Warner Brothers
Catalog number: F2316GTXCD
Format: book + CD
Songs: 21
14 – In Christ There Is No East Or West   1:14
15 – Take A Look At That Baby   0:52
16 – The First Noel   3:54
17 – Silent Night   3:17
Source: *The Guitar of John Fahey* – Stefan Grossman Guitar Workshop
Of note: (1) The accompanying book has the guitar tablature for Fahey's four songs.

TAKOMA ECLECTIC SAMPLER

Release date: 1997
Record company: Takoma
Catalog number: TAKCD-8904-2
Format: CD
Songs: 17
15 – Indian-Pacific R.R. Blues   4:43
Source: *Live in Tasmania* – Takoma 7089

ALTERNATIVE DISTRIBUTION ALLIANCE – SEPT. '97

Release date: 1997
Record company: Alternative Distribution Alliance
Catalog number: ADA 20011
Format: CD
Songs: 20
9 – New Red Pony 4:02
Source: *The Epiphany of Glenn Jones* – Thirsty Ear 57037

ACOUSTIC HOLIDAYS

Release date: 1998
Record company: EasyDisc / Rounder
Catalog number: 12136-7068-2
Format: CD
Songs: 11
10 – Medley: Hark The Herald Angels Sing / O Come All Ye Faithful 4:24
Source: *Christmas Guitar, Vol 1* – Varrick 002
Of note: (1) The digital information on the disc states John Fahey as the artist also for track 13, but it is actually Bill Keith, as stated on the liner notes.

VANGUARD COLLECTOR'S EDITION

Release date: 1997
Record company: Vanguard
Catalog number: 163/66-2
Format: CD (x4)
Songs: 22+22+20+20
CD3, track 11 – Requiem For John Hurt 5:04
Source: *Requia* – Vanguard VSD 79259

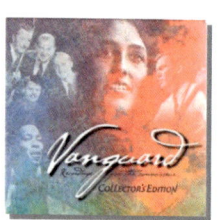

GENERATIONS OF FOLK, VOL. 2: PROTEST & POLITICS

Release date: 1998
Record company: Vanguard
Catalog number: 78001-2
Format: CD
Songs: 12
8 – March! For Martin Luther King 3:43
Source: *The Yellow Princess* – Vanguard VSD 79293

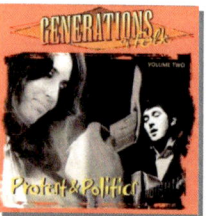

TAKOMA ECLECTIC SAMPLER - VOL. 2

Release date: 1998
Record company: Takoma
Catalog number: TAKCD-8906-2
Format: CD
Songs: 18
5 – Medley (Imitation Train Whistles / Po' Boy) 4:57
Source: *Railroad 1* – Shanachie 99003

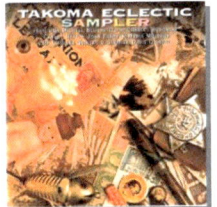

L.L. BEAN HOLIDAY SONGS

Release date: 1999
Record company: L.L. Bean / Rounder
Catalog number: LLB-1
Format: CD
Songs: 11
8 – Medley: Hark The Herald Angels Sing / O Come All Ye Faithful 4:27
Source: *Christmas Guitar, Vol 1* – Varrick 002

ACE SOUND CHOICE

Release date: 1999
Record company: ACE Records
Catalog number: PROMOJO 1
Format: enhanced CD
Songs: 14
14 – Brenda's Blues 1:50
Source: *The Transfiguration of Blind Joe Death* – Takoma CDTAK 7015

SAVAGE PENCIL PRESENTS ...
THE ANTIQUACK - A DEAD DUCK SELECTION

Release date: 1999
Record company: EMI
Catalog number: 7243 4 96606 2 5
Format: book CD
Songs: 19
5 – Dance of Death 2:42
Source: *Zabriskie Point* soundtrack
Of note: (1) page 8/9 has the illustration "John Fahey Meets Blind Joe Dead Duck."

TAKOMA SLIDE

Release date: 1999
Record company: Takoma
Catalog number: TAKCD-8910-2
Format: CD
Songs: 13
3 – Poor Boy 2:25
Source: *The Transfiguration of Blind Joe Death* – Takoma TAKCD-6504-2

DIGGIN' UP THE NEW ROOTS OF MUSIC - VOL. 2

Release date: 1999 (Japan)
Record company: Warner Music Japan & eastwest japan
Catalog number: PCS-363
Format: CD
Songs: 15
7 – Steamboat Gwine 'Round De Bend   4:14
8 – Funeral Song For Mississippi John Hurt   4:22
Source: *Of Rivers and Religion* – WPCR-10357

ROUTE 50

Release date: 2000
Record company: Vanguard
Catalog number: 79572-2
Format: CD (x2)
Songs: 21+18
CD #1, track 10 – Lion   5:06
Source: *Best of the Vanguard Years* – Vanguard VSD 79523-2

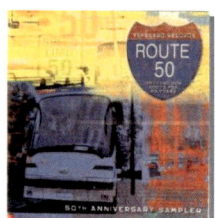

STRING ALCHEMY: FROM ECLECTIC TO ELECTRIC

Release date: 2000
Record company: Vanguard
Catalog number: 79563-2
Format: CD
Songs: 18
18 – Dance Of The Inhabitants Of The Invisible City Of
Bladensburg   4:08
Source: *The Yellow Princess* – Vanguard VSD 79293

DANGEROUS CURVES: THE ART OF THE GUITAR

Release date: 2000
Record company: Museum Music
Catalog number: MM110
Format: CD
Songs: 16
11 – Sunflower River Blues   3:20
Source: *Death Chants, Breakdowns and Military Waltzes* – Takoma 1003

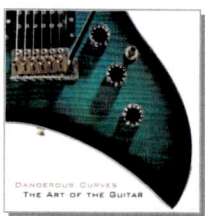

THE WIRE TAPPER 6

Release date: 2000
Record company: Wire
Catalog number:
Format: CD (x2)
Songs: 15+15
CD #2, track 3 – Dream Of The Origin Of The French Broad
River   2:58
Source: Fonotone
Of note: (1) This CD was given away with The Wire issue 200, October 2000. (2) This selection would be issued on *Your Past Will Come Back to Haunt You*.

L.L. BEAN HOLIDAY SONGS

Release date: 2001
Record company: L.L. Bean / Rounder
Catalog number: LLB-2
Format: CD
Songs: 11
8 – Medley: Hark The Herald Angels Sing/O Come All Ye
Faithful   4:27
Source: *Christmas Guitar, Vol 1* – Varrick 002
Of note: This is a re-issue of the 1999 version of *L.L. Bean Holiday Songs*.

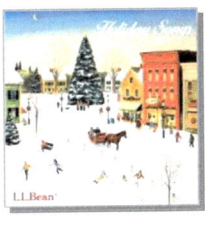

FINGERSTYLE GUITAR – NUMBER 45

Release date: 2002
Record company: Fingerstyle Guitar magazine
Catalog number:
Format: CD
Songs: 8
8 – St. Louis Blues   3:13
Source: *The Guitar of John Fahey* – Mel Bay MB95399CD

THE WIRE TAPPER 09

Release date: 2002
Record company: Wire
Catalog number:
Format: CD (x2)
Songs: 16+15
CD #2, track 5 – Red Cross, Disciple Of Christ Today   4:07
Source: *Red Cross* – Revenant 104
Of note: (1) given away with *The Wire* issue 225, November 2002.

THE WIRE 20

Release date: 2002
Record company: Wire
Catalog number: CDStumm220
Format: CD (x3)
Songs: 17+12+13
CD #3, track 12 – Some Summer Day   3:26
Source: *Death Chants, Breakdowns and Military Waltzes* – Takoma 1003

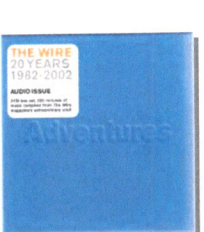

KOCH ENTERTAINMENT MUSIC SAMPLER - SPRING 2003

Release date: 2003
Record company: Koch Entertainment
Catalog number: KOC-XM-2003
Format: CD
Songs: 17
13 – Remember   4:46
Source: *Red Cross* – Revenant 104

VULTURE CULTURE MIX 2

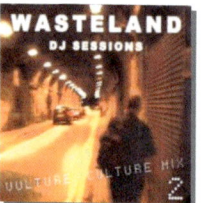

Release date: 2004
Record company: Transparent
Catalog number: promo 2
Format: CD
Songs: 31
31 – Untitled With Rain   2:00
Source: *Red Cross* – Revenant 104

TRANQUILITY: MUSIC FOR YOGA & MEDITATION

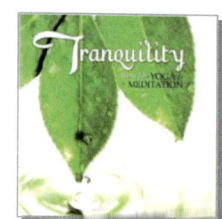

Release date: 2004
Record company: Vanguard
Catalog number: 79744-2
Format: CD
Songs: 14
10 – Dance Of The Inhabitants Of The Invisible City Of
Bladensburg   4:08
Source: *The Yellow Princess* – Vanguard VSD 79293

COUNTER CULTURE 03

Release date: 2004
Record company: Rough Trade Shops
Catalog number: CDSTUMM234
Format: CD (x2)
Songs: 20+25
CD 1, track 1 – Remember   4:41
Source: *Red Cross* – Revenant 104

ACOUSTIC SONGBOOK

Release date: 2004
Record company: Virgin Records
Catalog number: VTDCD 673
Format: CD (x3)
Songs: 19+23+23
CD#3, track 17 – Yellow Princess   4:51
Source: *The Yellow Princess* – Vanguard VSD 79293

THE ROOTS OF LED ZEPPELIN

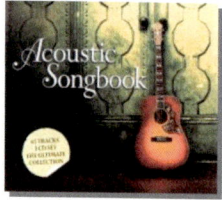

Release date: 2004
Record company: MOJO
Catalog number: MOJOAUG04
Format: CD
Songs: 15
14 – Dance Of The Inhabitants Of The Palace Of King Phillip
XIV Of Spain   3:20
Source: *The Best Of John Fahey: 1959-1977* – Takoma CDTAK 8915
Of note: (1) This CD was given away with the MOJO issue August 2004.

THE ROUGH GUIDE TO BOTTLENECK BLUES

Release date: 2005
Record company: Rough Guide
Catalog number: RGNET 1151 CD
Format: CD
Songs: 22
14 – Dance Of The Inhabitants Of The Palace Of King Philip XIV
Of Spain   3:16
Source: *Best Of John Fahey: 1959-77* – Takoma CDTAK 8915

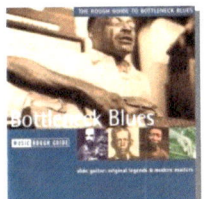

VANGUARD RECORDS VS. SUGAR HILL RECORDS

Release date: 2005
Record company: Vanguard & Sugar Hill Records
Catalog number: 79788-2
Format: CD
Songs: 12
4 – The Yellow Princess   4:50
Source: *Best of the Vanguard Years* – Vanguard 79513

BING CROSBY & FRIENDS: CHRISTMAS COLLECTION

Release date: 2005
Record company: Timeless Media Group
Catalog number: #18628
Format: CD
Songs: 13
11 – Medley: Hark The Herald Angels Sing/O Come All Ye
Faithful   3:12
Source: *The New Possibility* – Takoma 1020
Of note: (1) The digital information states a different album with the same songs: *The Great Songs of Christmas* from 1994 (see above). (2) It has the most illegible disc label seen: yellow writing on white background!

1973

Release date: 2005
Record company: Süddeutsche Zeitung
Catalog number:
Format: book + CD
Songs: 20
16 – Hawaiian Two-Step   2:42
Source: *After The Ball* – Reprise MS-2145

AN ECLECTIC CHRISTMAS

Release date: 2005
Record company: Concord Music Group
Catalog number: PRO-CJ-0109
Format: CD (x2)
Songs: 20+17
Disc #2, track 10 – Silent Night, Holy Night   1:18
Disc #2, track 12 – God Rest Ye Merry Gentlemen   2:50
Source: *The New Possibility* – Takoma 1020
Of note: (1) Track 12 is the same as "God Rest Ye Merry Gentlemen Fantasy."

IMAGINATIONAL ANTHEM
Release date: 2005
Record company: Near Mint Records
Catalog number: NM 0531
Format: CD
Songs: 16
13 – O' Holy Night   3:34
Source: *John Fahey Christmas Album* – Burnside BCD 0004-2

BING CROSBY: CHRISTMAS COLLECTION
Release date: 2006
Record company: Timeless Media Group
Catalog number: TMG #18637
Format: CD (x3) + DVD
Songs: 10+22+13
Disc #3, track 11 – Medley: Hark The Herald Angels Sing / O Come All Ye Faithful   3:12
Source: *The New Possibility* – Takoma 1020
Of note: (1) The digital information states a different album with the same songs: *The Great Songs of Christmas* from 1994 (see above).

MIDWINTER
Release date: 2006
Record company: Free Reed
Catalog number: FRQCD- 30
Format: CD (x4)
Songs: 27+24+22+26
Disc #1, track 4 – Skater's Waltz   1:51
Source: *Popular Songs of Christmas & New Year's* – Varrick VR-012

MBGU: BEST TRADITIONAL/FOLK SOLOS
Release date: 2006
Record company: Mel Bay
Catalog number: MB98165BCD
Format: book + CD (x2)
Songs: 24
Track 7 – In Christ There Is No East Or West   1:57
Track 9 – The Last Steam Engine Train   2:22
Source: *The Guitar of John Fahey* – Mel Bay MB95399
Of note: (1) The book has the guitar tablature for two Fahey songs: "In Christ There Is No East Or West" and "The Last Steam Engine Train."

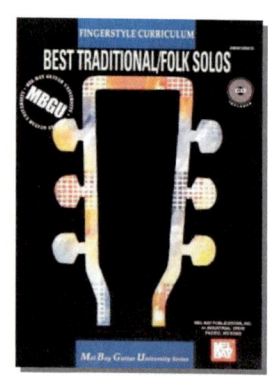

MBGU: BEST RAGTIME SOLO

Release date: 2006
Record company: Mel Bay
Catalog number: MB21362BCD
Format: book + CD (x2)
Songs: 20
Track 19 – Take A Look At That Baby   0:53
Source: *The Guitar of John Fahey* – Mel Bay MB95399
Of note: (1) The book has the guitar tablature for Fahey's song: "Take A Look At That Baby."

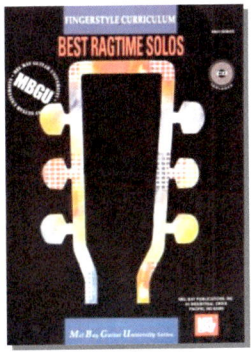

MBGU: BEST BLUES SOLO

Release date: 2007
Record company: Mel Bay
Catalog number: MB21365BCD
Format: book + CD (x2)
Songs: 26+5
Disc #1, track 21 – Some Summer Day   3:26
Disc #1, track 23 – St. Louis Blues   3:18
Source: #21: *Death Chants, Breakdowns & Military Waltzes* - Takoma 1003. #23: *The Guitar of John Fahey* – Mel Bay MB95399
Of note: (1) The book has the guitar tablature for three Fahey songs: "Some Summer Day," "St. Louis Blues" & "Beverly (Indian Pacific Railroad Blues)."

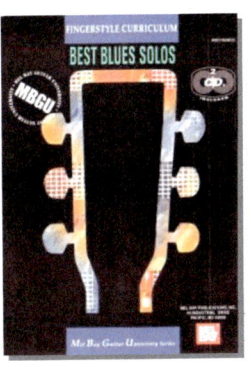

14 TRACKS FOR THE DUSTY VERANDA

Release date: 2008
Record company: Boomkat / 14 Tracks
Catalog number: Bundle 13
Format: mp3
Songs: 14
3 – O' Holy Night   3:34
Source: *Imaginational Anthem* – Near Mint Records NM 0531

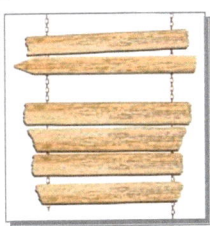

IMAGINATIONAL ANTHEM: VOLS 1-3

Release date: 2008
Record company: Tompkins Square Records
Catalog number:
Format: CD (x3)
Songs: 16+12+11
Disc #1, track 13 – O' Holy Night   3:34
Source: *The John Fahey Christmas Album* – Burnside BCD 0004-2

THE ROOTS OF LED ZEPPELIN

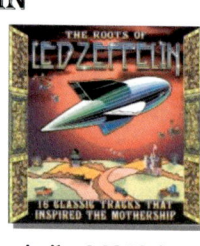

Release date: 2009
Record company: Great American Music Company
Catalog number: CD-GA-172
Format: CD
Songs: 16
9 – Dance Of The Inhabitants Of The Palace Of King Phillip XIV Of Spain   3:20
Source: *Best Of John Fahey: 1959-1977* – Takoma CDTAK 8915
Of note: Only three of the artists on this CD are represented on the similar MOJO issue from 2004 (see above), and Fahey is the only one with the same song.

BOB DYLAN: CHRISTMAS IN THE HEART

Release date: 2009
Record company: Columbia
Catalog number: CS7-762438
Format: 7" 45 rpm, stereo
Songs: 1+1
B1 – 'Twas The Night Before Christmas   3:12
Source: *The New Possibility* – TAKCD 8912-2 (see page 221)
Of note: This is a promo red vinyl record. Bob Dylan narrates the story with John Fahey's guitar music in the background. The two Fahey songs are excerpts of "Christmas Medley: Oh Tannenbaum /Angels We Have Heard On High/Jingle Bells" and "The Bells Of St. Mary's."

VANGUARD 50

Release date: 2009
Record company: Vanguard Records
Catalog number:
Format: mp3 digital download
Songs: 50
27 – When The Catfish Is In Bloom   7:41
Source: *The Yellow Princess* – Vanguard VSD 79293

VANGUARD RECORDS 60TH ANNIVERSARY SAMPLER

Release date: 2010
Record company: Vanguard Records
Catalog number: 78064-2
Format: promo CD
Songs: 9
4 – Yellow Princess   4:53
Source: *The Yellow Princess* – Vanguard VSD 79293

MAKE IT YOUR SOUND, MAKE IT YOUR SCENE:
VANGUARD RECORDS & THE 1960S MUSICAL REVOLUTION
Release date: 2012
Record company: Vanguard Records
Catalog number: VANBOX 14
Format: CD (x4)
Songs: 20+23+20+20
Disc #4, track 7 – March! For Martin Luther King   3:43
Source: *The Yellow Princess* – Vanguard VSD 79293

IMAGINATIONAL ANTHEM: VOLS 1-5
Release date: 2012
Record company: Tompkins Square Records
Catalog number:
Format: CD (x6)
Songs: 16+12+11+10+12+8
Disc #1, track 13 – O' Holy Night   3:34
Source: *John Fahey Christmas Album* - Burnside BCD 0004-2
Of note: Limited edition of 999 copies.

BEST OF GUITAR GODS
Record company: X5 Music Group   **Format**: *mp3*   **Release date**: 2012
5 – Requiem for John Hurt   5:10
14 – Fight On Christians, Fight On   1:55
Source: *Requia* – Vanguard VSD 79259

THE MASTERS OF EXPERIMENTAL GUITAR
Record company: X5 Music Group   **Format**: *mp3*   **Release date**: 2012
1 – Dance Of The Inhabitants Of The Invisible City Of Bladensburg   4:07
5 – The Yellow Princess   4:50
9 – Lion   5:10
13 – March! For Martin Luther King   3:42
Source: *Yellow Princess* – Vanguard VSD 79293

BLUEGRASS GUITAR MASTERS
Record company: X5 Music Group   **Format**: *mp3*   **Release date**: 2012
3 – The Yellow Princess   4:50
11 – Lion   5:10
Source: *Yellow Princess* – Vanguard VSD 79293

THE ANNIVERSARY OF THE LIGHT
Release date: 2013
Record company: Mississippi Records
Catalog number: MRC - 103
Format: cassette tape
Songs: 8+8
B4 – When The Springtime Comes Again   3:51
Source: *Death Chants, Breakdowns And Military Waltzes* – Takoma TAKCD-8908-2
Of note: (1) This is the 1963 version of "When the Spring Time Comes Again."

'TIS THE SEASON

Release date: 2013
Record company: Starbucks
Catalog number:
Format: CD
Songs: 15
8 – What Child Is This?   3:03
Source: *The New Possibility* – Takoma 1020

FOLK-SONGS OF THE CIVIL RIGHTS MOVEMENT
Record company: X5 Music Group   **Format**: *mp3*   **Release date**: 2013
15 – March! For Martin Luther King   3:42   **Source**: *The Yellow Princess* –VSD 79293

THE BEST OF INDIE FOLK
Record company: X5 Music Group   **Format**: *mp3*   **Release date**: 2013
14 – Requiem for John Hurt   5:08   **Source**: *Requia* – Vanguard VSD 79259

RARE FOLK GEMS
Record company: X5 Music Group   **Format**: *mp3*   **Release date**: 2013
15 – Dance of the Inhabitants of the Invisible City of Bladensburg   4:10
Source: *The Yellow Princess* –VSD 79293

ROOTS GUITAR ESSENTIALS
Record company: X5 Music Group   **Format**: *mp3*   **Release date**: 2013
7 – Steel Guitar Medley   9:15   **Source**: *The Yellow Princess* –VSD 79795-2

A BEGINNERS GUIDE TO ROOTS GUITAR
Record company: X5 Music Group   **Format**: *mp3*   **Release date**: 2013
5 – Charles A. Lee: In Memoriam   4:02   **Source**: *The Yellow Princess* –VSD 79293

A BEGINNERS GUIDE TO ACOUSTIC BLUES
Record company: X5 Music Group   **Format**: *mp3*   **Release date**: 2013
17 – Steel Guitar Medley   9:15   **Source**: *The Yellow Princess* –VSD 79795-2

FOLK MASTERS: GUITARISTS
Record company: X5 Music Group   **Format**: *mp3*   **Release date**: 2013
4 – Requiem for John Hurt   5:10   **Source**: *Requia* – Vanguard VSD 79259

COUNTRY GUITAR GEMS
Record company: X5 Music Group   **Format**: *mp3*   **Release date**: 2013
18 – Dance of the Inhabitants of the Invisible City of Bladensburg   4:07
Source: *The Yellow Princess* –VSD 79293

CHRISTIAN BLUES MUSIC
Record company: X5 Music Group   **Format**: *mp3*   **Release date**: 2013
16 – Fight On Christians, Fight On   1:57   **Source**: *Requia* – Vanguard VSD 79259

CHAPTER 8
JOHN FAHEY VIDEOS

JOHN FAHEY / ELIZABETH COTTEN
RARE INTERVIEWS & PERFORMANCES FROM 1969

#1
Release date: 1993
Edition: 1st issue
Producer: Stefan Grossman's Guitar Workshop
Catalog number: GW 2301
Format: VHS

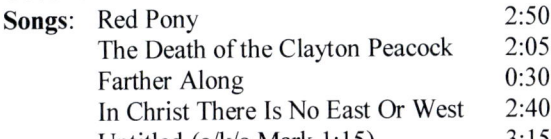

Front case cover: Fahey and Cotten
Cover credit: David Gahr
Songs: Red Pony   2:50
        The Death of the Clayton Peacock   2:05
        Farther Along   0:30
        In Christ There Is No East Or West   2:40
        Untitled (a/k/a Mark 1:15)   3:15
Recording Dates: 1969
Booklet: yes
Of note: (1) The segment with Fahey was first aired on the TV series *Guitar, Guitar* hosted by Laura Weber in December 1970. (2) The original 2" videotape made by KQED, a PBS station, is now held at the San Francisco State University.

#2
Release date: 1994
Edition: 2nd issue

Producer: Vestapol / Stefan Grossman's Guitar Workshop
Catalog number: Vestapol 13015
Format: VHS
Front case cover: Fahey and Cotten
Cover credit: David Gahr
Songs: same as #1
Recording Dates: same as #1.
Booklet: yes (16 pages), by Mark Humphrey

FINGERSTYLE GUITAR
NEW DIMENSIONS & EXPLORATIONS – VOL 1

#1
Release date: 1994
Edition: 1st issue
Producer: Vestapol Productions
Catalog number: Vestapol 13006
Format: VHS
Case front cover: two acoustic guitars

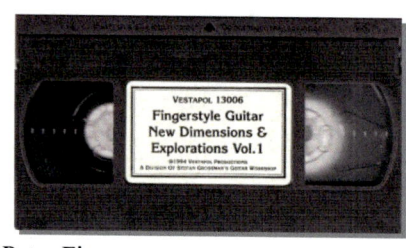

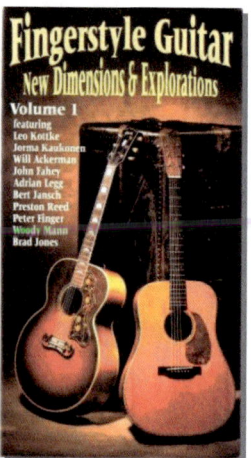

Cover credit: Peter Figen
Songs: three tunes by John Fahey

7 – Poor Boy	1:28	a
13 – Red Pony	2:55	b
17 – In Christ There Is No East Or West	2:40	b

Recording Dates: (a) ?, (b) 1969
Booklet: yes (16 pages), by Mark Humphrey.
Of note: (1) "Red Pony" and "In Christ" are excerpts from *John Fahey / Elizabeth Cotten: Rare Interviews & Performances from 1969.*

#2
Release date: 2003
Edition: 2nd issue
Producer: Vestapol Productions
Catalog number: Vestapol 13006
Format: DVD
Case front cover: five guitarists

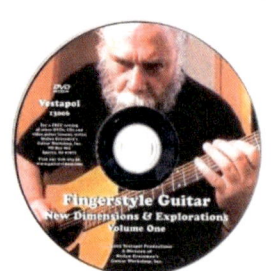

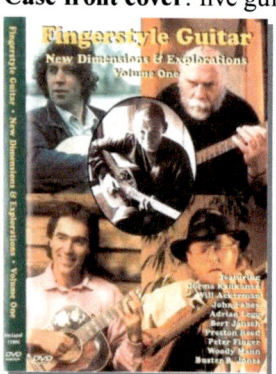

Cover credit:
Songs: four by J. Fahey

6 – Poor Boy	1:28	a
11 – Red Pony	2:55	b
15 – In Christ There Is No East Or West	2:40	b
17 – Some Summer Day		

Recording Dates: same as #1
Booklet: yes (32 pages and as a PDF file on the disc) by Mark Humphrey with guitar tab of "Some Summer Day."
Of note: (1) Track 17 is a bonus lesson from *The Guitar of John Fahey – Vol 1.*

WORLD OF SLIDE GUITAR

#1
Release date: 1996
Edition: 1st issue
Producer: Vestapol Productions
Catalog number: Vestapol 13061
Format: VHS
Case front cover: bottleneck guitar
Cover credit: Anna Grossman

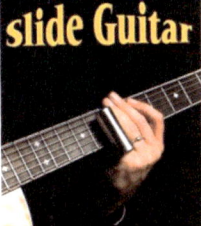

Songs:
11 – Steel Guitar Rag   2:30
12 – Discarded   5:10
Recording Dates: February 1996 concert at the Freight & Salvage, Berkeley, California.
Booklet: none
Of note: (1) This is an excerpt from Vestapol 13065 *John Fahey In Concert*.

#2
Release date: 2004
Edition: 2nd issue
Producer: Vestapol Productions
Catalog number: Vestapol 13061
Format: DVD
Case front cover: Debashish Bhattacharya

Cover credit: Anna Grossman
Songs: two songs by John Fahey
11 – Steel Guitar Rag   2:30
12 – Discarded   5:10
Recording Dates: February 1996 concert at the Freight & Salvage, Berkeley, California.
Booklet: yes (as a PDF file on the disc).
Of note: (1) This is an excerpt from Vestapol 13065 *John Fahey In Concert*.

JOHN FAHEY IN CONCERT

#1
Release date: 1996
Edition: 1st issue
Producer: Vestapol Productions
Catalog number: Vestapol 13065
Format: VHS
Case cover:
  - **Front cover**: Fahey playing guitar
Cover credit: Anna Grossman

Songs:
1 – City of Refuge	12:09
2 – *interview*	0:43
3 – Mexico	2:13
4 – *interview*	0:54
5 – Discarded	5:29
6 – *interview*	0:32
7 – Guitar Rag	2:37
8 – *interview*	0:34
9 – Who Will Rock The Cradle?	11:24
10 – 50's Medley: Blueberry Hill / Sea Of Love / Special Rider	7:45
11 – *interview*	0:33
12 – On The Sunnyside Of The Ocean	3:28
13 – *interview*	0:47
14 – St. Vitus Dance	3:17
15 – *interview*	0:53
16 – Dorothy	5:33
17 – Evening Not Night	2:50

Recording Dates: February 1996 concert at the Freight & Salvage, Berkeley, California.
Booklet: none
Of note: (1) In an interview at the Ash Grove the following year, Fahey said of this performance: "The best I played, up until that day." He also said: "Don't pay attention to the interview. I didn't mean anything I said."

#2

Release date: 2004
Edition: 2nd issue
Producer: Vestapol Productions
Catalog number: Vestapol 13065
Format: DVD
Case cover:
  - **Front cover**: Fahey with guitar in hand
Cover credit: Anna Grossman

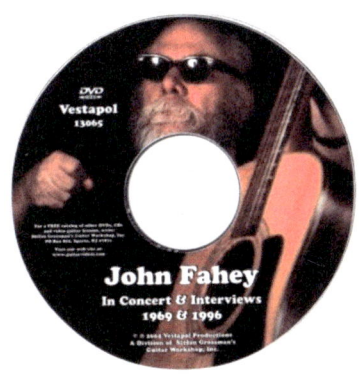

Songs:
see *John Fahey / Elizabeth Cotten* – Vestapol 13015
see *John Fahey In Concert* – Vestapol 13065
An informal *interview* (bonus addition)   18:05
Recording Dates: 1969 TV show *Guitar, Guitar* with Laura Weber; and February 1996 concert at the Freight & Salvage, Berkeley, California.
Booklet: none
Of note: (1) This DVD contains Fahey's segment on Vestapol 13015 and all of Vestapol 13065, as well as the complete interview from 1996.

THE GUITAR OF JOHN FAHEY - VOL 1

#1
Release date: 1996
Edition: 1st issue
Producer: Stephan Grossman's Guitar Workshop
Catalog number: GW 944
Format: VHS
Case front cover: Fahey playing guitar
Cover credit: Anna Grossman

Songs: 9 (duration: 77 minutes)
1 – ? (not a lesson)
2 – In Christ There Is No East Or West
3 – Claire
4 – Some Summer Day
5 – When The Springtime Comes Again
6 – Spanish Fandango
7 – Spanish Two-Step
8 – On The Sunny Side Of The Ocean
9 – How Long (not a lesson)

Recording Date: February 1996, backstage at the Freight & Salvage, Berkeley, California.
Booklet: yes (48 page booklet), with transcriptions by Alan Hager of all seven songs taught by Fahey plus "Sunflower River Blues."

#2
Release date: 2005
Edition: 2nd issue
Producer: Stephan Grossman's Guitar Workshop
Catalog number: GW 944
Format: DVD

Case front cover: Fahey playing guitar
Cover credit: Anna Grossman
Songs: 9 (duration: 77 minutes)
Same as #1
Recording Date: February 1996, backstage at the Freight & Salvage, Berkeley, California.
Booklet: yes (48 page booklet and as a PDF file on disc), with transcriptions by Alan Hager of all seven songs taught by Fahey plus "Sunflower River Blues."

THE GUITAR OF JOHN FAHEY - VOL 2

#1
Release date: 1996
Edition: 1st issue
Producer: Stephan Grossman's Guitar Workshop
Catalog number: GW 945
Format: VHS
Case front cover: Fahey playing lap-style slide guitar
Cover credit: Anna Grossman

Songs: 10 (duration: 64 minutes)
1 – ? (not a lesson)
2 – Poor Boy Long Way From Home
3 – My Prayer
4 – Marilyn
5 – The Red Pony
6 – Sunflower River Blues
7 – Joy To The World
8 – Steamboat Gwine Round De Bend
9 – Steel Guitar Rag
10 – Poor Boy (not a lesson)
Recording Date: February 1996, backstage at the Freight & Salvage, Berkeley, California.
Booklet: yes (56 page booklet), with transcriptions by Alan Hager of all eight songs taught by Fahey.

#2
Release date: 2005
Edition: 2nd issue
Producer: Stephan Grossman's Guitar Workshop
Catalog number: GW 945
Format: DVD

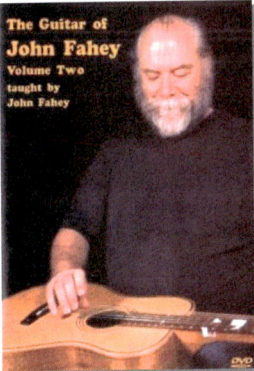

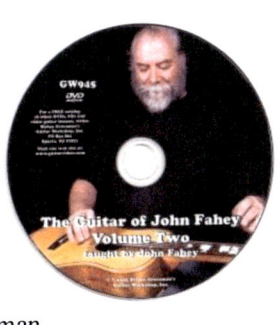

Case front cover: Fahey playing lap-style slide guitar
Cover credit: Anna Grossman
Songs: 10 (duration: 64 minutes)
Same as #1
Recording Dates: February 1996, backstage at the Freight & Salvage, Berkeley, California.
Booklet: yes (56 page booklet and as a PDF file on disc), with transcriptions by Alan Hager of all eight songs taught by Fahey.

CHRISTMAS SONGS & HOLIDAY MELODIES

#1
Release date: 1996
Edition: 1st issue
Producer: Stephan Grossman's Guitar Workshop
Catalog number: GW 946
Format: VHS
Case front cover: Fahey playing guitar
Cover credit: Anna Grossman

Songs: 11
1 – Joy To The World (not a lesson)
2 – Auld Lang Syne
3 – The Bells Of St. Mary's
4 – The First Noel
5 – Away In A Manger
6 – Medley: Jesus Won't You Come By Here / Go Tell It On The Mountain
7 – It Came Upon A Midnight Clear
8 – We Three Kings Of Orient Are
9 – Greensleeves (What Child Is This?)
10 – Silent Night
11 – Worried Blues (not a lesson)
Recording Dates: February 1996 concert at the Freight & Salvage, Berkeley, California.
Booklet: yes (36 page booklet) with transcriptions by Alan Hager of all nine songs taught by Fahey.

#2
Release date: 1996
Edition: 2nd issue
Producer: Vestapol Productions
Catalog number: GW 946
Format: DVD

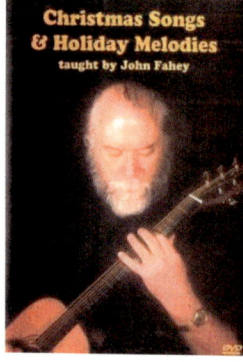

Case front cover: Fahey and Grossman arm wrestling
Cover credit: Anna Grossman
Songs: 11
Same as #1
Recording Dates: February 1996 concert at the Freight & Salvage, Berkeley, California.
Booklet: yes (36 page PDF file on disc), with transcriptions by Alan Hager of all nine songs taught by Fahey.

JOHN FAHEY LIVE – SANTA MONICA, APRIL '97

#1

Release date: 1997
Edition: 1st issue
Producer: Aes Nihil
Catalog number: no #
Format: VHS
Case cover:
  - **Front cover**: Fahey with guitar and sunglasses

Songs: (total: 1:31:35)
Guitar practice + informal interview — 4:35
Concert — 1:27:00
Recording Date: April 1997 concert at the Ash Grove, Santa Monica, California.
Booklet: no
Of note: (1) This concert was at the new Ash Grove which reopened in 1996 at the Santa Monica Pier. It would close soon after in 1997.
(2) John Fahey's concert followed a performance by Nels Cline that evening. During the pre-concert interview, Fahey complains about his show being so late, gives the finger to a couple of guys yapping while he is practicing, and in frustration says "C'mon, Nels. Just get the damn thing over with!"
(3) Some of pieces played by Fahey are: "City of Refuge I," "City of Refuge III," "Juana," "Song for Sara," and "Marilyn / My Prayer / Mood Indigo."

#2

Release date: 1997
Edition: 2nd issue
Producer: Aes-Nihil Productions
Catalog number: no #
Format: DVD
Case cover:
 - **Front cover**: Fahey with guitar

Songs: (total: 1:31:02)
Guitar practice + informal interview   4:01
Concert   1:27:00
Recording Date: April 1997 concert at the Ash Grove, Santa Monica, California.
Booklet: no
Of note: (1) The title now is "John Fahey – Live at the Ash Grove '97."

STRINGS AND FRETS

#1
Release date: 1999
Edition: 1st issue
Producer: Vestapol Productions
Catalog number: Vestapol 13088
Format: VHS
Front case cover: girl with guitar

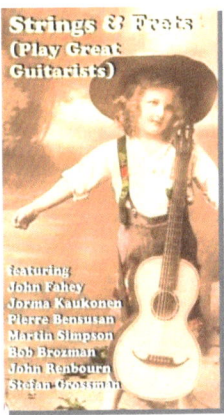

Back cover credit: Anna Grossman
Songs: two songs by Fahey
– *interview*   0:35
– On The Sunnyside Of The Ocean   3:31
– *interview*   0:54
– Who Will Rock The Cradle   11:15
Recording Dates: February 1996, live concert at the Freight & Salvage, Berkeley, California.
Booklet: yes (40 pages), by Jim Ohlschmidt.
Of note: (1) The Fahey tunes and interview clips are an excerpt from Vestapol 13065 *John Fahey In Concert*.

#2
Release date: 2007
Edition: 2nd issue
Producer: Vestapol Productions
Catalog number: Vestapol 13088
Format: DVD
Front cover: Fahey and Grossman arm wrestling
Cover credit: Anna Grossman

Songs: two songs by Fahey
– *interview*   0:35
– On The Sunnyside Of The Ocean   3:31
– *interview*   0:54
– Who Will Rock The Cradle   11:15
Recording Dates: February 1996, live concert at the Freight & Salvage, Berkeley, California.
Booklet: yes (40 page booklet, and a PDF file on the disc), by Jim Ohlschmidt.
Of note: (1) The Fahey tunes and interview clips are an excerpt from Vestapol 13065 *John Fahey In Concert*.

ROCKPALAST – 17 MARCH, 1978

#1
Release date: 2011
Edition: 1st issue
Producer: Blast First Petite
Catalog number: PTYT 037
Format: DVD
Front case cover: Fahey playing guitar
Cover credit: Manfred Mann

Songs: 11 (total 72 minutes)
1 – On The Sunny Side Of The Ocean	3:45
2 – Hawaiian Two-Step	2:05
3 – Lion	7:20
4 – Wine And Roses	5:00
5 – Poor Boy Long Ways From Home	5:00
6 – Steamboat Gwine 'Round De Bend	3:55
7 – How Green Was My Valley	3:05
8 – Candy Man / Brendas Blues / Take A Look At That Baby	4:00
9 – Beverly	4:48
10 – Medley	4:12
11 – *Interview*	5:00

Recording Dates: Audimax in Hamburg, Germany, on March 17, 1978.
Booklet: none
Of note: (1) Track 10 called "Medley" actually lasts over 22 minutes and is composed of the following tunes:
10a – When You Wore A Tulip / Ann Arbor	8:25
10b – The Revolt of the Dyke Brigade / Requiem for Mississippi John Hurt	6:30
10c – The Grand Finale	3:30
10d – Poor Boy / Steel String Guitar	3:40

(2) Several bootleg DVDs of this TV show, without interview, were previously released. (3) Audimax is a concert hall located on the University of Hamburg campus. (4) In 1980, Fahey told his friend Jürgen Kleine: "I do not like the way I played at Hamburg U. The backstage scene made me very nervous."

GUITAR ARTISTRY OF JOHN FAHEY
ON THE SUNNY SIDE OF THE OCEAN

#1
Release date: 2011
Edition: 1st issue
Producer: Vestapol Productions
Catalog number: Vestapol 13121
Format: DVD
Front case cover: Fahey with two guitars
Cover credit: Anna Grossman

Songs:
1 – Red Pony   a
2 – The Death of the Clayton Peacock   a
3 – In Christ There Is No East or West   a
4 – Poor Boy   b
5 – Medley: Twilight on Prince George's Avenue / O Holy Night / My Prayer   c
6 – Who Will Rock The Cradle?   c
7 – Steamboat 'Gwine Round The Bend   c
8 – The Story of Dorothy Gooch, Part One   c
9 – Guitar Rag   d
10 – On The Sunny Side of The Ocean   d
11 – Medley: Blueberry Hill / Special Rider   d
12 – St. Vitus Dance   d
13 – Dorothy   d
14 – City of Refuge   d
12 – Mexico   d
13 – Discarded   d
14 – Untitled (a/k/a Mark 1:15)   a
15 – *Interview* with Christian Roebling
16 – Some Summer Day (guitar lesson)

Recording Dates: (a) 1969 TV show *Guitar, Guitar* with Laura Weber; (b) ? (c) ? (d) February 1996 concert at the Freight & Salvage, Berkeley, California.
Booklet: none
Of note: (1) Each song is separated by a snippet of the backstage interview with Fahey. (2) The title of track 7 is spelled with a misplaced apostrophe.

IN SEARCH OF BLIND JOE DEATH
THE SAGA OF JOHN FAHEY

#1
Release date: 2012 (actually released in 2013)
Edition: 1st issue
Producer: First Run Features
Catalog number: FRF 915731D
Format: DVD
Case cover:
  - **Front cover**: Fahey with guitar
Cover credit:

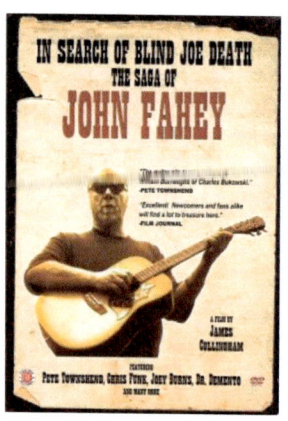
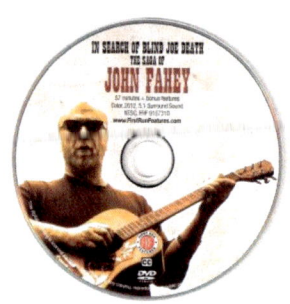

Movie: 57 minutes, Color
Director: James Cullingham
Bonus Features:
1) Rare John Fahey performance footage.
2) John Fahey Speaks – Woodburn Inn, 1999:
   a) The Great Koonaklaster
   b) Record Collecting
   c) The Factory
   d) Religion
3) Performances by Chris Funk, Jimmy Crosthwait, George Winston, Joe Bussard, Stefan Grossman, Terry Robb, Tim Knight, as well as by:
   John Fahey: a) Poor Boy   1:30
                   b) On The Sunny Side Of The Ocean   4:10
4) Extended interviews with Pete Townsend, Dean Blackwood, Chris Funk, and Joe Bussard.

JOHN FAHEY IN MOVIE SOUNDTRACKS

The following is a list of movies in which the soundtrack includes guitar pieces played by John Fahey.

1) **Zabriskie Point** (1970): "Dance of Death"

2) **Straight Time** (1978): "Desperate Man Blues"

3) **One Year Among the Many** (1980): "How Long," "Come To The Garden," "Lettuce and Tomatoes / Cold As Ice," "That New Song," "Come To The Garden (reprise)."

   An 11-minute film directed and produced by Este Gardner. "How Long" is from *Dance of Death*. The other titles were newly recorded on December 1, 1980, at The Sound Service in San Francisco, California. Another tune, "Doxology," was not included in the film score.

4) **Dogfight** (1991): "Sunflower River Blues"

4) **The Horse Whisperer** (1998): "Desperate Man Blues"

5) **One Nation Under** (2005): "Red Cross, Disciple of Christ Today"

6) **Following Sean** (2006): "Sligo River Blues"

7) **Idiotmaker's Gravity Tour** (2011): "When The Catfish Is In Bloom," "Impressions of Susan," "How Long," "Marilyn," "America," "The Portland Cement Factory At Monolith, California," "We Would Be Building," "America."

JOHN FAHEY ON TELEVISION

John Fahey's tunes were also used on soundtracks to documentaries, television programs, as well as several commercials.

1) **Bay View Massacre of 1886** – documentary (1987): "Requiem for Mississippi John Hurt," "When the Catfish is in Bloom."

2) **The Donner Party** – documentary (1992): "Fear And Loathing at 4th & Butternut"

3) **Skins** – season 2, episode 5 (2008): "Lion"

LIVE UNOFFICIAL RECORDINGS

Swarthmore College, Swarthmore, PA	April 5, 1968
Santa Barbara, CA	1968
Polytech, Worcester, MA	1969
Zabriskie Point session, Rome, Italy	1969
Matrix, San Francisco, CA	February 11 or November 2, 1969
Jabberwocky, Syracuse, NY	July 15, 1972
McCabe's Guitar Shop, Santa Monica, CA	September 1972
Paul Masson Winery, Saratoga, CA	September 17, 1972
Student Union at SUNY, Stonybrook, NY	October 1, 1972
University of Washington, Seattle, WA	January 1973
McCabe's Guitar Shop, Santa Monica, CA	April 1973
Live at Record Plant, Sausalito, CA	September 9, 1973
Live at Carnegie Hall, New York, NY	September 23, 1973
McCabe's Guitar Shop, Santa Monica, CA	June 7, 1974
Hunter College, New York, NY	May 31, 1975
Live at The Barn, UC-Riverside, CA	November 6, 1976
Live at the Great Midwestern Music Hall, Louisville, KY	December 13, 1977
Paradise Theater, Boston, MA	June 8, 1978
Late Show at Mr. Brown's, Columbus, OH	June 19, 1978
Jonathan Swift's, Cambridge, MA	November 19, 1979
McCabe's Guitar Shop, Santa Monica, CA	December 1979
Passim's, Cambridge, MA	July 15, 1981
Ironhorse Coffeehouse, Northampton, MA	July 19, 1981
Jonathan Swift's, Cambridge, MA	November 3, 1981
Boon's Treasury, Salem, OR	January 10, 1982
Recording Session, Milano, Italy	March 1982
Teatro delle Arti, Gallarate, Italy	March 8, 1982
Teatro Latina, Latina, Italy	March 15, 1982
Jonathan Swift's, Cambridge, MA	June 3, 1982
Berklee Center, Boston, MA	November 4, 1982
Cambridge Folk Festival, England	July 30, 1983
Villa Borghese, Rome, Italy	August 3, 1983
The Old Curch, Portland, OR	August 26, 1984
Holstein's, Chicago, IL	December 7, 1984
Live at Rum Doodle's, Madison, WI	December 9, 1984
Live at the Speakeasy, New York, NY	September 20, 1985
Passim's, Cambridge, MA	April 16, 1986

Live at the Cactus Café, University of Texas, Austin, TX	May 13, 1986
Skipper's Smokehouse, Tampa, FL	June 18, 1986
Palace Theater, Silverton, OR	July 2, 1987
The Birchmere, Alexandria, VA	August 26, 1987
University of Buffalo, Buffalo, NY	October 1, 1987
Gardner Arts Centre, Brighton, England	October 5, 1987
Town and Country, London, England	October 6, 1987
BBC Studios, London, England	October 8, 1987
WNYC - Summerstage in Central Park - NYC	June 18, 1988
Grand Theater, Salem, OR	December 12, 1991
WNYC – *New Sounds* Radio Show with John Shaefer	May 9, 1991
Boone's Treasury, Salem, OR	June 8, 1995
The Weathered Wall, Seattle, WA	May 31, 1996
The Empty Bottle, Chicago, IL	November 8, 1996
UNTITLED - From WFMU - John Allen Show [8-9 shows]	1997
John Fahey & Jim O'Rourke, Radio WNUR, Chicago, IL	1998
Lenora's Ghost, Independence, OR	June 5, 1998
Guiness Fleadh Fest, Randall's Island, NY	June 13, 1998
Live at the Stork Club, WFMU radio, NJ	July 19, 1998
Taku Taku, Kyoto, Japan	June 4, 1999
Dutch Radio, Amsterdam, NL	July 4, 1999
Christ Community Church, Aurora, OR	August 14, 1999
Live at Whelan's Bar, Dublin, Ireland	September 24, 1999
Stamford's Art Centre, Lincolnshire, England	September 27, 1999
Brudenell's Social Club, Leeds, UK	September 30, 1999
Queen Elizabeth's Hall, London, England	October 2, 1999
Cat's Cradle, 3rd Transmissions Festival, Carrborro, NC	July 15, 2000
The Empty Bottle, Chicago, IL	October 1, 2000
The Last Sessions	November 2000 – January 2001

LIVE UNOFFICIAL VIDEOS

"Fare Forward Voyagers" at Euphoria Tavern, Portland, OR	July 29, 1976
"Dance of the Inhabitants of the Palace of King Phillip XIV" at Euphoria Tavern, Portland, OR	July 29, 1976
Full concert at the New Varsity Theater, Palo Alto, CA	October 11, 1981
Full concert at the Horizon Theatre, Atlanta, GA	August 9, 1997

CONCERTS - GIGS

DATE	VENUE	CITY, COUNTRY
Mar 28, 1964	UCLA Folk Festival 3:30 pm – $2.00	Los Angeles, CA
Sep 4, 1964	Bitter Lemon	Memphis, TN
July 2, 1965	Folk City, USA WCRB radio, 11:15 pm	Boston, MA

Fahey participates as a live performance as a guest on the show.

July 5-17, 1965	Odyssey	Boston, MA

(This set of concerts was reviewed by no less than four different critics in the August 4th issue of *Broadside of Boston*)
From the review by Al Wilson we know that some of the pieces Fahey played were:
"When the Springtime Comes Again"
"The Death of the Clayton Peacock"
"The Portland Cement Factory in Monolith, California"
"Bicycle Built For Two"
"Dixie"

July 27-28, 30-31, 1965	Turks Head	Boston, MA
Aug 3, 1965	Club 47	Boston, MA
Sep 26, 1965	Jabberwock	Berkeley, CA
Nov 26-27, 1965	Jabberwock	Berkeley, CA

---

the ODYSSEY — Boston's Newest and Largest Coffeehouse

july 5-18
JOHN FAHEY

july 19-24
FOUR WOMEN ONLY

3 hancock st.   523-9457
corner of cambridge st. in boston

Dec 10-12, 1965	Ash Grove	Los Angeles, CA
Jan 7-8, 1966	Jabberwock	Berkeley, CA
Jan 28-29, 1966	The Folksinger	Portland, OR
Mar 11-12, 1966	Jabberwock	Berkeley, CA
Mar 27, 1966	Jabberwock	Berkeley, CA
Apr 15-16, 1966	Jabberwock	Berkeley, CA
Apr 23, 1966	Golden Ring	Claremont, CA
May 27-28, 1966	Jabberwock	Berkeley, CA
June 12, 1966	Ash Grove	Los Angeles, CA
June 20, 1966	Jabberwock 9:00 pm	Berkeley, CA
July 1, 1966	9th Annual Berkeley Folk Festival 8:00 pm – $2.25	Berkeley, CA

"Guitarist John Fahey ... employed radically altered guitar tunings to explore sonorities reminiscent of the zither and sitar. His unstructured offerings were casual to the point of unpreparedness."
Paul Hertelendy, *Oakland Tribune*

July 4, 1966	9th Annual Berkeley Folk Festival 2:00 pm – $2.25-$3.50	Berkeley, CA

At this festival John Fahey participated also in:
Workshop: "Robert Pete Williams and the Blues"
Panel: "Topical songs – Their role in politics and Folk Music"
Workshop: "New Directions in Guitar"
Workshop: "Guitar Workshop"

Sep 10, 1966	Church of St. Michael	Adelphi, MD
Nov 25-27, 1966	Jabberwock	Berkeley, CA
Dec 30-Jan 1, 1967	Jabberwock	Berkeley, CA
Jan 6, 13 & 14, 1967	Finnish Brotherhood Hall 8:00 pm – $2.00	Berkeley, CA
Feb 24-25, 1967	Jabberwock 9:00 pm	Berkeley, CA
Apr 10, 1967	Calif. College of Arts & Crafts 6-9 pm	Oakland, CA
Apr 14-16, 1967	Jabberwock	Berkeley, CA
Apr 29-30, 1967	Alexandra Palace 8:00 pm – £1.00 [Fahey probably cancelled]	London, England
May 21, 1967	Jabberwock	Berkeley, CA
May 27, 1967	Washington School Auditorium 9:00 pm – $2.00	Berkeley, CA
May 28, 1967	Jabberwock	Berkeley, CA
June 2-3, 1967	Jabberwock	Berkeley, CA
July 2-3, 1967	Jabberwock	Berkeley, CA

Poster for John Fahey concerts held in the Takoma Park area in 1967 (Design by Char Owens)

July 3, 1967	Berkeley Folk Music Festival (with Red Crayola)	Berkeley, CA
July 9, 1967	New Orleans House 6:00-10:00 pm	Berkeley, CA

Aug 25, 1967	Church of St. Michael 8:30 pm – $1.50	Adelphi, MD
Sep 1, 1967	Christ Church 8:30 pm – $1.50	Washington, DC
Sep 2, 1967	St. Stephen & the Incarnation Church 8:30 pm – $1.50	Washington, DC
Sep 3, 1967	Tyding's Auto Garage 8:30 pm – $1.50	Annapolis, MD
Oct 20, 1967	Bear's Lair 8:30 pm & 10:00 pm – $0.75	Berkeley, CA
Nov 14, 1967	Straight Theater	San Francisco, CA
Nov 17-19, 1967	Straight Theater 8/9:00 pm – $2.50	San Francisco, CA
Nov 25-27, 1967	Jabberwock	Berkeley, CA
Dec 8, 1967	Eagle's Auditorium 8-12:00 pm – $3.00	Seattle, WA
Jan 19, 1968	Bear's Lair 9:00 & 11:00 pm – $1.25	Berkeley, CA
Mar 10, 1968	New Orleans House 9:30-1:00 am	Berkeley, CA
Mar 17, 1968	New Orleans House	Berkeley, CA
Mar 24, 1968	New Orleans House	Berkeley, CA
Apr 5, 1968	Swarthmore College 8:15 pm	Swarthmore, PA

(reel tapes of this concert are preserved in the
Historical Library of Swarthmore College)

Apr 18-21, 1968	Café Au Go Go	New York, NY
Apr 27, 1968	Christ Church 8:00 pm – $2.50	Cambridge, MA
May 18, 1968	Campus Hall, UC at Irvine 8:30 pm – $1.50	Irvine, CA
Jun 9, 1968	Ash Grove	Los Angeles, CA
Jun 15-16, 1968	Ash Grove	Los Angeles, CA
July 4, 1968	Berkeley Folk Festival 1:00-5:00 pm – $1.50	Berkeley, CA
July 7, 1968	Berkeley Folk Festival 2:00 pm – $2.25	Berkeley, CA

". . . stone-faced John Fahey from UCLA, who plays his offbeat
harmonies and chromaticisms on his guitar laid flat on his lap.
Does he know something we don't?"
Paul Hertelendy, *Oakland Tribune*

July 16, 1968   [TV show "Berkeley Folk Festival" – Laura Weber host]
[Fahey, among others at this festival, was shown on this hour-long PBS TV
program]

Aug 31, 1968	Sky River Rock Festival	Sultan, WA
Oct 18, 1968		Santa Barbara, CA

APPENDIX C

Nov 16, 1968	LeConte School 8:30 pm – $2.25	Berkeley, CA
Dec 6-8, 1968	Ash Grove	Los Angeles, CA
Jan 1, 1969 ?	Polytech	Worcester, MA
Jan 24-Feb 2, 1969	Ash Grove	Los Angeles, CA
Feb 11, 1969 ?	Matrix	San Francisco, CA
Feb 14, 1969	Giannini High School 8:30-12:00 pm – $2.50	San Francisco, CA
Mar 7-8, 1969	Elks 99 8:00 pm & 2:00 am – $1.50	Los Angeles, CA
Mar 15, 1969	West Campus Auditorium 8:30 pm – $2.25-$2.75	Berkeley, CA
Mar 31-Apr 5, 1969	The Cellar Door	Washington, DC
May 2, 1969	Lisner Auditorium at GWU 8:00 pm – $3.00-$4.00	Washington, DC
May 6, 1969	Main Point	Bryn Mawr, PA
May 12, 1969	Hornsey Town Hall 7:45 pm – 10/- & 12/6d	London, England
May 15, 1969	Southampton University	Southampton, England
May 17, 1969	Institute of Science & Technology	Manchester, England
May 18, 1969	Camden Festival 2:00 pm-8:00 pm	Hampstead Heath, England
May 18, 1969	Collegiate Theatre 8:00 pm – 10/-	London, England
May …, 1969	[cancelled]	Sweden
May 25, 1969	Roundhouse 3 pm-6 pm – 10/-	London, England

One song Fahey played was "Special Rider Blues.".

May 26, 1969	The Dome 7:30 pm – 13/6d	Brighton, England
May 31, 1969	Mothers Club in Erdington 10s-12s/6p	Birmingham, England
June 6-7, 1969	Country Blues Festival	Memphis, TN

Some of the pieces Fahey played were:
"The Death of the Clayton Peacock,"
"How Green Was My Valley".
[Fahey, among others at this festival, was shown on the two hour-long PBS TV program *The Memphis Birthday Blues Festival* hosted by Steve Allen and first aired on June 29, 1969]

July 5, 1969	Viscount Records store 1:00-4:00 pm	Santa Monica, CA
Oct 4, 1969	Gold Rush Concert $3.50	Lake Amador, CA
Oct 10-12, 1969	Ash Grove 8:30-2:00 am – $2.50	Los Angeles, CA

APPENDIX C

Oct 18, 1969	Campbell Hall, UCSB 8:00 pm – $2.50	Santa Barbara, CA
Oct 23-26, 1969	UC Berkeley Folk Festival	Berkeley, CA

Workshop "An Hour with John Fahey": Oct 24 at 4:00 pm
Concert: Oct 24 at 8:00 pm
Concert: Oct 26 at 2:00 pm:

Nov 7, 1969	Giannini High School	San Francisco, CA
Nov 8, 1969	Poppycock 9 pm-2 am – $2.50	Palo Alto, CA
Nov 16, 1969	Canterbury House 7:00 & 9:00 – $2.00	Ann Arbor, MI
Nov 20, 1969	Holy Family Church 8:00 pm	Omaha, NE

"His opening number was a long and demanding piece called "The Death and Resurrection of Our Lord Jesus Christ"
James Bresette, *Omaha World Herald*

Nov 22, 1969	Cal State 8:00 pm – $3.50	Fullerton, CA
Jan 10, 1970	University of California 8:00 pm – $2.50	Riverside, CA
Apr 24, 1970	Washington Square Church 8:30 pm	New York, NY
Apr 28, 1970	Main Point	Bryn Mawr, PA
Apr 30-May 2, 1970	Boston Tea Party	Boston, MA

"Make sure to arrive early enough to hear all of John Fahey's beautiful set. No vocals — just an expressive, enormously gifted guitarist who concentrates on making his instrument sing."
Timothy Crouse, *Boston Herald*

May 14-17, 1970	Ash Grove $2.50	Los Angeles, CA
Jun 5-6, 1970	Matrix	San Francisco, CA
Jun 19-20, 1970	McCabe's Guitar Shop 8:00 pm & 10:30 pm	Santa Monica, CA
Jul 25-26, 1970	Reading Folk Encaenia	Swallowfield, England

[concert festival was postponed / cancelled]

Aug 2, 1970	The Golden Bear	Huntington Beach, CA
Aug 23, 1970	New Orleans House	Berkeley, CA
Sep 10-12, 1970	Matrix	San Francisco, CA
Sep 25-26, 1970	McCabe's Guitar Shop 8:00 pm	Santa Monica, CA
Oct 10, 1970	Antioch College 8:30 pm – $3.00	Yellow Springs, OH
Oct 16-18, 1970	Winterland 8:30 pm – $3.50	San Francisco, CA

[John Fahey rescheduled for December]

Oct 26, 1970   Washington Square Church   New York, NY
8:30-12:00 pm – $2.00
"When Mr. Fahey put down his bottle, balanced his cigarette on its tray & got down to business, he produced a most remarkable session of guitar playing."
John S. Wilson, *The New York Times*

Nov 28, 1970	Southampton University	Southampton, England
Dec 11, 1970	[Fahey on "Guitar, Guitar" TV show with Laura Weber]	
Jan 15, 1971	University of California	Santa Barbara, CA
Jan 22-23, 1971	Pepperland	San Rafael, CA
	8:30-2:00 am – $3.50	
Feb 4-6, 1971	Matrix	San Francisco, CA
Feb 20-21, 1971	U. of Pittsburgh Blues Festival	Pittsburgh, PA

Concert: Feb 20 at 8:00 pm – $4.00
Blues Workshop: Feb 21 at 1:30 pm - with John Fahey
"John Fahey whose lengthy guitar works assimilating countless blues chords and modes is almost concerto and symphonic in its approach."
Len Kunstadt, *Record Research*

John Fahey's workshop at the Pitt's Student Union during the Pittsburgh Blues Festival, 1971.

"John Fahey in a talkathon making with the Fahey philosophy which is quite complicated and bewildering at times – but very entertaining."
Len Kunstadt, *Record Research*

Feb 24, 1971	Main Point	Bryn Mawr, PA
Mar 3, 1971	The Whole Coffeehouse	Minneapolis, MN
	9:00 pm-1:00 am – $2.50	
Mar 8, 1971	St. Paul Student Center	St. Paul, MN
	8:00 pm – $2.00	
Mar 11, 1971	Civic Hall	Guildford, England
	7:30 pm – 40p-80p	
Apr 12-13, 1971	Ash Grove	Los Angeles, CA

May 3, 1971	Ledbetter's	Los Angeles, CA
May 6-9, 1971	Ash Grove	Los Angeles, CA
Jun 18-20, 1971	Sunrise Concert (? cancelled) $7.00	WA
Aug 7-8, 1971	Quiet Knight	Chicago, IL
Aug 26, 1971	33rd National Folk Festival	Vienna, VA

Blues Workshop: 11:00 am - with Taj Mahal and John Fahey
" 'Weep Like A Willow And Moan Like A Morning Dove' which [Taj Mahal] sang with guitarist John Fahey."
Hollie West, *The Washington Post*

"Accompanying [Taj Mahal] is John Fahey . . . They play three traditional numbers, including 'Fishin' Blues.' "
Tom Zito, *The Washington Post*

Aug 28, 1971	33rd National Folk Festival 7:30 pm – $1.00-$5.00	Vienna, VA

"John Fahey . . . tended to drag compositions out beyond the attention span of most in the audience — an audience unusually boorish . . ."
Tom Zito, *The Washington Post*

Aug 29, 1971	Main Point	Bryn Mawr, PA
Sep 6, 1971	Washington Square Methodist Church 8:30 pm	New York, NY
Oct 10, 1971	New Monk	Berkeley, CA
Oct 14, 1971	Earth 8:00 & 11:00 pm	San Diego, CA
Nov 12, 1971	Berkeley Community Theatre 8:00 pm – $2.50	Berkeley, CA

"John Fahey opened the set and . . . superbombed. . . . he was a real bumber and we couldn't wait to get him off the stage."
K. Staska & G. Mangrum, *The Daily Review*

Nov 27-28, 1971	Ash Grove	Los Angeles, CA
Dec 3, 1971	St. Aidan's Episcopal Church	San Francisco, CA
Jan 17, 1972	Sunset Canyon Rec. Ctr. - UCLA 8:00 & 10:00 pm - $0.50	Los Angeles, CA
Apr 6-8, 1972	The Boarding House	San Francisco, CA
Apr 14, 1972	California Lutheran College 8:15 pm	Oxnard, CA
Apr 17, 1972	Lighthouse	Hermosa Beach, CA
Apr 20-23, 1972	Ash Grove	Los Angeles, CA
Apr 28-30, 1972	The Golden Bear	Huntington Beach, CA
May 7, 1972	Queen Elizabeth Theatre 7:30 pm & 10:30 pm – $3.50-$5.50	Vancouver, Canada
May 19-20, 1972	Palace of Fine Arts 8:30 pm – $3.00	San Francisco, CA
June 16-17, 1972	Summertime Blues Concert 7:00 pm	Ann Arbor, MI

July 10, 1972	Washington Square Church 8:30 pm	New York, NY
July 15, 1972	Jabberwocky	Syracuse, NY
July 25, 1972	Main Point	Bryn Mawr, PA
Aug 16, 1972	Community Church, 40 E 35th St 7:30 pm	New York, NY

[Celebration 1: a benefit concert for the Integral Yoga Institute]

Aug 18, 1972	Sherwood Lodge 8:00 pm – $2.00-$2.50	Rockford, IL
Sep 1, 1972	McCabe's Guitar Shop	Santa Monica, CA
Sep 5-9, 1972	The Boarding House	San Francisco, CA

[The September 7 show at 10:30 pm was aired live on KPFA]
[The concerts were organized by Warner Bros to promote Fahey's new album *Of Rivers and Religion*]

"The Warner's junket was obviously self-defeating, assembling an inattentive audience guaranteed to antagonize a temperamental performer and almost to ensure a poor performance."
Peggy Baker, *Daily Bruin*

Sep 16-17, 1972	Paul Masson Mountain Winery 3:00 pm	Saratoga, CA
Sep 25, 1972	The Lighthouse	Hermosa Beach, CA
Sep 29-Oct 1, 1972	Max's Kansas City	New York, NY

"There were no words from Fahey or the audience as both shared in a sound that said whatever needed saying at the moment."
Ira Mayer, *Village Voice*

Oct 1, 1972	SUNY Student's Union	Stonybrook, NY
Oct 7, 1972	Bristol Bay Club	Long Beach, CA
Oct 27-29, 1972	McCabe's Guitar Shop 8:00 & 10:00 pm	Santa Monica, CA
Dec 3, 1972	Shimer College 7:30 pm – free	Chicago, IL
Dec 6, 1972	Northwestern U. - Cahn Auditorium 8:30 pm – $2.50	Evanston, IL

"Living legend John Fahey . . . managed to be stunning and uncharismatic at the same time. After an hour, he finally spoke – to announce the intermission. But his playing says it all. It is a hypnotic thing and haunts the mind long afterward. He seems to be meditating through his fingers and transfiguring his blues and classical themes from a state of grace."
Al Rudis, *Melody Maker*

Jan or Feb, 1973	University of Washington	Seattle, WA
Feb 23, 1973	Palace of Fine Arts 8:00 – $3.00	San Francisco, CA

"Benefit Concert: Satchidananda Ashram – Yogaville West
Sponsored by Integral Yoga Institute"

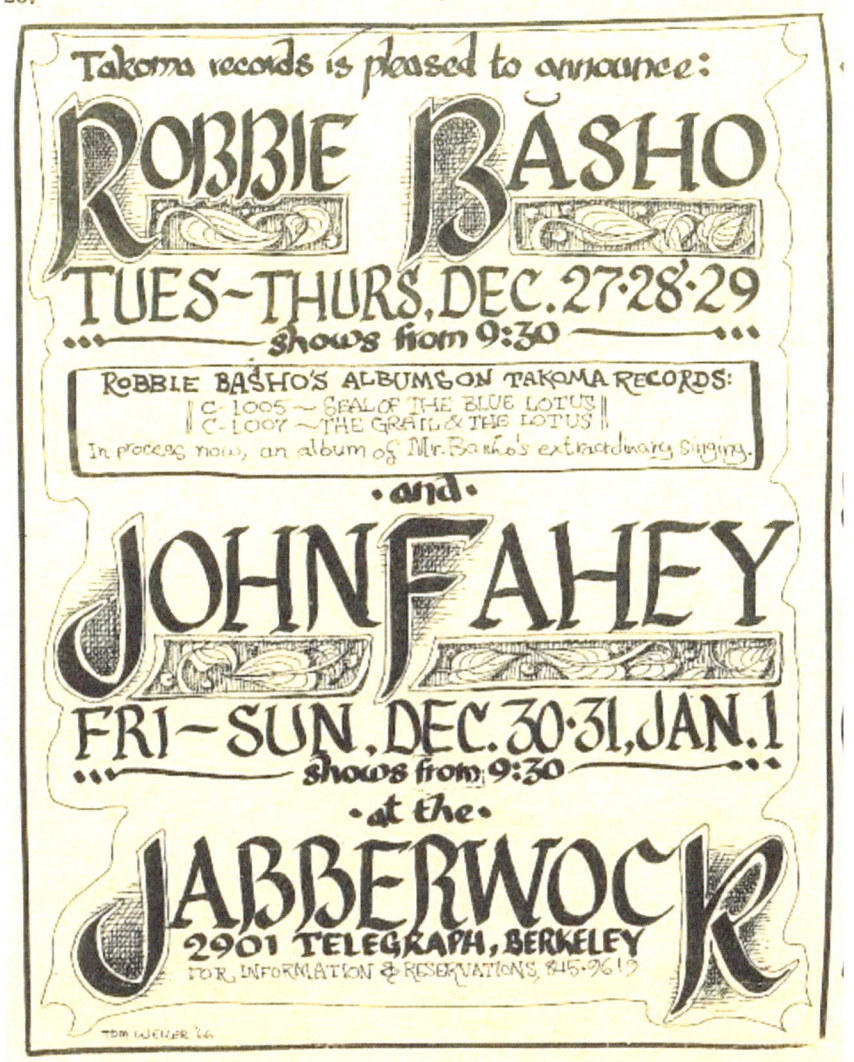

Poster of Fahey & Basho concerts in December 1966-January 1967 (Design by Tom Weller)

Mar 16-18, 1973	The Boarding House $2.50	San Francisco, CA
Mar 23, 1973	Oxford Hotel	Denver, CO
Mar 30-31, 1973	McCabe's Guitar Shop 8:00 & 10:00 pm – $3.50	Santa Monica, CA
Apr 20, 1973	University of Washington 7:00 & 10:00 pm – $2.00-2.50 [aired by radio station KOL-FM]	Seattle, WA

Apr 24, 1973	Univ. of Minnesota 7:00 pm – $3.00	Minneapolis, MN

"The John Fahey concert had come out $400 off budget . . . part of the problem had been the dumb old *Daily*'s failure to print two major ads."
Minutes of the Union Program Council

May 5, 1973	Lisner Auditorium at GWU 8:00 pm – $3.50-$4.50	Washington, DC

"At the end he rose abruptly and left the stage without a word, and would not come back despite the ovation and cheers of the crowd."
Mark Spivak, *Washington Post*

May 11-12, 1973	Buffalo Folk Festival (transmitted on the radio on June 1, 1974)	Buffalo, NY
May 13, 1973	Ingle Auditorium at RIT 8:00 pm – $2.50-$4.00	Rochester, NY
May 17, 1973	WNUR-FM radio show of concert taped at Northwestern U.	
Sep 9, 1973	Record Plant 11:00 pm [aired live on KSAN-FM radio]	Sausalito, CA
Sep 21, 1973	Carnegie Hall 8:00 pm – $4.50-$8.50	New York, NY

"Fahey's music is obsessive, with its strumming drones and compulsive reiteration of short fragments, and the effect is mystically hypnotic."
John Rockwell, *The New York Times*

Sep 28, 1973	Humboldt State Gym	Eureka, CA
Oct 7, 1973	Queen's College 10:00 pm – $4.50	Queens, NY
Dec 7-10, 1973	Amazingrace Coffeehouse	Evanston, IL
Jan 1-2, 1974	Main Point	Bryn Mawr, PA
Mar 2, 1974	Univ. of Missouri-Columbia 8:00 pm - free	Jefferson City, MO
Mar 4-5, 1974	Quiet Knight	Chicago, IL
Mar 21-23, 1974	Ebbets Field	Denver, CO
Apr 23, 1974	Main Point	Bryn Mawr, PA
May 10, 1974	Schoenberg Hall - UCLA	Los Angeles, CA
May 16, 1974	Schoenberg Hall - UCLA	Los Angeles, CA
May 31, 1974	Portland State University 8:00 pm – $3.50	Portland, OR
June 1, 1974	U. of Washington - Roethke Aud. 7:30 pm – $1.50-$3.50	Seattle, WA
June 7-8, 1974	McCabe's Guitar Shop 8:00 & 10:00 pm	Santa Monica, CA
July 19, 1974	Great American Music Hall 9:00 & 11:30 pm	San Francisco, CA
Aug 19, 1974	Lighthouse	Hermosa Beach, CA

APPENDIX C   403

*Concert ad for Fahey concerts at the Jabberwock in November 1966
(Design by Tom Weller)*

Aug 23-25, 1974   Amazingrace Coffeehouse   Evanston, IL
                         8:30 & 11:00 pm
"Fahey, speaking in a strange mongrel of an accent, not really Latin, nor French, nor Asian Indian ... was imagining himself to be the Brazilian guitarist Bola Sete. Then he ... began to play. All that was left was the Fahey sound, coming out of his guitar, and sweeping into the mind. It was another triumph."
              Al Rudis, *Melody Maker*

Aug 30-Sep 1, 1974   Good Karma   Madison, WI
                          9:00 pm
"John Fahey came on stage ... wearing levis with the cuffs rolled up wide and a grey t-shirt ... he was heavier ... wore glasses, and had an intimidating physical intensity about him."
              Robert LaBrasca, *Madison Capital Times*

Sep 4, 1974   Teddy's   Milwaukee, WI
"An audience nearly frozen in mute appreciation attentively followed the hypnotic meanderings of Fahey's fingerpicking for more than two hours."
              Stephen Wiest, *The Milwaukee Journal*

Sep 13-14, 1974   Charlotte's Web   Rockford, IL
                          8:30 & 11:00 pm – $2.50
                          [cancelled]
Sep 21, 1974   Memorial Union University   Madison, WI
                          8:00 pm
Oct 10, 1974   Great American Music Hall   San Francisco, CA
                          9:00 & 11:30 pm

Oct 19, 1974	Memorial Auditorium, Stanford U. 7:30 & 10:00 pm – $3.50	Stanford, CA
Oct 25, 1974	Carnegie Hall 8:00 pm – $4.50-$6.50	New York, NY

". . . a drawn-out ordeal of three 20 minute pieces, technically superior but
thematically piecemeal and rather boring . . ."
C. Ornstein & D. Clubock, *The Miscellany News*

"Expressionless as usual, Fahey played but three extended numbers
during his 48-minute set."
Kirb, *Variety*

Oct 28, 1974	Great SouthEast Music Hall 8:00 & 10:30 pm	Atlanta, GA
Oct 31, 1974	Old Cambridge Baptist Church	Cambridge, MA
Nov 11, 1974	Lighthouse	Hermosa Beach, CA
Dec 22, 1974	Wilshire-Ebell Theatre 8:00 pm	Los Angeles, CA

[60th Birthday Celebration of Swami Satchidananda]

Feb 8, 1975	Lane Fairgrounds Agricult. Bldg. 8:30 pm	Eugene, OR
Feb 9, 1975	University of California 8:00 pm	Riverside, CA
Mar 8, 1975	Great American Music Hall 9:00 & 11:30 pm	San Francisco, CA
May 31, 1975	Hunter College Assembly Hall 8:00 pm	New York, NY

"Without a word, he picked up his guitar and played the first song.
It lasted 45 minutes and was quite remarkable,
as was the rest of his three-hour concert."
Paul Nelson, *The Village Voice*

Aug 4, 1975	Lighthouse	Hermosa Beach, CA
Aug 8, 1975	Great American Music Hall 9:00 & 11:30 pm	San Francisco, CA
Sep 26-27, 1975	McCabe's Guitar Shop 8:30 pm	Santa Monica, CA
Oct 19, 1975	Lighthouse	Hermosa Beach, CA
Nov 17-18, 1975	Cellar Door	Washington, DC

"John Fahey failed to appear on opening night."
Larry Rohter, *Washington Post*

Nov 21, 1975	Main Point	Bryn Mawr, PA
Nov 30, 1975	Bottom Line	New York, NY

"John Fahey . . . remains as impressive and distinctive a master of
the acoustic guitar as he ever was."
John Rockwell, *The New York Times*

Dec 8-9, 1975	Paul's Mall	Boston, MA

Dec 21, 1975	QE Playhouse	Vancouver, Canada
	7:00 & 10:00 pm – $5.00	
Feb 7, 1976	Royce Hall, UCLA	Los Angeles, CA
	8:30 pm – $5.50-$6.50	
Feb 8, 1976	U. C. Berkeley	Berkeley, CA
	8:00 pm – $5.50-$6.50	
Feb 11, 1976	"Studio None" TV show	Madison, WI
Feb 27, 1976	Cal State University	Fullerton, CA
	7:30 & 10:00 pm	
Mar 25, 1976	Great American Music Hall	San Francisco, CA
Apr 10, 1976	The Grove, Ambassador Hotel	Los Angeles, CA
	9:00 pm to 1:00 am – $5.00	
June 1, 1976	Lighthouse	Hermosa Beach, CA
	9:00 pm	
June 11-12, 1976	Harry Hope's	Chicago, IL
June 18-19, 1976	Amazingrace	Evanston, IL
	8:00 & 11:00 pm – $3.50	
June 23, 1976	Charlotte's Web	Rockford, IL
	8:00 & 10:30 pm – $3.00	
July 9, 1976	Great American Music Hall	San Francisco, CA
	8:30 & 11:30 pm	
July 14, 1976	Great American Music Hall	San Francisco, CA
	8:30 & 11:30 pm	
July 16-17, 1976	McCabe's Guitar Shop	Santa Monica, CA
	8:30 pm	
July 29, 1976	Euphoria Tavern	Portland, OR
July 30, 1976	WOW Hall	Eugene, OR
	8:30 & 11:00 pm – $3.50	
Aug 22-23, 1976	Bottom Line	New York, NY
Aug 28, 1976	My Father's Place	Roslyn, NY
	8:30 & 11:30 pm – $4.00	
Sep 2, 1976	U. of Nebraska - Sheldon Gallery	Lincoln, NB
	7:30 pm – free	
Sep 4, 1976	University of Wisconsin	Madison, WI
	8:00 pm – $4.00	
Sep 10-11, 1976	Poplars	Bloomington, IN
	8:00 pm	
Sep 14, 1976	Main Point	Bryn Mawr, PA
Oct 30, 1976	Stanford University	Palo Alto, CA
	7:00 & 9:30 pm	
Nov 2, 1976	Great American Music Hall	San Francisco, CA
	8:30 & 11:30 pm	
Nov 6, 1976	The Barn	Riverside, CA
Mar 17, 1977	Golden Bear	Huntington Beach, CA
	9:00 pm	
Mar 25-26, 1977	Bob Baxter's Guitar Workshop	Santa Monica, CA

Apr 1, 1977	Univ. of Washington - Meany Hall 8:00 pm – $6.00	Seattle, WA

"We and our guests felt ripped off, as though he were teasing his audience with scales and guitar exercises most of the concert. Then to get up and go to the bathroom in the middle of the second half wasn't even funny."
John D. Brown, *Seattle Daily Times*

Apr 3, 1977	Earth 9:30 pm	Portland, OR
Apr 5-9, 1977	The Old Roller Rink	Vancouver, Canada

"(Fahey) attacks the instrument with the determination of a drill-press operator and moves his fretting finger and steel slide about the strings with the casual precision of an expert backgammon player laying stones."
Vaughn Palmer, *Vancouver Sun*

Apr 14, 1977	Great American Music Hall 8:30 & 11:00 pm – $5.00	San Francisco, CA
Apr 29-30, 1977	Humboldt State University 8:00 & 11:00 pm – $4.00	Arcata, CA
June 10-11, 1977	The Cellar Door	Washington, DC
June 16, 1977	Main Point	Bryn Mawr, PA
June 20-21, 1977	Bottom Line 8:30 & 11:30 pm – $5.00	New York, NY

"Mr. Fahey offered his customary excellence. His music unfolded slowly, sometimes almost ponderously, like a vaguely familiar ritual, only to burst suddenly into coursing, sunny lyrical passages."
Robert Palmer, *The New York Times*

June 28-29, 1977	Passim 8:00 & 10:30 pm – $4.00	Cambridge, MA
July 22-24, 1977	Amazingrace	Evanston, IL
Oct 16-17, 1977	Rainbow Tavern	Seattle, WA
Oct 23, 1977	Eugene Hotel 7:30 & 9:30 pm – $5.50	Eugene, OR
Oct 26, 1977	Great American Music Hall 8:00 & 10:30 pm	San Francisco, CA
Oct 28, 1977	Backdoor - San Diego State Univ. 8:00 & 10:30 pm	San Diego, CA
Nov 3, 1977	Golden Bear 9:00 pm	Huntington Beach, CA
Nov 11-13, 1977	The Whole Coffeehouse 8:30 pm – $3.00	Minneapolis, MN
Nov 16, 1977	Charlotte's Web	Rockford, IL
Nov 18, 1977	University of Chicago	Chicago, IL
Nov 22, 1977	Bunky's	Madison, WI
Nov 28, 1977	El Mocambo	Toronto, Canada
Dec 3-4, 1977	Salt Theatre	Newport, RI

Poster advertising a John Fahey & Robbie Basho concert in 1967. (Design by Tom Weller)

Dec 6-7, 1977	Passim 8:00 & 10:30 pm	Boston, MA
Dec 9, 1977	Main Point 8:00 & 10:00 pm	Bryn Mawr, PA
Dec 11-12, 1977	The Cellar Door	Washington, DC

"There is a tension, a voltage, in what Fahey does . . .
Fahey makes it look a lot simpler than it really is."
    Joseph McLellan, *The Washington Post*

Dec 13, 1977	The Great Midwestern Music Hall	Louisville, KY
Dec 21-22, 1977	Troubadour	Los Angeles, CA

"He plays a personalized folk music that sees pieces of traditional songs
entering the Fahey sensibility and emerging magically transformed.
On stage, Fahey appears to be asleep from the elbows up."
    Richard Cromelin, *Los Angeles Times*

Dec 31, 1977	Great Midwestern Music Hall	Louisville, KY
Mar 17, 1978	Audimax at Hamburg University	Hamburg, Germany
Mar 20, 1978	Radio Bremen	Bremen, Germany
May 18, 1978	Amazingrace	Evanston, IL
May 24, 1978	Armadillo World Headquarters 9:00 pm – $4.50	Austin, TX
May 29, 1978	Bottom Line 8:30 & 11:30 pm – $5.00	New York, NY
May 31-June 1, 1978	El Mocambo	Toronto, Canada

"The crowd held Fahey in such reverence that at no time, not even
between numbers, did I hear one person talk above a whisper."
    Alan Niester, *The Globe and Mail*

June 8, 1978	Paradise Theater 8:30 & 11:00 pm – $3.50-$4.50	Boston, MA
June 10-11, 1978	Cellar Door	Washington, DC
June ..., 1978	Great Hall	Madison, WI
June 19, 1978	Mr. Brown's 8:00 & 11:00 pm – $3.50	Columbus, OH
Aug 27, 1978	Earth Tavern 9:00 & 11:00 pm – $6.00	Portland, OR
Sep 17, 1978	Quiet Knight	Chicago, IL
Sep 22, 1978	Finney Chapel, Oberlin College 8:30 pm – $2.00	Oberlin, OH
Oct 20-21, 1978	The Whole Coffeehouse 8:30 pm – $3.50	Minneapolis, MN
Nov 30, 1978	Bottom Line 8:30 & 11:30 – $5.00	New York, NY
Dec 3, 1978	Paradise Theater 8:30 pm – $3.50-$4.50	Boston, MA
Dec 4, 1978	Cellar Door	Washington, DC

Dec 6, 1978	Long Beach Arena 8:00 pm	Long Beach, CA

"The nearly empty house not only spelled financial disaster for the promoters but also stripped the artists of much of their motivation."
Dennis Hunt, *Los Angeles Times*

Feb 21, 1979	Earth Tavern 7:30 & 10:00 pm	Portland, OR
June 10-11, 1979	Cellar Door	Washington, DC

"Playing a steel-string guitar, he presented several extended songs that leap from one style to the next while never forsaking a sense of musical coherence."
Harry Sumrall, *Washington Post*

June 15, 1979	["Concert Special: John Fahey" WUSB radio program]	
June 29-30, 1979	Cellar Door	Washington, DC
July 2, 1979	Bottom Line 8:30 & 11:30 pm – $5.50	New York, NY

"Drinking beer, chatting drunkenly and playing his steel-string acoustics as nimbly as legend demands."
Davitt Sigerson, *Melody Maker*

July 11, 1979	Jonathan Swift's Pub 8:00 & 10:30 pm – $4.50	Cambridge, MA
July 14, 1979	The Venue 7:00 pm – £4.00	London, England

"His playing exudes a craftman's assurance, complementing an extraordinary technical skill with a great sensitivity to the importance of emphasis, balancing surges of power with moments of quiet reflection."
Mick Brown, *The Guardian*

"He came on stage, opened his guitar case, picked up his axe, and then didn't play a note for 4 minutes and 33 seconds . . . This did not go down well with the habitues of the Venue, who presumably have dropped in to get tanked up before the disco starts."
Karl Dallas, *Melody Maker*

Sep 7, 1979	McCabe's Guitar Shop 8:00 & 10:30 pm	Santa Monica, CA
Oct 31, 1979	Great American Music Hall	San Francisco, CA
Nov 16, 1979	Los Angeles Convention Center $4.00	Los Angeles, CA

"The New Earth Exposition . . . And there too was John Fahey, called upon to play for this assemblage of blissed-out Lotophagi. . . . John had a tough act to follow: a chimpanzee in a space suit, a bear that danced the cha-cha, and a tiger."
Mark Humphrey, *LA Reader*

Nov 18, 1979	Jonathan Swift's Pub 9:00 & 11:00 pm – $5.00	Cambridge, MA
Nov 24-25, 1979	Cellar Door	Washington, DC

Nov 28-29, 1979	Bottom Line 8:30 & 11:30 pm – $5.50	New York, NY

"I'm not sure when I noticed Fahey's great failing. Perhaps it was at the
Bottom Line, where his sloppy, subtly derisive banter betrayed
the music he finally got around to playing."
Jan Hoffman, *Village Voice*

". . . blunt, unpretentious, funny, occasionally rude, always down-to-earth,
anything but a guru. Mr. Fahey once again reminded the faithful
that he was a minimalist, a conceptualist and
perhaps even a punk long before anybody realized it.
Robert Palmer, *"The New York Times*

Dec 1, 1979	Market House Music Hall 8:00 and 10:30 pm – $4.00-$5.00	Oswego, NY
Dec 13-16, 1979	McCabe's Guitar Shop 8:00 & 10:30 pm	Santa Monica, CA
Dec 23, 1979	McCabe's Guitar Shop	Santa Monica, CA

["Christmas at McCabe's" radio show, produced by National Public Radio]

Dec 25, 1979	McCabe's Guitar Shop	Santa Monica, CA

["Christmas at McCabe's" radio show, produced by National Public Radio]

Dec 29, 1979	McCabe's Guitar Shop	Santa Monica, CA

["Christmas at McCabe's" show aired on FM radio]

Jan 11, 1980	Earth Tavern 8:00 & 10:00 pm – $4.50	Portland, OR
Feb 18, 1980	Earth Tavern 8:00 & 10:00 pm – $4.50	Portland, OR
Feb 23, 1980	Student Union Ballroom 8:00 pm – $6.00	Albuquerque, NM
Mar 30, 1980	The Lighthouse	Hermosa Beach, CA
Apr 9-10, 1980	Cellar Door 8:00 & 10:30 pm – $6.00	Washington, DC
Apr 12, 1980	Main Point	Bryn Mawr, PA
Apr 14, 1980	Jonathan Swift's 9:00 pm – $5.00	Cambridge, MA
Apr 16, 1980	Bottom Line 8:30 & 11:30 pm – $6.00	New York, NY
June 21, 1980	McCabe's Guitar Shop 8:00 & 10:30 pm	Santa Monica, CA
July 18, 1980	White Mountains Festival	Bretton Woods, NH
July 20, 1980	Hancock County Auditorium 8:00 pm	Bangor, ME
July 25-26, 1980	Main Point	Bryn Mawr, PA
July 27, 1980	Guthrie Theater 7:30 pm	Minneapolis, MN
Aug 3, 1980	Jonathan Swift's 8:30 & 11:00 pm – $5.00-$6.00	Cambridge, MA

Sep 1, 1980	The Basement	Sydney, Australia
Sep 2, 1980	Universal Workshop Theatre 7:30 pm	Melbourne, Australia
Sep 5, 1980	And Now For Something Completely Different 8:30 pm	Chatswood, Australia
Sep 6, 1980	Universal Workshop Theatre 10:30 pm	Melbourne, Australia
Sep 7, 1980	The Basement 8:30 pm – $6.00	Sydney, Australia
Sep 12 or 13, 1980	Hobart University	Tasmania, Australia
Dec 11, 1980	[cancelled]	Bergamo, Italy
Feb 13, 1981	Community Center - CCPA 8:00 & 11:00 pm – $7.00	Eugene, OR
Mar 29, 1981	New Earth Tavern 8:00 pm – $5.00	Portland, OR
Mar 30, 1981	Jazz Alley	Portland, OR
Apr 30, 1981	Country Club	Reseda, CA
May 15, 1981	McCabe's Guitar Shop	Santa Monica, CA
May 16, 1981	Ice House	Pasadena, CA
May, 1981	Cellar Door	Washington, DC
July 7, 1981	Cellar Door 8:00 & 10:30 pm – $5.00	Washington, DC
July 15, 1981	Passim's 8:00 & 10:30 pm – $4.50	Cambridge, MA
July 18, 1981	Folk City	New York, NY
July 19, 1981	Iron Horse Coffeehouse	Northampton, MA
July 31, 1981	Twilight Theater, Lyndon College	Lyndonville, VT
Aug 6, 1981	El Mocambo Tavern	Toronto, Canada

"Fahey didn't say much . . . and didn't bother introducing the numbers by title.
His unique technique was merely to sit down
and play incredibly complex pieces."
Alan Niester, *The Globe and Mail*

Sep, 1981	McCabe's Guitar Shop	Santa Monica, CA
Oct 8, 1981	Ice House	Pasadena, CA
Oct 11, 1981	New Varsity Theater	Palo Alto, CA
Nov 3, 1981	Jonathan Swift's Pub	Cambridge, MA
Nov 11-12, 1981	The Other End	New York, NY
Nov 27, 1981	["Backstage Pass" TV show at midnight]	
Dec 23, 1981	Luis' La Bamba Club 8:00 & 11:00 pm – $5.00	Portland, OR
Jan 10, 1982	Boon's Treasury	Salem, OR
Jan 17, 1982	Belly Up Tavern 9:00 pm	Solana Beach, CA
Jan 22, 1982	Whole Coffeehouse 7:00 pm – $5.00-7.00 [cancelled]	Minneapolis, MN

APPENDIX C

Jan 23, 1982	Old Town School of Folk Music 8:00 & 10:00 pm – $6.50	Chicago, IL
Jan 24, 1982	Old Town School of Folk Music Guitar workshop: 1-4:00 pm – $10.00	Chicago, IL
Jan 29, 1982	Whole Coffeehouse 8:00 pm – $5.00-7.00	Minneapolis, MN
Jan 30, 1982	Maintenance Shop	Ames, IA
Feb 10, 1982	W.O.W Hall (cancelled)	Eugene, OR
Feb 23, 1982	W.O.W Hall	Eugene, OR
Mar 6, 1982	Teatro Cristallo 9:30 pm – £5000	Milano, Italy
Mar 7, 1982	Teatro Cristallo 4:00 pm – £5000	Milano, Italy
Mar 8, 1982	Teatro delle Arti	Gallarate, Italy
Mar 15, 1982	Cinema Teatro Tirreno	Latina, Italy
Mar 19, 1982	Teatro Massimo 9:30 pm – £6000	Genoa, Italy
Mar 28, 1982	Moonshadow Saloon	Atlanta, GA
Mar 31, 1982	Bottom Line 9:00 & 12:00 pm	New York, NY
Apr 2, 1982	My Father's Place 8:30 & 11:30 pm – $8.00	Roslyn, NY
Apr 6, 1982	Jonathan Swift's Pub 9:00 & 11:00 pm	Cambridge, MA
Apr 9, 1982	Bijou Café	Philadelphia, PA
Apr 11, 1982	Iron Horse Coffeehouse 7:00 & 10:00 pm	Northampon, MA
May 7, 1982	McCabe's Guitar Shop	Santa Monica, CA
May 7, 1982	[an informal concert appearance on the TV show "Video West: Backstage Pass"]	
May 9, 1982	Golden Bear 8:30 pm	Huntington Beach, CA

"Fahey '82 is a bald, burly Falstaffian character. Fueled by the eight beers he drank on stage, the set was spliced by rambling anecdotes and intermittent intermissions. For all Fahey's on-stage informality,
he was dead-on when he played."
C. P. Smith, *Santa Ana Orange County Register*

May 27, 1982	Folkstudio	Rome, Italy
June 3, 1982	Jonathan Swift's Pub	Cambridge, MA
June 4, 1982	Folk City 9:30 & 11:00 pm	New York, NY
June 26, 1982	The General Store 8:00 & 10:00 pm	Stone City, IA
July 16-18, 1982	5th Annual Folk Music Festival	Vancouver, Canada
Aug 22, 1982	Silver Spoon 8:00 pm	Duvall, WA

APPENDIX C

Sep 12, 1982   Euphoria Tavern   Portland, OR
8:30 pm – $5.00
Sep 16, 1982   Victoria Street Theater   Santa Barbara, CA
"A slightly weather-beaten, shy-with-words kind of performer . . .
But once his left forefinger begins dancing up and down the frets on the
finger board of a guitar, the real John Fahey begins to emerge."
     Sheila Kennedy, *Santa Barbara News-Press*

Oct 3, 1982   Old World Center   Corvallis, OR
7:30 & 10:00
Nov 1, 1982   Bottom Line   New York, NY
8:30 & 11:30 pm – $7.50
Nov 4, 1982   Berklee Center   Boston, MA
Nov 22, 1982   Wisconsin Conservatory of Music   Milwaukee, WI
Guitar workshop: 6-9:00 pm – $15.00
Nov 23, 1982   Bunky's   Madison, WI
$5.00
Dec 11, 1982   McCabe's Guitar Shop   Santa Monica, CA
8:00 & 10:30 pm
Dec 12, 1982   Sonoma County Fairgrounds   Santa Rosa, CA
4:00 pm
Dec 19, 1982   Fat Little Rooster Tavern   Portland, OR
7:00 & 10:00 pm
Dec 21, 1982   Silver Spoon   Duvall, WA
Dec 24, 1982   First United Presbyterian Church   McMinnville, OR
8:00 pm
Dec 24, 1982   McCabe's Guitar Shop   Santa Monica, CA
["Christmas at McCabe's" radio show, produced by National Public Radio]
Feb 20, 1983   Soft Rock Café   Vancouver, Canada
"The balding, chubby man . . . looks more like the Beverly Hillbillies' Jed Clampet
than a solo guitarist attributed with the birth of contemporary fingerpicking.
But when John Fahey took the stage . . . the audience . . . was held spellbound."
     Robby Robertson, *The Ubyssey*
Mar 8, 1983   Bayou   Washington, DC
Apr 12, 1983   "Faces and Places" Radio show "Meet guitarist John Fahey"
aired on the KATU channel (an ABC affiliated TV channel in Portland, OR)
Apr 22, 1983   Holstein's   Chicago, IL
8:30 & 10:30 pm – $5.00
May 29, 1983   Cotati Cabaret   Cotati, CA
June 3, 1983   Seattle Concert Theater   Seattle, WA
8:00 pm
July 23, 1983   Catlin Gable School   Portland, OR
KBOO World Music Festival
11:00 am - 11:00 pm – $9.00-$11.00
Workshop: "Guitar Styles"; July 23 at 3:45-5:15 pm.
Concert: July 23: 12:45 to 1:20 pm

July 25, 1983   Ahab's Whale Tavern   Spokane, WA
"What Fahey did for the Monday night crowd was to provide the musical equivalent of poetry."
Ken Maffitt, *The Spokesman-Review*

July 30, 1983   Cambridge Folk Festival   Cambridge, England
£8-15£
"John Fahey's full length set was quite simply a masterpiece."
Music; by Lynda Morrison & Judy Wheway

Aug 3, 1983   Villa Borghese   Rome, Italy
9:00 pm

Aug 31, 1983   Wisconsin Conservatory of Music   Milwaukee, WI
Guitar workshop: 7-11:00 pm – $15.00

Sep 1, 1983   Jazz Gallery   Milwaukee, WI
Sep 16, 1983   Poor David's Pub   Dallas, TX
Dec 2, 1983   Folk City   New York, NY
Dec 3, 1983   Birchmere   Alexandria, VA
"Many of the pieces possessed an introspective quality a curious mixture of Southern Blues and Indian mysticism—that proved entrancing at times."
Mike Joyce, *Washington Post*

Dec 7, 1983   Peabody's DownUnder   Cleveland, OH
7:30 & 10:30 – $7.50

Dec 10, 1983   Walker Art Center Auditorium   Minneapolis, MN
8:00 pm

Dec 11, 1983   Benson High School Auditorium   Portland, OR
8:00 pm – $7.50-$8.50

Dec 17, 1983   McCabe's Guitar Shop   Santa Monica, CA
8:00 & 10:30 pm

Dec 18. 1983   Cotati Cabaret   Cotati, CA
8:00 pm

Dec 22, 1983   Museum of History & Industry   Seattle, WA
8:00 pm – $6.50-$7.50

Dec 24, 1983   Key Largo   Portland, OR
7:30 pm

Feb 28, 1984   Club West   Santa Fe, NM
8:30 & 10:30 pm – $6.50

Feb 29, 1984   Poor David's Pub   Dallas, TX
8:30 pm – $7.00

Mar 3, 1984   Fitzgerald's   Houston, TX
"a splendid night of Fahey at his best — two sets of incomparable guitar-picking . . . the music was scintillating."
Bob Claypool, *The Houston Post*

APPENDIX C

Mar 4, 1984 Soap Creek Saloon Austin, TX

" 'Sounds like some guy practicing,' opined a spectator ... which only serves to emphasize that the most vital element of Fahey's subtle, unpretentiously innovative approach to traditional blues-based guitar styles is his capacity to make each tune a vision quest in which the listener may at any moment drown in a quicksand of seething, droning dissonance or ascend a shimmering chordal pathway to the most rarefied instrumental bliss."
L. E. McCullough, *Austin Chronicle*

Date	Venue	Location
Apr 11, 1984	KBOO radio – live 9:00 - 12:00 pm	Portland, OR
May 15, 1984	Caspar Inn $5.00	Caspar, CA
June 8, 1984	Folk City 8:00 & 11:00 pm – $8.00	New York, NY
June 9, 1984	Birchmere	Alexandria, VA
June 11, 1984	Hippodrome 8:00 pm – $7.00	Gainesville, FL
June 15-16, 1984	Café Exchange	Miami, FL
July 3, 1984	The Backstage $6.00	Ballard, WA
Aug 21, 1984	Hunts's	Burlington, VT
Aug 24, 1984	Lyndon State College	Lyndonville, VT
Aug 26, 1984	The Old Church	Portland, OR

"A sparsely attended concert ... showed why he is known well only in a small circle."
Alan R. Hayakawa, *Oregonian*

Date	Venue	Location
Dec 7, 1984	Holstein's 8:30 & 10:30 pm – $5.00	Chicago, IL
Dec 9, 1984	Rum Doodle's	Madison, WI

"In the first [set] ... he spun dazzling patterns of notes around simple, folky melodies, extending and transforming them into compositions of real substance. In the second set, however, he played like a nervous amateur at a school recital."
Tom Strini, *The Milwaukee Journal*

Date	Venue	Location
Dec 14, 1984	McCabe's Guitar Shop 8:00 & 10:30 pm	Santa Monica, CA
Dec ..., 1984	Willamette Univ. Auditorium	Salem, OR
Dec 16, 1984	Starry Night 8:30 pm	Portland, OR
Dec 18-19, 1984	The Backstage	Ballard, WA
Dec 21, 1984	Folk City 8:30 & 11:30 pm – $8.00	New York, NY
Dec 22, 1984	Arlington Town Hall 7:00 pm & 9:45 pm – $8.50	Arlington, MA
Dec 23, 1984	Iron Horse Coffeehouse 7:00 & 10:00 pm – $6.00	Northampton, MA
Dec 29, 1984	Birchmere	Alexandria, VA

September 1985 calendar for the Speakeasy Club in NYC (Design by Jeff Tiedrich)

Jan 3, 1985	Rockefeller's	Houston, TX
Jan 15, 1985	Caspar Inn	Caspar, CA
	$6.00	
Jan 27, 1985	Golem	Montreal, Canada
Apr 26, 1985	Birchmere	Alexandria, VA
May 6, 1985	Pentacle's Theater	Salem, OR
	8:00 pm – $10.00	
May 19, 1985	University of Oregon	Eugene, OR
	15th Annual Willamette Valley Folk Festival	
	1:00 pm	
June 1, 1985	Museum of History & Industry	Seattle, WA
	8:00 pm	
July 5, 1985	Anderson Fair	Houston, TX
July 11-14, 1985	12th Annual Folk Festival	Winnipeg, Canada

At this festival John Fahey participated in:
Workshop: "Candy Man: Mississippi John Hurt"; July 12: 2:00-3:00 pm
Workshop: "The New Acoustic Music"; host; July 12: 5:00-6:00 pm
Workshop: "Folk-Jazz, Where They Come Together"; July 13: 11:00-12:00 am
Workshop: "Master Guitar Styles"; July 13: 2:00-3:00 pm.
Evening Concert: July 13: 11:05 to 11:30 pm
Workshop: "Love, Life, and Hard Times"; July 14: 12:00-1:00 pm.
Workshop: "I Learned This A Long Time Ago"; July 14: 6:00-7:00 pm.

July 21, 1985	Peter Britt Gardens	Jacksonville, OR
Aug 3, 1985	Towne Crier Café	Beekman, NY
	9:30 pm	
Sep 17, 1985	The Ark	Ann Arbor, MI
	8:00 pm – $7.00	
Sep 20, 1985	Speakeasy	New York, NY
	9:00 & 11:00 pm – $5.00	
Sep 22, 1985	Iron Horse Coffeehouse	Northampton, MA
	$6.00	
Sep 21, 1985	Towne Crier Café	Beekman, NY
	8:00 pm	
Oct 30, 1985	Birchmere	Alexandria, VA
Dec 5, 1985	Anderson Fair	Houston, TX
Dec 8, 1985	Cherry Tree Music Co-op	Philadelphia, PA
	8:00 pm – $6.00	
Dec 14, 1985	The Barns at Wolf Trap	Vienna, VA
	8:00 pm – $10.00	
Dec 21, 1985	Peakes Auditorium	Bangor, ME
	8:00 pm – $7.00	

"Fahey disappoints . . . much of his music Saturday night was unlistenable."
Dick Shaw, *Bangor Daily News*

Feb 14, 1986	Pine Street Theatre	Portland, OR
	8:30 pm – $8.50	

APPENDIX C

Date	Venue	Location
Mar 8, 1986	Pine Street Theatre 8:30 pm – $8.00	Portland, OR
Apr 11, 1986	Post and Beam 7:30 & 9:30 pm – $7.00	Kingston, RI
Apr 16, 1986	Passim's	Cambridge, MA
Apr 17, 1986	Iron Horse Coffeehouse 7:00 pm – $7.00	Northampton, MA
May 9-10, 1986	Conley's Nostalgia	Denver, CO
May 13, 1986	Cactus Café	Austin, TX
May 23, 1986	Felten-Start Theater 8:00 pm – $5.00	Hays, KS
June 6, 1986	Second Fret [cancelled]	Oklahoma City, OK
June 24, 1986	Tipitina's 9:30 pm	New Orleans, LA
June 26, 1986	Second Fret 9:00 pm	Oklahoma City, OK
June 27, 1986	Musikworks 8:00 & 10:00 pm – $8.00	Atlanta, GA
July 17, 1986	Holiday Cabaret and Restaurant 9:00 pm	Grass Valley, CA
Aug 30, 1986	Backstage 9:00 pm – $8.50	Seattle, WA
Oct 8, 1986	Springfield City Library 7:00 pm – free	Springfield, MA
Oct 10, 1986	John & Peter's Place 9:30 pm – $7.50 / $9.50	New Hope, PA
Oct 11, 1986	Towne Crier Cafe 9:30 pm	Beekman, NY
Oct 18, 1986	McCabe's Guitar Shop 8:00 & 10:30 pm	Santa Monica, CA
Oct 22, 1986	Fitzgerald's 9:00 & 11:00 pm – $6.00	Berwyn, IL
Oct 24, 1986	Church of the Holy Communion $6.00	St. Louis, MO
Oct 25, 1986	Barns of Wolf Trap 8:00 pm – $10.00	Vienna, VA
Nov 21, 1986	P.S. 41 Auditorium 8:00 pm – $8.00	New York, NY
Nov 23, 1986	Caffe Lena 6:00 & 9:00 pm	Saratoga Springs, NY
Nov 23, 1986	"Mountain Stage" radio show on NPR	
Dec 6, 1986	"Mountain Stage" radio show on NPR	
Dec 11, 1986	Colony Theater 7:30 pm – $10.00-$12.00	Miami, FL
Dec 13, 1986	Sweet Baby Jane's	Tampa, FL

Dec 22, 1986	Key Largo 8:00 & 10:00 pm – $6.50	Portland, OR
Jan 17, 1987	Merry Widow Restaurant 8:00 pm – $9.00	Bridgeport, CT
Feb 15, 1987	Anderson Fair	Houston, TX
Mar 14, 1987	Holstein's 8:30 & 10:30 pm – $6.00	Chicago, IL
Mar 29, 1987	Backstage 8:30 pm – $8.50	Seattle, WA
Apr 25, 1987	Fret House	Covina, CA
May 8, 1987	Pine Street Theatre 9:00 pm – $7.00-$8.00	Portland, OR
June 10, 1987	Town & Country	London, England
July 2, 1987	Palace Theater	Silverton, OR
July 10, 1987	Old Time Café 7:00 & 9:00 pm	Encinitas, CA
July 11, 1987	McCabe's Guitar Shop 8:00 & 10:30 pm – $10.00	Santa Monica, CA
Aug 7-9, 1987	Edmonton Folk Music Festival	Edmonton, Canada

Workshop: "Folk, Blues & Beyond"; Aug 8: 12:00-1:00 pm
Workshop: "Guitar Improvisation by Example"; Aug 8: 2:00-3:30 pm
Concert: Aug 9: 1:00-1:30 pm
Workshop: "Jazz & Improvisation"; Aug 9: 3:00-4:00 pm

Aug 21, 1987	Club Bene' Dinner Theater	Sayreville, NJ
Aug 26, 1987	Birchmere	Alexandria, VA
Sep 6, 1987	Towne Crier Café 9:30 pm – $10.00	Beekman, NY
Oct 5, 1987	The Art's Theatre	London, England
Oct 6, 1987	Town & Country Club	London, England

"... the music ebbed and flowed from the dogged and occasionally faltering through the somnolent to the near-inspired."
Richard Williams, *The Times*

Oct 5, 1987	Gardner Arts Centre	Brighton, England
Oct 8, 1987	Andy Kershaw BBC Radio	London, England
Dec 5, 1987	Chimes	Baton Rouge, LA

"... such a fiasco. The guy could hardly even play."
Calvin Gilbert, *The Advocate*

Dec 21, 1987	Gerdes Folk City	New York, NY
Dec 27, 1987	Ballard Firehouse 8:00 pm	Seattle, WA
Jan 8, 1988	ACL Club 9:00 pm – $10.00	St. Petersburg, FL
Jan 10, 1988	Wine Gallery 8:00 & 10:30 pm – $11.00	Indialantic, FL
Jan 23, 1988	McCabe's Guitar Shop	Santa Monica, CA

Mar 13, 1988	St. Mary' Church 8:00 pm	Philadelphia, PA
Mar 20, 1988	C&O Club	Charlottesville, VA
June 18, 1988	Central Park – Summer Stage 3:00 pm – free	New York, NY
Aug 6, 1988	Old Town School of Folk Music 7:30 pm – $10.00	Chicago, IL
Dec 11, 1988	Prospect Park Picnic House 3:00 pm – $5.00	Brooklyn, NY
Dec 16, 1988	Pine Street Theatre 9:00 pm – $8.00	Portland, OR
Jan 14, 1989	McCabe's Guitar Shop	Santa Monica, CA
Mar 10, 1989	Skipper's Smokehouse	St. Petersburg, FL
May 21, 1989	University of Oregon 5:00 pm	Eugene, OR
Jan 6, 1990	Iron Horse Coffeehouse 7:00 pm	Northampton, MA
June 21, 1990	Freight & Salvage Coffeehouse	Berkeley, CA
June 23, 1990	Palms 8:30 pm – $9.50	Berkeley, CA
Aug 18, 1990	WOW Hall 9:30 pm – $7.00	Eugene, OR
Dec 19, 1990	Melody Ballroom	Portland, OR
Aug 31, 1991	Winningstad Theatre 4:00 pm	Portland, OR
Sep 4, 1991	Belly Up Tavern	Solana Beach, CA

"Fahey's playing was a marvel of taut, economical virtuosity."
John D'Agostino, *Los Angeles Times*

Dec 20, 1991	Freight & Salvage Coffeehouse	Berkeley, CA
Apr 12, 1992	West End Cultural Centre	Winnipeg, Canada

[cancelled due to illness; Fahey was hospitalized
due to diabetes related problems]

Sep 23-26, 1992	The Senator	Toronto, Canada
Oct 17, 1992	Abbey Pub 8:00 & 10:30 pm – $14.00	Chicago, IL
Oct 29, 1992	Scuffers	Toronto, Canada
Nov 1, 1992	Bottom Line	New York, NY
Nov 4, 1992	Berklee Performance Center	Boston, MA
Nov 7, 1992	Brown University	Providence, RI
Nov 11, 1992	Yale University	New Haven, CT
Nov 21, 1992	West End Cultural Centre	Winnipeg, Canada
Dec 2, 1992	Backstage	Seattle, WA
June 26, 1993	Inter-Media Art Center 9:00 pm – $17.50	Huntington, NY
Aug 5, 1993	Melarkey's Place	Sacramento, CA

Apr 2, 1994	"Folk Festival Kansas" radio show	
	[selections from Fahey's concert in Hays, KS]	
Sep 15, 1994	Tractor Tavern	Seattle, WA
Oct 8, 1994	McCabe's Guitar Shop	Santa Monica, CA
Dec 17, 1994	East Avenue Tavern	Portland, OR
	6:30 pm – $10.00-$12.00	
Dec 22, 1994	Tractor Tavern	Seattle, WA
	8:30 pm – $8.00-$12.00	
Mar 30, 1995	Community Center - WOW hall	Eugene, OR
	8:30 pm – $6.00-$7.00	
Jan 5, 1996	CSPS Hall	Cedar Rapids, IA
	8:00 pm – $10.00	
May 30, 1996	WNUR radio show	Chicago, IL
	4:00-7:00 pm [with Jim O'Rourke]	
May 31, 1996	Weathered Wall	Seattle, WA
Aug 1, 1996	The Casbah	Middletown, CA
	9:00 pm – $6.00	
Aug 2, 1996	Spaceland	Los Angeles, CA
Aug 30, 1996 ?	Tractor Tavern	Seattle, WA
Oct 19, 1996	Benson	Portland, OR

[North by Northwest Music and Media Conference]
Panel Discussion: "Artists: Why Can't We Just Play Music?"
". . . there was one truly alternative set - John Fahey on Saturday night at the Benson."
The Oregonian

John Fahey live at CBGB, East Village, New York City, 1996

Nov 8, 1996	Empty Bottle 9:00 pm – $10.00	Chicago, IL
Dec 3, 1996	Iron Horse 10:00 pm	Northampton, MA

"... he mumbled, stumbled and fumbled his way through a 30 minute set that contained little more than echoes of greatness."
                Kembrew McLeod, *www.MTV.com*

Dec 6, 1996	Five Spot 8:00 pm – $10.00	Philadelphia, PA
Dec 7, 1996	CBGB $10.00	New York, NY
Jan, 1997	Empty Bottle	Chicago, IL
Jan 26, 1997	["All Things Considered" – NPR radio show]	
Feb 6, 1997	Aladdin Theater	Portland, OR
Feb 7, 1997	Capitol Theater 8:00 pm – $5.00	Olympia, WA
Feb 14, 1997	Cactus	Austin, TX
Mar 19, 1997	Gargoyle – Washington Univ. 8:30 pm – $5.00	St. Louis, MO
Apr 4, 1997	Ash Grove	Santa Monica, CA

"... one wonders what the people who walked out expected to hear. ... It was sometimes lovely, sometimes crude, sometimes smooth, sometimes stumbling, sometimes transporting, sometimes leading nowhere ... just like life."
                Steve Hochman, *Los Angeles Times*

Aug 9, 1997	Horizon Theatre 8:00 pm – $12.00	Atlanta, GA
Nov 2, 1997	Tramps 8:00 pm – $10.00	New York, NY
Dec 23, 1997	[as JF Trio]	Portland, OR ?
Feb 1, 1998	Sam Bond's Garage 9:00 pm – $5.00 to $8.00	Eugene, OR
Apr 11, 1998	Freight & Salvage	Berkeley, CA
May 23, 1998	Unity Temple	Oak Park, IL

"Challenging, trying, rewarding, surprising and decidedly non-New Age, the performance was, in all of its irascible contradiction, pure John Fahey."
                Rick Reger, *Chicago Tribune*

June 5, 1998	Lenora's Ghost	Independence, OR
June 13, 1998	Guinness Fleadh Festival $40.00 (festival price)	Randall's Island, NY
June 13, 1998	Cooler	New York, NY
July 19, 1998	["Stork Club" radio show on WFMU]	Jersey City, NJ
July 25, 1998	Stephen Talkhouse 8:00 pm – $20-$25	Amagansett, NY
Aug 21, 1998	Green Onion 1:00 am – $20.00	Portland, OR

[as the John Fahey Trio in the North By Northwest Music Conference]

Dec 3, 1998	Iron Horse Coffeehouse	Northampton, MA
Dec 5, 1998	Lenora's Ghost	Independence, OR
	9:00 pm - $8.00	
Dec 11, 1998	1201 Café & Lounge	Portland, OR
Dec 23, 1998	Satyricon	Portland, OR
Feb 28, 1999	Swiss	Tacoma, WA
Apr 15, 1999	Khyber	Philadelphia, PA
	9:30 pm	
Apr 17, 1999	Tonic	New York, NY
	1:30 pm – $10.00	
Apr 18, 1999	Middle East	Cambridge, MA
	$7.00	
May 1-2, 1999	Schuba's Tavern	Chicago, IL
	8:00 pm – $15.00	

"John Fahey played open-ended, discursive medleys on his electric guitar and sported a prankish sense of humor and a highly idiosyncratic reinterpretation of the blues."
Bill Meyer, *Chicago Tribune*

May 8, 1999	St. John's Pub	Portland, OR
	9:00 pm – $10.00	
June 4, 1999	Taku, Taku	Kyoto, Japan
June 5, 1999	Hosei University	Tokyo, Japan
	7:00 pm – 2500 yen	
June 12, 1999	Guinness Fleadh – Motor Speedway	Chicago, IL
	4:15 pm – $45.00 (festival price)	
June 17-18, 1999	Ritz	Austin, TX
June 29, 1999	Tractor Tavern	Ballard, WA
July 3, 1999	Paradiso	Amsterdam, Netherlands
July 4, 1999	[Radio Show]	Amsterdam, Netherlands
July 5, 1999	Klopothek im Studio	Cologne, Germany
	10:00 pm	
Aug 14, 1999		Aurora, OR
Sep 16, 1999	Queen's Hall	Edinburgh, Scotland
	8:00 pm – £12	

"John Fahey let his guitar do all the talking and it proved to be more expressive than any human voice."
Rory Ford, *Evening News*

"John Fahey's guitar playing was ... incoherent competence."
Rob Adams, *The Herald*

Sep 18, 1999	Royal Northern College of Music. [cancelled]	Manchester, England
Sep 21, 1999	Live Theatre [cancelled]	Newcastle upon Tyne, England
Sep 23, 1999	Adrian Boult Hall [cancelled]	Birmingham, England

Sep 24, 1999	Whelan's	Dublin, Ireland
Sep 25, 1999	Elmwood Hall	Belfast, N. Ireland
Sep 27, 1999	Stamford Arts Centre [cancelled]	Stamford, England
Sep 30, 1999	Brudenell Social Club	Leeds, England
Oct 2, 1999	Queen Elizabeth Hall 7:45 pm – £12.50-£15.00	London, England
Oct 5, 1999	Cork Lobby [?cancelled]	
Oct 6, 1999	Roisin Dubh [?cancelled]	Galway, Ireland
Dec 23, 1999	Roseland Grill 8:00 pm – $10.00	Portland, OR
Jan 15, 2000	Grants Brewery Pub 9:45 pm – $12.00	Yakima, WA
May 1, 2000	Schuba's	Chicago, IL
July 8, 2000	Venetian Theater $15.00	Albany, OR
July 15, 2000	Cat's Cradle 6:30 pm	Carrboro, NC
July 17, 2000	Knitting Factory [cancelled] 8:00 pm – $14.00	New York, NY
July 21, 2000	Empty Bottle [cancelled] 10:00 pm – $8.00-$10.00	Chicago, IL

"The concert was canceled because Fahey is ill."
Chicago Tribune

Sep 22, 2000	Green Onion (JF Trio) 11:00 pm – $30.00 (festival price)	Portland, OR

[as the John Fahey Trio in the North By Northwest Music Conference]
"among the acts who made the biggest splash were . . . arty veteran John Fahey."
Chris Riemenschneider, *Austin American Statesman*

Sep 29, 2000	Medicine Hat Gallery	Portland, OR

"Tonight, it's John Fahey, playing a live improv score to the silent film *The Thief of Bagdad* . . . the decadent 1924 Douglas Fairbanks classic."
Julianne Shepherd, *The Portland Mercury*

Oct 1, 2000	Empty Bottle 10:00 pm – $10.00	Chicago, IL

"[Fahey] used his sure and subtle touch to weave a compelling stream of consciousness blues tapestry that was wrung dry of sentimentality, but teeming with remembered hope and despair."
Steve Knopper & Bill Meyer, *Chicago Tribune*

Oct 25, 2000	GH Gallery	Fukuoka, Japan
Oct 27, 2000	Deluxe	Tokyo, Japan
Nov 8, 2000	Viscount Ballroom 3:00 pm	Portland, OR

JOHN FAHEY WRITINGS

BOOKS (by John Fahey)

1966: *A Textual and Musicological Analysis of the Repertoire of Charley Patton*; 176 pp; M. A. Thesis; University of California in Los Angeles.

1971: *Charley Patton*; Studio Vista, London.
Note: This is the book edition of Fahey's post-graduate thesis. Also reprinted as part of the CD box set "Screamin' and Hollerin' the Blues: The Worlds of Charley Patton"; Revenant, 2001.

1978: *The Best of John Fahey*; Guitar Player Books.

1988: *Admiral Kelvinator: Clockworks Factory*; unpublished manuscript.

1999: *The Nature of Reality*; www.johnfahey.com

2000: *How Bluegrass Music Destroyed My Life*; Drag City.

2003: *Vampire Vultures*; Drag City (posthumous).

ARTICLES (by John Fahey)

1955: (under the pseudonym of "Aggregate Execrable Nemesis"); *Iota*, vol 1.

1956: (under the pseudonym of "Aggregate Execrable Nemesis"); *Iota*, vol 2.

1964: "Bukka White – Musicological Notes"; *Blues Unlimited*, #8; pg 13; January 1964.

1966: "Abstracts of Academic Dissertations: John Aloysius Fahey, A Textual and Musicological Analysis of the Repertoire of Charley Patton"; *JEMF*, vol 2, pt 1; November 1966.

1966: Album review of *Today!* by Mississippi John Hurt (Vanguard VRS-9220); *The Little Sandy Review*, vol 2, no. 2; November 1966.

1966: "The John Fahey Collectanea"; *The Little Sandy Review*; vol 2, no. 3; November 1966.

1967: Album review of *Blues and Country Dance Tunes* by John Jackson (Arhoolie F1025); *The Little Sandy Review*, vol 2, no.3; 1967.

1968: "The John Fahey Collectanea – cont."; *The Little Sandy Review*, vol 2, no. 4; 1968.

1968: "The New Herwin Blues Records"; *The Little Sandy Review*, vol 2, no. 4; 1968.

1972: "Exfoliative Saprophagony of the Existential John Fahey" by Elijah P. Lovejoy (alias John Fahey), 1972.

MISSISSIPPI JOHN HURT - TODAY! (Vanguard VRS-9220)

It is with great joy that I see that John Hurt has somehow escaped the contractual entanglements of his former "manager", Mr. Tom Hoskins. It was due to Hoskins that no records of Hurt have been made since his former Piedmont issues. Hopefully Vanguard will give us more of John in the future, for he seems to have lost none of his ability since he made his Okeh records in 1928.

This excellently recorded album is certainly proof of that. The sound is better than on the Piedmonts. The selection of songs is far superior to that of the second Piedmont record, Worried Blues, and slightly exceeds that of his first album, Folk Songs and Blues. John knows hundreds of songs, and I hope that Vanguard will make many more of them available to us.

Some of the Piedmont songs are duplicated here: TALKING CASEY, CANDY MAN, LOUIS COLLINS and SPIKE DRIVER'S BLUES. The middle two are played a trifle more slowly than on the Piedmonts, perhaps for the best since there are fewer mistakes. TALKING CASEY also sounds much better than it did on Piedmont.

The spiritual BEULAH LAND (a version of DO LORD REMEMBER ME, a song many of us used to sing at summer camp) is well done. IF YOU DON'T WANT ME, BABY adequately demonstrates that John can play blues. COFFEE BLUES is a variant of 'BOUT A SPOONFUL, known to practically every old songster and bluesman.

Most of John's stanzas are traditional and occur on other commercial and field-collected recordings. PAY DAY is an excellent example of this; Henry Thomas' 1927 Vocalion recording (entitled SHANTY BLUES, currently available on Origin OJL-3) may have been the source for John's version, which is beautiful. I'M SATISFIED is a delightful song in a happy lighter vein. MAKE ME A PALLET ON THE FLOOR has the same tune and guitar part as John's AIN'T NO TELLING (a 1928 recording not currently available); it is excellently performed—as is most everything on this album.

CORRINNA, CORRINNA is perhaps the weakest cut on this record. It suffers from something, I know not what.

A 4 or 4½ star album, this Vanguard set suffers only from a lack of informative notes regarding the songs and their origin, bibliographical and discographical information. Not to mention a discussion of where John Hurt fits into the Negro (and white) music traditions in the United States. Nat Hentoff's brief and stupid notes only make a reference to the fact that John "is not a raw, harsh chronicler of the human condition in the manner of many Mississippi shaped blues story-tellers." What the hell is a "blues story-teller" anyway, Nat? And who was one? Hentoff's explanation of what Hurt is supposedly trying to tell us in his songs is equally ridiculous, but somewhat amusing. But nobody reads record notes anyway so who cares. The Record is great! (if you like songsters like I do). Someone even made sure that John's guitar was in tune.

John's singing suffers not from a sense of the dramatic but because it is so low in pitch. He frequently misses the pitch he intends to sing, but his quiet subtlety and great guitar cancel that out. Buy this record so they'll make some more of them.

john fahey

John Fahey's review of Mississippi John Hurt's *Today!* in *The Little Sandy Review* from November 1966.
Reproduced with kind permission from Barret Hansen & The John Fahey Trust.

1974: "Performance as War"; *Georgia Straight,* October 3-10, 1974.

1975: "Horizontal and Vertical Playing"; *Guitar Player*, vol 9, no. 2; pg 48; February 1975.

1976: "Bola Sete, The Nature of Infinity, and John Fahey"; *Guitar Player*, vol 10, no. 2; pg 10,36-44; February 1976.

1979: "Takoma Records Newsletter"; *Guitar Player,* pg 67; December 1979.

1980: "Takoma Records Newsletter"; *Guitar Player,* pg 57; January 1980.

1980: "Takoma Records Newsletter"; *Guitar Player*, pg 45; July 1980.

1982: "The Historical Subjectivity of the Guitar"; *Grinning Idiot,* pg 29-32; 1982.

1984: "Vignettes, Digressions, and Screens"; *Grinning Idiot*, pg 7-14; 1984.

1986: "Growing Up in Perversity Park"; *Grinning Idiot,* pg 28-33; 1986.

1997: "Fish"; *Halana*, vol 1, no. 3; pg. 59-67; winter 1997.

Note: later included in *How Bluegrass Music Destroyed My Life.*

1998: "Antonioni" in *Popwatch*, No 9, spring-summer; pg 25-29; 1998.

Note: later included in *How Bluegrass Music Destroyed My Life.*

2000: "Hank Williams – Too Late, Too Late"; *Gadfly*, vol 4, no 5, Sep/Oct; pg 14-17,73; 2000.

Note: excerpt from *How Bluegrass Music Destroyed My Life.*

2001: "The Dream"; *Ecstatic Peace Poetry Journal,* #2, summer 2001.

LINER NOTES (by John Fahey)

1972: John Miller's LP, *First Degree Blues*; Blue Goose BG 2007.

1975: Steve Calt & Dave Mann's LP, *Looney Tunes*; Blue Goose BG 2017.

1979: Michael Gulezian's LP, *Unspoken Intentions*; TAKCD-6510-2.

1994: Woody Mann's CD, *Stories*; Greenhays GR 70724.

1997: *The Anthology of Amercan Folk Music, Vol 1-3*; pg 8-12, Folkways FP 251-253.

1997: *American Primitive Vol. 1, Raw Pre-War Gospel (1926-36)*; Revenant RVN 206.

2000: Robbie Basho CD *Bashovia*; Takoma TAKCD-8913-2.

2000: *Harry Smith's Anthology of American Folk Music, Volume Four*; Revenant RVN 211.

Fahey on the Front Page

John Fahey's image has graced the front cover of music magazines eight times, six of which times during his lifetime.

1965: **Rag Baby**

December; vol. 1, no. 3.

No article; only Fahey concert ad and Takoma record ad.

1980: **Frets**

August; vol. 2, no. 8.

Inside article, pg 22-26: "John Fahey" by Mark Humphrey.

1980: **FolkScene**

Sep-Oct, vol. 8, no. 4.

Inside article, pg 16-19: "John Fahey On Record: A Retrospective" by John Kally.

1984: **Guitar**

February; vol. 12, no. 7.

Inside article, pg 11-14: "John Fahey – In conversation with …" by Michael Grenfell.

APPENDIX E   429

1995: **9X**

March, no. 6.

Inside article, pg 22-23: "John Fahey – Dry Bones in the Valley" by Bryan Sale.

1998: **The Wire**

August, issue 174.

Inside article, pg 22-31: "Blood on the Frets" by Edwin Pouncey.

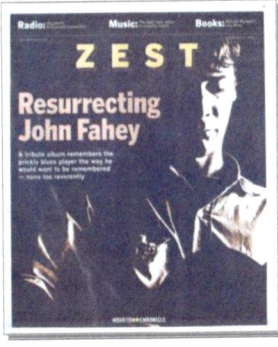

2006: **ZEST** (Arts magazine of the Houston Chronicle)

Feb 12, 2006

Inside article, pg 8-9, 21: "Channeling John Fahey" by Andrew Dansby.

2014: **Blow Up**

February, issue #189

Inside article, pg 46-51: "La voce della tartaruga" by Riccardo Bertoncelli.

FAHEY SONGS ACCORDING TO GUITAR CHORD TUNING

STANDARD = EADGBE

101 Is A Hard Road To Travel
900 Miles
Ann Arbor / Death By Reputation
Assassination of Stephan Grossman, The
Barbara Namkin Blues
Beautiful Linda Getchell
Beverly
Bicycle Built For Two
Black Mommy
Brenda's Blues
Buckdancer's Choice
Bucktown Stomp
Carol of the Bells
Christmas Fantasy – part one
Christmas Fantasy – part two
Christ's Saints of God Fantasy
Claire
Come Labour On
Dorothy / Calvert Street Blues
Episcopal Hymn
Faith Of Our Fathers
For All The Beauty Of The World
For All The Saints
Franklin Blues
God Rest Ye Merry Gentlemen Fantasy
Good King Wenceslas
Goodbye Old Paint
Green River Blues
Greensleeves
Guitar Lamento
Hill High Blues
Holy, Holy, Holy
I'm Gonna Do All I Can For My Lord
In A Persian Market
In Christ There is No East or West
Indian Pacific R.R. Blues (= Beverly)
Irish Setter
It Came Upon a Midnight Clear
Jesus Christ Is Risen Today
Joe Kirby Blues
John Henry
Just As I Am
Knott's Berry Farm Molly
Last Steam Engine Train, The
Let All Mortal Flesh Keep Silence
Little Hat Blues
Lo How A Rose E'er Blooming
Lonely Gaucho in the Pampas Awaiting the Advent of Christmas, The
Lord, I Want To Be A Christian In My Heart
Medley: Come Thou Almighty King / Wild Western Hero
Medley: Hark, The Herald Angels Sing / O Come All Ye Faithful
Medley: Lord Of All Hopefulness / All Through The Night
Medley: Oh Tannenbaum / Angels We Have Heard on High / Jingle Bells
My Grandfather's Clock
My Shepherd Will Supply My Needs
Nobody's Business
O Jesus I Have Promised
Ocean Waves
Oh Come, Oh Come Emmanuel
Oh Holy Night
On Doing An Evil Deed Blues
Praise To The Lord
Pretty Polly / Shortnin' Bread
Reinumeration Blues
Requiem for Molly – part one
Requiem for Molly – part three
Russian Christmas Overture
Silver Bell / Cheyenne
Simple Gifts
Sligo River Blues

Smoketown Strut
Some Summer Day
Spanish Dance
Stak 'O Lee Blues
Stand Up, Stand Up For Jesus
Stomping Tonight on the
　Pennsylvania/Alabama Border
Story of Dorothy Gooch – part one, The
St. Patrick's Hymn
Sun Gonna Shine in my Back Door
　Some Day
Take A Look At That Baby
Tell Her To Come Back Home
Transcendental Waterfall, The
Two American Folk Hymns

Waltzing Matilda
Waltz That Carried Us Away &
　Then a Mosquito Came and Ate
　Up My Sweetheart, The
We Three Kings of Orient Are
We Would Be Building
What Child is This?
When You Wore A Tulip (And I
　Wore A Big Red Rose)
Will The Circle Be Unbroken
Yazoo Basin Blues
Yellow Princess, The
Yes! Jesus Loves Me
You Take The E Train
Zekiah Swamp River Blues

OPEN C = CGCGCE

Atlantic High
Auld Lang Syne
Bells of St. Mary's, The
Commemorative Transfiguration and
　Communion at Magruder Park
Dalhart Texas, 1967
Dance of the Inhabitants of the
　Invisible City of Bladensburg
Discovery of the Sylvia Scott, The
Fare Forward Voyagers
Funeral Song for Mississippi John Hurt
Grand Finale, The (* then switches to
　open C modal)
Horses
I Wish I Knew How It Would Feel
　To Be Free
Interlude

Jaya Shiva Shankarah
Joy to the World
Melody McBad
Old Southern Medley
Portland Cement Factory At
　Monolith California, The
Requiem for Mississippi John Hurt
Return of the Tasmanian Tiger (=
　Revolt of the Dyke Brigade)
Revolt of the Dyke Brigade, The
Sail Away Ladies
Smoky Ordinary Blues (1)
Song
Sunflower River Blues
Thus Krishna on the Battlefield
Union Pacific, The (= The Revolt
　of the Dyke Brigade)

OPEN C var = CCCGCE

Dance of the Inhabitants of the Palace of King Phillip XIV of Spain
Smoky Ordinary Blues (2)

OPEN C modal = CGCGCC

A Raga Called Pat – part one, two, three and four
When the Catfish is in Bloom

DROPPED D = DADGBE

America
Days Have Gone By
Fahey Sampler, The
I Am A Rake And Rambling Boy
Let Go
Mark 1:15
Old Country Rock
St. Louis Blues
When the Springtime Comes Again
White Christmas

OPEN D = DADF♯AD

Away In A Manger
Blind Blues
Come Back Baby
Chris's Rag
Dry Bones In The Valley
Go Tell It On The Mountain
Gulf Port Island Blues
I'm a Poor Boy a Long ways from Home
Jesus Won't You Come 'Round Here
John Henry
John Henry Variations
Knoxville Blues
Lay My Burden Down
Long Time Town Blues
Marilyn
Medley: Imitation Train Whistle / Po' Boy
My Prayer
Orinda-Moraga
Over The Hill Blues
Poor Boy
Requiem for Russell Blaine Cooper
Steve Talbot on the Keddie Wye
Steel Guitar Rag
Takoma Park Pool Hall Blues
Twilight On Prince George's Avenue

OPEN D7 = DADF♯AC

Uncloudy Day (* then switches to open D)

OPEN D modal = DADGAD

Guitar Excursion into the Unknown
My Station Will Be Changed After While
Night Train To Valhalla
Variations on the Coocoo
Voice of the Turtle
When the Fire and the Rose Are One

OPEN Dm = DADFAD

Approaching of the Disco Void, The
Charles A. Lee: In Memoriam
Red Pony
Wine and Roses

OPEN G = DGDGBD

Banty Rooster
Blind Thomas Blues
Chelsey Silver, Please Come Home
Death of the Clayton Peacock, The

Discarded
Dream Of The Origin Of The French Broad River
Enigmas and Perplexities of the Norfolk and Western
Evening, Not Night
Farther Along
First Noel, The
Give Me Corn Bread When I'm Hungry
Go I Will Send Thee
Going Crabbing Talking Blues
Hawaiian Two-Step (= Spanish Two-Step)
House Carpenter
How Green Was My Valley
How Long
It Came Upon a Midnight Clear
Jesus Gonna Make Up My Dyin' Bed
Libba's Rag
Lion
Medley: By The Side Of The Road / I Come, I Come
Medley: Deep River / Ol' Man River
Mississippi Boweavil Blues
New Mind Reader Blues
New Newport News Blues
Night Train To Valhalla
On the Banks of the Owchita
On the Beach at Waikiki
On the Sunny Side of the Ocean
Poor Boy Blues
Racemic Tartrate River Blues
Revelation on the Banks of the Pawtuxent
Silent Night, Holy Night
Snowflakes
Spanish Fandango
Spanish Two-Step
Special Rider Blues
Steamboat Gwine 'Round De Bend
St. Vitus Dance
Tasmanian Two-Step (= Spanish Two-Step)
The Blues You Saved For Me
Thing at the End of New Hampshire Avenue, The
Tiger (= Lion)
Tom Rushen Blues
Tuff
Weissman Blues
What The Sun Said
Wissenschaftlich River Blues
Worried Blues
You Better Get Right So God Can Use You
You Gonna Miss Me

OPEN Gm = DGDGBbD

Dance of Death
Great San Bernardino Birthday Party, The (* first section is in standard tuning)
Impressions of Susan

OPEN G modal = DGDGGD

I Am The Resurrection
Fight On Christians, Fight On

OPEN G variant = GGDGBD

Desperate Man Blues

OPEN G6 = DGDGBE

View

GUITARS USED BY JOHN FAHEY

1) **Silvertone:**

    John Fahey bought this guitar for $17.00 in 1953 from Sears & Roebuck. He later said: "... it had a high action."

    The Sears & Roebuck catalog of 1953 advertised three acoustic guitars at this price:
    (1) Silvertone Flat Top Spanish Guitar: #57 D 0614L, price: $16.95
    (2) Silvertone Arched Spanish Guitar, dark: #57 D 0710L, price: $16.95
    (3) Silvertone Arched Spanish Guitar, blonde: #57 D 0702L, price: $16.95

2) **Kay** arch-top, f-hole

3) **Gibson** arch-top, 14 fret, f-hole

    This guitar is depicted on pages 44-45 of the book included with *Your Past Comes Back To Haunt You*.

    John Fahey said: "It had a lousy tone."

4) **Martin** "New Yorker," 12 fret, small bodied, rosewood, model O-18.

    This is the guitar he played on the 1959 version of the *Blind Joe Death* album.

5) **Holzapfel.** 12-string guitar.

    John Fahey bought this guitar from Carl C. Holzapfel & Son on July 29, 1959, and paid $80.00.

6) **Bacon & Day** "Senorita," 14 fret, rosewood, ~1935.

    This guitar is depicted on the covers of *Requia*, *The Essential John Fahey*, *Your Past Comes Back To Haunt You*, and *The Transcendental Waterfall*. John Fahey plays it on the video from the TV show *Guitar, Guitar* hosted by Laura Weber.

This rare guitar was made in the mid 1930s by the Bacon Banjo Company based in Groton, Connecticut. It was found in a New York pawn shop priced at $10.00 and then owned by Stefan Grossman who brought it to California in the mid 1960s (probably 1965). He traded it to Jon Lundberg (1935-2011) of Fretted Instruments guitar shop in Berkeley who, after making some modifications to it, sold it to Pat Sullivan.

John Fahey bought this guitar for $350.00 from Pat in 1966. That year Fahey considered it the best sounding guitar he had ever played. He told Susan Turner that he was offered $1,000 for it: "I didn't sell it – nor will I, come hell or high water." Much later Fahey told an interviewer: "It didn't have any bass though," so in 1971 he traded it in to Lundberg for a Ray Whitley Recording King. The Bacon & Day guitar was promptly bought by Country Joe McDonald who eventually sold it to a British fan.

7) **Martin** 0028, 1928, 12 fret.

    This guitar is depicted on the cover of *Days Have Gone By*.

8) **Yamaha** FG-180, rosewood.
9) **Kona** Hawaiian 6-string lap steel guitar.

   This guitar is depicted on the cover of *The Essential John Fahey* and *Railroad I*. John Fahey can be seen playing it on *Guitar, Guitar* hosted by Laura Weber.

   This guitar was made in the 1920s by Hermann Weissenborn. It was made out of Koa wood which is derived from the trunk of the *Acacia koa*, a tree endemic to the Hawaiian Islands. The guitars were produced in Los Angeles. They had a solid neck as opposed to the hollow neck of the original Weissenborn acoustic guitars. John Fahey owned a style 3 version of the Kona guitar.

   Fahey would play slide with this guitar on his lap. In the 1950s he played with a slide that he had made out of a glass bottle neck, while later he would use a Stevens steel bar. In earlier days, he would sometimes use a woman's lipstick case instead of the glass bottleneck when playing slide guitar.

10) **Recording King** "Ray Whitley" model, 14 fret.

    John Fahey bought this guitar at Lundberg's in 1971. It was destroyed in a quarrel with his girlfriend Marilyn.

    The story of its restoration by Fred Sheppard can be found at www.johnfahey.com and at www.parachodelnorte.com.

    This guitar was made by Gibson in 1939 and endorsed by Country & Western singer and movie star Ray Whitley. It was sold by the mail-order company Montgomery Ward.

11) **Martin** D-35, 14 fret.
12) **Martin** D-76.

    This guitar is depicted on the cover of *Best of John Fahey: 1959-1977*.

13) **Bozo**
14) **Laguna**, model L-60S

    John Fahey played this guitar from the mid 1980s to the early '90s.

15) **Alvarez**
16) **Fender Telecaster**, electric guitar.
17) **Washburn**, "Festival" series, acoustic electric guitar.

    John Fahey can be seen playing this guitar (and the following Marrs RGS), on the video *Live in Santa Monica, April 1997*.

18) **Marrs RGS** (Resophonic Guitar Simulator) lap steel "Cat-Can."

TAKOMA RECORDS CATALOGUES

Takoma Records put out a number of catalogues during its lifetime. The first catalogue listing known is on page 3 of the Summer 1964 issue of the International Blues Records newsletter by Chris Strachwitz:

```
Takoma Records    $5 each

1   - John Fahey - guitar solos - vol.1
2   - John Fahey - guitar solos - vol.2
B 1001 - Bukka White - Mississippi Blues
```

Thereafter, the lists of records issued by Takoma were printed on the back page of booklets included with the LPs or on the back cover of the album jackets.

RECORD*	Jacket or Booklet	LISTING	YEAR
C-1002[2]	booklet	B-1001 to C-1003	4/1965
C-1003[2]	booklet	B-1001 to C-1003	4/1965
C-1004[1]	booklet	B-1001 to C-1005	9/1965
C-1005[1]	booklet	B-1001 to C-1005	9/1965
C-1003[4]	booklet	B-1001 to C-1005	12/1965
C-1002[4]	booklet	B-1001 to C-1009	3/1966
C-1003[6]	booklet	B-1001 to B-1009	1966
C-1004[2]	booklet	B-1001 to C-1005	1966
C-1004[3]	booklet	B-1001 to B-1009	6/1966
C-1007[1]	jacket	B-1001 to B-1009	1966
C-1008[1]	jacket	B-1001 to B-1009	6/1966
C-1009[1]	booklet	B-1001 to B-1009	6/1966
C-1010[1]	booklet	B-1001 to C-1015	1966
C-1014[1]	booklet	B-1001 to C-1015	1967
C-1006[1]	jacket	B-1001 to C-1015	1967
C-1017[1]	jacket	C-1005 to C-1018	1967
C-1018[1]	jacket	C-1005 to C-1017	1967
C-1007[2]	jacket	C-1005 to C-1018	1967
C-1001[2]	jacket	B-1001 to B-1020	1968
C-1011[2]	jacket	B-1001 to B-1020	1968
C-1006[2]	jacket	B-1001 to B-1020	1968
C-1014[2]	booklet	B-1001 to C-1021	1968

* The number in superscript refers to the edition of that particular album.

#1:

The first true stand-alone catalogue with an order form came out in the summer of **1968**. It was included with many LPs at the time and is relatively easy to find. It listed the albums from B-1001 to B-1020. It has the Berkeley, CA, address. The price of the records is $5.00.

This is an interesting catalogue for various reasons:

(1) The Takoma albums are divided into 3 prefix categories:

A = Authentic American Folk Music
B = Blues
C = Contemporary guitarists/composers.

(2) It states that B-1020 would be *One String Blues*, though this slot would eventually belong to C-1020 by the end of 1968. The album *One String Blues* would become B-1023 and would be issued in 1969.

(3) It mentions 5 LPs in preparation, 4 of which never became Takoma issues:

    a) **Slim Critchlow** – who would eventually issue his record *Cowboy Songs – The Crooked Trail To Holbrook* as Arhoolie Records 5007 in 1969.

    b) **Bruce Jackson** – who would issue his record of negro toasts *Get Your Ass In The Water And Swim Like Me* as Rounder Records 2014 in 1976.

    c) **Tox Drohar & M.T. Void** – Tox Drohar (a/k/a Dick Scott) is a jazz drummer. He would accompany Charlie Nothing on his 2nd LP *Outside/Inside* on Everit Enterprize Records in 1969. M.T. Void (as in Empty Void) may have been another pseudonym for Charlie Nothing a/k/a Charles Martin Simon.
Tox Drohar would continue with a jazz career in Europe (and still does as of 2014) and is present on several jazz albums:
- *Your Friendly Neighborhood Rhythm Section* on Wave Records LP7 (1974).
- *No Kidding* on Wave Records LP9 (1974)
- *Timespan* on Wave Records LP14 (1977).

    d) **Phil Yost** would issue a second LP *Fog Hat Ramble* on Takoma C-1021 in 1968.

    e) **Harry Taussig** – would not issue any record on Takoma. His 1965 album *Fate is Only Once* (Talisman Records, TM 1001) was re-issued in 2006 by Tompkins Square Records (TSQ 1523 –CD; TSQ 2042 – LP) and Vinyl Lovers Records (900892 – LP). His second record *Fate is Only Twice* came out in 2012 (Tompkins Square; TSQ 2738 – LP; TSQ 2745 – CD).

#2:

The second catalogue with order form was from **1969**. It listed the albums from B-1001 to A-1022. The address listed is now P.O. Box 5403 in Santa Monica, CA. The price of the records is $5.00.

#3:

The third catalogue with order form was from **1970**. It listed the albums from B-1001 to A-1027. The address listed is P.O. Box 5403 in Santa Monica, CA. The price of the records is $5.00.

#4:

The fourth catalogue with order form was from **1972**. It listed the albums from B-1001 to D-1033. The D prefix probably stands for Devi Records. The address listed is P.O. Box 5403 in Santa Monica, CA. The price of the records is now $5.98, except for C-1019 ($6.98) and C-1030 & C-1031 ($6.95).

#5:

The fifth catalogue with order form was from **1975**. It listed the albums from B-1001 to D-1043. Also listed are Symposium and Thistle Records. The address listed is P.O. Box 5403 in Santa Monica, CA. No price is given for the records.

#6:

The sixth catalogue with order form was from early **1976**. It listed the albums from C-1002 to C-1049. Also listed are Takoma/Briar and Thistle Records. The address listed is now P.O. Box 5369 in Santa Monica, CA. No price is given for the records.

#7:

The seventh catalogue with order form was from late **1976**. It listed the albums from C-1002 to C-1054. Also listed are Takoma/Briar, Briar, Thistle, and Guitar Player Records. The address listed is P.O. Box 5369 in Santa Monica, CA. The price of the records is now $6.98.

#8:

The eighth catalogue with order form was from **1977**. It listed the albums from C-1002 to D-1060. Also listed are Takoma/Briar, Briar, and Long Neck Records. The address listed is P.O. Box 5369 in Santa Monica, CA. The price of the records is $6.98.

#9:

The ninth and last catalogue with order form was from **1980**. It listed the albums from TAK-7001 to TAK-7083. Also listed are Takoma/Briar, Briar, and Long Neck Records. The address listed is Los Angeles, CA. The price of the records is now $7.98.

TAKOMA RECORDS LP WEIGHT

The weight of an LP is said to be one of the parameters that can influence the quality of a vinyl recording. In truth, it is debatable whether a heavier and thus thicker LP contributes to the LP's sound quality. Certainly, grooves can be cut deeper on thicker vinyl and, if cut farther apart from neighboring tracks, will allow for a louder playback with less interference. Other factors obviously also contribute to the vinyl quality, such as the purity of the vinyl and, most importantly, the actual mastering by the engineer. Today, vinyl LPs often come with a 150 gm or 180 gm sticker that implicitly advertises a premium quality of the record. One undeniable value of a heavier vinyl disc is that it is less prone to warping.

Takoma Records consistently issued vinyl LPs over a period of 25 years from 1963 to 1988. A total of 434 Takoma albums were evaluated to determine the variation in weight of Takoma LPs over this period of time and, consequently, to see what impact the so-called "oil crisis" of 1973 and the "energy crisis" of 1979 had on the weight of LPs, a period when record companies supposedly thinned the LPs in order to reduce costs.

One can notice how the 1973 oil crisis had little impact since there was already a decreasing trend in the weight of LPs during the preceding years. However, the 1979 energy crisis significantly impacted the weight of LPs. These never returned to their prior figures, probably since record companies realized that they could still produce good quality albums while using a smaller amount of vinyl.

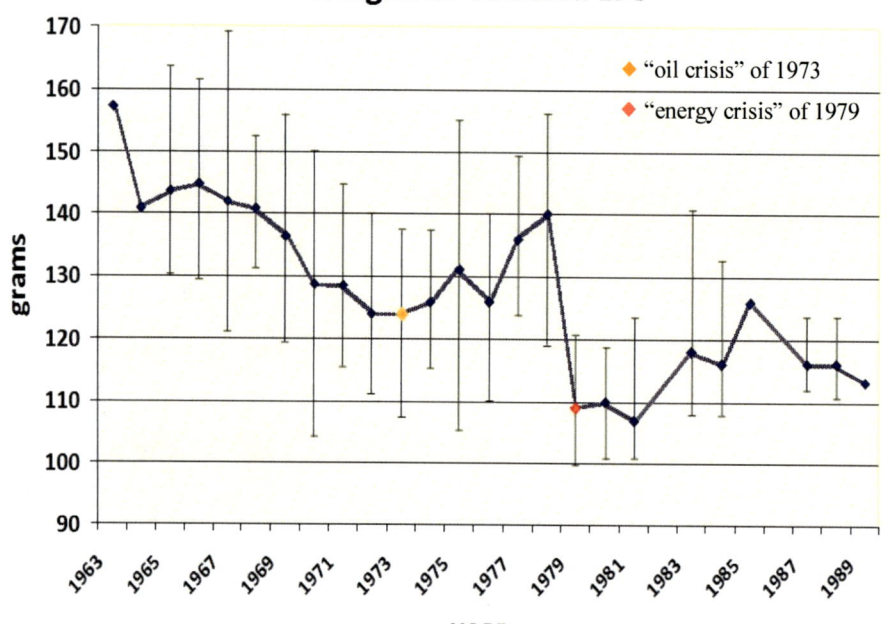

SÄVEL

Sävel Records was a record company based in Helsinki, Finland, that put out recordings from 1948 up to 1976. It specialized predominantly in Finnish folk music.

Sävel began by issuing 10" 78 rpm records from 1948 to 1949 (Sävel S 9001-S 9022).

It released titles on 7" 45 rpm records from 1963-1965 (Sävel 1500-1517), as well as two 7" 33⅓ rpm EPs (1518 & 1519) in 1968 and 1971, respectively. The SÄ 1518 issue is the Finlandia EP by John Fahey.

Other formats issued were 8-tracks from 1967 to 1971 (Sävel 400-415), cassette tapes from 1967 to 1975 (Sävel 2002-2133) and 12" 33⅓ LPs from 1967 to 1976 (Sävel Sälp 601-734).

REFERENCES

Chapter 5

Brooks, Michael. "John Fahey: Turtle Blues"; *Guitar Player*, pg 20-21, 40-42; Mar 1972.

Campbell, Tom. "Movie Soundtracks Again Becoming Hits"; *The Stars And Stripes*; pg 19, Nov 27, 1971.

Eliot TS. *Four Quartets* Harvest Books/Harcourt, New York, 1971.

Fahey, John: epistolary correspondence with Sam Charters, 1967-1969.

Fahey, John: epistolary correspondence with Glenn Jones.

Fahey, John. "Takoma Records Newsletter"; *Acoustic Guitar*: pg 67; Dec 1979.

Finnerty, W Patrick. "Community Structure and Trade at Isthmus Cove: A Salvage Excavation on Catalina Island"; Pacific Coast Archaeological Society Occasional Paper, #1, 1970.

Gadd, Steve. "Recollections: John Fahey Live in Tasmania"; *Acoustic Guitar Community* blog; posted Aug 2, 2009.

Gewertz, Daniel. "Folk Guitarist John Fahey enjoys the bounty of Christmas"; *Boston Herald*, Dec 22, 1984.

Golden, Eve. *Anna Held and the Birth of Ziegfield's Broadway*, The University Press of Kentucky, 2000.

Greenblatt, Alan. "Fahey 'Original' at Caffe Lena"; *Schenectady Gazette*, Nov 25, 1986.

Grenfell, Michael. "John Fahey – In conversation with …"; *Guitar*; Feb 1984.

Nilsson, BA. "Guitarist 'steels' the show"; *The Cavalier Daily*, Mar 22, 1988.

Thede, M & Preece, H. "The Story Behind The Song: Red River Valley"; *Real West*: pg 24-30, 51; No. 129, Aug 1974.

Chapter 6

Morse Steve. "John Fahey: Genius of the acoustic guitar"; *Boston Globe*; pg A11, July 10, 1977.

Thomas, Tony. *Oklahoma's Longest Pony Express*. (self-published); 1962.

Appendices

Angeletti, Maurizio. *American Guitar* Gammalibri, 1982.

Elder, Ben. "Born Again – Unraveling the mysteries of the Weissenborn steel, the ultimate Hawaiian guitar"; *Acoustic Guitar*: Jan 1996.

Kunstadt, Len. "Pittsburgh Blues . ."; *Record Research*: pg 6-7; No. 110, May 1971.

ILLUSTRATION CREDITS & ACKNOWLEDGEMENTS

The author would like to thank the following persons and institutions for their kind permission to reproduce the following images:

(Key: t=top; b=bottom; m=middle; l=left; r=right)

Front cover: photograph by Marvin Lyons; courtesy of the Samuel B. Charters Archives, Dodd Research Center, University of Connecticut.
14-15: David Wilson and Ralph Earle.
25-t: courtesy of Vanguard Records.
28: courtesy of R. Anthony Lee and The Associated Press.
33: courtesy of Southern Folklife Collection, UNC.
60: courtesy of Patrick Finnerty and PCAS Occasional Paper #1 *Community Structure and Trade at Isthmus Cove: A Salvage Excavation on Catalina Island*, Pacific Coast Archaeological Society (1970).
88-b: courtesy of Vintage Jazz Mart & Mark Berresford.
95-b: courtesy of Jon Monday.
98: photograph by Jon Monday.
109: Wikipedia Commons.
147: courtesy of Joe Bussard.
185-b: photograph by Adrain Studer, (http://commons.wikimedia.org/wiki/File:KeddieWye.JPG).
196-mr: Wikipedia Commons.
196-ml: Wikipedia Commons.
262: courtesy of the University of Tasmania.
308: source: 1967 Berkeley Folk Festival brochure - courtesy of Barry Olivier.
392-b: courtesy of David Wilson.
394: courtesy of Chris Downes.
398: source: Record Research magazine - photograph by Len Kunstadt.
401: courtesy of Tom Weller.
403: courtesy of Tom Weller.
407: courtesy of Tom Weller.
416: courtesy of Jeff Tiedrich.
421: photograph by Claudio Guerrieri.
426: courtesy of Barret Hansen and the John Fahey Trust.
428-t: courtesy of Joe McDonald.
428-ml: courtesy of Roz Larman.
429-mr: courtesy of Tony Herrington.

INDEX

Entries in *italics* indicate a John Fahey album title; entries in SMALL CAPS indicate a song title (its page number refers only to its first appearance on a particular recording).

4 Men with Beards: 66, 286, 303
50'S MEDLEY: BLUEBERRY HILL / SEA OF LOVE / SPECIAL RIDER: 275, 378
900 MILES: 282

A

A MINOR BLUES: 205
Addendum: 272
Admiral Kelvinator Clockworks Factory: 156
After The Ball: 81-89, 253-254
AFTER THE BALL: 81
AFTERNOON ESPEE THROUGH SALEM: 179, 185
Amazingrace Concert: 294-296
AMAZING GRACE: 66, 70
America: 58-71
AMERICA: 58, 143
Americana Masters: 260-262
Americana Masters, Vol. 2: 263
Americana Masters, Vol. 3: 264-265
ANANAIAS: 247
Andes, Mark: 27
Andes, Matt: 27
ANGELS FROM THE REALMS OF GLORY: 219
ANN ARBOR / DEATH BY REPUTATION: 145
Antonioni, Michelangelo: 355
APPLE BLOSSOM TIME: 187
APPROACHING OF THE DISCO VOID, THE: 162, 175
ARE YOU FROM DIXIE?: 205
ASSASSINATION OF STEPHAN GROSSMAN, THE: 108
Astor Records: 8
AT THE NAME OF JESUS: 158
ATLANTIC HIGH: 200
AULD LANG SYNE: 37, 171, 175, 203
AWAY IN THE MANGER #1: 36, 171, 203
AWAY IN THE MANGER #2: 171, 203
Azalea City Memories: 256

B

BACK UP AND PUSH: 304, 309
Backporch Drifters: 36
BANTY ROOSTER BLUES: 198, 281
BARBARA NAMKIN BLUES: 280
Barth, Bill: 312

Basho, Robbie: 299
BASTROP WALTZ: 27
BEAN VINE BLUES: 282
BELLS OF SAINT MARY'S, THE: 37, 171, 175, 203
Belmont, Bill: 70, 227
Best of John Fahey, 1959-1977: 129-144
Best of John Fahey, Vol 2: 255-257
Best Of The Vanguard Years: 240
BEVERLY: 81
BICYCLE BUILT FOR TWO: 57, 197, 282
Big Boy Cleveland: 5
BILL CHEATUM: 223
BITTER LEMON, THE: 56, 197, 282
BLACK MOMMY: 191
BLACK SWAMPERS BLUES, PART 1: 199
BLACK SWAMPERS BLUES, PART 2: 199
Blackwood, Dean: 225, 247, 283
Blazek, Douglas: 283
BLIND BLUES [MARTIN'S ESSO BLUES]: 198, 281
Blind Brand X: 36
BLIND THOMAS BLUES PART 1-4: 198, 281
BLUEBERRY HILL: 218
BLUES MEDLEY: 275
BLUES YOU SAVED FOR ME, THE: 57, 197, 282
Boarding House club: 192
Bogas, Ed: 32
BOODLE AM SHAKE: 108
BOTTLE NECK NO. 1, TAKE 1: 264
BOTTLE NECK NO. 1, TAKE 2: 264
BOTTLE NECK NO. 1, THE VIRGINIAN: 264
BOTTLE NECK NO. 2 ILLINOIS CENTRAL: 264
BOTTLE NECK NO. 3 (IN OPEN D): 264
BOTTLE NECK NO. 4 (IN OPEN D): 264
BOTTLENECK BLUES: 283
BOTTLENECK BLUES (AKA RAINY DAYS DOWN METZEROTT ROAD): 56, 197
Bradley, Charley: 33
BRENDA'S BLUES: 57, 197, 223, 282
Brown, Herschel: 85
Bruce, Denny: 27, 72, 81, 350
BUCK DANCER'S CHOICE: 280, 282
BUCKTOWN STOMP: 81

BURY ME NOT ON THE LONE PRAIRIE: 56, 197, 283
Bussard, Joe: 34, 147

C
CANDY MAN: 81
Canned Heat: 219, 310-311
CAROL OF THE BELLS: 120
CARROLL COUNTY BLUES: 304, 309
Carson, Lori: 342-343
CAT, TAKE 1, THE: 264
CAT, TAKE 2, THE: 264
Catudal, Donald: 156
CENTER WILL NOT HOLD, THE: 243, 246
CHARLES A. LEE: IN MEMORIAM: 4, 102
CHARLEY BRADLEY'S 1066: 32-33
CHARLEY BRADLEY'S TEN SIXTY-SIX BLUES: 247
CHARLIE BECKER'S MEDITATION:179, 185
Charters, Sam: 9, 16, 26, 32, 103, 286
CHELSEY SILVER, PLEASE COME HOME: 226
CHESSIE: 264
CHICKEN: 304
CHINATOWN, MY CHINATOWN: 263
CHRIS'S RAG: 281
Christ Church: 157
CHRIST IS BORN AS CHILD OF MAN: 214
CHRIST IS BORN ON CHRISTMAS DAY: 214
CHRIST'S SAINTS OF GOD FANTASY: 37
CHRISTMAS FANTASY – PART I: 120
CHRISTMAS FANTASY – PART II: 120
Christmas Guitar: 203-204
Christmas Guitar, Volume One: 171-174
CHRISTMAS MEDLEY: SAMUEL: BARBER'S "LARGO" / IT CAME UPON A MIDNIGHT CLEAR / WE THREE KINGS / GREENSLEEVES / IN THE BLEAK MIDWINTER / HARK! THE HERALD ANGELS SING / O COME ALL YE FAITHFUL / SAMUEL BARBER'S "LARGO": 214
CHRISTMAS MEDLEY (OH TANNENBAUM, ANGELS WE HAVE HEARD ON HIGH, JINGLE BELLS): 120
Christmas Soli: 293
CHRISTMAS SONG, THE: 187
CHRISTMAS TIME IS HERE: 187
Christmas With John Fahey, Vol II: 52, 55, 120-128, 221
City Of Refuge: 226-227
CITY OF REFUGE I: 226
CITY OF REFUGE III: 226
CLAIRE: 218

COELACANTHS: 232
Colburn, Scott: 228, 232
Coley, Byron: 270, 283
Comet Records: 11, 19
COME LABOR ON: 158
COME ON IN MY KITCHEN: 234
COMMEMORATIVE TRANSFIGURATION & COMMUNION AT MAGRUDER PARK: 4, 102
Connors, Loren Mazzacane: 352
Contemporary Guitar: 299-303
Cooper, Stoney: 155
Cooper, Wilma Lee: 155
Crosby, Bing: 38
Cul de Sac: 235
Curtis, Thomas: 157, 454

D
DALHART, TEXAS; 1967: 58, 66, 70-71
DAMNED IF I KNOW THE DOG: 264
DANCE OF DEATH: 255
DANCE OF THE CAT PEOPLE, THE: 241
DANCE OF THE INHABITANTS OF THE INVISIBLE CITY OF BLADENSBURG: 4, 102
DANCE OF THE INHABITANTS OF THE PALACE OF KING PHILIP XIV OF SPAIN: 5, 129
DARK AND LONELY NIGHT BLUES: 199
DARK IS THE NIGHT, COLD IS THE GROUND: 352
DASEIN RIVER BLUES: 199, 281
DAYS HAVE GONE BY: 282, 292
Dean, Eddie: 283
DEATH OF THE CLAYTON PEACOCK, THE: 223
Decker, Doug: 108, 120
Definitive John Fahey, The: 285
DELTA BLUES: 339
DELTA DOG THROUGH THE BOOK OF REVELATION: 179, 186
DELTA FLIGHT 53: 241
DELTA FLIGHT 54: 241
DELTA SERENADE: 29
Demon Records: 75
DeSousa, Bob: 32
DESPAIR: 241
DESPERATE MAN BLUES: 143
DIANNE KELLY: 218
Dilleshaw, John: 85, 130
DISCARDED: 377-378
DISCOVERY OF THE SYLVIA SCOTT, THE: 145
DISERTATION ON "OBSCURITY", A: 162

Disneyland: 73
DIXIE PIG BAR-B-Q BLUES: 72
DO YOU HEAR WHAT I HEAR: 187
DOLLS INSIDE THE WALLS: 345
DON'T: 218
DOROTHY: 275
DOROTHY (PART TWO): 275
DOROTHY / CALVERT STREET BLUES [BRENDA'S BLUES]: 282
DREAM OF THE ORIGIN OF THE FRENCH BROAD RIVER: 281
DREAMING UNDER THE B & O TRESTLE: 282
DRILL: WHAT'S YOUR CURSE?: 347
DRUNKEN TALE TO HIDE, A: 243, 246
DRY BONES IN THE VALLEY: 108
DURGAN PARK: 56, 197, 283
DVORAK: 66, 70, 191, 265
DVORSACK: 264
DYING DEATH BLUES: 199

E

Earle, Ralph: 14-15
EAST MEETS WEST: 241
Edsel: 75
EELS: 232
Eldridge, Greg: 155
Elektra demo tape: 22-23, 29-30
Elektra Records: 29-30
Eliot, T.S.: 91
ENIGMAS AND PERPLEXITIES OF THE NORFOLK AND WESTERN: 179, 185
Epiphany of Glenn Jones, The: 234-235
EPITHALAMIUM: 28, 32-33
Essential John Fahey, The: 102-103
Eteenpäin!: 35
EVENING MYSTERIES OF FERRY STREET, THE: 205
EVENING, NOT NIGHT (PT. 1): 225
EVENING, NOT NIGHT (PT. 2): 225
EVERMORE AND EVERMORE (OF THE FATHER'S LOVE BEGOTTEN): 171
Exil, Levoy: 219

F

Fahey, Melody: 158, 179, 191, 211, 219
FAHEY BLOWS HIS NOSE: 258
FAHEY ESTABLISHES RAPPORT WITH THE TASMANIANS: 162
FAHEY SAMPLER, THE: 255, 299
FAITH OF OUR FATHERS: 158
Falcon, Joseph F: 67
FANFARE: 226

Fare Forward Voyagers: 90-101
FARE FORWARD VOYAGERS: 90, 143
FARE FORWARD VOYAGERS, 1965: 22, 30
FARTHER ALONG: 375
FEAR & LOATHING AT 4TH & BUTTERNUT: 218
Ferguson, Jay: 27
Festival Records: 146, 165
FIGHT ON CHRISTIANS, FIGHT ON: 102
FINAL SONG LIVE: 246
FINALE: 66, 70
FINLANDIA: 34-35
FINN & THE SALMON OF KNOWLEDGE: 344
Finnerty, Patrick: 59-71, 259
FIRST NOEL, THE: 37
Fisher, Kenneth: 154
FIX ME A PALLET ON THE FLOOR: 264
Flynn, Tommy: 156
Fonotone: 3, 56-57, 197, 357
FOR ALL THE BEAUTY OF THE EARTH: 158
FOR ALL THE SAINTS: 158
FRANKLIN BLUES: 280
FRISCO LEAVING BIRMINGHAM: 179, 185
FRISCO LEAVING BIRMINGHAM (LONGER VERSION): 264
FRISCO LEAVING BIRMINGHAM, TAKE 1: 264
FRISCO LEAVING BIRMINGHAM, TAKE 2: 264
FRISCO LEAVING BIRMINGHAM, TAKE 3: 264
Fuccillo, Jeff: 351
FUNERAL SONG FOR MISSISSIPPI JOHN HURT: 72, 162

G

Gadd, Steve: 261
GAMELAN COLLAGE: 234
GAMELAN GUITAR: 234
GARBAGE: 228
Gardner, Este: 391
GAUCHO: 205
Georgia Stomps, Atlanta Struts, and Other Contemporary Dance Favorites: 237-239, 270
GHOSTS: 228
GIVE ME CORNBREAD WHEN I'M HUNGRY: 129
Give Me Wings: 337-338
Glasswing Media: 344
GO I WILL SEND THEE: 37
GOD REST YE MERRY GENTLEMEN FANTASY: 37
God, Time and Causality: 211-212
GOING AWAY TO LEAVE YOU BLUES: 198, 281

GOING CRABBING TALKING BLUES, PT 1: 281
GOING CRABBING TALKING BLUES, PT 2: 281
Gooch, Dorothy: 156
GOOD CHRISTIAN MEN REJOICE: 171, 203
GOOD CHRISTIAN MEN, REJOICE, REJOICE: 214
GOOD KING WENCESLAS: 37, 171
Good Luck: 243-244
GOODBYE OLD PAINT: 283
GOODBYE OLD PAINT #1 / WHOOPEE-TI-YI-YO: 56, 197
GOODBYE OLD PAINT #2: 56, 197
GOODBYE OLD PAINT #3: 56, 197
GOPINATHA: 337
Gordon, Kim: 348
GRAND FINALE, THE: 145
Great American Music Hall: 279, 294-298
GREAT EIGHT, THE: 275
Great Santa Barbara Oil Slick, The: 59, 258-259
GREAT SANTA BARBARA OIL SLICK, THE: 258
GREEN BLUES: 199, 282
GREEN, GREEN: 29
GREEN RIVER BLUES: 280
GREENSLEEVES: 382
Grinning Idiot: 156
Gronow, Pekka: 35
Grossman, Stefan: 175, 192
GUITAR LAMENTO: 145, 237
Guitar of John Fahey, The: 175-178
Guitar Masters Collection: John Fahey, The: 277
GUITAR RAG: 378
GUITAR SOLO TITLE UNKNOWN #1 [REVELATION ON THE BANKS OF THE PAWTUXENT]: 3, 282
GUITAR SOLO TITLE UNKNOWN #2 [NIGHT TRAIN TO VALHALLA]: 3, 282
GULF PORT ISLAND BLUES: 198, 281

H
Halfant, Jules: 5, 25
Halfway House Orchestra: 88
Hamersveld, John Van: 145, 162
Hansen, Barrett: 4, 26-28, 33, 103, 224
Hard Time Empty Bottle Blues: 252, 270
HARD TIME EMPTY BOTTLE BLUES 1-4: 252
Hardy, Caroline: 156
Harris, Charles K: 89
HAWAIIAN TWO-STEP: 81, 163
Hawn, Goldie: 154
Held, Anna: 109

Henson, Jim: 155
HIGH SHERIFF BLUES: 334
HILL HIGH BLUES: 198, 281
HISTORY OF TOKYO RAIL TRACTION, A: 241
Hitomi: 241-242
HITOMI: 241
HITOMI CRIES: 246
HITOMI SMILES: 241
Hobart: 162, 262
HOLY, HOLY, HOLY: 158
HOPE SLUMBERS ETERNAL: 226
HORSES: 81
HOUSE CARPENTER: 57, 197, 282
HOUSE OF THE RISING SUN / NIGHTMARE: 237
HOW GREEN WAS MY VALLEY: 261
How Bluegrass Music Destroyed My Life: 155
HOW LONG: 57, 197, 282
HS2: 346
Hurt, Mississippi John: 426

I
I AM A RAKE AND RAMBLING BOY: 56, 197, 283
I Remember Blind Joe Death: 205-210
I SHALL NOT BE MOVED: 281
I SING A SONG OF THE SAINTS OF GOD: 57, 197, 282
I WISH I KNEW HOW IT WOULD FEEL TO BE FREE: 81
ICKWEISSNKT RIVER BLUES: 199
I'LL BE HOME FOR CHRISTMAS: 188
I'M GOING TO DO ALL I CAN FOR MY LORD: 129, 223
IMITATION TRAIN WHISTLES: 175
IMPROV IN E MINOR: 205
IMPROVISATION FOR FLUTE AND GUITAR: 282
IN A PERSIAN MARKET: 108
IN CHRIST THERE IS NO EAST OR WEST: 129
IN DARKEST NIGHT: 218
IN THE BLEAK MIDWINTER: 171
IN THE PINES: 282
INDIAN PACIFIC RAILROAD BLUES: 162, 175
INTERVIEW WITH JOHN FAHEY: 280
INTRO / SHE / THINGS FALL APART: 246
INTRO TO "LION": 258
INTRO TO OCEAN WAVES: 200
INTRODUCTION BY STEFAN MARKOVITCH: 162
IRISH CHRISTMAS MEDLEY: 275
IRISH MEDLEY: 214

IRISH SETTER: 4, 102
IT CAME UPON A MIDNIGHT CLEAR: 37, 171, 175

J

JACK THE MILLER'S SON: 344
Jakoila, Antero: 213
JAYA SHIVA SHANKARAH: 108
JESUS CHRIST IS RISEN TODAY: 158
JESUS GONNA MAKE UP MY DYIN' BED: 198, 291
JESUS IS A DYING BED MAKER: 66, 70
JESUS IS A DYING BED MAKER 2: 66, 70
JESUS WON'T YOU COME BY HERE? / GO TELL IT ON THE MOUNTAIN: 171, 204
JINGLE BELLS: 214
Jo Jo Gunne: 27
JOE KIRBY BLUES: 258
John Fahey Christmas Album, The: 214-217
JOHN FAHEY RECORDED IN CHICAGO MAY '98: 348
JOHN FAHEY SAMPLER, THEMES AND VARIATIONS, THE: 22-23, 30
John Fahey Trio – Vol 1: 246
John Fahey Visits Washington, DC: 145-156
JOHN HENRY: 198, 280, 281
JOHN HENRY BLUES: 282
Johnson, Blind Willie: 227
Johnston, Ralph Cameron: 34, 36, 172
JOLLY OLD SAINT NICHOLAS: 187
Jones, Glenn: 22-23, 30, 43, 234-235, 248, 259, 283
JOULUYÖ, JUHLAYÖ (SILENT NIGHT): 213
JOY TO THE WORLD: 37, 171, 175, 203
JUANA: 232, 237
JUROSCHO ASCOPI: 200
JUST AS I AM: 158

K

Kaiser, Henry: 143, 255, 266
KBOO Radio Live Session: 236, 241, 245
KBOO RADIO LIVE RECORDING: 245
KEEP YOUR LAMPS TRIMMED & BURNING: 108
Kelley, Kevin: 27,
Kelly, Jo Ann: 334-336, 340-341
Kennedy, Robert F: 27
Kensett, John F: 196
Kerrick, George: 155
Ketelbey, Albert W: 111
King, Martin Luther: 27, 31
Kirton, Malcolm: 283

Kleine, Jürgen: 58
Knight, Tim: 236, 243, 245
KNOTT'S BERRY FARM MOLLY: 223
KNOXVILLE BLUES: 58, 223
Kottke, Leo: 318

L

Lane, Fitz Hugh: 196
Lang, Peter: 318
LANGLEY TWO-STEP, THE: 281
Larrabee Sound: 58
LAST STEAM ENGINE TRAIN, THE: 129, 175
LAVA ON WAIKIKI: 205
LAY MY BURDEN DOWN: 198, 281
LAYLA: 191
Lebow, Jan: 103
Led Zeppelin: 131
Ledbetter, Steven Lance: 283
Lee, Charles F: 28
Lee, R. Anthony: 157, 283
Leo Kottke/Peter Lang/John Fahey: 130
LET ALL MORTAL FLESH KEEP SILENCE: 158
Let Go: 191-196
LET GO: 191
LET ME CALL YOU SWEETHEART: 205
Levine, Mark: 33
LIBBA'S RAG: 281
LIFE IS LIKE A MOUNTAIN RAILROAD: 179, 186
LIGHTS OUT: 191
LIKE BEING REBORN AGAIN: 243, 246
LION: 4, 102, 163, 211
LITTLE DRUMMER BOY, THE: 214
LITTLE HAT BLUES: 281
LITTLE RIVER STOMP, THE: 304
Live at Studio KAFE: 275
Live in Tasmania: 162-170
Livings, Louise: 155
LO HOW A ROSE E'ER BLOOMING: 37, 172
LONG TIME TOWN BLUES: 198, 281
LORD, I WANT TO BE A CHRISTIAN IN MY HEART: 158
LORD HAVE MERCY: 172
LOST LAKE: 191, 194
LOVE SONG: 264
Lovejoy, Elijah P: 218, 425
LULLABY AND FINALE FROM THE FIREBIRD: 200
Lunsford, Bascom Lamar: 112
Lyons, Marvin: 102, 103, 273

M

MAGGIE CAMPBELL BLUES: 234
Mahoney, Tinh: 205, 352

MARCH! FOR MARTIN LUTHER KING: 4, 31, 102
MAGIC MOUNTAIN: 234
MAGRUDER PARK: 258
MANICURE: 349
Mann, Woody: 108
MARIE: 350
MARILYN: 108
MARK 1:15 : 59
Markovitch, Stefan: 162, 262
MARY HAD A BABY: 214
McClay, Carole: 155
McGee, Sam: 64
McVicker, Charles (Chuck): 5, 24-25
MAY THIS BE LOVE / CASEY JONES: 200
MEDLEY: BY THE SIDE OF THE ROAD / I COME, I COME: 72
MEDLEY: CHRISTMAS TIME'S A–COMING / RUDOLPH THE RED-NOSED REINDEER: 187
MEDLEY: COME THOU ALMIGHTY KING / WILD WESTERN HERO: 158
MEDLEY: DECK THE HALLS WITH BOUGHS OF HOLLY / WE WISH YOU A MERRY CHRISTMAS: 188
MEDLEY: DEEP RIVER / OL' MAN RIVER: 72, 191
MEDLEY: GOODBYE OLD PAINT/WHOOPEE TI-YI-YO, GIT ALONG LITTLE DOGGIES: 283
MEDLEY: HARK, THE HERALD ANGELS SING / O COME ALL YE FAITHFUL: 37, 171, 203
MEDLEY: IMITATION TRAIN WHISTLES / PO' BOY: 179, 185
MEDLEY: INTERLUDE / THE PORTLAND CEMENT FACTORY / REQUIEM FOR MISSISSIPPI JOHN HURT: 211
MEDLEY: JESUS WON'T YOU COME BY HERE?/GO TELL IT ON THE MOUNTAIN: 171
MEDLEY: LET IT SNOW, LET IT SNOW, LET IT SNOW / WINTER WONDERLAND: 187
MEDLEY: LORD OF ALL HOPEFULLNESS / ALL THROUGH THE NIGHT: 158
MEDLEY: PRETTY POLLY / SHORTNIN' BREAD: 280
MEDLEY: SANDY ON EARTH / I'LL SEE YOU IN MY DREAMS: 211
MEDLEY: SILVER BELL / CHEYENNE: 145
MEDLEY: SNOWFLAKES / STEAMBOAT 'GWINE AROUND THE BEND / DEATH OF THE CLAYTON PEACOCK / HOW GREEN WAS MY VALLEY: 211
MEDLEY: THE HOLLY AND THE IVY / THE CHERRY TREE CAROL: 187

MEDLEY: TWILIGHT ON PRINCE GEORGES AVENUE / O HOLY NIGHT / MY PRAYER: 387
MEDLEY: UNTITLED / O JESUS I HAVE PROMISED: 283
MELODY MCBAD: 145
MELODY MCOCEAN: 200
MEMPHIS RAG: 312
MEXICO: 378
Mill Pond, The: 228-231
MILL POND, THE: 226
MILL POND DROWNS HOPE, THE: 228
MINUTES SEEM LIKE HOURS, THE HOURS SEEM LIKE DAYS, THE: 205
Miss Murgatroid: 345, 347
MISSISSIPPI BOWEAVIL BLUES: 280
Mitchell, Charlie: 192
Mojave Desert: 59
Monday, Jon: 90, 93, 95
MORE NOTHING: 234
Morning / Evening: 225
MORNING (PT. 1): 225
MORNING (PT. 2): 225
Moses Mason: 249
MOTHERLESS CHILD: 247
MY PRAYER: 381

N
NEW MIND READER BLUES: 334
NEW NEWPORT NEWS BLUES #2: 281
NEW ORLEANS SHUFFLE: 32, 81
New Possibility, The: 37, 172, 221
NEW RED PONY, THE: 234
NEW YORK CENTRAL, TAKE 1: 264
NEW YORK CENTRAL, TAKE 2: 264
NIGHT TRAIN TO VALHALLA: 3, 34, 199, 223, 282
NIGHTMARE / SUMMERTIME: 205
Nitzsche, Jack: 350
Noble, Peter: 162, 261-262
NOBODY'S BUSINESS: 281
NOTHING: 234

O
O' COME LITTLE CHILDREN / ACH DU LIEBER AUGUSTINE: 214
O' HOLY NIGHT: 214
O JESUS I HAVE PROMISED: 56, 197, 282
O' LITTLE TOWN OF BETHLEHEM: 214
O'Rourke, Jim: 232, 348
OF THE FATHER'S LOVE BEGOTTEN: 203
Of Rivers and Religion: 72-79, 253-254
OH COME, OH COME EMMANUEL: 158

OH HOLY NIGHT: 120
OKEFENOKEE SWAMP RAINTREE, THE: 32
OLD COUNTRY ROCK: 191, 280
Old Fashioned Love: 108-119
OLD FASHIONED LOVE: 108
Old Girlfriends and Other Horrible Memories: 218-219
OLD JOE CLARK: 304, 309
OLD SOUTHERN MEDLEY (FRAGMENT): 283
OM SHANTHI NORRIS: 81
On Air: 266
ON DOING AN EVIL DEED BLUES: 223
ON THE BEACH AT WAIKIKI: 255
ON THE DEATH AND DISEMBOWELMENT OF THE NEW AGE: 226
ON THE SUNNY SIDE OF THE OCEAN: 130, 162
ONEONTA: 179, 185
ORINDA-MORAGA: 223, 255
OUR PUPPET SELVES: 234
OVER THE HILL BLUES: 280-281
OVERCOME: 353
Owens, Don: 155

P
PAINT BRUSH BLUES: 198, 281
PARTHENOGENESIS: 310
PAT SULLIVAN'S BLUES: 281
Perls, Nick: 308, 334, 340
Pick It Baby: 278
PLANARIA: 232
POOR BOY: 223
POOR BOY A LONG WAY FROM HOME: 129, 175
POOR BOY BLUES: 198, 281
Popular Songs of Christmas and New Year's: 187-190
PORTLAND CEMENT FACTORY AT MONOLITH, CALIFORNIA, THE: 57, 197, 282
PRAISE TO THE LORD: 158
PRAYING ON THE OLD CAMP GROUND & LONESOME BLUES: 312
PRETTY AFTERNOON: 191
PRETTY POLLY: 282
PRINCE GEORGE'S DANCE: 282
Pure Pleasure Records: 12
Pyren, Stephanie: 52, 55, 120-121

Q
Quill Blues: 5
Quonset: 36

R
RACEMIC TARTRATE RIVER BLUES, PART 1 & PART 2: 199, 281
Radha Krishna Temple: 337
RAGA CALLED PAT, A: 34
RAGA CALLED PAT, A – PART ONE: 223
Ragtime Ralph: 34, 36
Railroad I: 179-186
RAIN FOREST: 200
Rainforests, Oceans and Other Themes: 200-202
Ranaldo, Lee: 349
Red Crayola: 346
RED CRAYOLA WITH JOHN FAHEY: 346
Red Cross: 33, 247-251
RED CROSS, DISCIPLE OF CHRIST TODAY: 247
RED PONY, THE: 211, 279, 432
RED ROCKING CHAIR: 237
REINUMERATION BLUES: 280
REMEMBER: 187, 247
RENO: 350
Requia: 103
REQUIEM FOR JOHN HURT: 102, 175
REQUIEM FOR MISSISSIPPI JOHN HURT: 258
REQUIEM FOR MOLLY, PART 1: 102
REQUIEM FOR MOLLY, PART 2: 102
REQUIEM FOR MOLLY, PART 3: 102
REQUIEM FOR MOLLY, PART 4: 102
REQUIEM FOR MOLLY, PART 5: 32
REQUIEM FOR RUSSELL BLAINE COOPER: 102
Return Of The Repressed: 223-224
RETURN OF THE TASMANIAN TIGER, THE: 162
REVELATION: 211
REVELATION ON THE BANKS OF THE PAWTUXENT: 3, 223, 282
REVOLT OF THE DYKE BRIGADE: 129, 163
REVOLT OF THE BRONTOSAURUS: 29-30
Riedrer, Friedrich: 252
Rimsky-Korsakov: 5
RIVER MEDLEY: 191
Robb, Terry: 172, 188, 191, 200, 211, 215, 218
ROSE AND A BABY RUTH, A: 218
Ruskin, Rick: 120
RUSSIAN CHRISTMAS OVERTURE: 120

S
SAIL AWAY LADIES: 282
St. Aidan's Church: 157
ST. CLEMENT'S: 158
SAINT JOHN'S HORNPIPE: 282
ST. LOUIS BLUES: 129, 175, 280

ST. LOUIS TICKLE: 281
St. Michael's and All Angels Church: 157
ST. PATRICK'S: 158
ST. PATRICK'S HYMN: 57, 197, 200, 282
St. Paul's Church: 157
ST. VITUS DANCE: 378
SAMBA DE ORFEO: 200
SANTA CLAUS IS COMING TO TOWN: 187
SANTISIMA: 214
Savel records: 34-35, 441
SCHERZO: 243
SCHERZO / OREGON CAPITOL INN: 246
Schmidt, Charlie: 30, 256
Scrivner, Rob: 155
Sea Changes And Coelacanths: 269-271
SEA OF LOVE, THE: 218
Seaton, Donald: 155, 157
Segura Brothers: 67
Sete, Bola: 192-193
SHARKS: 232
SHAVE 'EM DRY: 340
Shaw, Don: 156-157
Sibelius, Jean: 35
Sierra Sound Labs: 14,26,28
SILENT NIGHT: 175, 214
SILENT NIGHT, HOLY NIGHT: 37, 172
SIMPLE GIFTS: 56, 197, 283
SINGING BRIDGE OF MEMPHIS TENNESSEE, THE: 4, 31, 102
SITTING ON TOP OF THE WORLD: 304
SKATER'S WALTZ, THE: 187
SLIGO MUD: 255
SLIGO RIVER BLUES: 223
SLOUCHING TOWARD JERUSALEM: 243
SMOKETOWN STRUT: 280
SMOKY ORDINARY BLUES: 5, 199, 281-282
Solo Records: 80
Some Summer Day: 267
SOME SUMMER DAY: 129, 175, 178, 199
Some Sunny Day: 276
SON HOUSE / MARILYN / MY PRAYER / MOON INDIGO: 237
SONG: 72
SONG #3: 66, 70
SONG FOR SARA: 237
SPANISH CAROL: 214
SPANISH DANCE: 129
SPANISH FANDANGO: 85, 380
SPANISH TWO STEP: 85, 130, 163, 175
SPECIAL RIDER BLUES: 66, 70
Spirit: 27
Spongebob Squarepants: 36

Sror, Joey: 154
STAK 'O LEE BLUES [LOUIS COLLINS]: 280
STAND UP, STAND UP FOR JESUS: 158
STEAMBOAT GWINE 'ROUND DE BEND: 72, 162, 175
STEEL GUITAR MEDLEY: 22, 30
STEEL GUITAR RAG: 175, 205, 280
STEEL STRING GUITAR: 386
STEVE TALBOT: 264
STEVE TALBOT ON THE KEDDIE WYE: 179, 185
STOCKING FEET BLUES: 334
STOMPING TONIGHT ON THE PENNSYLVANIA / ALABAMA BORDER: 266
STOMPING TONIGHT ON THE (OLD) PENNSYLVANIA / ALABAMA BORDER: 282
STONE PONY: 199, 282
Storey, Carl: 155
Strachwitz, Chris: 312-317
SUMMER CAT BY MY DOOR: 179, 185
SUMMERTIME: 247
SUN GONNA SHINE IN MY BACK DOOR SOMEDAY BLUES: 223
SUNFLOWER RIVER BLUES: 129, 223
Sunny Side Of The Ocean, The: 268
SUNSET ON PRINCE GEORGE'S COUNTY: 191
Surfdusters: 36

T
TAKE A LOOK AT THAT BABY:129, 175, 178
TAKE THIS HAMMER: 282
TAKOMA PARK POOL HALL BLUES: 280
TANAKA JUN: 241
Tasmania: 162, 262
TASMANIAN TWO-STEP: 85, 162
TELEVISION BLUES: 34-35
TELL HER TO COME BACK HOME: 223
TEXAS AND PACIFIC BLUES: 72, 197
TEXAS & PACIFIC BLUES [MY BUCKET'S GOT A HOLE IN IT]: 282
THEMES AND VARIATIONS: 200
THEME AND VARIATIONS FOR GUITAR FROM DVORAK'S 4TH SYMPHONY: 32
THING AT THE END OF NEW HAMPSHIRE AVENUE, THE: 218
THINGS FALL APART: 243
Things To Come: 236
Thomas, Rod: 304-308
Thomas, Tony: 304-309
THUS KRISHNA ON THE BATTLEFIELD: 90
TIGER: 162
TINA IN THE RAIN: 243, 246

TOM RUSHEN BLUES: 198, 281
Tom Sawyer's Island: 73
TRAIN: 197
Transcendental Waterfall, The: 286-292
TRANSCENDENTAL WATERFALL, THE: 280
TRY ME ONE MORE TIME: 340
TUFF: 234, 255
Twilight on Prince Georges Avenue: 274
TWILIGHT ON PRINCE GEORGES AVENUE: 218, 255
TWILIGHT TIME: 218
TWO AMERICAN FOLK HYMNS: 158

U

UNION PACIFIC: 175
UNKNOWN TANGO: 205
UNTITLED: 283
UNTITLED #1: 56, 197
UNTITLED #2 / O JESUS I HAVE PROMISED: 56
UNTITLED #3: 56, 197
UNTITLED WITH RAIN: 247
UNTITLED (HIDDEN TRACK): 247
UNTITLED (*AKA* MARK 1:15): 375, 387

V

van Kalkar, Stefan: 206
Vanguard Records: 4-28, 31-32
Vanguard Visionaries: John Fahey: 273
Vesalius, Andreas: 206
VIEW: 218
VIEW (EAST FROM THE TOP OF THE RIGGS ROAD/B & O TRESTLE): 4, 102
VIEW EAST FROM THE B&O RAILROAD VIADUCT AND THE RIGGS ROAD INTERSECTION: 258
VOICE OF THE TURTLE, THE: 58

W

WALTZ THAT CARRIED US AWAY & A MOSQUITO CAME ALONG AND ATE UP MY SWEETHEART, THE: 58
WALTZ YOU SAVED FOR ME, THE: 188
WALTZING MATILDA: 162
WANDA RUSSELL'S BLUES: 198, 281
Watson, Rosa Lee: 316
WE THREE KINGS: 171
WE THREE KINGS OF ORIENT ARE: 37, 203
WE WOULD BE BUILDING: 34
Weber, Laura: 375, 395
Weisburd, Sherman: 81
WEISSMAN BLUES 199, 281
Weller, Tom: 37-38, 293, 299-300
WESTERN MEDLEY: 56, 197, 283

WHAT CHILD IS THIS?: 37, 171, 203
Wheeling Records: 147
WHEN THE CATFISH IS IN BLOOM: 102
WHEN THE FIRE AND THE ROSE ARE ONE: 90
WHEN THE SPRING TIME COMES AGAIN: 129, 175, 258
WHEN YOU WORE A TULIP: 81
WHICH WAY BE BROADWAY: 342
WHITE CHRISTMAS: 120, 187
WHO WILL ROCK THE CRADLE?: 378
WHY HAVEN'T I HEARD FROM YOU: 352
Wickham, Graham: 304, 308
Williams, Doc: 147
Williams, Elmer: 156
Wilson, Al: 219, 310
Wilson, David: 14
Windham Hill Records: 196
WINE & ROSES: 163, 432
Wiseman, Mac: 154
WISSENSCHAFTLICH RIVER BLUES, PART 1 & PART 2: 199, 281
Womblife: 232-233, 270
WORLD IS WAITING FOR THE SUNRISE, THE: 191
Worrall, Henry: 85
WORRIED BLUES: 223
Wright, Tim: 155

Y

YALLABOOSHA RIVER BLUES: 281
YAZOO BASIN BLUES: 282
Yeats, William B: 244
Yellow Princess, The: 4-28, 103
YELLOW PRINCESS, THE: 4, 102
Yes! Jesus Loves Me: 158-161
YES, JESUS LOVES ME: 158
YOU CAN'T COOL OFF IN THE MILL POND, YOU CAN ONLY DIE: 228
YOU BETTER GET RIGHT SO GOD CAN USE YOU: 281
YOU GONNA MISS ME: 199, 281
YOU GONNA NEED SOMEBODY ON YOUR BOND: 198, 281
YOU TAKE THE E TRAIN: 57, 197, 282
YOU'LL FIND HER NAME WRITTEN THERE: 205
Young, Izzy: 259
Your Past Comes Back To Haunt You: 56-57, 59, 280-284

Z

Zabriskie Point: 354-355
ZEKIAH SWAMP BLUES: 281
Ziegfield, Florenz: 109

> *"My best to you . . . and anybody else who can remember me ----*
> *and even those who don't remember me*
> *or never knew me."*

John Fahey

(from a letter to Dr. Robert Georges, UCLA Folklore & Mythology Dept., 1985)

> *"As Flea told me in a recent letter,*
> *we're still haunted by the memory of Fahey."*

"Blind" Thomas Curtis

(Thomas Curtis, August 2013)

About the Author

Claudio Guerrieri is a co-author of the notes in the John Fahey book/CD set *Your Past Comes Back To Haunt You* (Dust-to-Digital, 2011), and has been a consultant for the release on CD of the John Fahey albums *The Yellow Princess* (Vanguard, 2006) and *The Great Santa Barbara Oil Slick* (Water, 2004).

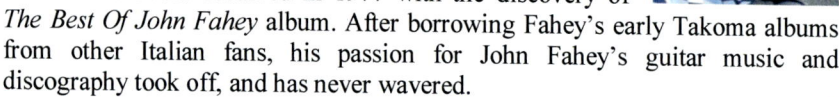

Claudio's taste in music has evolved over time, but a momentous event occurred in 1977 with the discovery of *The Best Of John Fahey* album. After borrowing Fahey's early Takoma albums from other Italian fans, his passion for John Fahey's guitar music and discography took off, and has never wavered.

He was born in London, England, and graduated from the University of Rome "La Sapienza" with a degree in Medicine. His profession includes a brief period as Medical Lieutenant in the Italian Armed Forces, and working as an Anatomic Pathologist for more than 20 years. He has published research papers principally in the field of gynecologic pathology. For the past 15 years, his secondary focus has been representational oil painting.

Claudio Guerrieri has lived in England, Italy, USA, the Netherlands, and Sweden. He currently lives and works in the New York/New Jersey area of the U.S. with his wife Aly and daughter Lucia.

Made in the USA
San Bernardino, CA
11 November 2016